DISCOVER *the* ART *of* FIELD SKETCHING

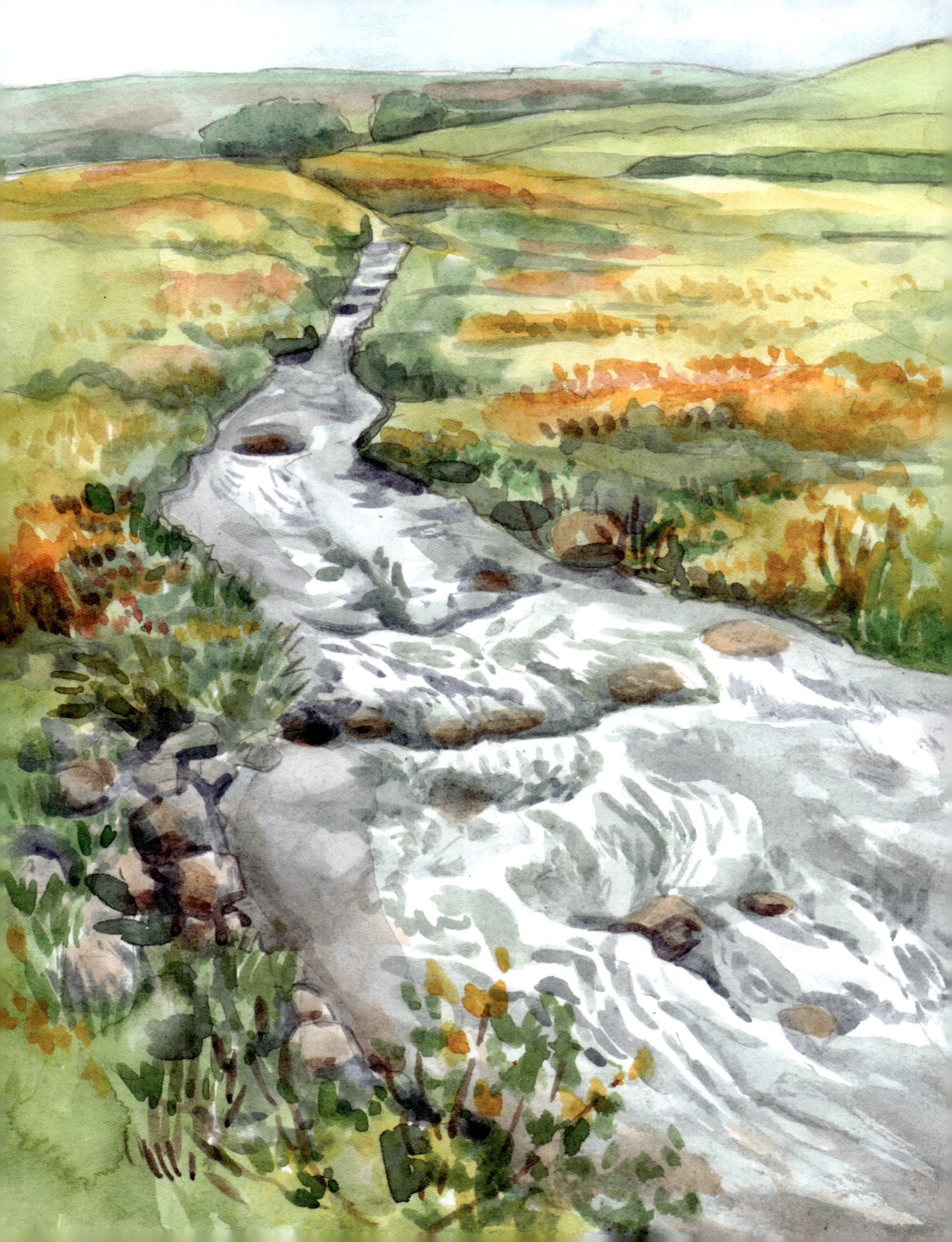

DISCOVER *the* ART *of* FIELD SKETCHING

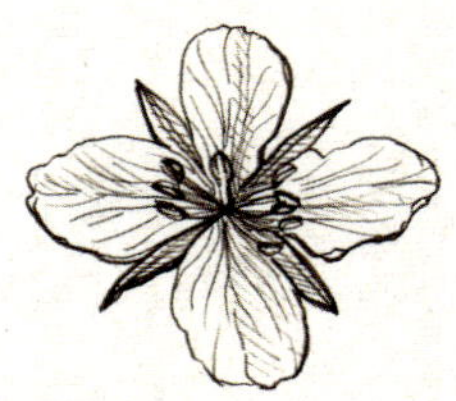

NATURE-INSPIRED TECHNIQUES FOR PENCIL, PEN & WATERCOLOR

Kristin Link

TIMBER PRESS
Portland, Oregon

Land Acknowledgement

With my whole heart, I want to acknowledge that I live and work on Atna Nenn', Ahtna Athabaskan land. The photos in this book are from Alaska on Ahtna land in the upper Copper River Watershed, Eyak/dAXunhyuu Land on Kayak Island, Dena'ina land in the Anchorage area, Nunamiut land at Toolik Field Station, Dena land in the Fairbanks area, and Kaska Dena land in British Columbia. I am grateful to the Indigenous people for being caretakers and stewards of these places so that we all might enjoy and learn from them, whether in person or through the photos in this book.

Photo credits appear on page 289.

TIMBER PRESS
Workman Publishing
Hachette Book Group, Inc.
1290 Avenue of the Americas
New York, New York 10104
timberpress.com

Timber Press is an imprint of Workman Publishing, a division of Hachette Book Group, Inc. The Timber Press name and logo are registered trademarks of Hachette Book Group, Inc.

Printed in Shenzhen, China (APO), on responsibly sourced paper.
Text design by Laura Shaw Design
Cover design by Vincent James

ISBN 978-1-64326-379-3
A catalog record for this book is available from the Library of Congress.

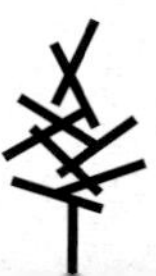

For my teachers, for sharing your patience,
wisdom, and experience

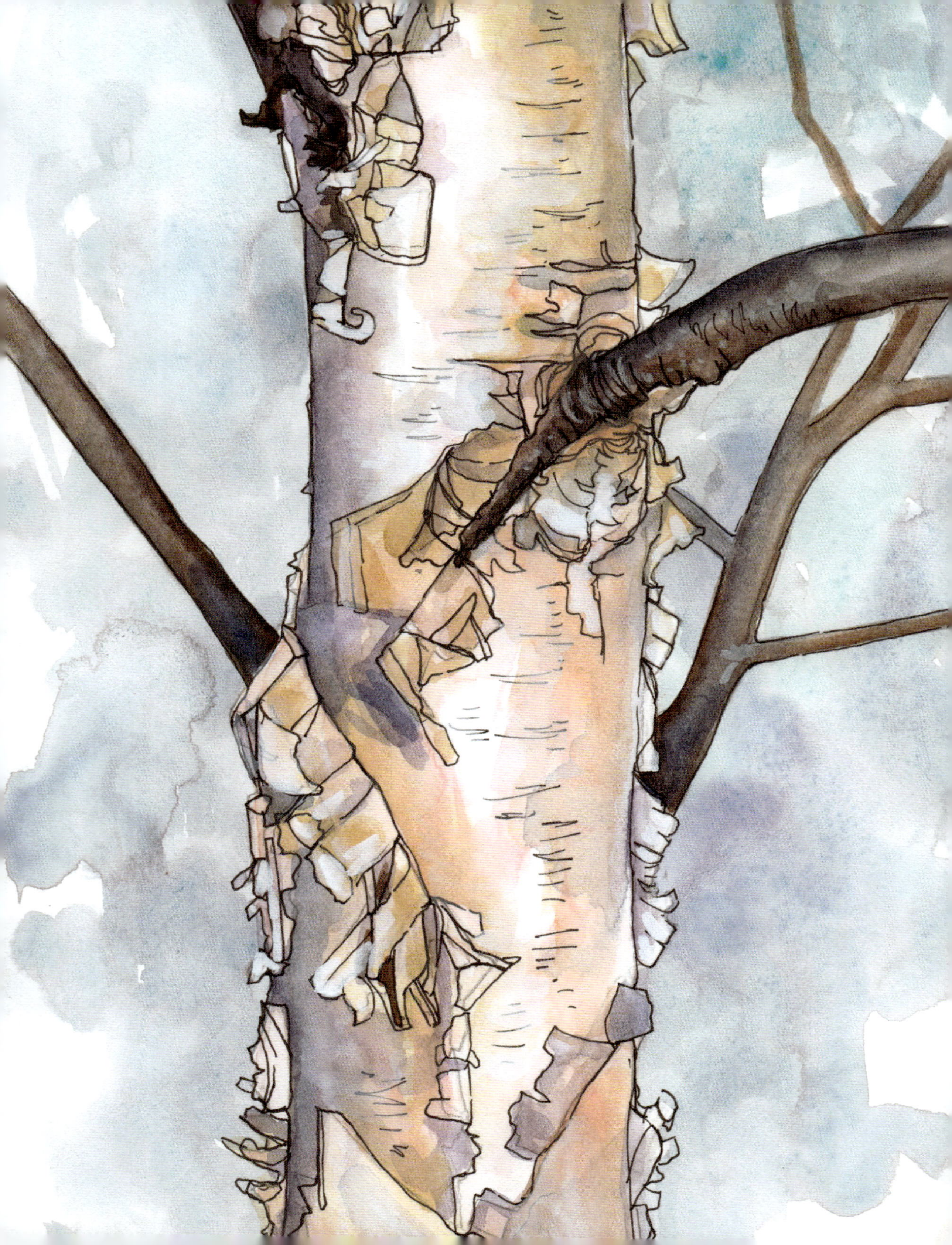

Contents

INTRODUCTION: SUNSET AT DONOHO BASIN 11

CHAPTER 1 **Why Field Sketching? 14**

CHAPTER 2 **Materials 22**

CHAPTER 3 **Getting Started with Drawing 34**

Project 1 Line drawing of a leaf 42

CHAPTER 4 **Drawing with Shading and Value 48**

Project 2 Owl feather with pencil 53

Project 3 Drawing and shading a skull 59

Project 4 Jawbone in pen 64

CHAPTER 5 **Watercolor Basics for Sketching 70**

Project 5 Paint a flat leaf with watercolor 79

Project 6 Monochromatic shell with blue and brown 84

CHAPTER 6 **Using Color to Build Up Texture and Form 92**

Project 7 Anemone flower 100

Project 8 Watercolor and pencil botanical study of lupine 104

Project 9 Fall leaves with complementary colors with fireweed 112

CHAPTER 7 **Putting It Together and Mixing Media 120**

Project 10 Hummingbird moth with pen and watercolor 129

Project 11 Sketching round subjects: Rocks 136

Project 12 Adding in white and black ink: Black morel mushroom 139

Project 13 Building up texture with colored pencil and watercolor: Robin's nest 143

CHAPTER 8 **Animals and Moving Subjects 146**

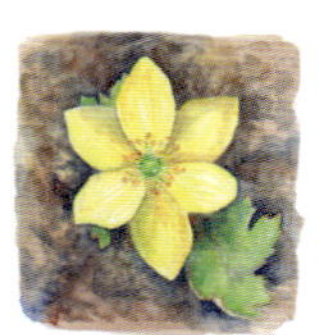

Project 14 Gesture sketching animals: Moose 152
Project 15 Studying anatomy with an owl skull 157
Project 16 Capturing fur: Red squirrel 160
Project 17 Iridescence and feathers: Raven 164

CHAPTER 9 **Sketching Landscapes and Creating the Illusion of Space 172**

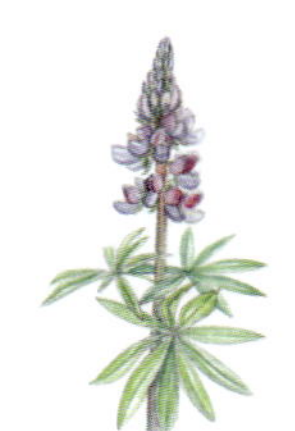

Project 18 Sketching trees 179
Project 19 Color and space: Meadow 184
Project 20 Landscape gesture sketch of sunset and lake 189
Project 21 Meditative sketching: K'esugi Ridge 194

CHAPTER 10 **More Approaches for Sketching Landscapes 202**

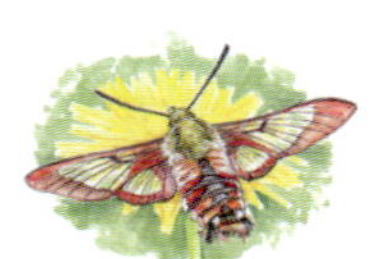

Project 22 Working with a grid: Glacier lake 206
Project 23 Sketching near and far in the alpine tundra 211
Project 24 Working on toned paper: Glacial moraines 216
Project 25 Sketching moving water: Arctic tundra stream 221

CHAPTER 11 **Sketching Through the Seasons and Celebrating Winter 230**

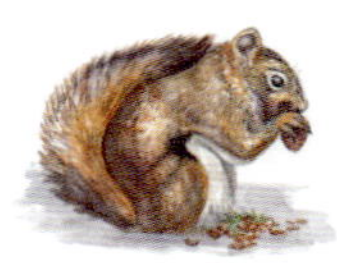

Project 26 Dormant plants and winter trees: Birch tree 238
Project 27 Animal tracks in the snow 244
Project 28 Night skies: Orion constellation 250
Project 29 Winter landscapes, winter light, and alpenglow 254

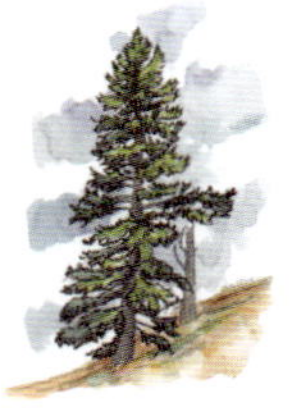

CHAPTER 12 **Taking It with You and Making It Your Own** 260

Project 30 One plant drawing a day in late spring 270

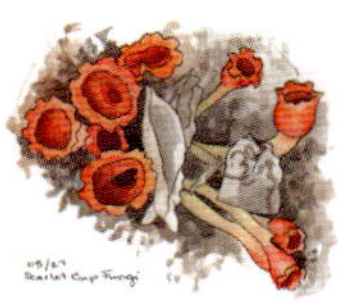

GLOSSARY 285

ACKNOWLEDGMENTS 287

RESOURCES 288

PHOTOGRAPHY AND ART CREDITS 289

INDEX 290

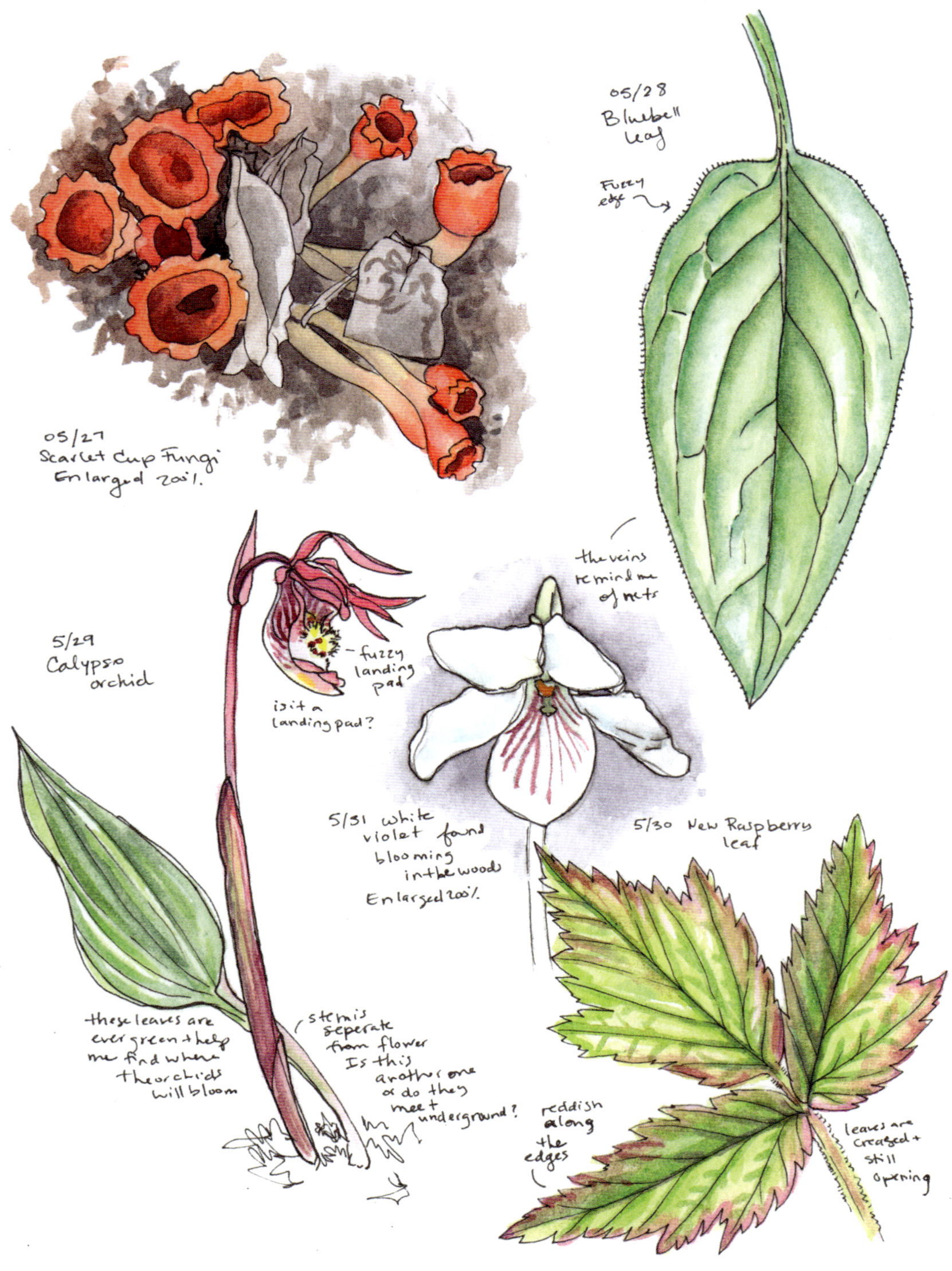

05/27
Scarlet Cup Fungi
Enlarged 200%.
05/28
Bluebell leaf
Fuzzy edge
the veins remind me of nets
5/29
Calypso orchid
fuzzy landing pad
is it a landing pad?
5/31 white violet found blooming in the woods
Enlarged 200%.
5/30 New Raspberry leaf
these leaves are evergreen + help me find where the orchids will bloom
stem is seperate from flower Is this another one or do they meet underground?
reddish along the edges
leaves are creased + still opening

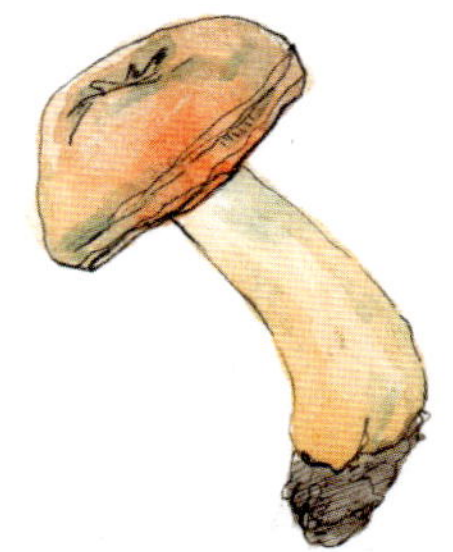

Introduction

Sunset at Donoho Basin

AFTER HIKING ALL AFTERNOON, I got to where I intended to camp. The sun was going down at 11 pm on this Alaskan July evening. The landscape where I live is often so overwhelming that it breaks me apart to take it in. I had hiked across blue ice and rocky moraine to get to a nunatak (an island of land surrounded by glaciers) to sit on the shore of a turquoise alpine lake and look out at the purple and pink shining white peaks illuminated by the descending sun. It was late and I was tired, but I pulled out my sketchbook to savor the moment. I sketched with immediacy, making broad strokes with a brush pen and then filling the shapes with dabs of color from my tiny palette, emphasizing the mauve and violet hues. I noticed the light change, emphasizing different shapes on the icefalls. I heard rocks fall as the glaciers moved, and birds sang about this time of summer, which is fleeting for all of us. I relished how the stillness of my relatively quiet sketching helped me arrive at this place.

While sipping my coffee the following day, I sketched a similar view on a larger paper spread. This practice was slower. I created contour lines thoughtfully with my pencil, not so much worrying about every piece of the mountain being in the right place but feeling the peak, creating a small meditation and prayer as my hand moved, fusing the mountain into a part of myself as I drew. I went over the pencil with pen, repeating this practice and my prayer. Then I carefully added some watercolors to remember the blue of the sky on that sunny morning, the dusty green of the willow leaves moving in the midsummer breeze, the neon colors of the sedges at the edge of the water, and the many shades of pink, brown, and violet-gray of the moraine. My favorite part was trying to capture how the glaciers shine under the sun in the summer with a few carefully placed movements of Cobalt Teal Blue.

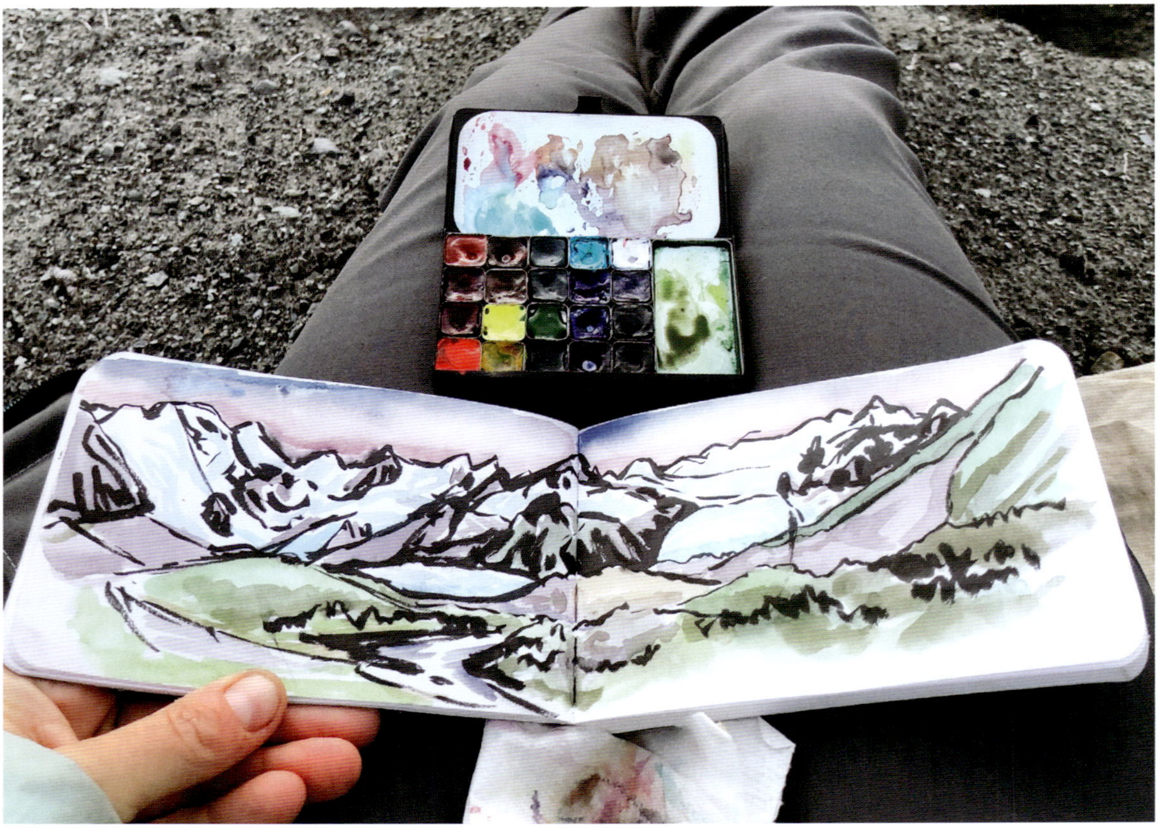

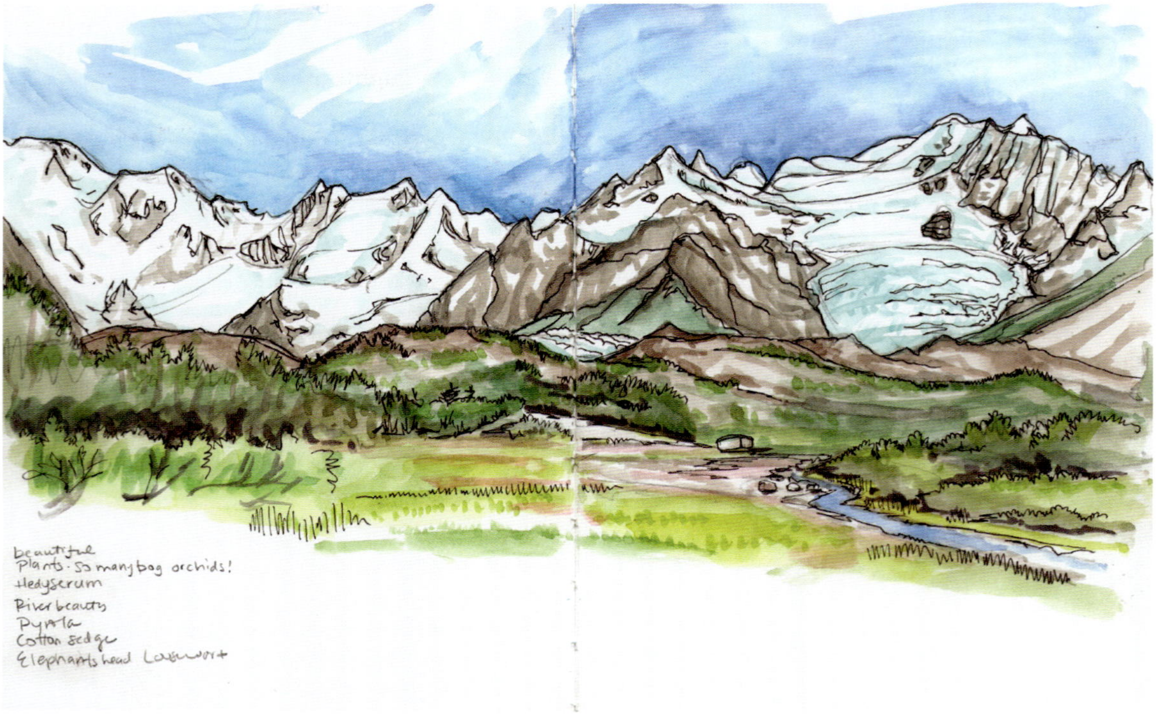

beautiful
Plants. So many bog orchids!
Hedyserum
River beauty
Pyrola
Cotton sedge
Elephants head Lousewort

These sketches were different experiences with different results and embodied responses to a place and time. They each required sustained attention, and because of that, I can recall that time three years later. This is the same way I remember walking my regular trail near my cabin, making small discoveries to capture in my sketchbook. Day after day, that attention has led me to learn the patterns of my neighbors: what the squirrel is eating in January, how the glacier river channel moves, how to recognize dormant plants, and that mosquitos carry pollen. I've created a record to reference yearly to remember how the river froze last November or when the snow buntings stopped by on their spring migration.

Sketching has also helped me remember the places I travel. I remember sitting on a wall sketching ancient temples in Cambodia while listening to the conversations of the people around me. I studied the different layers of rock in the Grand Canyon with pen and watercolor while floating down a calm section of the Colorado River perched on the bow of a raft. I asked questions about an orange tree in midtown Tucson after noticing that every time an orange fell, even if it wasn't ripe, some opportunist was ready to drill a small hole and suck out the nutrients from the inside of the fruit. I wandered through the Northern Hardwood Forest in Vermont and recorded the distinct rectangular holes of the Pileated Woodpecker, with accompanying piles of woodchips below.

Two artists I admire have quotes about drawing, attention, and love:

"Love is sustained compassionate attention." —John Muir

"Drawing is looking and looking is love." —Wendy MacNaughton

This book is an opening, an invitation to fall in love with the world around you—and find that that world includes you.

◀ **Two approaches to sketching the same landscape at different times of the day: a quick gesture sketch at sunset (*top*) and a slower, meditative approach the next day (*bottom*).**

Why Field Sketching?

Instructions for living a life.
Pay attention.
Be astonished.
Tell about it.

—MARY OLIVER

Sketching combines art, place, and nature.

Developing a sketching practice helps us slow down and be present in the places we inhabit by establishing attention and focus. We often think about what is next or ruminate on past events. It is powerful to cultivate a practice in the present. Sketching can be a tool for grounding, reflection, and noticing at a slower pace.

Sketching creates a record of observations and questions about the natural world. It can challenge us to look at nature and make new discoveries. Sketching helps create a natural history record that can be referenced over time. It can help us develop a practice for curiosity and get better at asking questions.

▶ Sketching Fireweed Mountain in the evening light

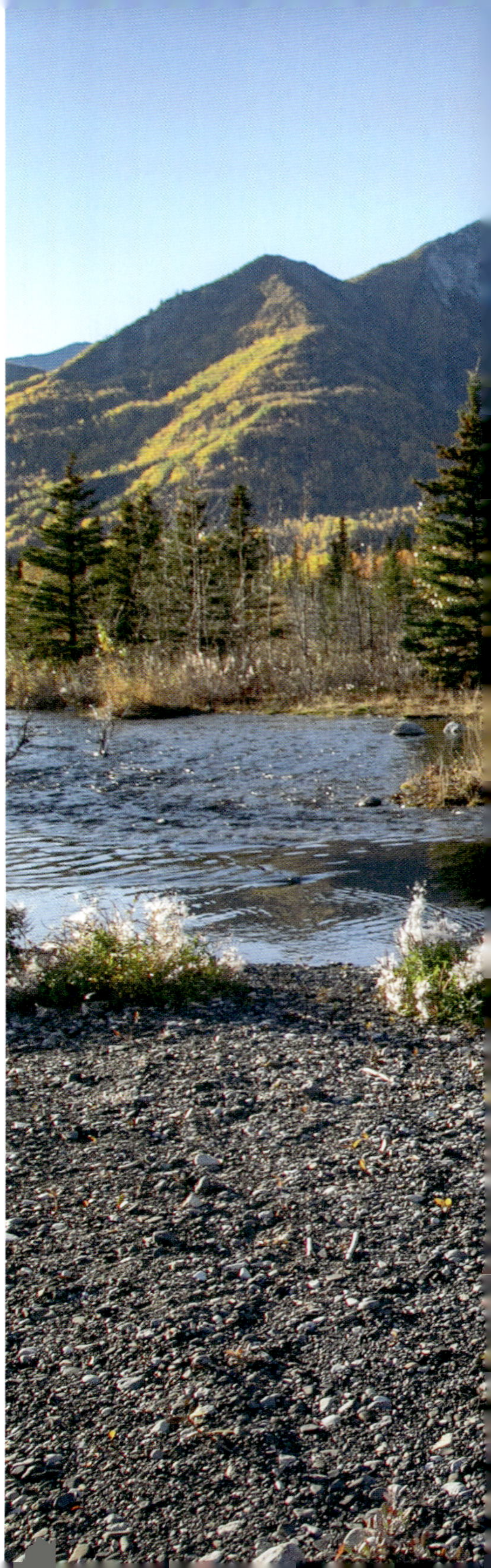

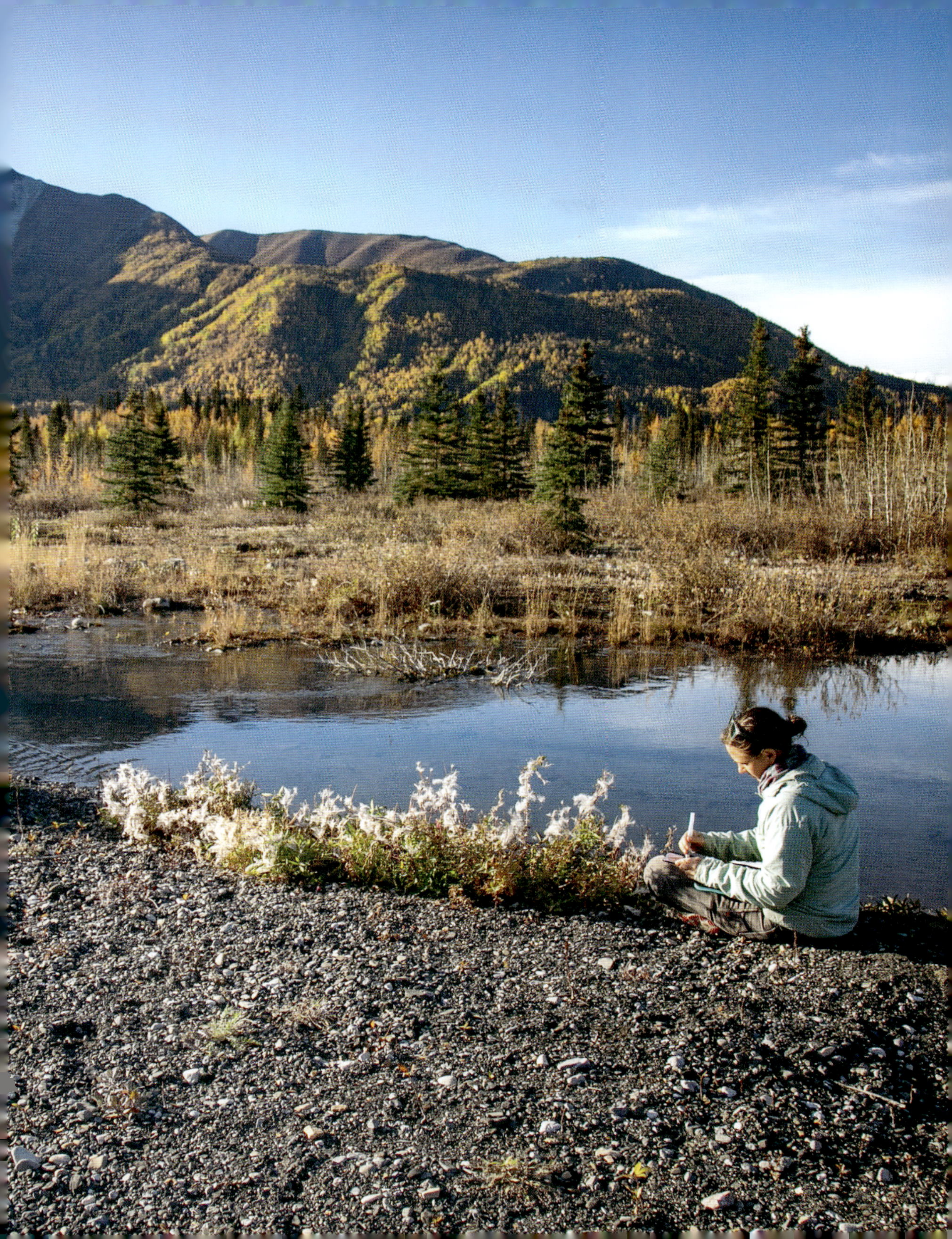

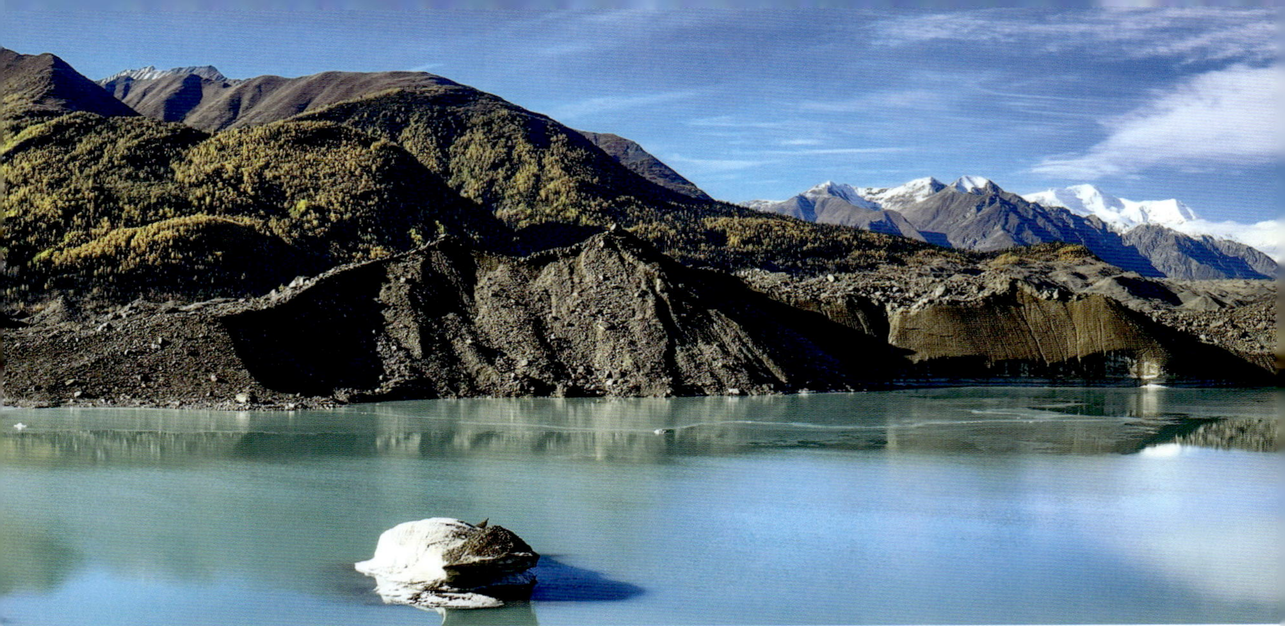

You can develop your style and voice as an artist by creating a regular practice and paying attention to what you enjoy. If you feel so inclined, you can share your sketching with others and be a part of a community of people interested in nature, art, and journaling.

LOCATION

I am located in rural Alaska, where I live in an off-the-grid cabin on the Nizina River, Atna Nenn', which is part of the largest national park in the United States, Wrangell–St. Elias. The landscape outside my door is stunning, dynamic, and breathtaking. I appreciate this every day, yet I am often drawn to the tiny details of the world that might be found anywhere. I am excited to share this special place with you through the photo references and projects. I tried to pick reference photos that will help you travel to Alaska but which will also feel familiar, as if they might have been taken right outside your door.

I want to encourage you to sketch where you are and to fall in love with the world around you. I've lived in cities and know that they have vibrant nature in their parks, their skies, the cracks in their pavement, and their people. The internet is an excellent resource for traveling and experiencing nature from your chair. So, whether it is out your window, on your screen, on your neighborhood walk, or at a UNESCO World Heritage Site, sketch and draw inspiration from what is around you.

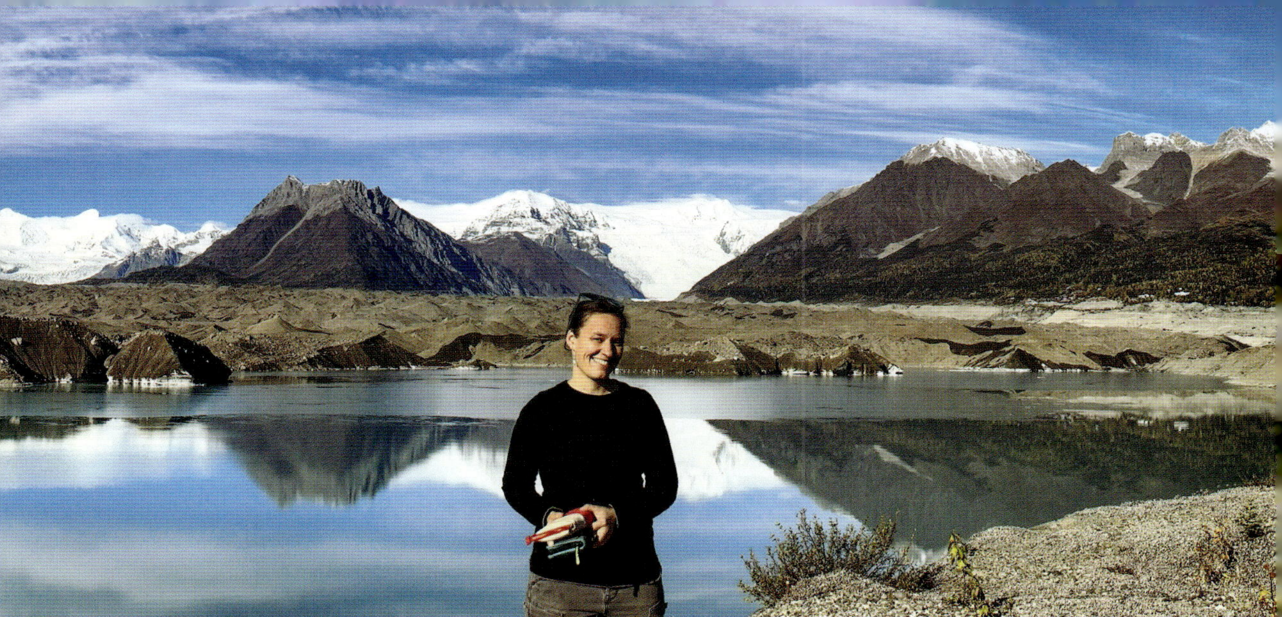

HOW TO USE THIS BOOK

The lake at the toe of the Kennicott Glacier on Ahtna land near McCarthy, AK

This book is instructional, with step-by-step projects, but I hope you can work through it as a guided, moving meditation ritual. Sketching involves attention and focus that help us ground in the present and connect with nature to feel peaceful and relaxed. Like mediation, sketching can take hours and years of exercise and still may not be mastered, but an imperfect practice is worthwhile and makes us better humans. I've been working on sketching and drawing for over thirty years and as my primary vocation for more than ten years, and I am still getting better at it every day and learning new things all the time. I hope you use my process as a set of guidelines but not as a means of comparison. Be kind to yourself and celebrate that you are on your unique art journey.

START IN THE BEGINNING

After discussing the materials, the first chapters (chapters 3 through 7) build on each other progressively, beginning with line drawing, working with shading, adding watercolor, and working in mixed media. The second part of the book (chapters 8 through 11) dives deeper into specific subjects, such as sketching animals, landscapes, and different seasons. The last chapter discusses some ways to use the skills you have gained outside.

Even though the skills build progressively, you can skip projects and move around. You can go back to some of the earlier reference photos and try other techniques with them, for example, using watercolor for some of the subjects in chapters 3 and 4. If you feel stuck or overwhelmed, move on to another project.

PROCESS, PERFECTIONISM, CURIOSITY, AND PRACTICE

In my practice of making art and sketching, I alternate between being a creator and an editor, but I try not to do both at once.

I open my sketchbook when I see something intriguing or beautiful or something I want to spend some time on. Next, I make a series of initial decisions about what I want to capture, why, and roughly how I will do it. Am I interested in the patterns of a specific leaf? Am I sketching a flower to represent and better understand that species in general or that particular individual? Am I grounding in the landscape, or do I want to capture how the wind is blowing through the trees? Each of these intentions would yield a different process and a different result. Having gone through that thought process, I can focus on the intuitive practice of making art.

When I finish my sketch, I'll look down at my creation and find that it differs from what I imagined or expected. It is the human imperfections in this process that make art enjoyable. We interpret the world around us, deciding what textures, colors, and details are essential and what we can physically create with our bodies and materials.

I will transition from focusing on creating to thinking like an editor for a bit; I will make a change or two and then close my book, put it away, and revisit it with a different mindset, maybe at my desk with a cup of tea in the evening. Then, I will add notes and another layer to the artwork. Separating the editor and the creator helps me quiet perfectionism and focus on making things. It has also been helpful to approach the resulting work with curiosity and wonder instead of a set of expectations.

Throughout this book, you may be pushed outside of your comfort zone. You will create some work that you feel is a failure or did not meet your expectations of what you initially imagined. I hope you also create work that surpasses your expectations and delights you! I can be a perfectionist; every time I accept a failure, I try to remember that I am becoming a better artist who is not afraid to try something new and learn from it. Remember that sketching is about process and building up a practice of doing it repeatedly. This can help us step away from the importance of the product or what the final sketch looks like. Consider the journey through the whole sketchbook and how you have changed as a person by filling it out.

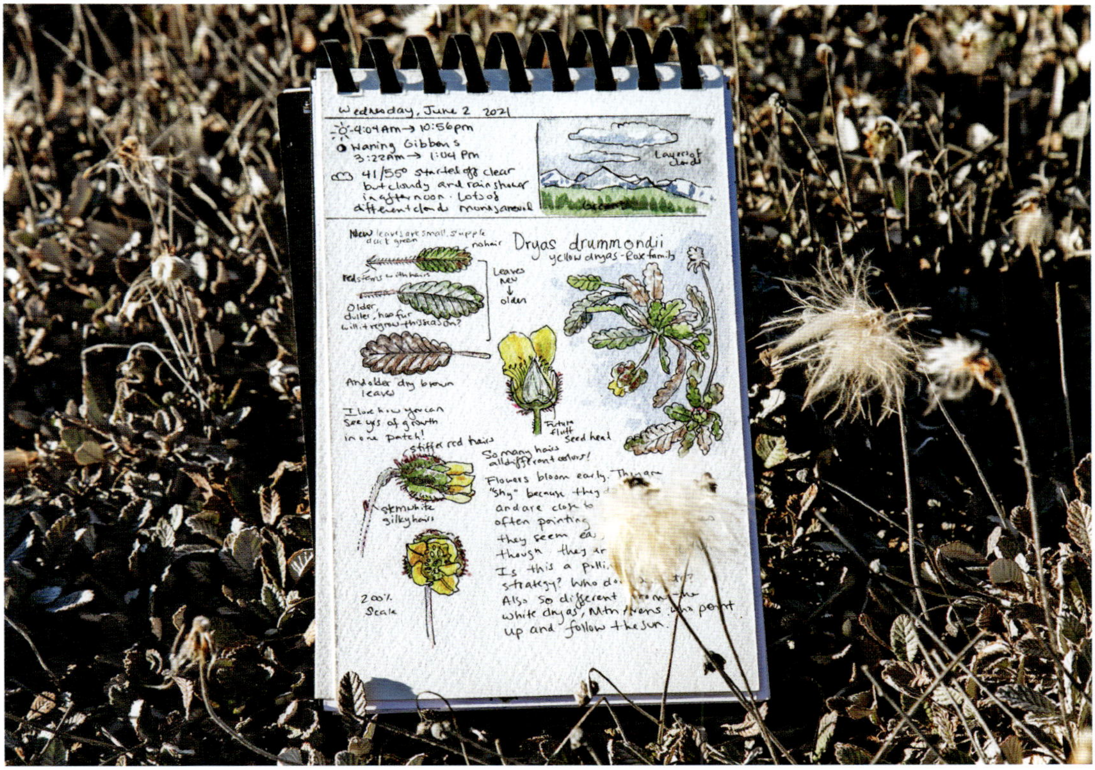

ADDING NOTES TO YOUR SKETCHES—SKETCHING AND NATURE JOURNALING

Sketchbook page of *Dryas drummondii* surrounded by that plant gone to seed

As a science illustrator, my sketching expertise is in visual art, and most of the instruction in this book revolves around the visual aspect of creating pictures for your page. I use some of the tools from nature journaling in my sketchbook and include words, pictures, and numbers in my sketchbooks. Words can consist of information about the day, location, how I am feeling, observations, and questions that come to me. I often use the prompts: "I notice . . .", "I wonder . . .", and "It reminds me of . . ." to figure out what to write. Numbers can include measurements, temperature, date, speed, quantity, duration, etc.

It can be helpful to dance between these tools when you want to change the pace or the challenge level of your sketching practice. If you feel out of your comfort zone with drawing, try using another form of language or switch to recording numbers or words, which can take some pressure off the artwork. Likewise, if you feel too comfortable and want a challenge, stretch

Sketchbook page from Marion Creek in the Brooks Range: study of a willow leaf up close and the faraway landscape

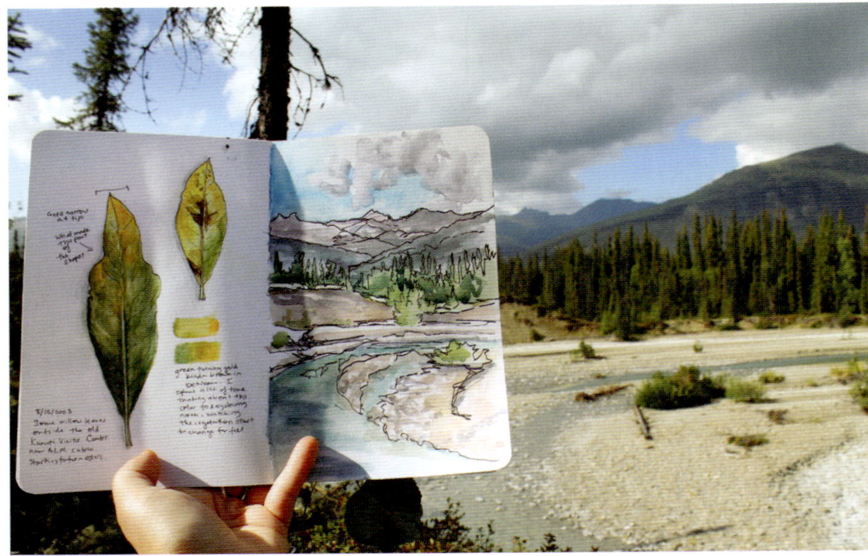

yourself to work in another format you don't usually think in. My comfort zone is drawing, and a stretch for my brain is to include numbers. The more I practice using numbers and asking questions, the more naturally it comes to me. I am often surprised by what I discover by pushing my brain to think differently.

WORKING FROM PHOTOS

Since I can't take you outside with me, the projects in this book are based on photo references that I took while wandering around my home in Alaska. As a professional artist, I've learned that both drawing from life and working from photos are valuable practices. Sketching from life will teach you how photos tend to flatten the subject, but sketching from photos will help you see the shapes and colors standing still. As I sketch, I make changes to my photo references based on my experience to bring in a bit more life or tell a particular story. I hope that in practicing drawing from photos and using tools from field sketching, you feel prepared to take your art practice outdoors and sketch subjects from life (maybe the apple in your fridge). As your art journey continues beyond this book, I encourage you to try different methods: draw from life outside, make your own photo references, or work with other people's photos if they have extended permission.

NOTE ABOUT MY INITIAL DRAWINGS

Many of the initial pencil drawings in this book are printed darker than I would make them so they are easier to see. The lighter the initial pencil drawing, the easier it is to modify, paint, or draw over with a pen. I recommend starting your initial sketches with a light touch. You can lighten a pencil drawing by dabbing the graphite with a kneaded eraser. I often leave these light pencil lines in my sketchbook as an archive of my process, but you may erase yours at some point if you want a cleaner look.

DEVELOPING YOUR STYLE AND VISUAL VOCABULARY

I am excited to share the techniques and steps I use in observational drawing as a science illustrator to capture subjects in my sketchbook accurately. I will explain why I make certain decisions along the way and share all the techniques I work with so that you can try them out and decide how you like to work. The instructions are specific, and I will note which colors I use if that information is helpful to you. Following along with my process will help you figure out what works for you, and you will make up your steps and color choices as you develop your practice. You are always welcome and encouraged to deviate from my steps. I will prompt you to stop and reflect along the way to decide what works for you as a sketcher, and I hope that as you progress, you lean into the subjects, media, and techniques you love and enjoy doing.

Reflection

Why have you decided to pick up this book and start on this journey? What are you unsure of? What are you excited about? What do you hope to accomplish?

Materials

As each new skill is learned, you will merge it with those previously learned until, one day, you are simply drawing—just as, one day, you found yourself driving without thinking about how to do it.
—BETTY EDWARDS

You can begin working through this book with materials you have on hand, and I encourage you to use what is available. The first few projects can be done with a pencil and any paper, so you can start immediately as you collect some extra supplies to add color and ink.

You do not need to go out and buy fancy watercolors or brushes; however, you are welcome to. Student-grade watercolors are a great place to start. I began sketching with a Cotman travel watercolor palette with twelve student-grade colors. When I used them up, I got more concentrated artist watercolor paint in tubes and refilled the pans. The supplies worth investing in are a pen with permanent ink and watercolor paper that is smooth and

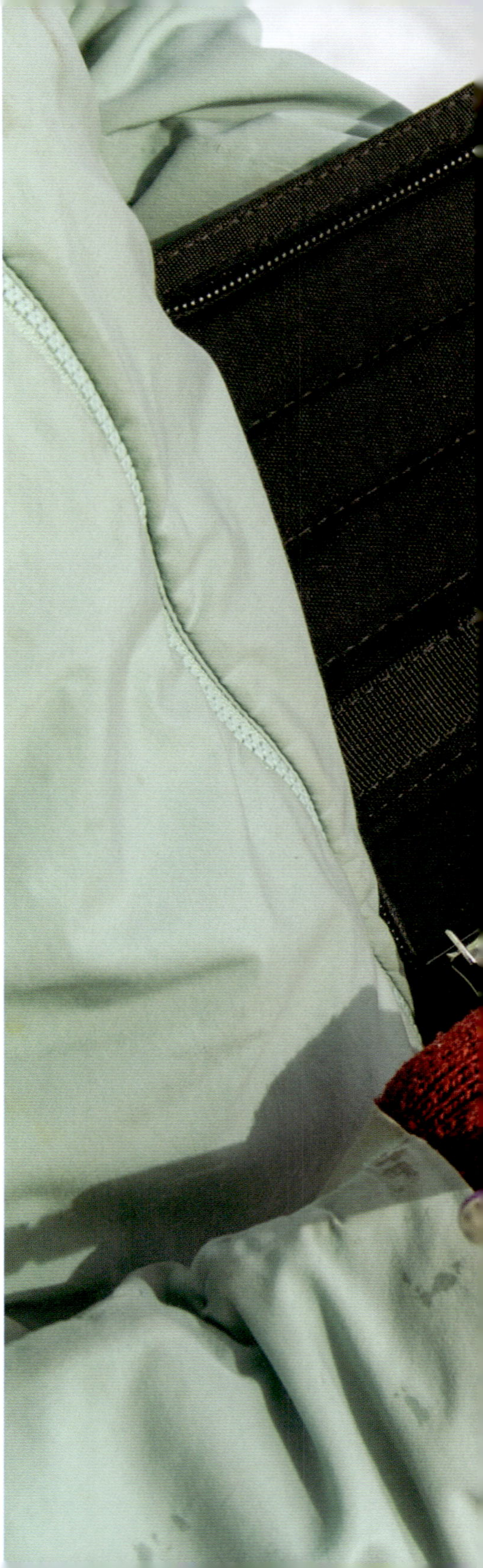

► Sketching in the winter with pencil and colored pencils that work even when it is below 0°F outside

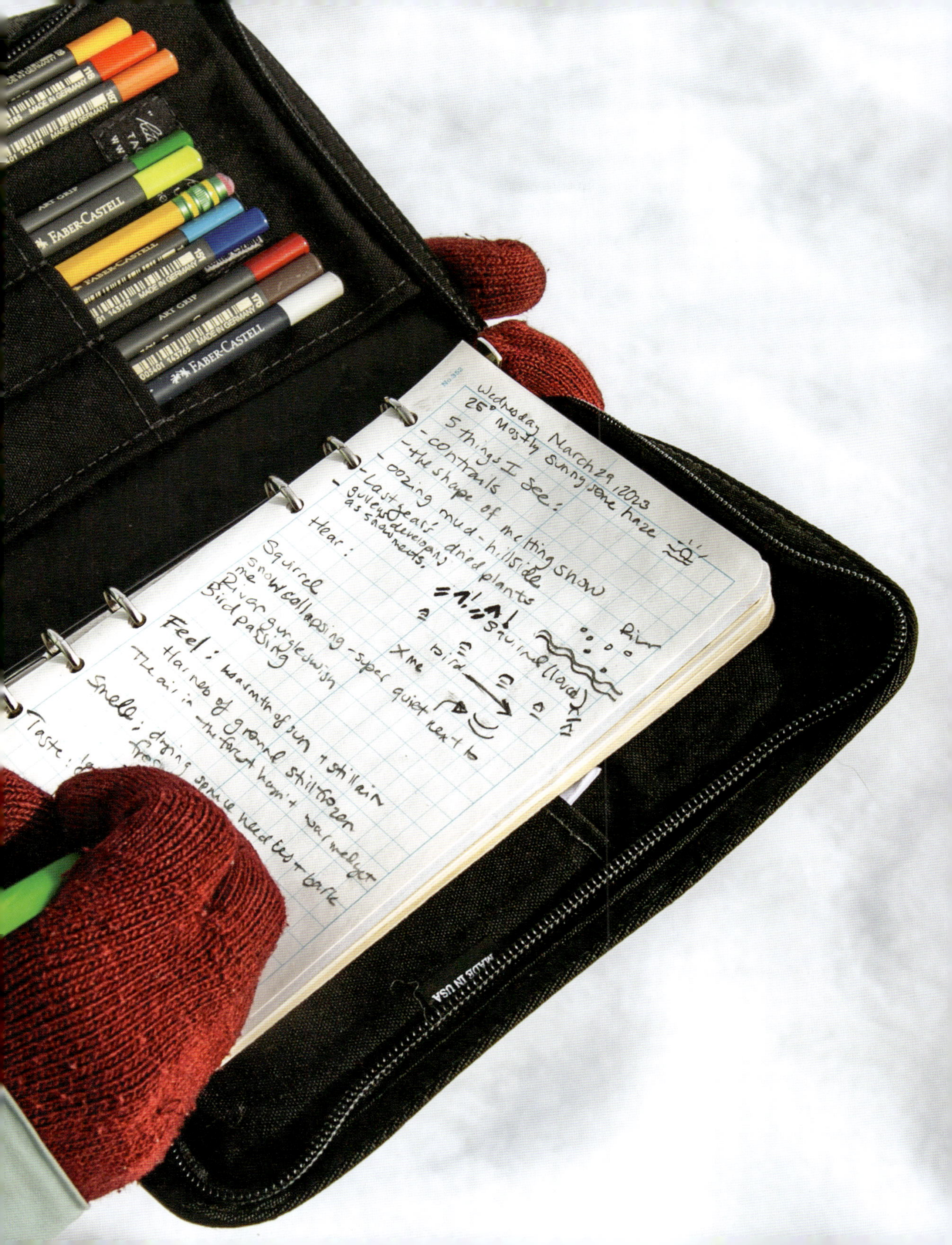

FABER-CASTELL
ART GRIP
MADE IN GERMANY
Wednesday March 29, 2023
25° Mostly sunny, some haze
5 things I see:
- contrails
- the shape of melting snow
- oozing mud-hillside
- Last year's dried plants
Hear:
Squirrel
River
Feel:
Smell:
Taste:
MADE IN USA

thick enough to take a series of washes. If you struggle to achieve a specific technique and it is frustrating, consider upgrading your materials.

There is also something freeing about working with affordable and readily available materials. If you find yourself scared to touch your fancy sketchbook or palette, try using a ballpoint pen and some cheap watercolor paints from the drugstore. Also, have a conversation with yourself about the worthiness of this endeavor. Life is too short to hoard fancy paper, as I often need to remind myself. Again, there are no rules; do what works for you!

WHAT I BRING WITH ME

These are the specific tools that I've tested and loved over many years of sketching. They are the tools that I use for all the projects in this book. The ones marked with an asterisk (*) are optional, and I will bring them along when I have extra space.

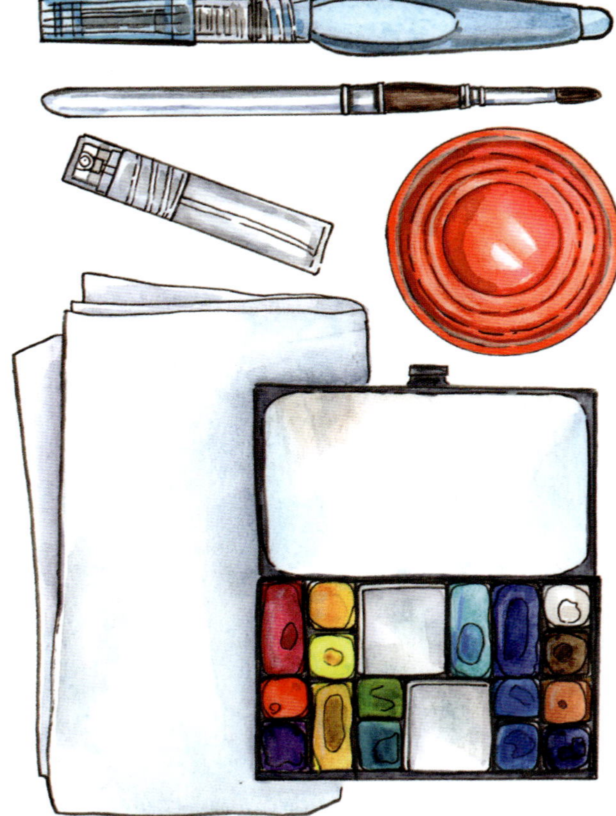

WATERCOLOR MATERIALS: brushes, palette, towel, spray bottle, and a small cup

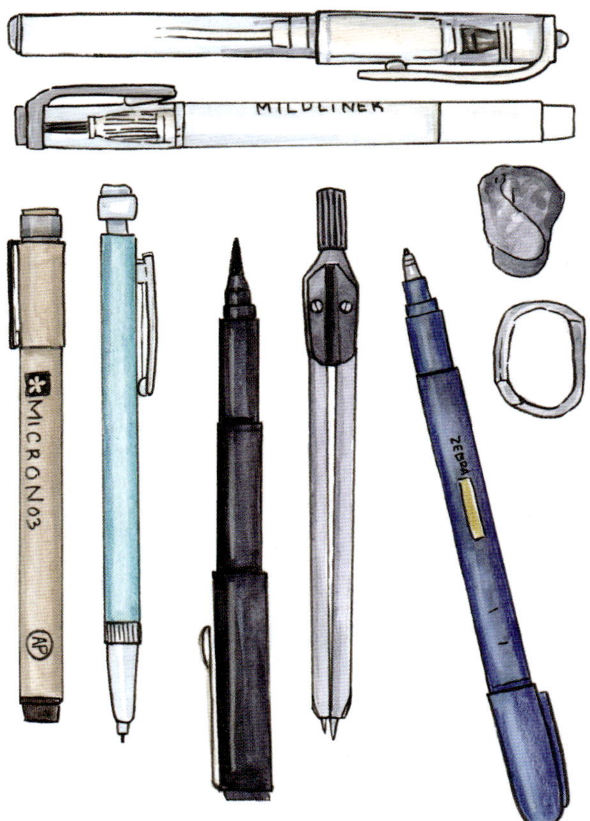

DRAWING TOOLS: pens, pencil, measuring dividers, and erasers

DRAWING IMPLEMENTS

MECHANICAL PENCIL. I use a BIC #2, 0.9 or 0.5 mm, which never gets dull and can be reloaded with graphite refills.

FINE PEN WITH WATERPROOF INK. I use a black 03 or 05 Pigma Micron by Sakura. Waterproof ink is essential so your lines won't smudge when adding watercolor.

BRUSH PEN(S) WITH PERMANENT INK. I use a Zebra Fude brush pen with a fine tip and a Pentel pocket brush pen.

LIGHT GRAY BRUSH PEN WITH WATER-SOLUBLE INK*. I use the Zebra Mildliner and Tombow pens

WHITE PEN*. I have mixed results with the ink drying up on these and don't always carry them, but they can be great for specific effects. My favorite is the uniball Signo.

PLASTIC AND KNEADED ERASERS. Use a plastic eraser to completely rub out lines and a kneaded eraser to lighten graphite.

MEASURING DIVIDERS*. This is a helpful drawing instrument for measuring things and transferring lengths into my sketchbook.

RULER. I carry a transparent 6-inch ruler

SET OF COLORED PENCILS*. I use a set of 24 Faber-Castell Polychromos pencils. I keep them in a case that telescopes down so the pencils are easy to see and access. I also carry a travel pencil sharpener and a small baggie to pack out pencil shavings on longer trips.

WATERCOLOR

I have a travel watercolor palette that I fill with paint from tubes and then let it dry in the pan so I can take it with me. The more mixing space the palette has, the better, but I also love a tiny palette that fits in my pocket.

My condensed and basic palette has a warm and cool version of each primary color. I also usually bring some neutrals and secondary colors to speed up mixing and a few extra blues because I like the range of colors I can get mixing with them. I use Daniel Smith watercolors. I also have a few palettes with natural pigment and sometimes make my own paint, but for this book, I'll work with colors that are commercially available and pretty easy to find.

Primary Colors

PYRROL SCARLET: warm red

QUINACRIDONE ROSE: cool red (magenta)

NEW GAMBOGE: warm yellow

HANSA YELLOW LIGHT: cool yellow

QUINACRIDONE GOLD: ranges from warm, bright yellow to almost brown.

FRENCH ULTRAMARINE: warm blue

PHTHALO BLUE (GREEN SHADE): cool blue

CERULEAN BLUE, CHROMIUM: cool blue, similar to a toned-down Phthalo; terrific for mixing light grays and painting skies

COBALT TEAL BLUE: greenish blue that granulates beautifully

INDANTHRONE BLUE: extra-deep blue that is almost purple-black. I love mixing dark grays with it.

Secondary Colors

SAP GREEN: warm green. I usually mix my own, but sometimes there is a lot of green in the world, which is a good baseline for a natural green.

PHTHALO TURQUOISE: cool green that is great for iridescent subjects and night skies

CARBAZOLE VIOLET: purple that is helpful for iridescent subjects and night skies

Neutral Colors

RAW UMBER: cool brown

BURNT SIENNA: warm reddish brown

BUFF TITANIUM: warm, semitransparent whitish brown

ZINC WHITE GOUACHE: More opaque than watercolor, gouache is great for layering on top when bringing some lighter tones back. You can also mix it with watercolor to make an opaque, lighter version of a color.

NO BLACK? I am not opposed to black paint, but I learned how to mix color without having black and got used to it. Mixing my own blacks and dark tones creates another layer of color that adds depth.

BRUSHES AND TOOLS

Carry a small paper towel or absorbent rag, or cut off a cotton sock to wear around your wrist and wipe your brushes off with.

Bring along a tiny spray bottle filled with water to wet your palette and paper.

My go-to brush is a plastic water brush where I can load water into the barrel. I usually work with small or medium sizes and like several different brands. I also love having a traditional brush because they hold more paint and create a greater variety of lines. I have a set of round Escoda travel brushes in sizes 2, 6, and 10, where the handle becomes the cap to protect the bristles. I carry a small container to put water in when I use these brushes. Because it is a little fussier than using a water brush, I use this setup when making a bigger sketch or if I have more time and a comfortable place to sketch.

Primary colors

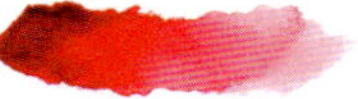
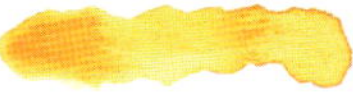

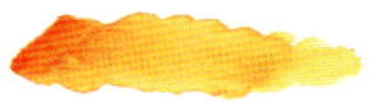
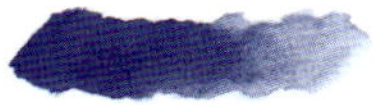
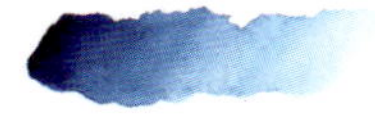

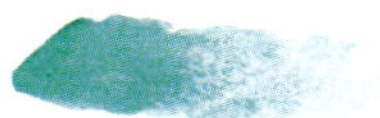

Secondary colors and neutrals

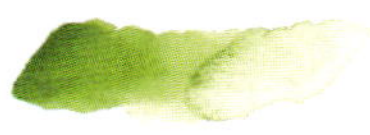
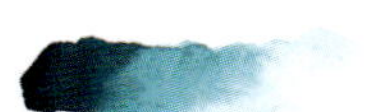
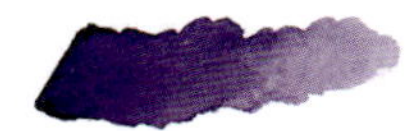
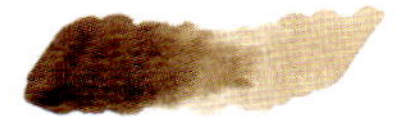
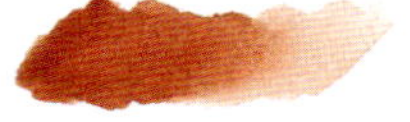

► Color swatches painted from a palette.

PAPER AND SKETCHBOOKS

I almost always have a small, lightweight sketchbook for taking notes and making small drawings and something with heavier-weight paper for watercolor. I switch back and forth between sketching in a sketchbook and on loose watercolor paper. I prefer working on smooth, hot-pressed paper because I like a smooth paper to draw on. I look for watercolor or mixed media paper that is 140 lbs (255 grams per square meter) or thicker.

If I sketch on loose watercolor paper, I store the finished sketches in accordion folders organized by month of the year or by place. This becomes an archive of information I can reference based on the season, which gets added to over the years. I did the projects for this book on a block of 7 x 9–inch hot-pressed watercolor paper, which is portable and high-quality. A block has glued edges so the paper is held in place and stretched flat as it dries.

Sometimes, I also like to sketch on toned paper, like Canson Mi-Teintes gray pastel paper. This paper can take a light wash and works well with colored pencils and a bit of gouache.

I enjoy the freedom of sketching on loose paper or in binders or spiral-bound books where I can move the pages around. It is easy for me to scan the pages for work or to frame and give away my sketches. Sometimes I also enjoy keeping a bound sketchbook.

PAPER SIZE

My preference is to find the balance of something portable but also big enough to spread out and have space for detail and notes when sketching. I often work in a 5.5 x 8.5–inch sketchbook, which creates a spread the size of a full sheet of paper. I did the project work in this book on 7 x 9–inch paper, except for some landscapes where I intentionally worked smaller to force myself to simplify. For the projects in this book, I encourage you not to go too small so that your sketches don't get cramped. If you struggle to get the detail you want in your sketches, try working on a larger piece of paper; 7 x 9 or 9 x 12–inch should work well.

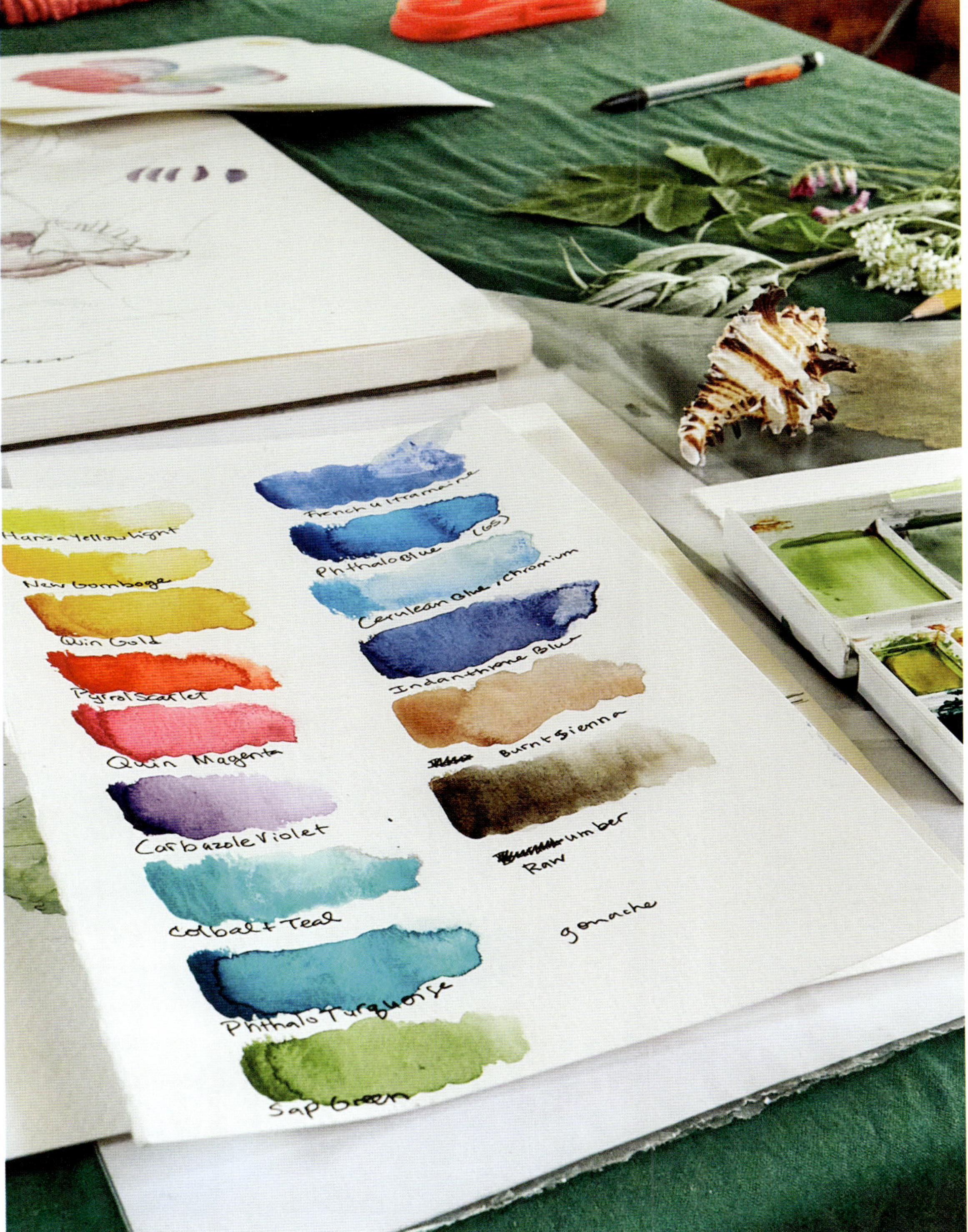
Hansa Yellow Light
New Gamboge
Quin Gold
Pyrol Scarlet
Quin Magenta
Carbazole Violet
Colbalt Teal
Phthalo Turquoise
Sap Green
French Ultramarine
Phthalo Blue (GS)
Cerulean Blue Chromium
Indanthrone Blue
Burnt Sienna
umber
Raw
gouache

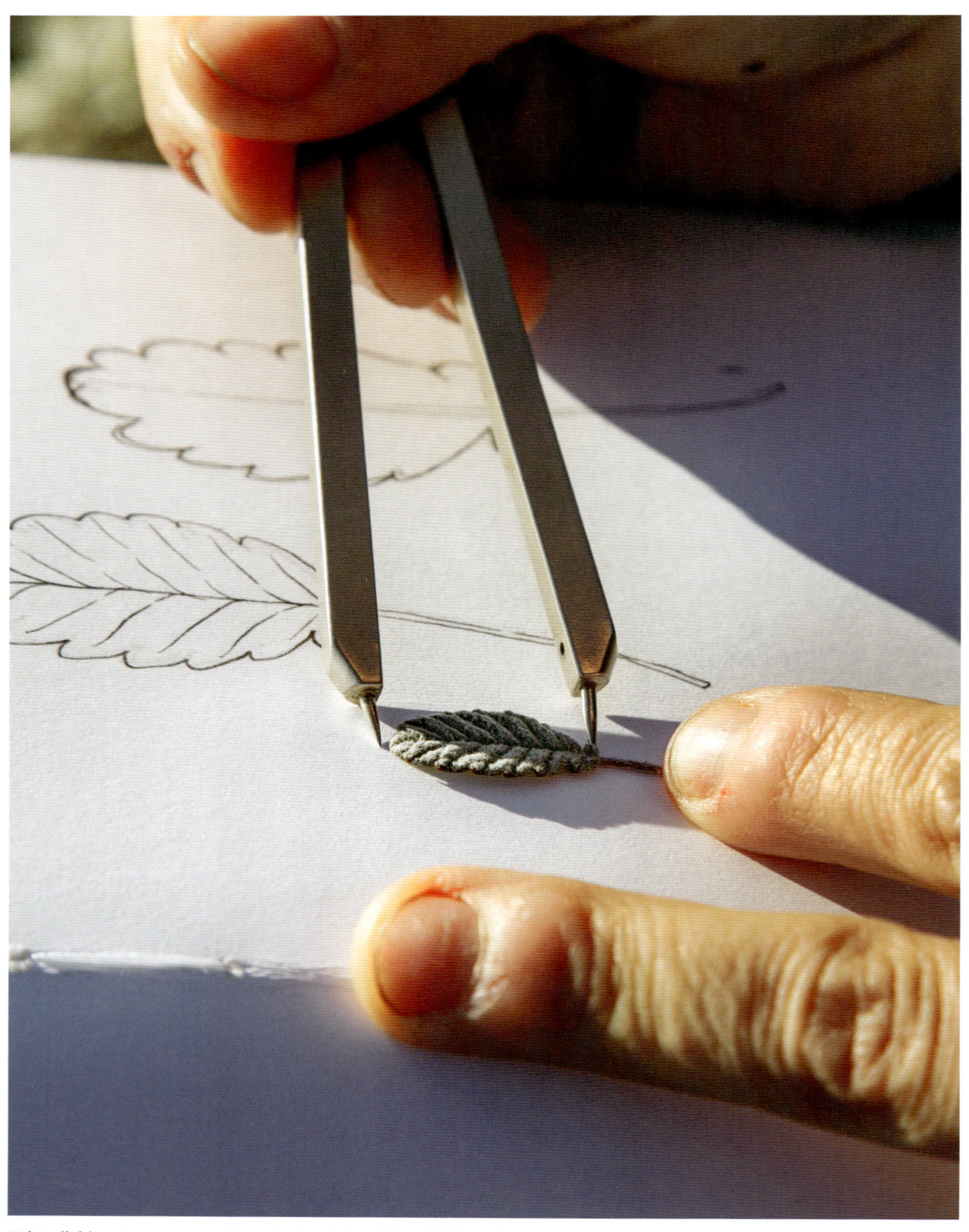

Using dividers to measure a dryas leaf and sketch it at 200% scale

Sketchbooks

I prefer the Stillman and Birn Zeta series and Hahnemühle watercolor sketchbooks. I also like the Bee Paper Company Super Deluxe Mixed Media sketchbook. I enjoy trying out different sketchbooks with different paper and page sizes.

I usually keep sketchbooks for specific trips and chunks of time. I love sketchbooks that focus on a place or season, which I have continued adding to over several years. I have sketchbooks for plants I found traveling through the Southwestern United States and for autumn observations. I have one for the area around the Root Glacier, where I live. There is something special about having all my drawings bound into one book. All my sketchbooks have pages that turned out poorly or were started and never finished (maybe it started raining). I like to keep those pages to curb my perfectionism as an artist. Those outlier pages also tell the story of a trip and an experience. If a page bothers you, you can collage over a page or turn it into something different.

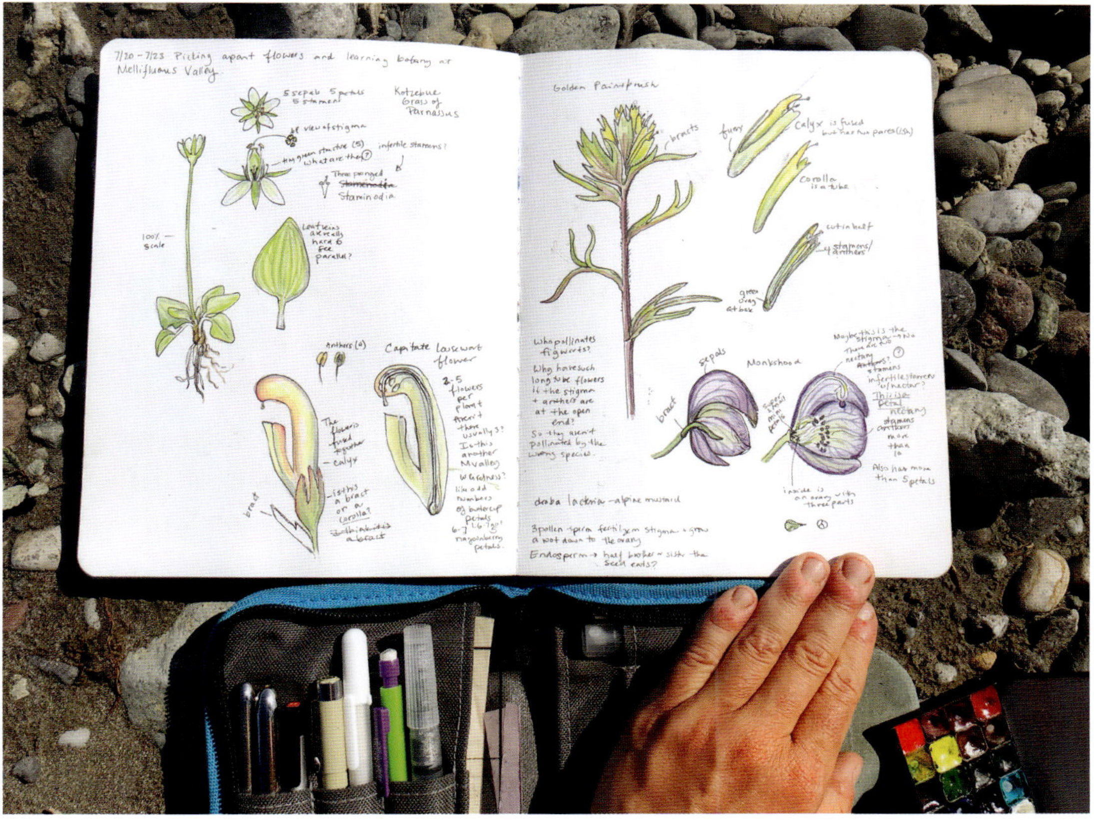

My sketchbook page exploring alpine botany and my portable kit with watercolor and drawing supplies

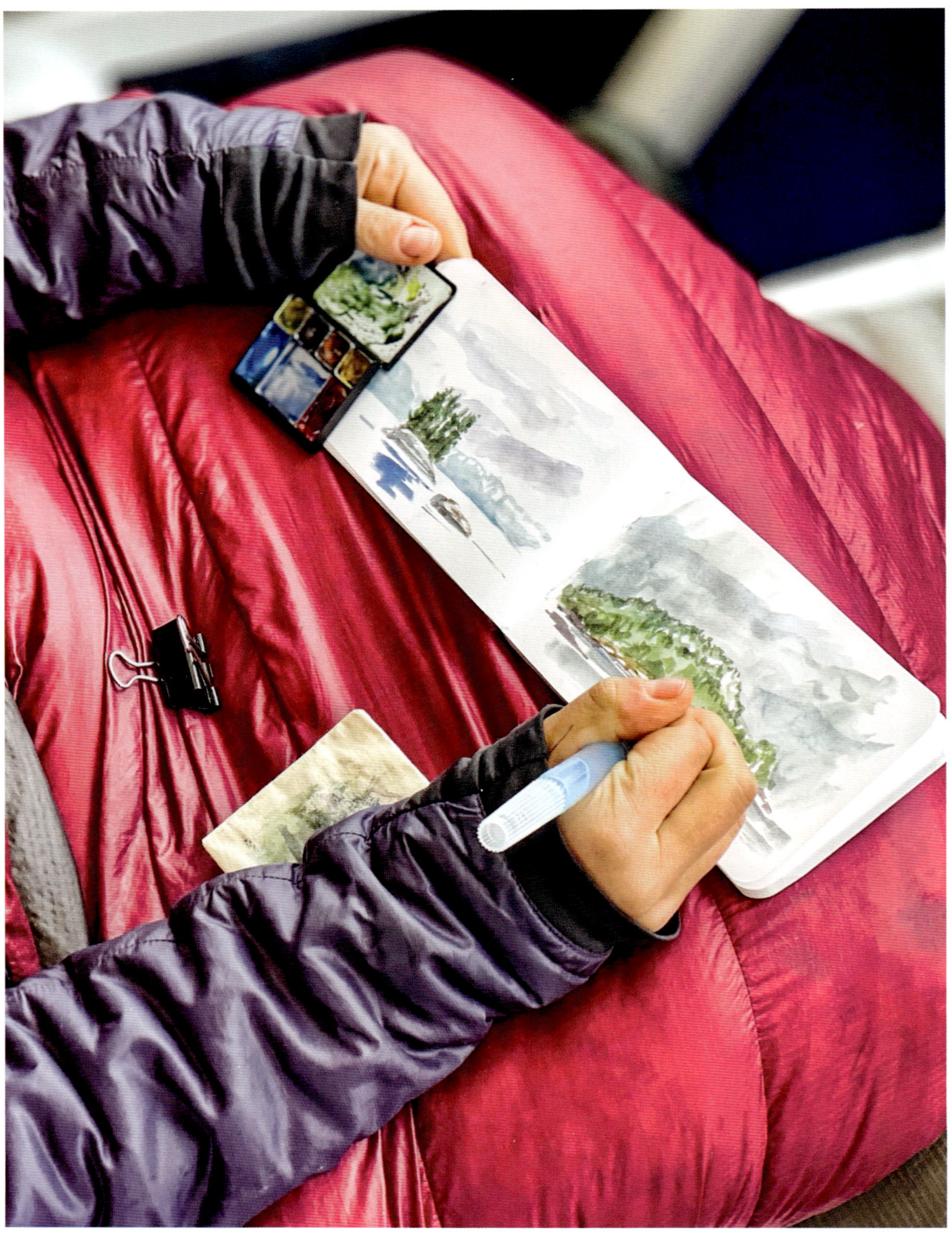

OTHER

When I return to the studio, I sometimes add some white details with Dr. Ph. Martin's Bleedproof White.

I also have a good pencil sharpener to ensure that my pencils are sharp when I head out.

I make sure to bring along a phone or camera to take pictures with.

I also carry along a Bodelin microscope lens attachment for my phone camera or a hand lens to look at small details (about 20x).

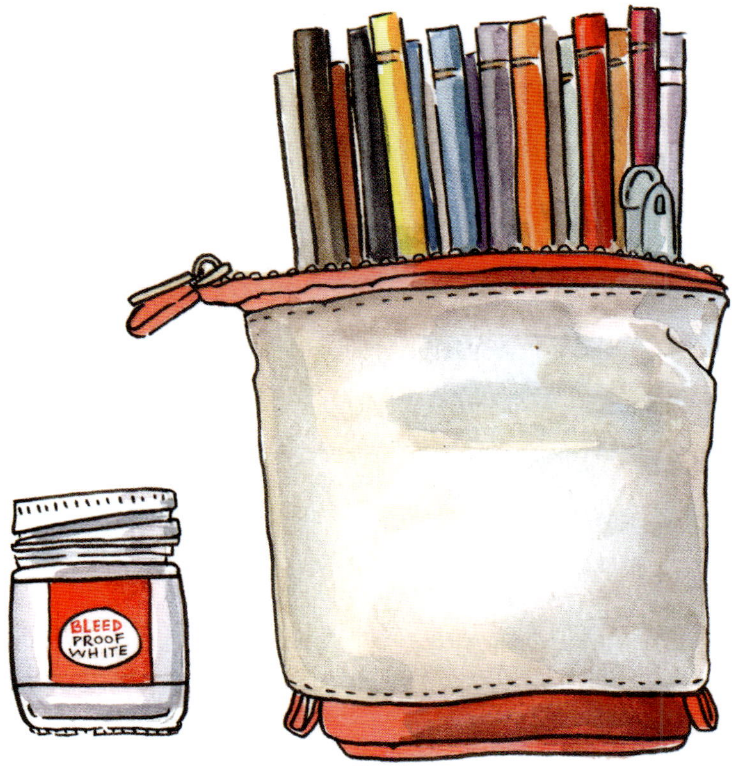

◀ Using a small portable sketching kit to paint from the back deck of a ferry while snuggled in a sleeping bag to stay warm

Getting Started with Drawing

A drawing is simply a line going for a walk.
—PAUL KLEE

We begin with drawing because it can provide time to slow down, observe, and map out the structure of a subject. With a light pencil mark, you can describe the main shapes that can get filled in later with shading, color, and texture. A line drawing can also be a finished work in its own right. A line can convey so much information and feeling, depending on its weight and character. A thick, straight stroke will read differently than a thin, wavering passage, and both can be beautiful. I love the act of drawing because it feels like a meditation on paper. Most of the work in this book begins with drawing, usually with a pencil but sometimes with a pen.

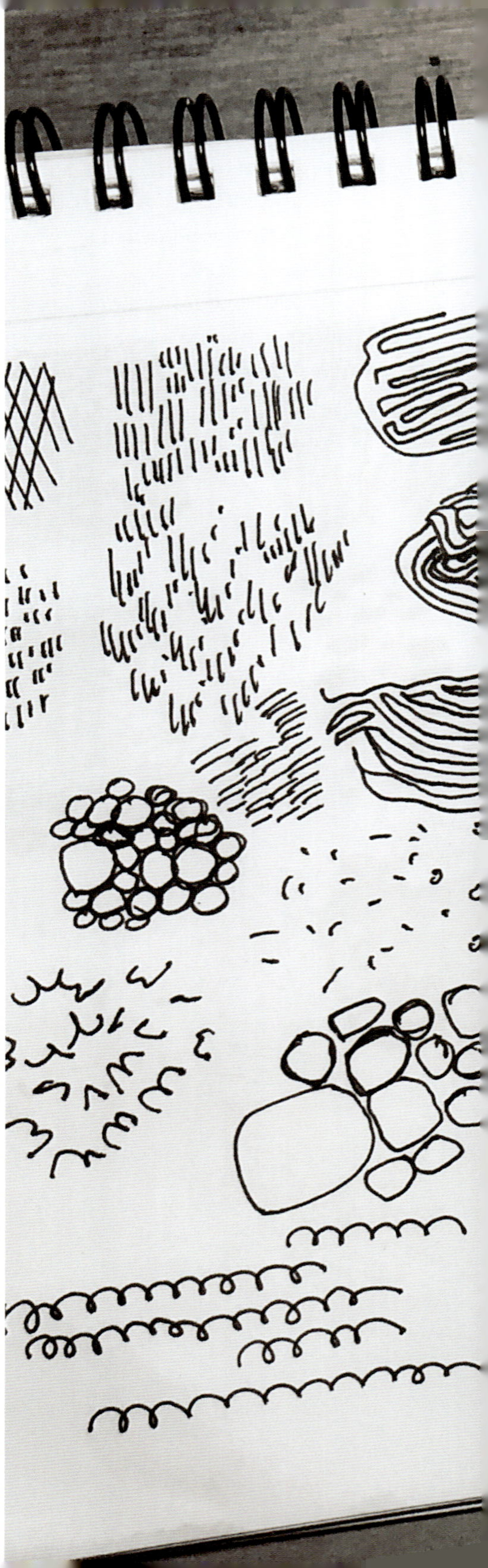

► Warming up by drawing different lines, marks, and textures with pen

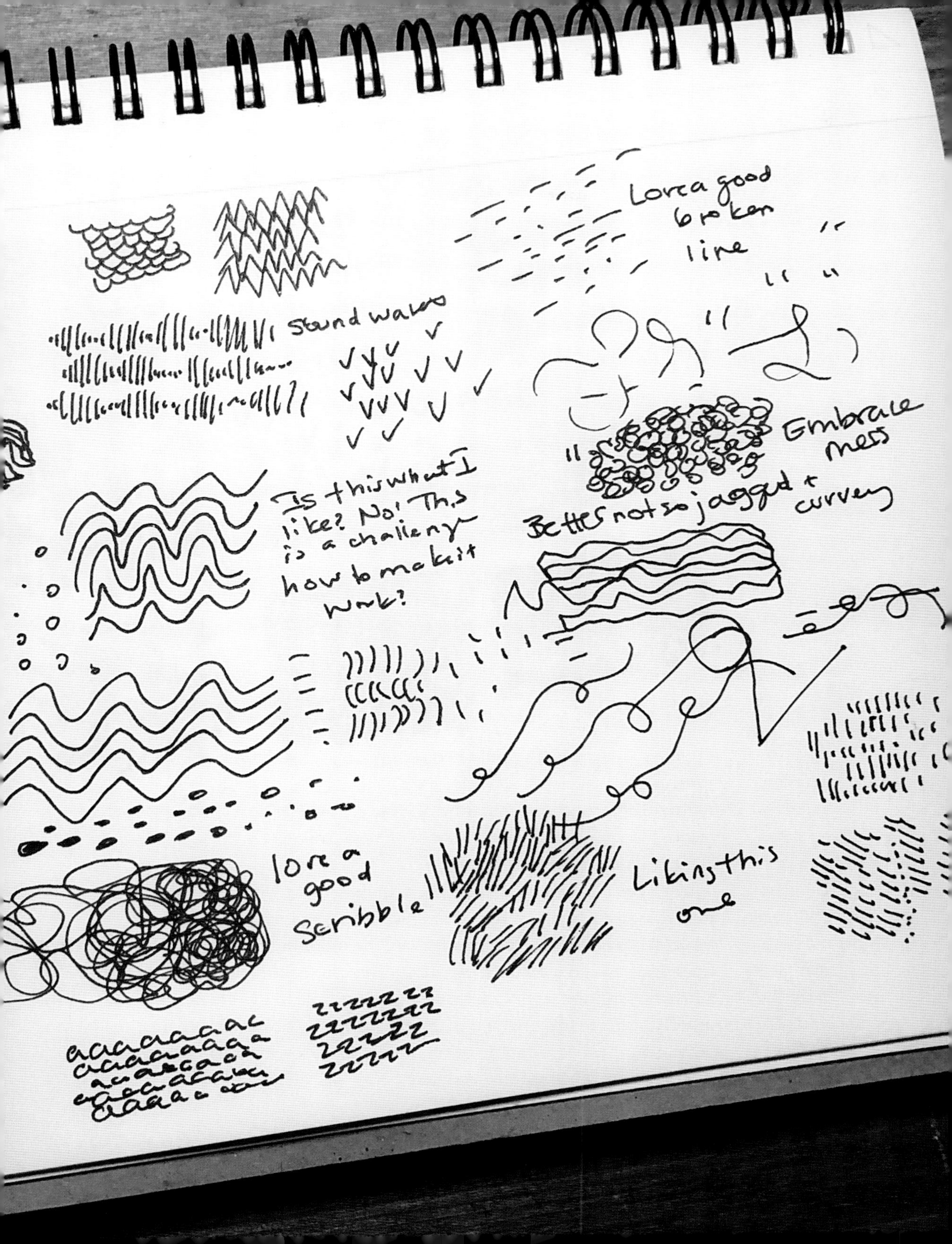

Love a good broken line

"

" "

Sound waves

Embrace mess

Is this what I like? No! This is a challenge how to make it work?

Better not so jagged + curvey

love a good Scribble

Liking this one

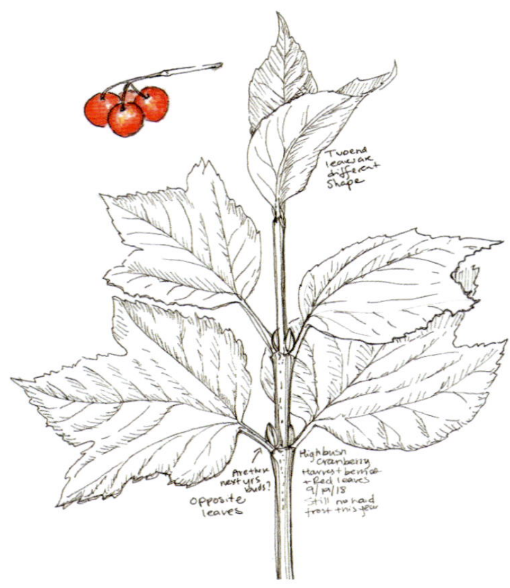

Pen sketch of a highbush cranberry plant with minimal color

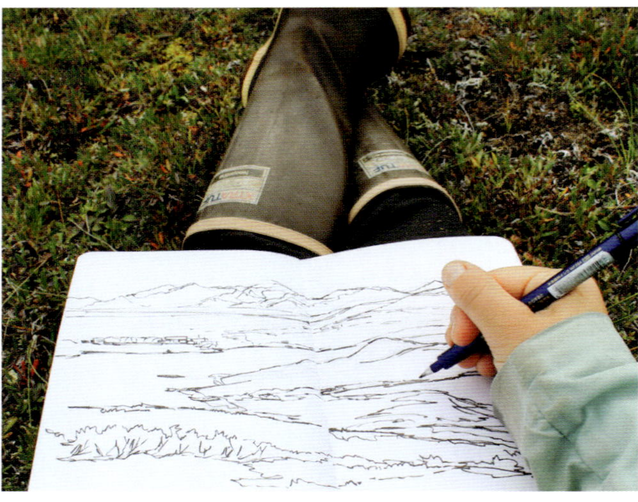

A line drawing with brush pen is the foundation of this landscape sketch of the tundra near Toolik Field Station.

For the following two chapters, you will need a drawing implement (pen or pencil) and drawing paper, which can be lighter in weight than watercolor or mixed media paper. It is also helpful to have a timing device. We will begin with a few exercises to warm up our drawing muscles. Sketching is a connection between the brain and the body, so working on hand-eye coordination is essential. The goal for the first exercise is to trick ourselves out of perfectionism and to focus on the process rather than the resulting drawing.

WARMING UP

A blank page can be intimidating. When I am struggling to find a place to begin, I warm up by drawing a series of lines. This gets my pen, hand, arm, and brain talking to each other.

Fill a piece of paper, or a section, with lines. Start with a straight line, then draw a curvy line, a jagged line, and a dashed line. How many different types of lines can you make? Vary the weight and thickness of your lines. Play around with drawing marks. You can make little circles, dashes, X-marks, scribbles, etc. Notice that when multiple marks are next to each other, they form textures and patterns. The more you practice these, the better your hand-eye coordination becomes and the more you'll learn what types of marks you like to make.

CONTOUR AND GESTURE DRAWING

These two exercises focus on drawing what you observe instead of what you think you see. For example, when I imagine drawing a human eye, I would create an almond shape with a circle in the middle. However, if I look closely, I notice that there is more to it. The eyelid has folds and creases. There is a tear duct, and the circle of the iris is not complete, etc. We will practice slowing down and speeding up to get outside our comfort zones.

Use the two photos below as references for the contour and gesture drawing exercises that follow.

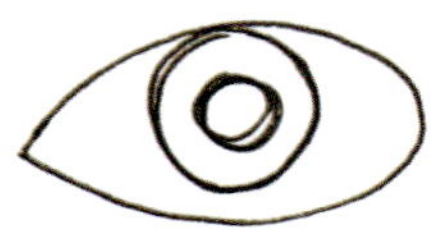

A drawing of what I think an eye looks like

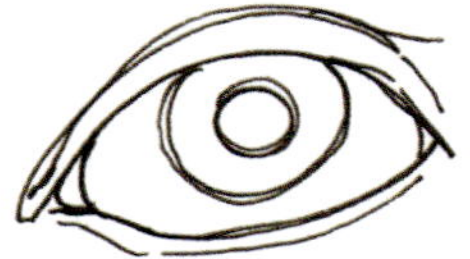

A drawing of an eye when drawn from observation

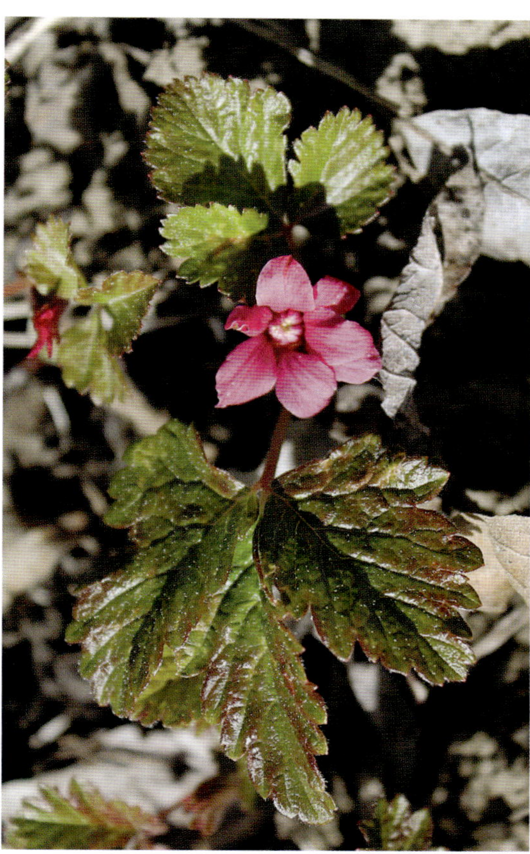

A nagoonberry flower

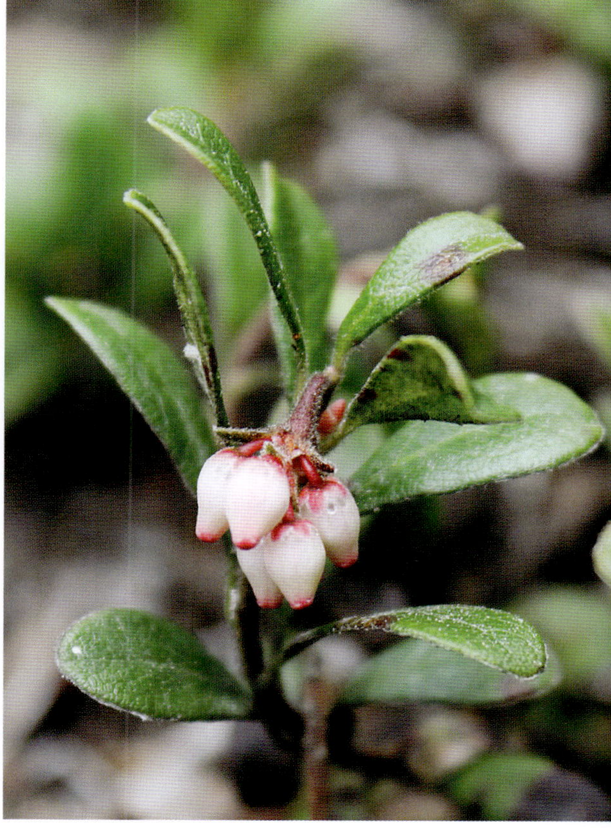

A kinnikinnick inflorescence.

CONTOUR DRAWING

This is an exercise in slowing down. Begin by drawing without looking at your paper to challenge yourself to focus entirely on the subject. Draw one continuous line without picking up your pen, feeling the subject's shape with the pen's tip as you go. Travel slowly, like a tiny creature walking across the subject, moving your pen with small motions in your fingers and wrist. Focus on the shape and structure of the subject and delve into the details that seem important to you. I will often go over a line or shape more than once to keep my hand moving and connect different parts of the subject. When I don't look at my paper, the drawing will get skewed and out of place, which is OK. The drawing is abstract, but when I look closely, I see moments of truth in the scribbles.

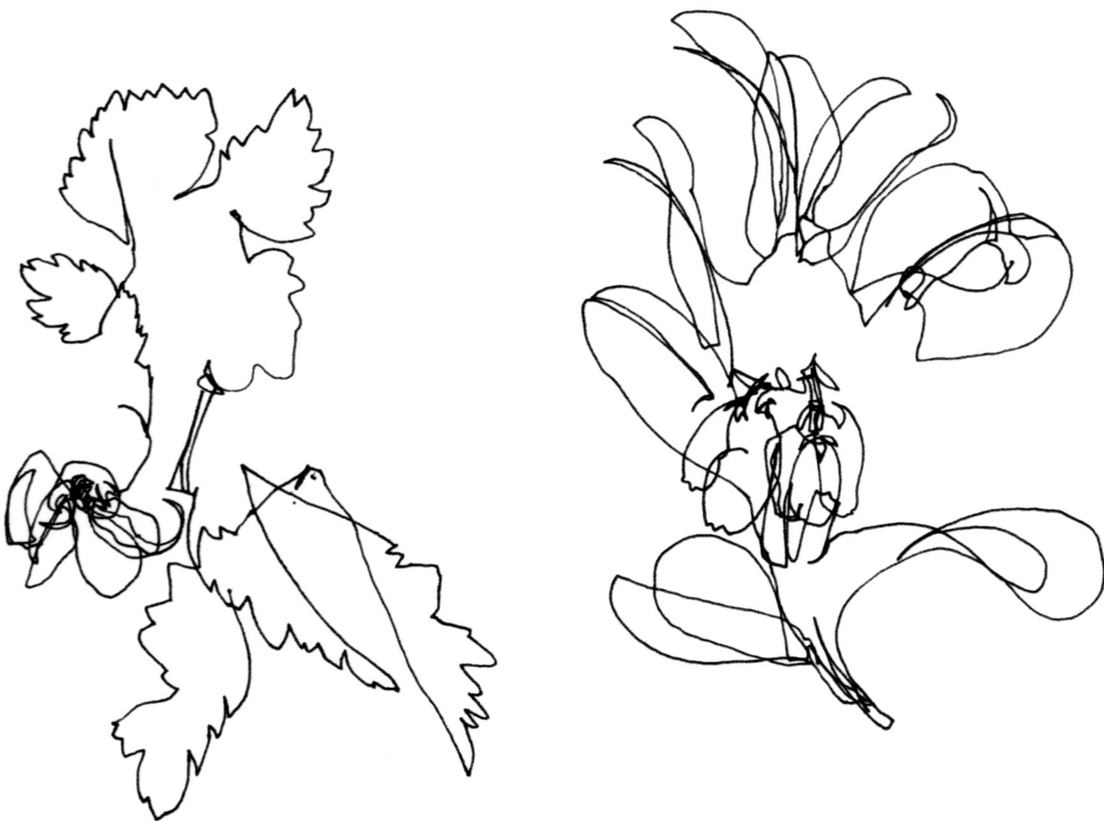

Contour drawings done without looking at the paper

GESTURE DRAWING

This is an exercise in speeding up. I will set my timer for 30 seconds and work as quickly as possible. Practice drawing with your whole arm hinging at the shoulder and blocking in the big shapes that make up your subject. For example, if I am drawing a plant, I start with the main stem as a simple line, then add other lines for the leaves and maybe some blobby circles for flowers or big shapes. If I have time, I'll go over those shapes again with the pen to refine them and add more detail.

Gesture sketching is excellent for moving animals. Start with the main body chunks by drawing ovals and circles for the shoulders, hips, and head and then connect them with lines for the limbs. Once you have a stick figure of sorts, you can "flesh it out" and add more information.

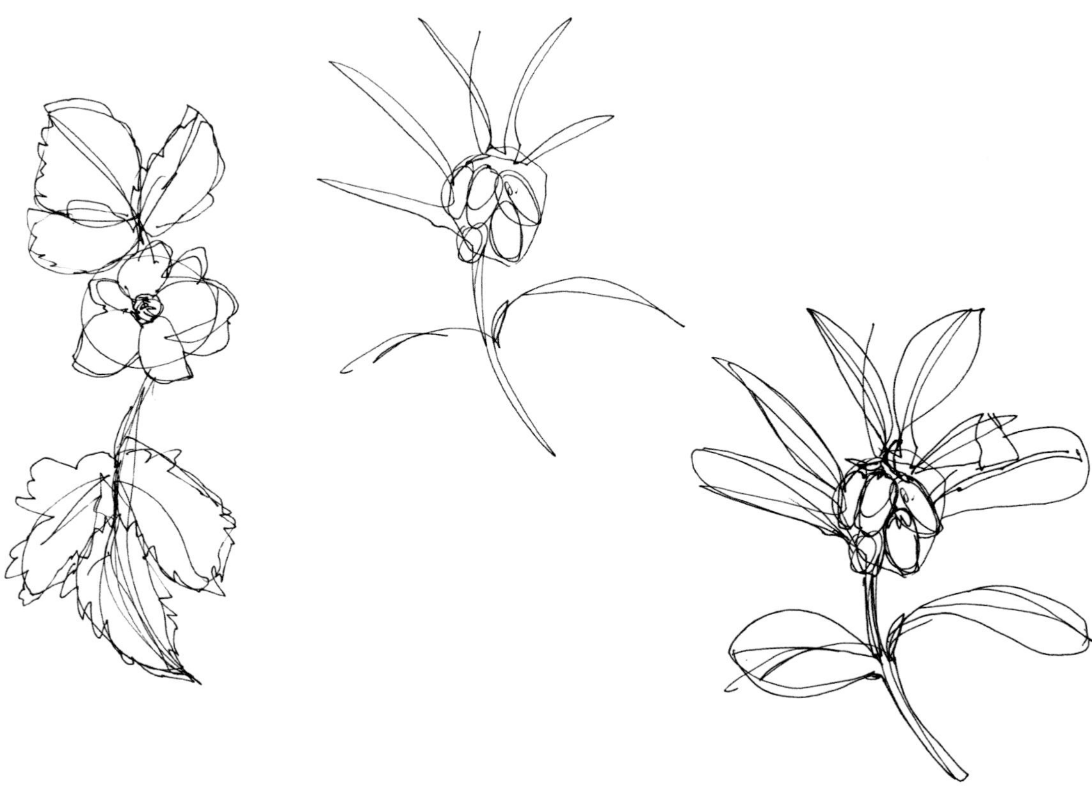

Gesture drawings. In the kinnikinnick plant example, there are two steps: I began with the simple shapes and lines, then filled out the leaves and details of the flower shapes.

HOW I WORK WITH CONTOUR AND GESTURE

I use contour and gesture sketching as warm-ups, but I also incorporate them into my regular practice because they help me change how I draw and see more deeply. Contour drawing is the foundation of my work because it feels like a peaceful meditation connecting my hand and the world. I often warm up by making contour drawings without looking at my paper, but I will also practice contour drawing when I glance at my paper from time to time. I like using this for landscapes, plants, and organic subjects with many squiggly lines and organic shapes. It is helpful for foreshortened subjects, when a leaf or other structure appears to come straight at you.

I use gesture sketching to capture something changing or moving (animals, sunsets, weather, trees in the wind). Sometimes, I'll make gesture sketches with paint. Gesture sketching tends to give the drawing life, and sometimes that is more important than accurately rendering every angle and proportion.

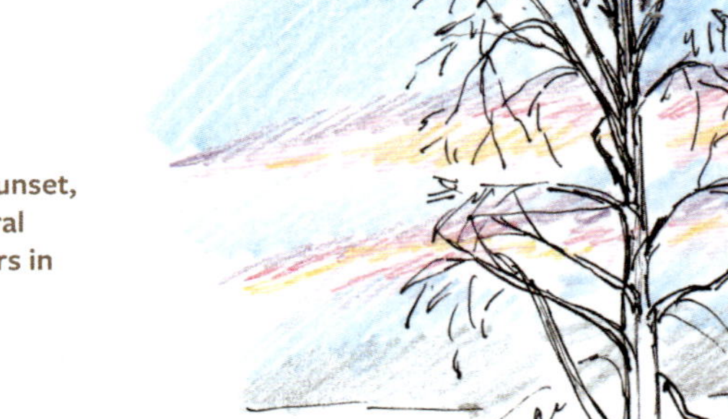

In this quick sketch of a birch tree at sunset, I used gesture sketching to get a general sense of the tree and to mark the colors in the background with colored pencils.

MEASURING TECHNIQUES

Contour and gesture sketching help us see and notice the shapes in the subject we are trying to draw, but incorporating some measurements can help us get those shapes into the right places and proportions. Below are some of my favorite measuring tricks to use in the field.

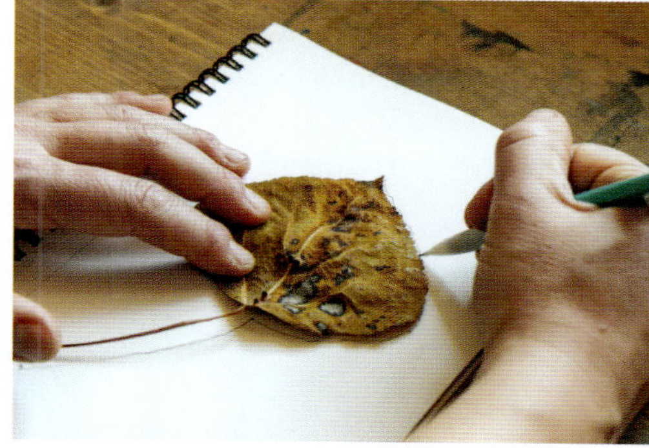

Using a pencil to trace a cottonwood leaf

TRACING: Trace when you can. If you can safely pick up a leaf, put it on your paper, and draw around it, that can be the quickest way to get the right shape. I don't have the most drawing control when I trace something, so I make my tracing very light and then go over my lines with more detail by looking at my subject. If you cannot trace the whole thing, you can still mark the size or main angles using tracing.

USING A PENCIL TO MEASURE PROPORTIONS: If you can't trace something, you can measure the size with your pencil. If you can hold your pencil (or a similar object) next to the subject, make a mark with a finger and transfer that mark. Maybe the thing you are drawing is far away. You can still use this technique to compare and measure proportions. For example, a distant mountain could be 2.5 times as wide as it is tall.

USING A PENCIL TO MEASURE ANGLES: You can also hold your pencil out in front of you, squint one eye, measure the angle of something (such as that distant mountain ridge), and then transfer that angle onto your paper.

USING DIVIDERS: I carry measuring dividers and a clear plastic ruler for more precise measurements. The ruler helps record measurements and capture numbers. Those measurements can be helpful later on when identifying a specific plant or animal track. Doubling your measurements can enlarge things by 200%, which can be beneficial for sketching tiny subjects.

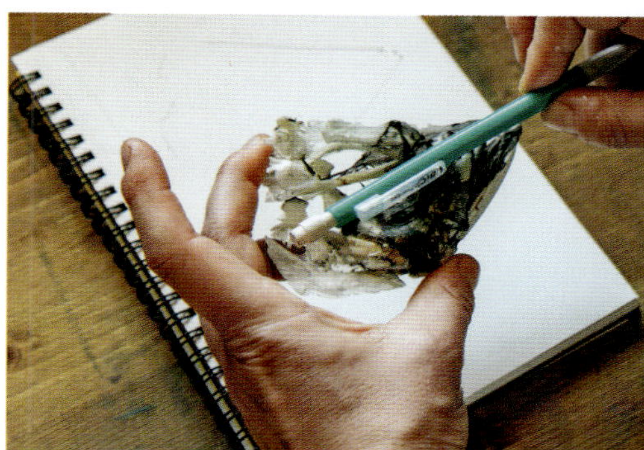

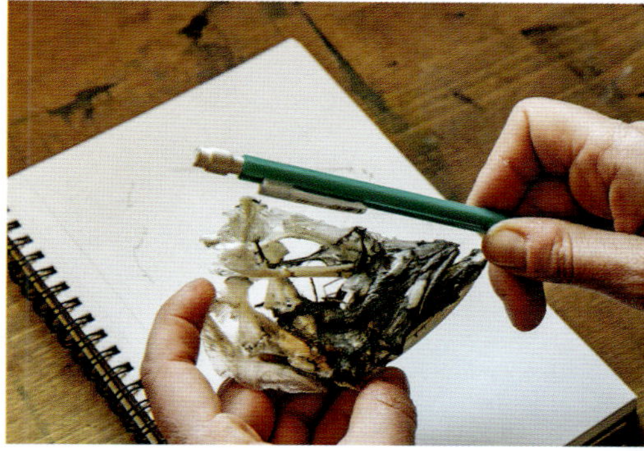

Using a pencil to measure the width and angle of a salmon bone

Project 1

LINE DRAWING OF A LEAF

We will practice drawing a brown cottonwood leaf using lines in this project. When the leaf dried, the edges curled, giving us some interesting shapes to capture.

MATERIALS: a pencil and drawing paper

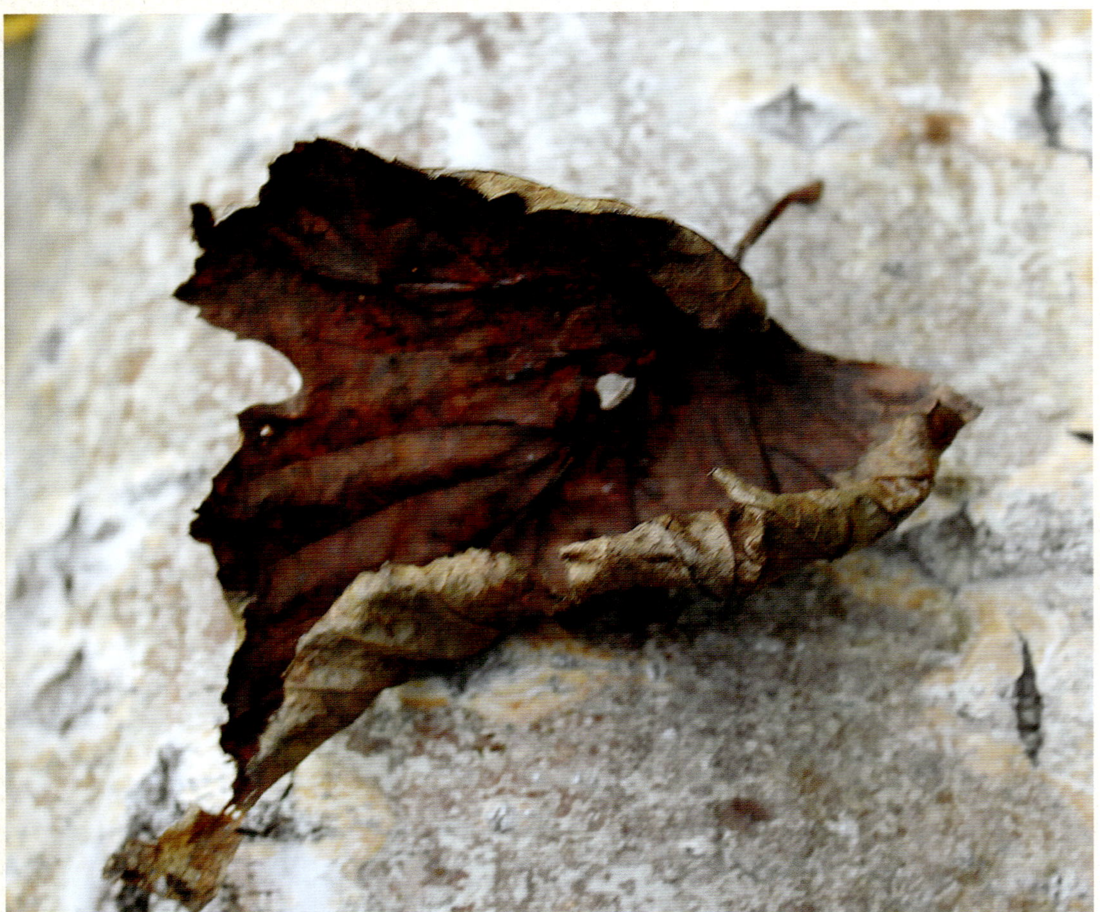

Leaves may be most vibrant when green in the spring and summer, but they are still exciting subjects to study when they have fallen from the tree onto the ground.

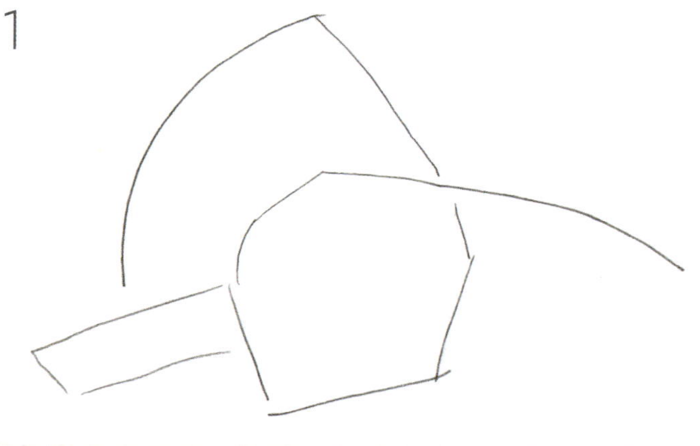

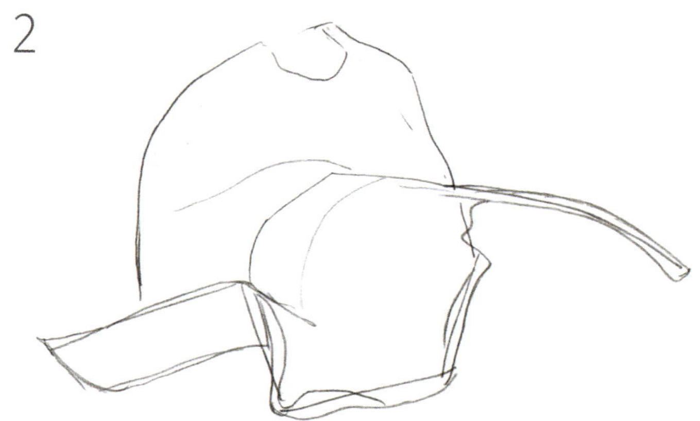

STEP 1: Start with a pencil sketch of the basic shapes you observe. I started with the stem and mid-rib vein and then outlined a triangle shape where I noticed the edges of the leaf on the top section. I will come back to sketch in the chunk that is missing. The bottom section of the leaf is drawn as a rectangle on the left, where you can see the top part and three lines coming together to form the other section.

STEP 2: Refine the first sketch by adding the shapes where the leaf edges are curled over. I added in the section where the leaf is missing at the top. In the second step of a rough sketch, I refined the straight lines into curves, but I will focus on the fine details next, such as the margin of the leaf.

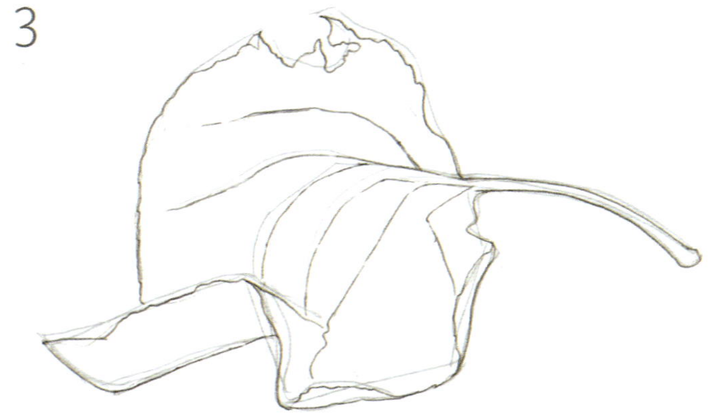

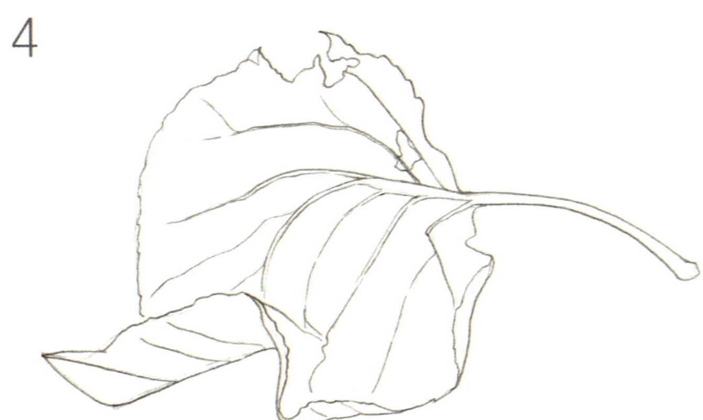

STEP 3: Go over the straight lines to add detail and texture, such as the jagged, toothed margin of the leaf. Refine the shapes as you go, erasing where needed. I moved some of the veins slightly as I went.

STEP 4: Add more lines and detail to capture the shape of the holes in the leaf and the secondary veins that are important to the structure. Pay attention to the shape and curve of these lines and how they help define the shape of the leaf in your drawing.

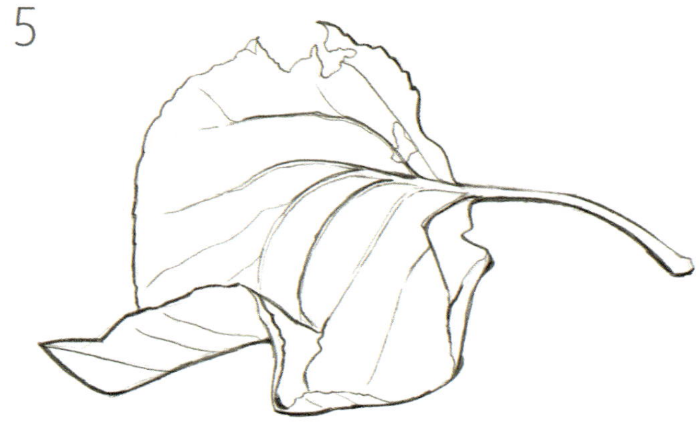

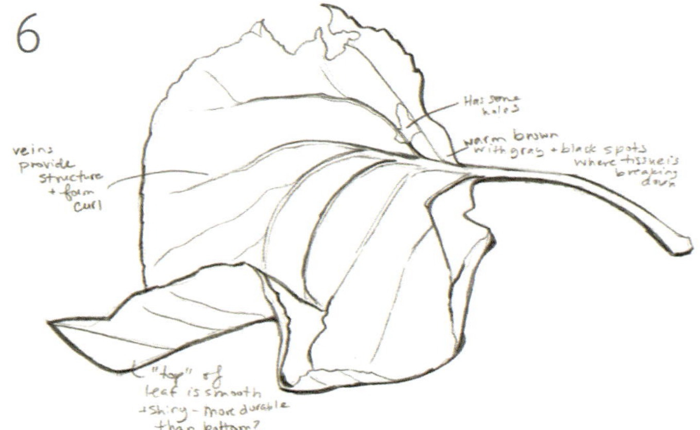

STEP 5: Go over some lines to add thickness in places. Variation in line weight makes the drawing more dynamic. Heavy lines are darker and will appear to pop forward. Thicker lines can also indicate areas in shadow.

STEP 6: Add some written notes about your observations while creating the sketch. What did you notice at first when you looked at the leaf? What else did you notice as you spent more time observing it while making the drawing? A line drawing can capture a lot of information, but not everything. You can add notes about color, texture, patterns, and other observations.

FINDING BEAUTY IN THE "UGLY"

I create a weekly sketch for my local newspaper, *The Copper River Record*, to highlight some aspects of what is happening in the natural world around us during that time of year. I love this job, but sometimes it is a challenge to come up with a subject to draw. I feel like I have sketched it all before, even though I know that isn't true. I also know there is always a new way of looking at something. The same tree on the river might have changed since the last time I drew it; maybe it is flowering now or dropping its leaves, or a vole has cached some berries in the nook in its trunk.

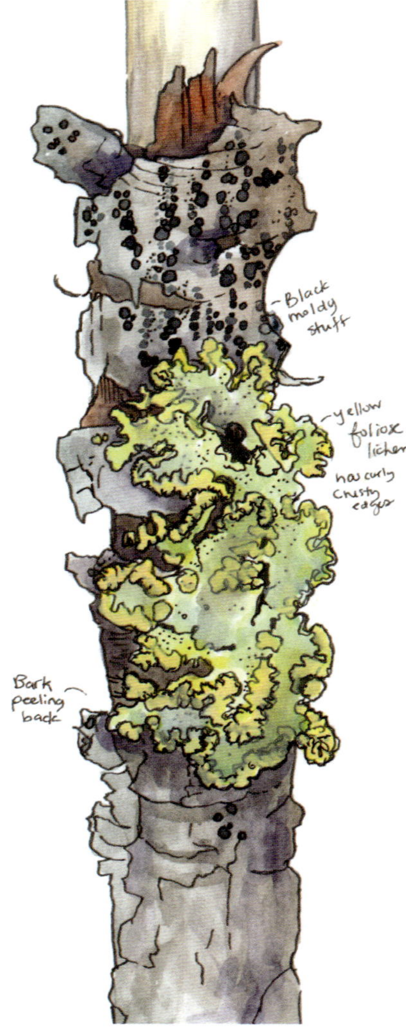

Watercolor and pen sketch of a rotting stick with peeling bark, mold, and lichen

One week, searching for something to sketch, I picked up a decaying stick that had broken off a branch of a willow tree. It had some interesting shapes and one pretty patch of yellow lichen that drew me in, but mostly, it appeared dead, peeling, and somewhat ugly. I decided to sketch it anyway, and in the process, I started to fall in love with all the beauty I found through spending time and attention on it. The yellow of the lichen complemented the purple of the shadows in the bark, making it even more vibrant after the recent storm. The shapes of the peeling bark tell the story of a branch that was once contributing to part of a tree or shrub but is now home to the decomposers there, these lichens and molds. There were also probably insects inside and bacteria that I couldn't see working on that wood and bark, releasing nutrients that other things in the forest would appreciate. I noticed all these tiny black spots, which looked like a random pattern, like freckles or stars scattered across the sky. I thought they might be slime mold or regular mold; I didn't know, but I wanted to look it up and see if I could learn. What is the difference between mold and slime mold? I wondered. I asked myself what other questions I had. What makes that lichen so yellow? Does that mean something? Is it poisonous? Do people use it for dye? Would that dye be yellow if it came from a yellow thing? What is going on under the peeling bark? With each question, I honed my curiosity. With each observation, I deepened my understanding, and I fell more in love with this ugly little stick and the world that it contained. I forgot myself and became a part of that world.

Reflection

As you draw, pay attention to what feels comfortable to you. What feels challenging? What is exciting or pleasing to look at? The combination of what feels fun to make and what is interesting to look at can become your personal visual vocabulary. We will build on this and add moments for personal reflection throughout this book to encourage you to think about how to make this practice your own.

Drawing with Shading and Value

Drawing is the discipline by which I constantly rediscover the world. I have learned that when I have not drawn, I have never really seen and that when I start drawing an ordinary thing, I realize how extraordinary it is.
—FREDERICK FRANK

Adding shading to a line drawing can provide important information, make a drawing appear more dimensional, and help us understand textures and shadows. In art, the word "value" refers to the lightness or darkness of a color or tone. An excellent place to begin practicing shading is to create different values with your pencil, pen, and watercolors. This value scale can then be used as a reference for shading in your drawings and the projects in this chapter.

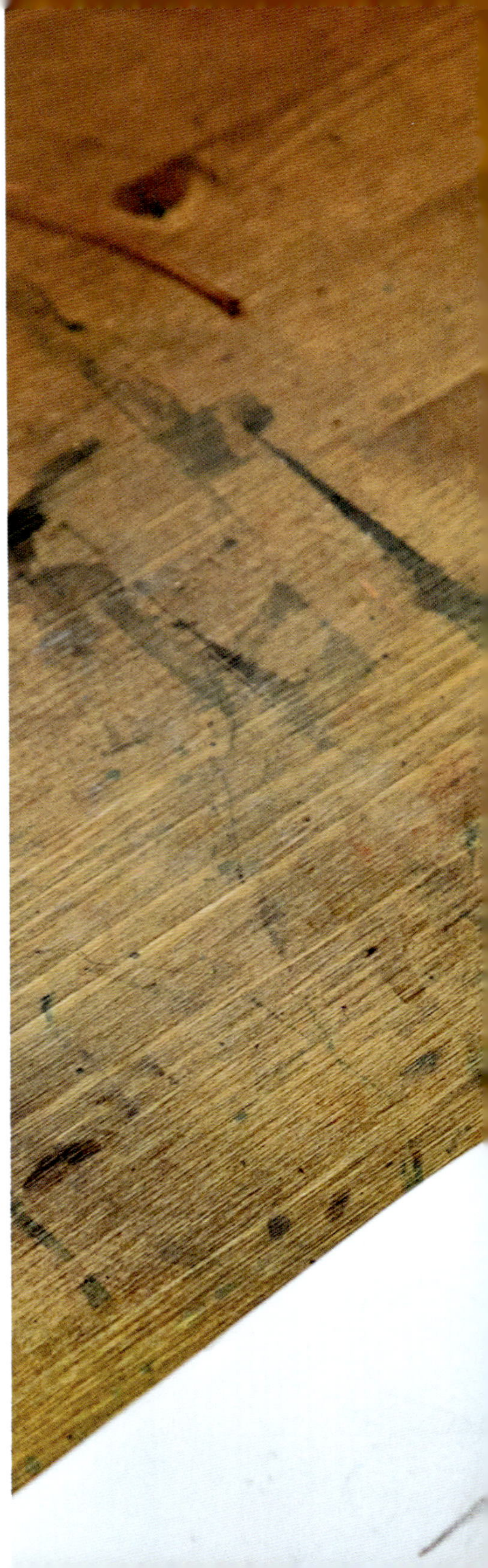

▸ Sketching Donoho Peak using a pen. I vary the thickness and direction of my pen lines to indicate shadow and form.

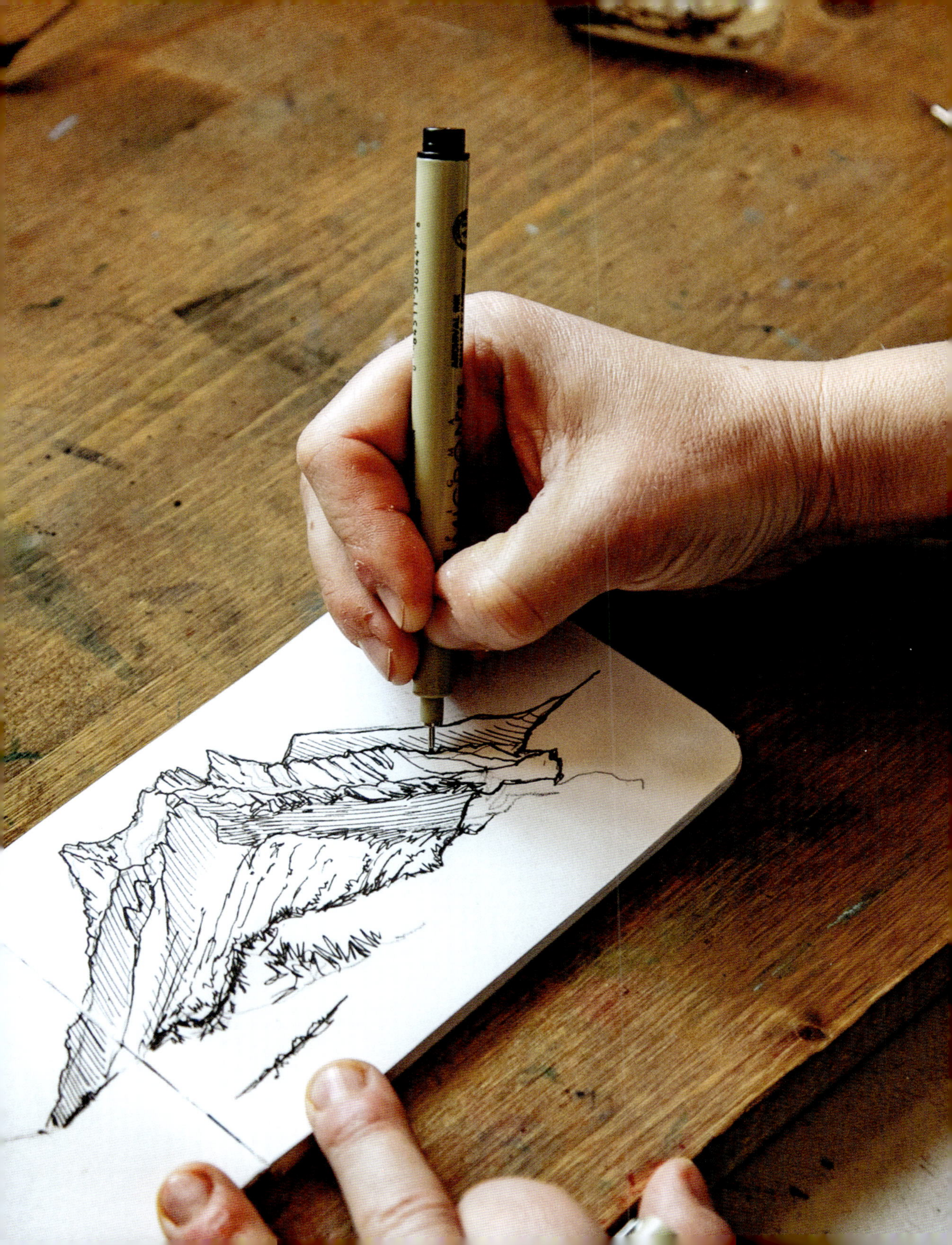

VALUE SCALES

A value scale is a useful way to practice achieving different shades, going from light to dark. Make your own value scale by drawing a rectangle with five boxes to fill in. Use the white of the paper as your lightest value. Then use very light pressure and make marks that are farther apart to get light values. Make darker values by pressing harder and putting lines and marks closer together to cover up the white of the paper.

There are many different ways to shade with a pencil or pen. You can rub a pencil lightly and try smudging the graphite with a tissue or a small scrap of paper. You can also make a series of marks. Stippling is made up of lots of tiny dots. Hatching is made up of parallel lines. Crosshatching is made with multiple groups of parallel lines going in perpendicular directions to one another. The closer and heavier the marks, the more the white of the paper is covered, resulting in a darker value.

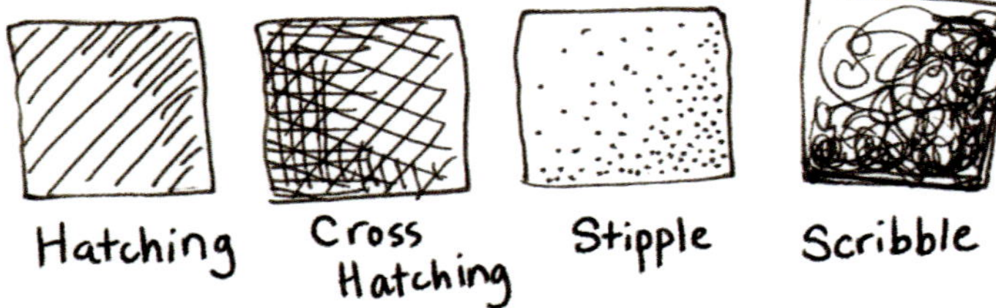

▲ Different types of marks are used in shading. Hatching is made with parallel lines, crosshatching is made of intersecting sets of parallel lines, stipple is made of tiny dots, and scribble is filling space with loose lines.

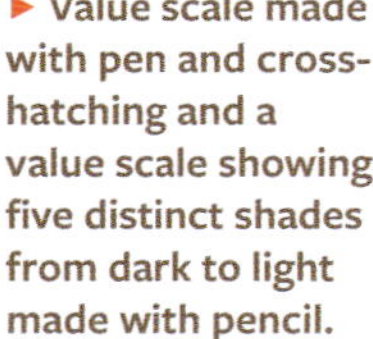

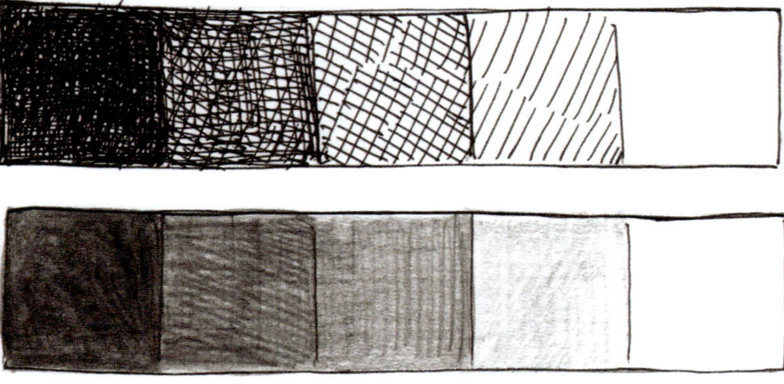

► Value scale made with pen and crosshatching and a value scale showing five distinct shades from dark to light made with pencil.

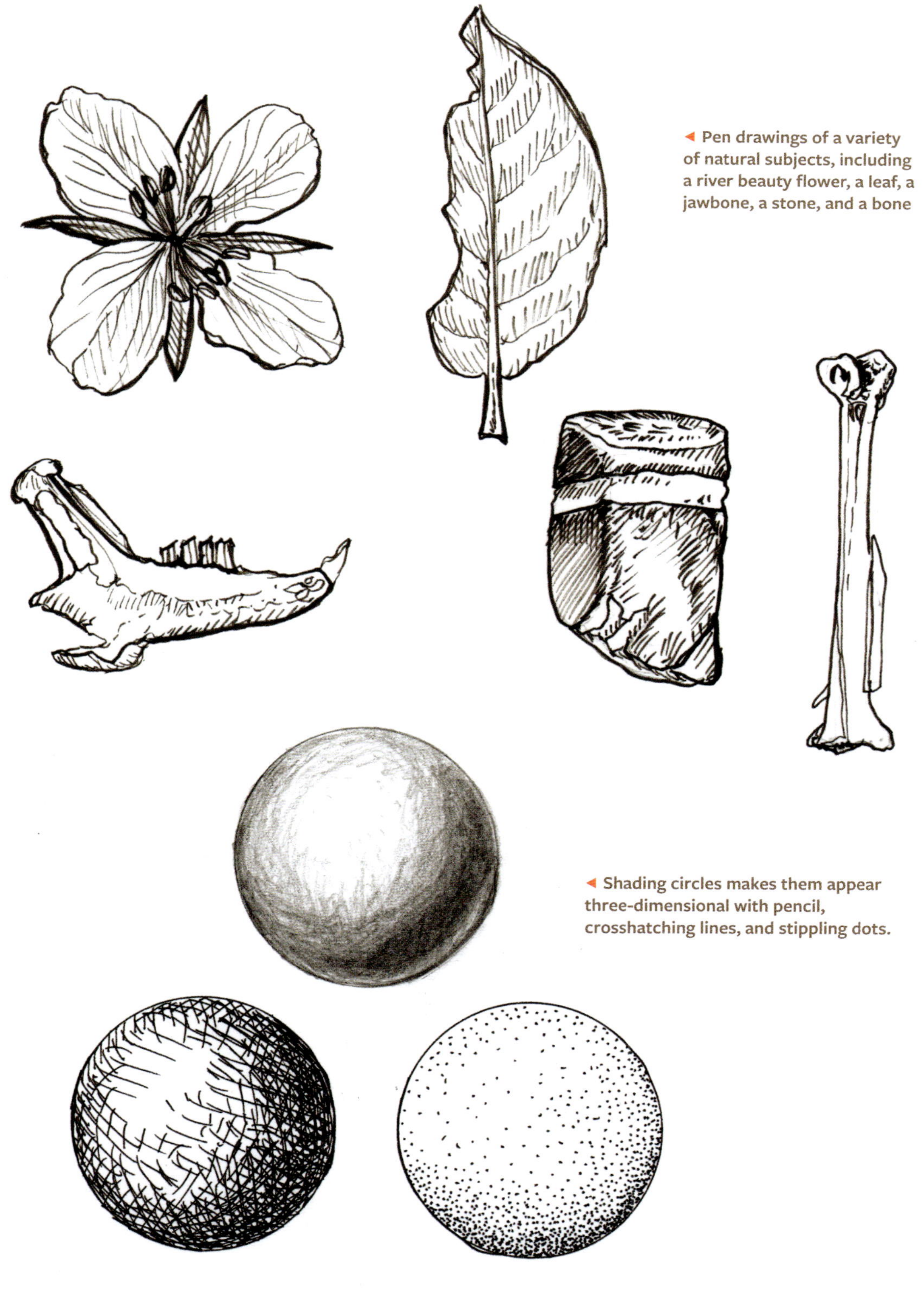

Pen drawings of a variety of natural subjects, including a river beauty flower, a leaf, a jawbone, a stone, and a bone

Shading circles makes them appear three-dimensional with pencil, crosshatching lines, and stippling dots.

VALUE SCALE IN PEN

To shade with pen, make different marks to build up value, using hatching, stipple, and scribble marks. The shape and direction of the marks can help describe the shape of the form.

Once you feel comfortable making different values, try shading geometric objects and turning circles into spheres to make them appear round. If the light source is in the upper left corner, which is traditional lighting in Western illustration, the value will transition gradually from a highlight in the upper left to a deep shadow on the bottom right.

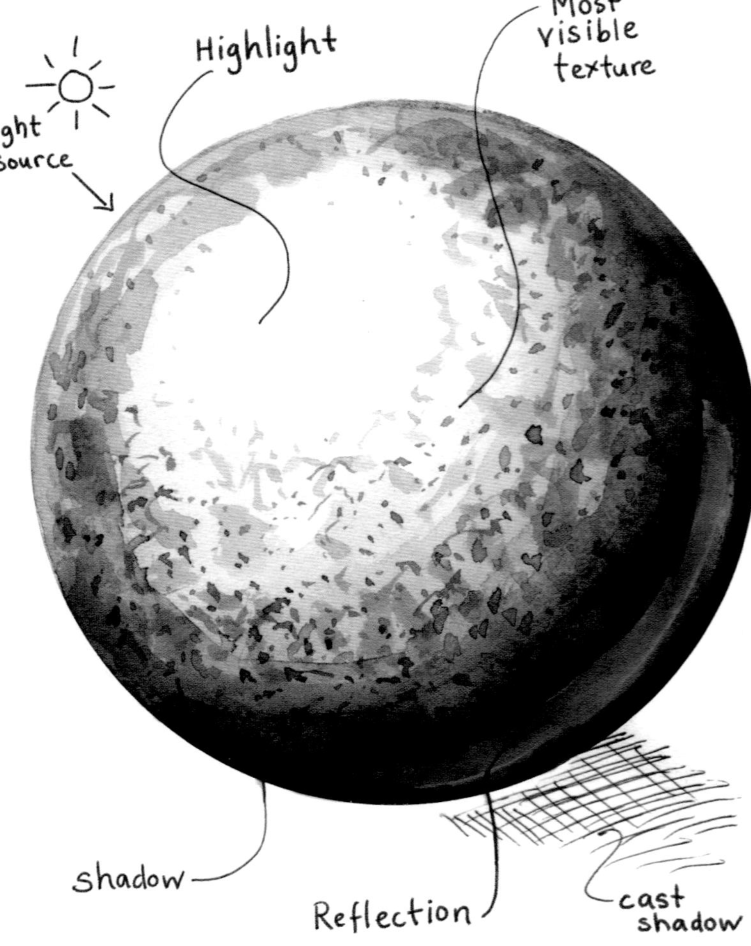

SHADING A SPHERE: We see the most texture in the area between the highlight and the shadow, in the mid-tone area. This is also usually the space that is the furthest in the foreground and has the most contrast (light next to dark). Putting the most detail, texture, and contrast in this mid-tone area will make your drawing more dimensional. In addition to a shadow, you may also see a cast shadow on the surface where the object is sitting and a reflection of that surface in the deepest part of the shadow.

Project 2

OWL FEATHER WITH PENCIL

Practice using value to build up texture and describe the pattern on this relatively flat subject.

MATERIALS: a pencil and drawing paper

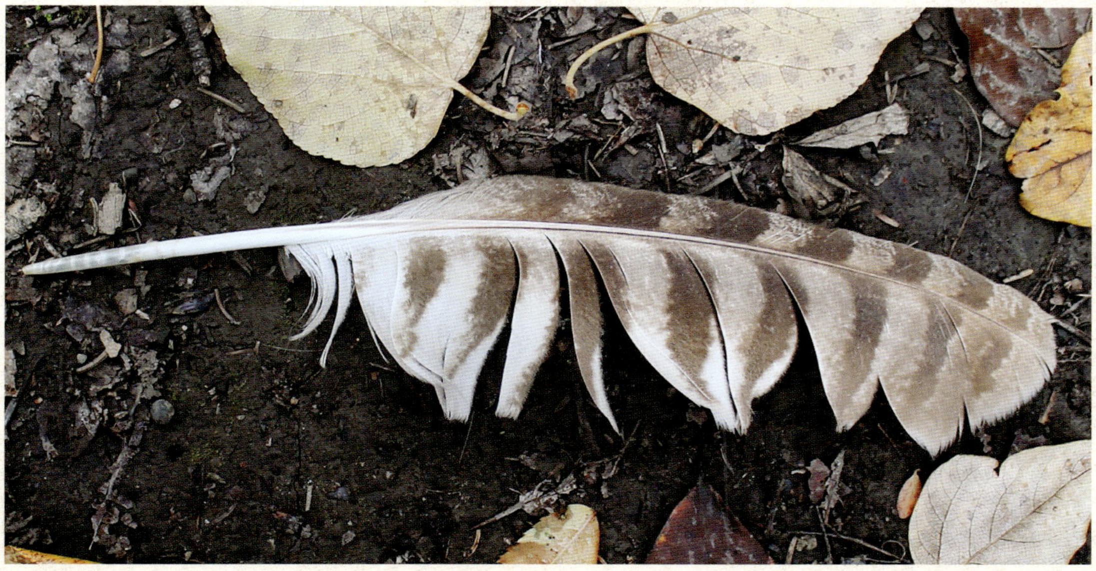

Owl feathers have patterning that helps the raptors camouflage into their environment. They also have soft, fluffy edges to reduce noise so the owl can fly more quietly and hunt prey. What else do you notice about this feather as you draw it?

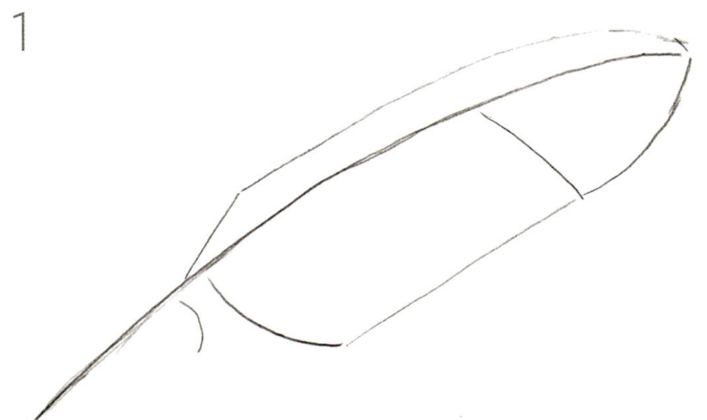

STEP 1: Begin by drawing the main shapes lightly in pencil. Start with a slightly curved line for the middle shaft on the feather, then draw an outline of the inner and outer vanes. I decided to draw my feather on a diagonal angle to make the sketch bigger and more interesting.

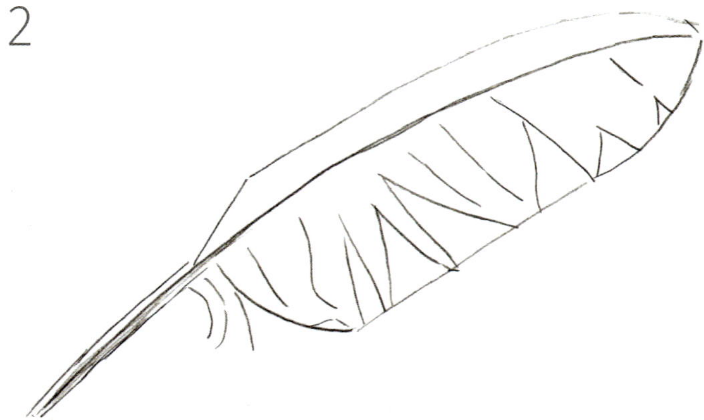

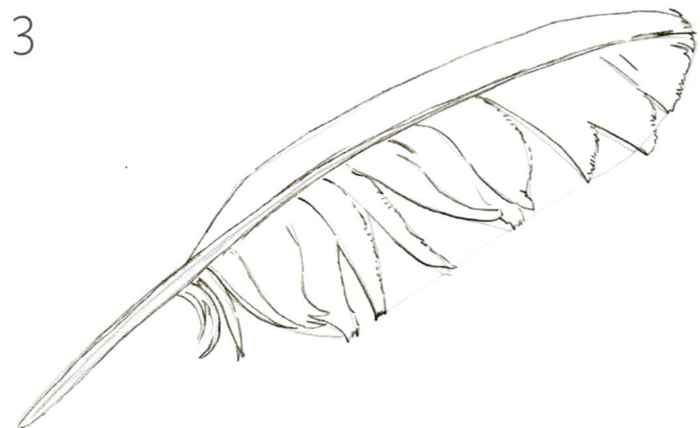

STEP 2: Refine the shape of the vanes where some barbs are pulling apart from each other and separating. These look like triangles.

STEP 3: Erase any marks that aren't needed. Refine the shapes to soften the curves along the edges and add a bit of texture along the margins. Owls have soft, irregular edges on their feathers so that they can fly quietly.

4

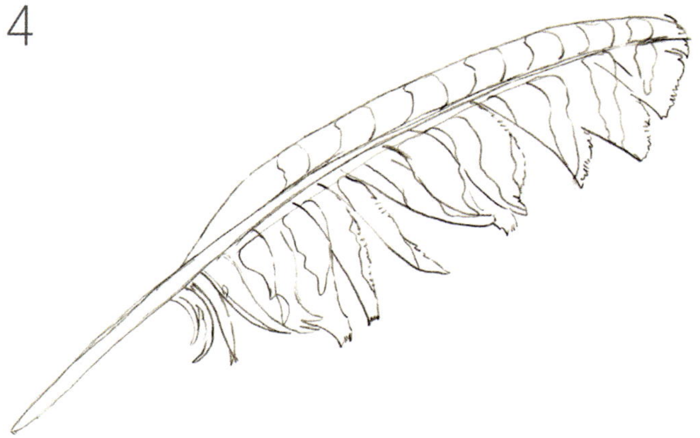

5

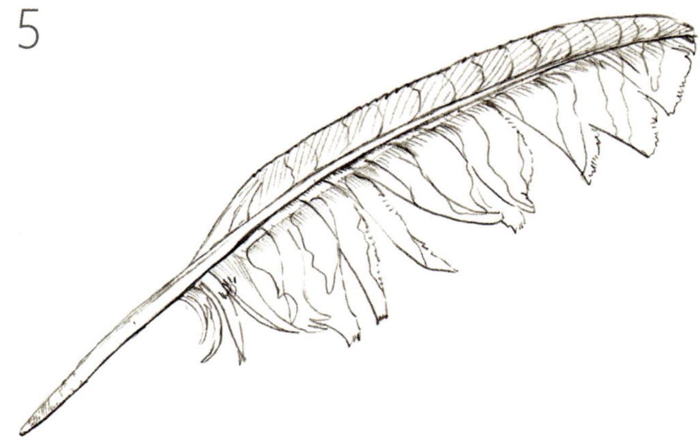

STEP 4: Notice dark brown and lighter brown stripes on the feather that form a pattern. Mark the main shapes of the pattern with outlines in light pencil.

STEP 5: Start shading in the light values of the feather. You can use parallel hash marks to show the structure of the feather. In general, we work from light to dark because it is easier to add more value and make a drawing darker than to take value away and make it lighter.

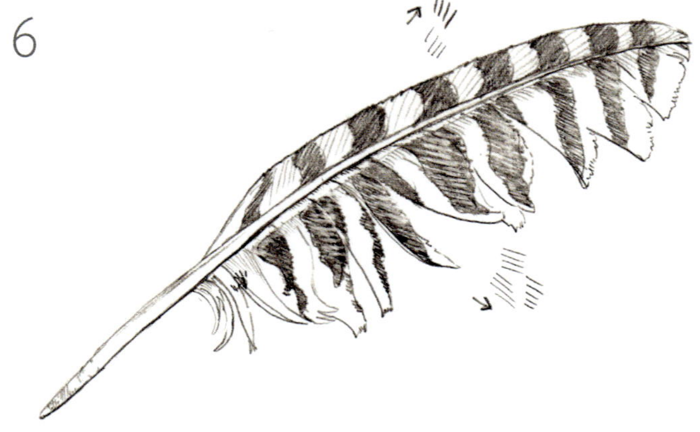

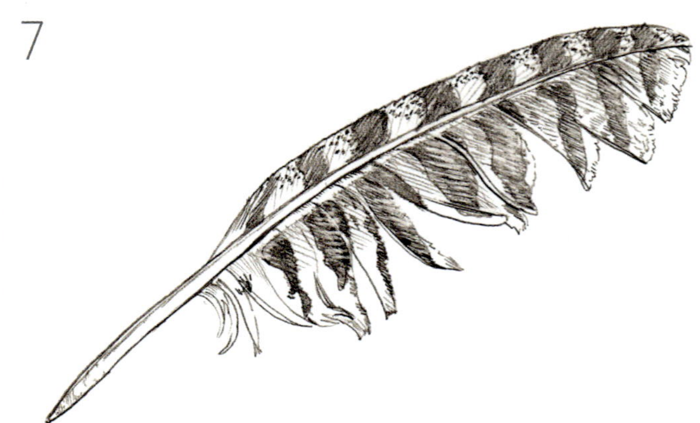

STEP 6: Shade in the darker parts of the pattern. Again, use hash marks or parallel lines to show the structure of the feather and the direction of the barbs.

STEP 7: Add mid-tones between the light and dark values marked so far. Draw some spots to describe the texture in the middle-brown areas.

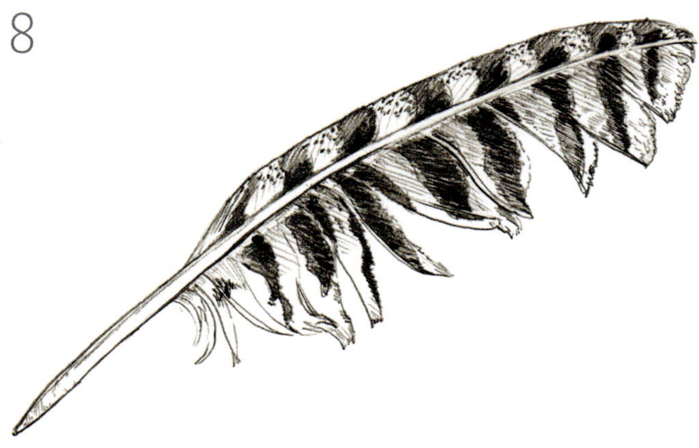

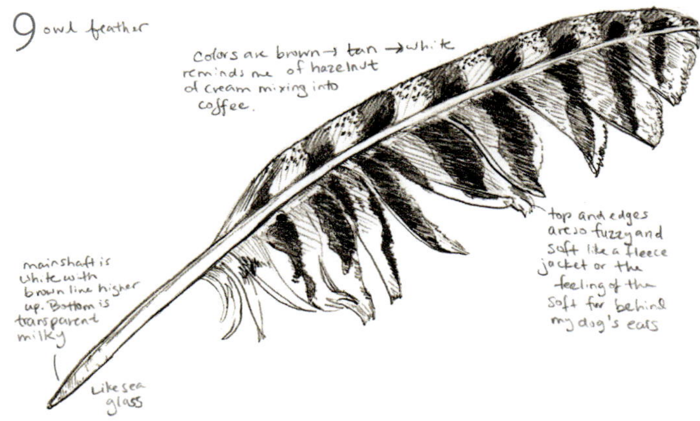

STEP 8: Darken up the darkest values in certain places. I notice the darkest values in the stripes along the middle shaft, also called a rachis.

STEP 9: Add some notes about what the characteristics of the feather remind you of. These can be based on observations from other feathers or birds or completely unrelated. I wrote about the textures and the colors, since the drawing is black and white. The colors transition from white to tan to dusty brown, reminding me of cream mixed into coffee. The texture on the top of the feather is very soft, reminding me of a fleece jacket or the back of my dogs' ears. This helps the owl stay quiet in flight. Situating these things in my personal experience allows me to relate to them and will remind me of my observations. It can also be a little bit of poetry in your sketchbook.

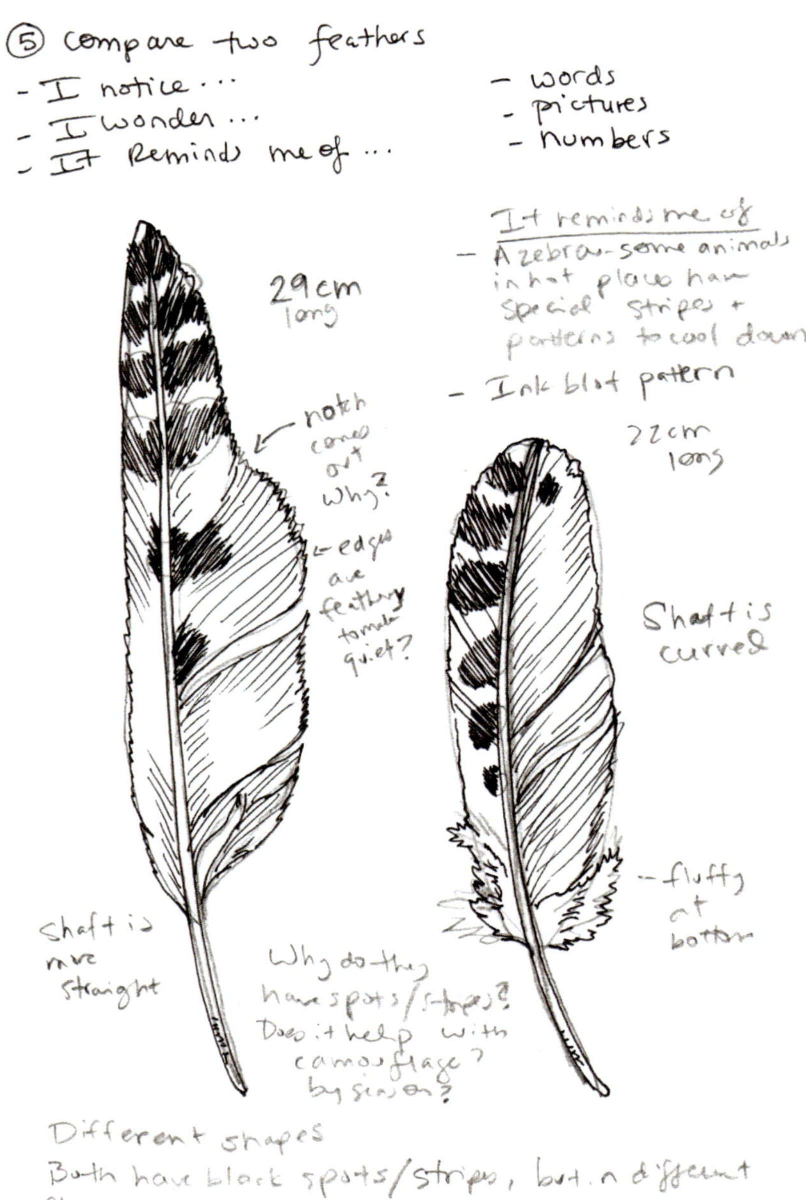

Sketchbook page comparing two feathers from a Snowy Owl. This is a quick study, but I try to include words, pictures, and numbers as well as what I notice, what I wonder, and what it reminds me of.

Project 3

DRAWING AND SHADING A SKULL

Build up different values with pencil shading to show the dimensionality of this round form.

MATERIALS: a pencil and drawing paper

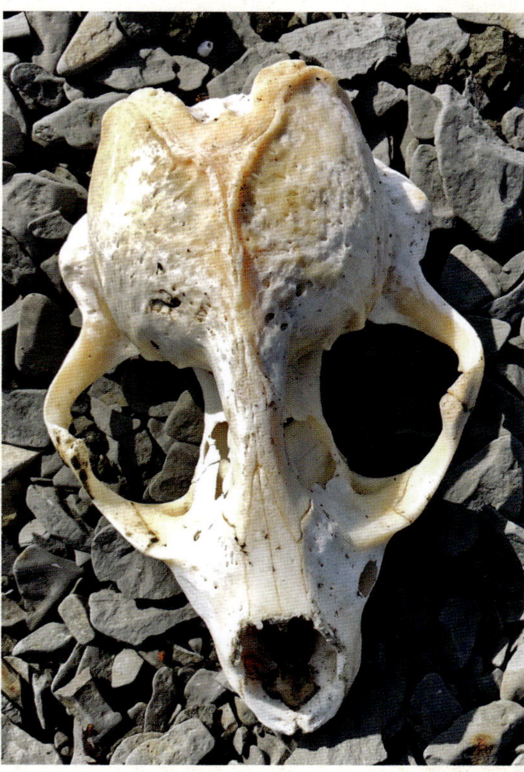

▲ I found this skull on a beach on Kayak Island, which juts out into the Gulf of Alaska and collects a lot of interesting marine debris. The angle of this photo, looking down at it from the top, gives us some information, but many mysteries remain. Sometimes you need to create a sketch with the information that you have, and it is OK to have unanswered questions.

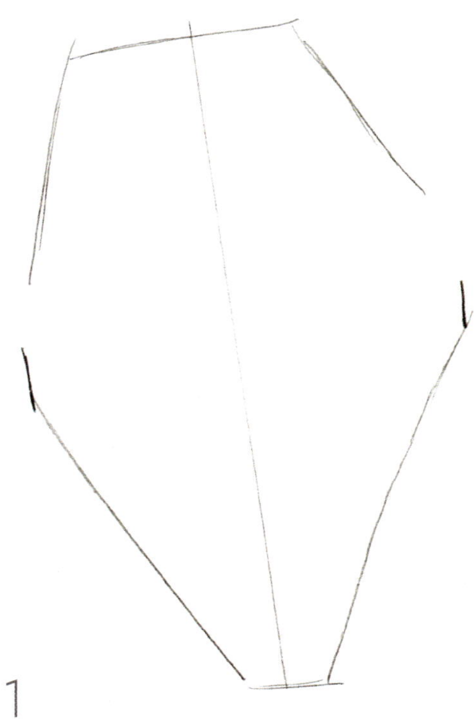

STEP 1: Lightly mark out the space the drawing will occupy on the paper in pencil. Since the subject is almost symmetrical, I drew a middle line and then marked the top and sides to indicate how big the skull would be. Then, I connected those marks with diagonal lines.

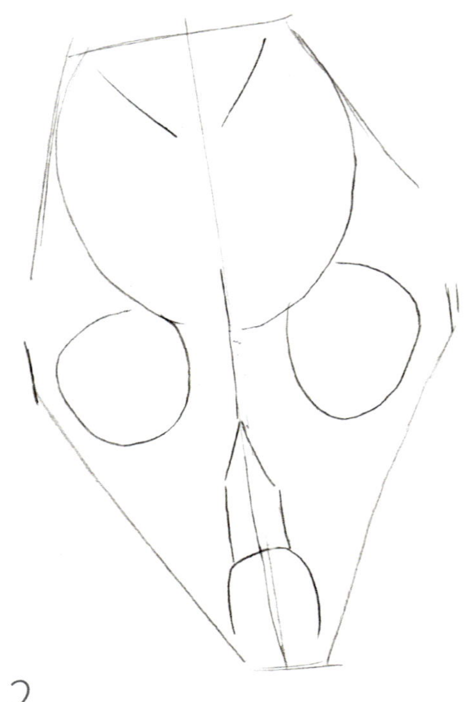

2

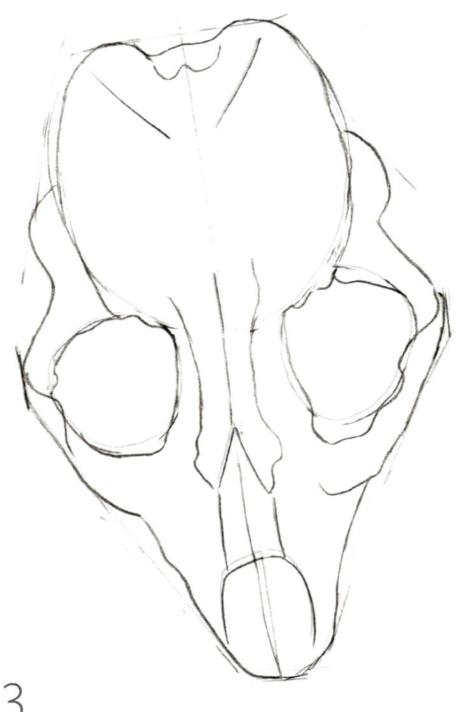

3

STEP 2: What shapes do you notice that make up the skull? I drew an oval for the braincase, two circles for the eye orbits, and a half circle and pentagon for the nose.

STEP 3: Refine the drawing to describe the main shapes of the skull more accurately. For example, the braincase is almost an oval, but it has a little notch at the top. The bones around the eye sockets are curved inward, so they are not perfect ovals.

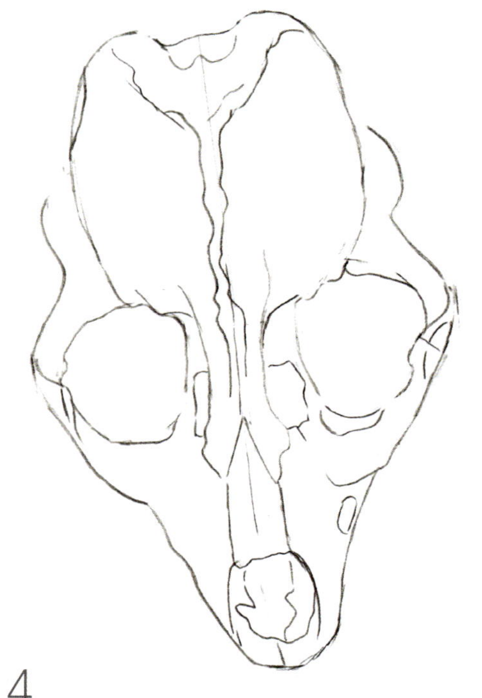

4

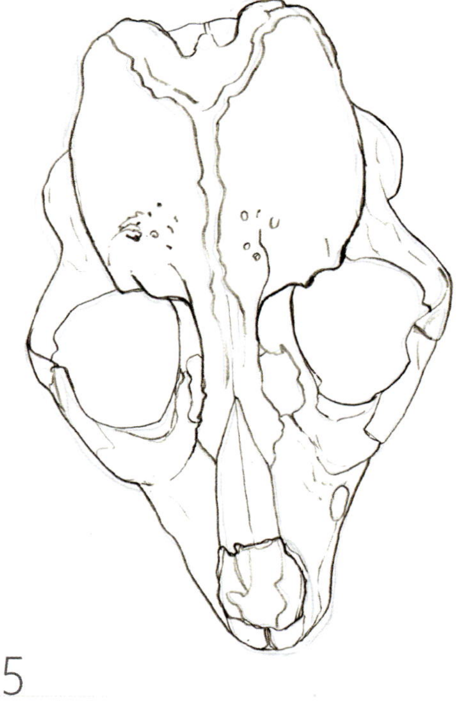

5

STEP 4: Continue to refine the shapes and add any more important structures, such as the sagittal crest or ridge on the top of the skull and some places where there are holes and cracks. Erase the pencil marks you don't need as you go.

STEP 5: Go over your line drawing again to thicken some lines and ensure everything holds together. This creates more variation in the drawing. I thickened the lines around the edges of the braincase and the top of the nose to make them appear to come forward. I used some thin lines to add detail and texture for some of the cracks and bumps on the skull.

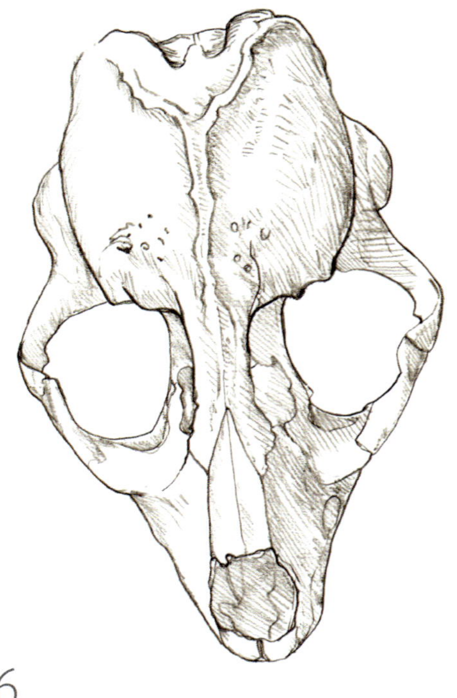

6

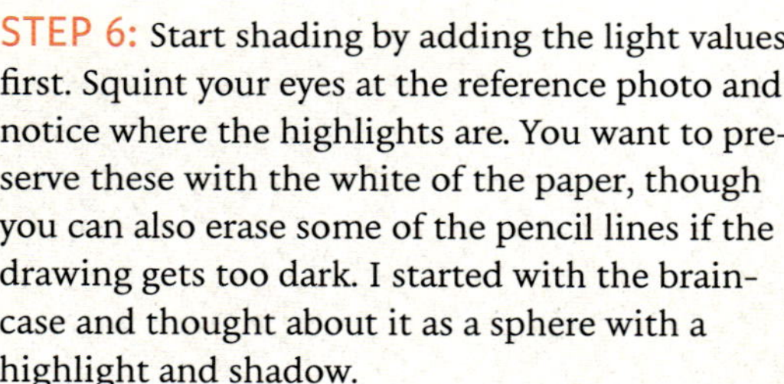

STEP 6: Start shading by adding the light values first. Squint your eyes at the reference photo and notice where the highlights are. You want to preserve these with the white of the paper, though you can also erase some of the pencil lines if the drawing gets too dark. I started with the braincase and thought about it as a sphere with a highlight and shadow.

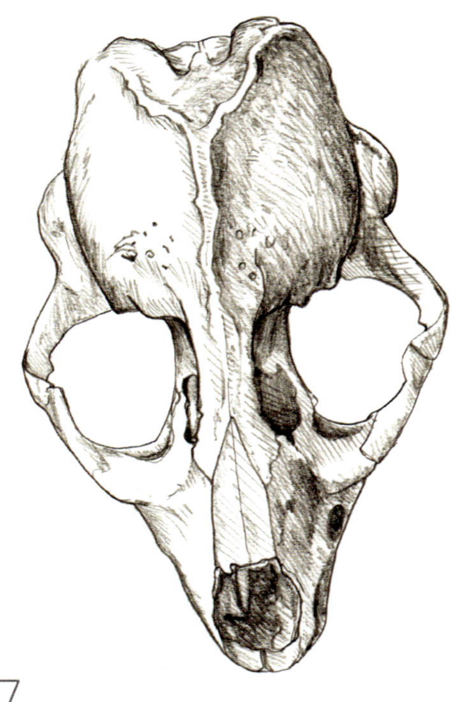

7

STEP 7: Build up the mid-tones with your pencil, making some areas darker. I used cross-hatching and made marks with my pencil, going perpendicular to the marks in the previous step. I thought about how the direction of my marks would help define the form of the skull, so they are slightly curved in some places and follow the roundness of the shape.

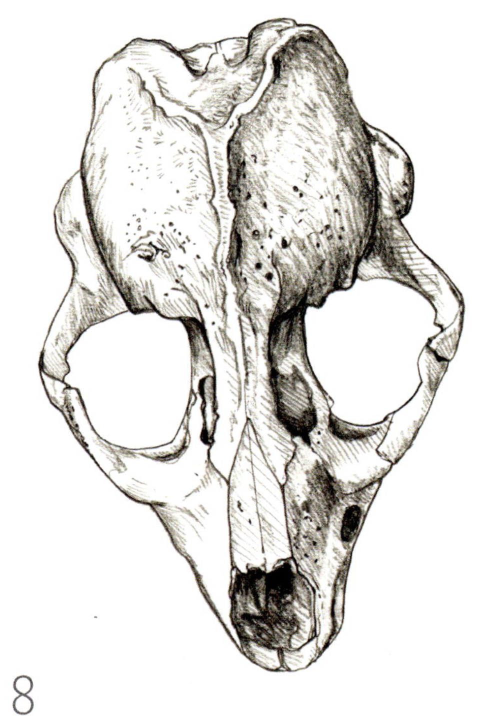

8

lambdoidal crest
cranium (braincase)
Skull is cracked + weathered
Sagital crest pretty tall powerful jaws?
zygomatic arch
orbit (eye socket) Eyes face forward and top
nose is on top also - easier to breath? Many tiny plates + bones good sense of smell?

9

STEP 8: Add the darkest values where you see the deepest shadows. Next, add some more texture to some parts of the skull. Erase any pencil marks or areas where your drawing got too dark or where you want high contrast. The areas with the most detail and contrast will appear to pop forward.

STEP 9: This subject is more complicated than some of the others. It can be nice to take some focus off of the drawing and pretend it is a diagram. Label the parts of the skull that you notice. Come up with your own names based on what you notice or look up the names for parts of a skull. Paying attention to form and structure often leads to questions about why things are shaped that way and how form relates to function. Spend some time thinking about what questions you have about this skull. What kind of animal do you think it came from? What other information do you wish you had? How do you think it ended up on this island in the Gulf of Alaska?

Project 4

JAWBONE IN PEN

Shading with a pen is similar to shading with a pencil, but it has a darker and more precise line. In this project, we will use a pencil for the initial sketch, but we will go over it and do the shading with ink.

MATERIALS: a pencil, a pen, and drawing paper

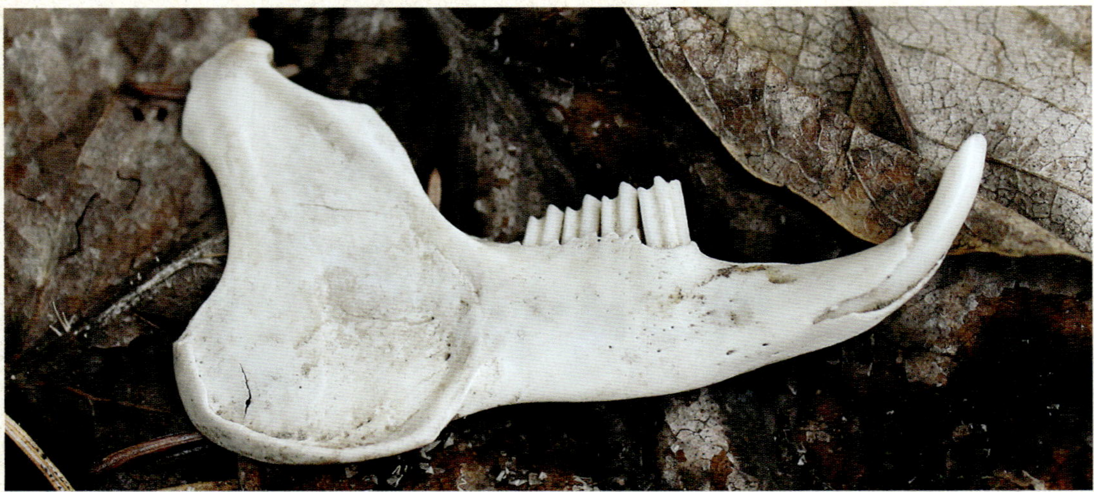

This is part of a snowshoe hare's lower jawbone or mandible.

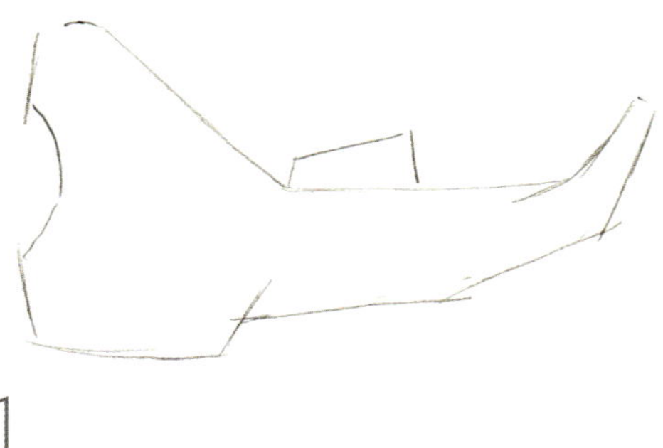

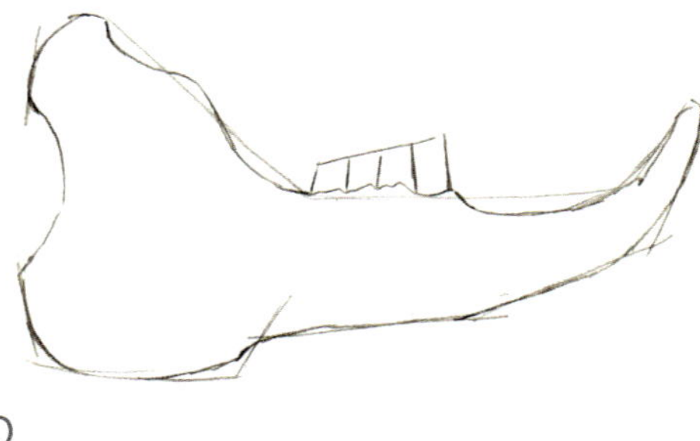

STEP 1: Start with a pencil, drawing lightly with straight lines to show the area the subject will take up on your paper. You can use your pencil to measure the angles from the photo reference.

STEP 2: Modify the straight lines to add curves. My brain finds it much easier to observe angles and straight lines first, then think about curves, and finally refine the curves to add detail along the edges and margins.

STEP 3: Continue working with a pencil to add detail to the line drawing. Add the jagged edge along the top of the molar teeth and some of the interior shapes on the skull, such as the incisor tooth socket.

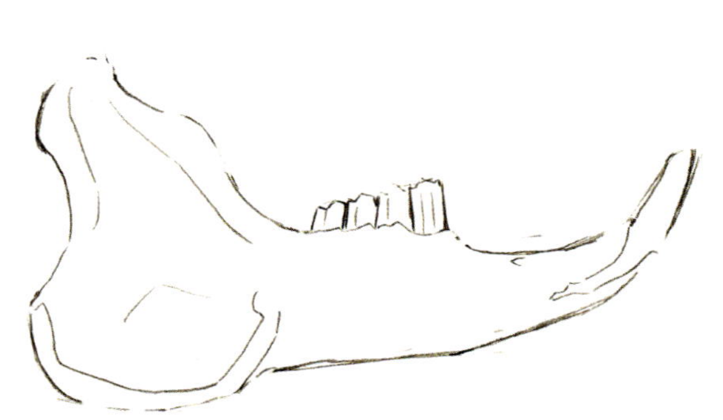

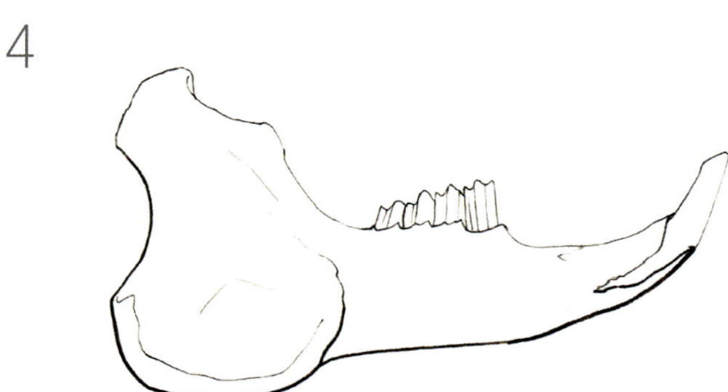

STEP 4: Go over the line drawing with a pen. I used a thicker line along the bottom of the skull to indicate a shadow there. I made sure the pen ink dried and erased the pencil. Sometimes, I leave the pencil lines underneath my pen drawing to tell the story of my sketch.

STEP 5: Start shading where you notice lighter values. I tried to keep the highlights white and created hatch marks that helped describe the form.

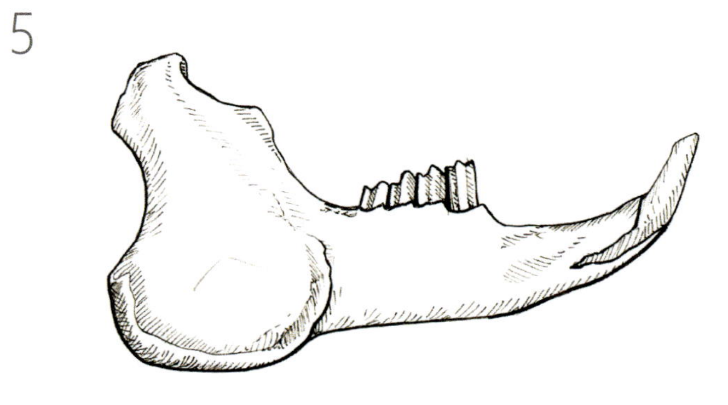

STEP 6: Build up darker values by adding more hatching and crosshatching where you notice the darkest shadows. Add some circles and stipple dots in the middle of the bone where you notice texture.

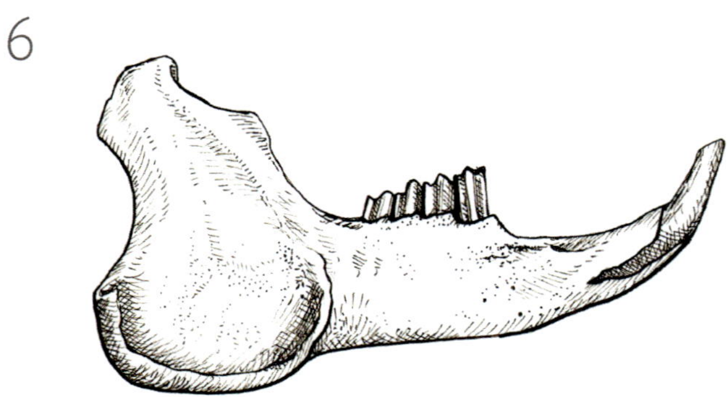

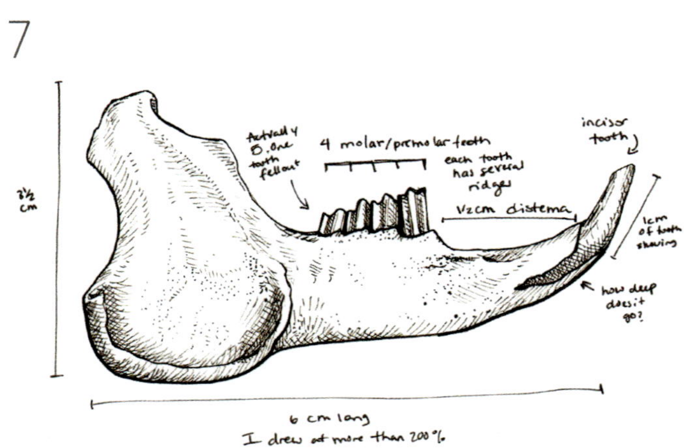

STEP 7: Take some time to make observations with numbers. Since I had this physical mandible in addition to the photo of it, I was able to hold it and measure it with a ruler. As soon as I started counting, I noticed that I saw four back teeth, but one was missing, so there were actually five, and I couldn't see the socket from the angle the photo was taken from. I would not have noticed this if I didn't think about numbers. You may include the measurements I took in your sketch.

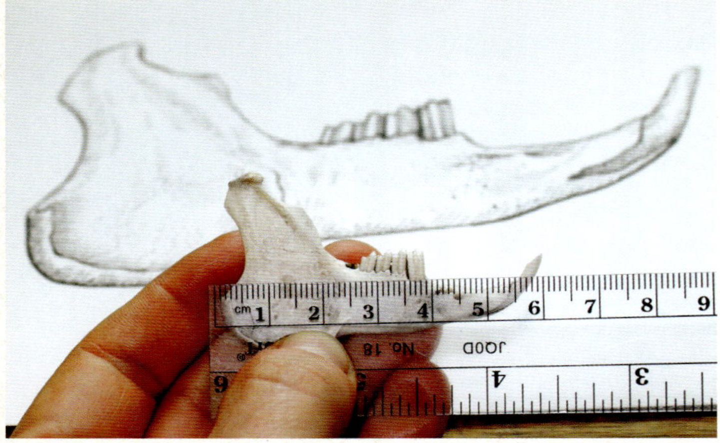

► **Measuring with a clear plastic ruler to add some numbers to my sketch**

SKETCHING A MYSTERY PLANT

Sometimes, I like to play a game and sketch a plant or other subject I don't recognize. I try to capture as much information as possible using words, pictures, and numbers and then look it up in a field guide based on my sketch. This is a terrific way to hone your observation skills because you realize what you forget to notice and learn about new species. Once I sketch a plant, I will almost always remember it forever.

One day, I was walking through a forest clearing with some sedges and wildflowers growing in it. I noticed a small, unassuming purple flower and decided to sketch it so that I could look it up. I saw it had square stems and opposite leaves, which reminded me of mint growing in my garden. I sketched the elliptical shape of the leaves. I looked closely and noted their edges and texture. I looked at the flowers and discovered they were a kind of tube with four parts that fringed off the top. It reminded me of the gentian plants I had seen up in the alpine, but those were much bigger and a different color. I only had time to make a quick drawing and a few color notes, but when I looked it up later, I found it was a type of gentian, *Gentianella amarella*. I also learned that people work with the roots to create bitters. I checked this with another trusted source and remembered the plants later in the fall, harvesting some of the roots to make a bitter tincture. Now that I know them, I often look for and recognize these flowers in meadows and other clearings. Recognizing plants helps me feel grounded in a place.

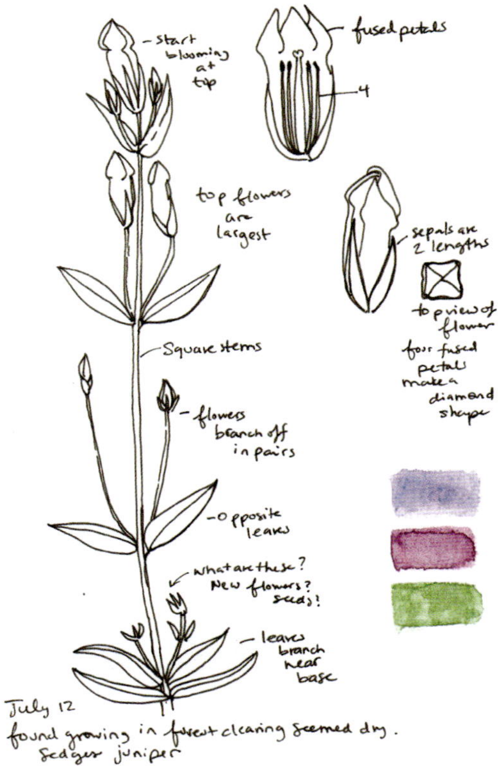

Describing an unknown plant with words, pictures, and numbers to look up later from my sketch

FOCUSING ON TEXTURE

Value can help define three-dimensional form in a sketch, but it is also great for describing the subject's surface. Sometimes, focusing solely on the surface texture and ignoring the whole shape is helpful. I like to do this with a 1- or 2-inch square window cut out of cardstock. I hold the window close to my subject and view an abstract square that zooms in on a portion of the surface. You can do the same thing by cropping photos, such as the ones provided here. I created a series of pen drawings inspired by the textures I noticed in the photos to explore mark-making and value. This is a good exercise for challenging yourself to make different types of marks and to expand your visual vocabulary.

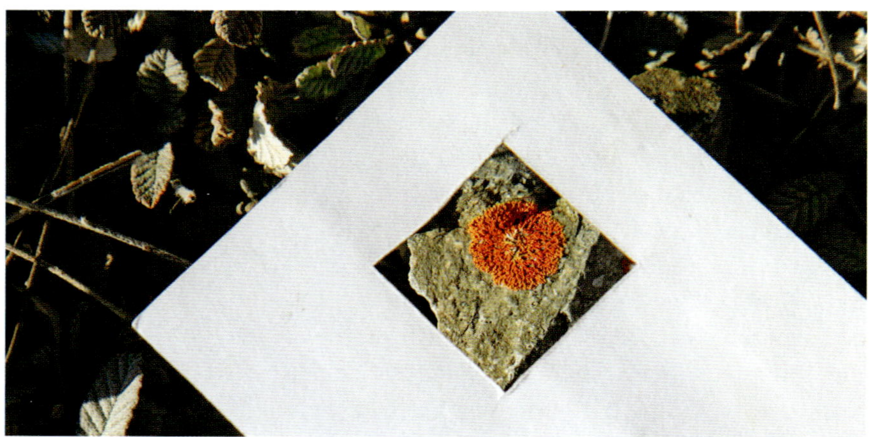

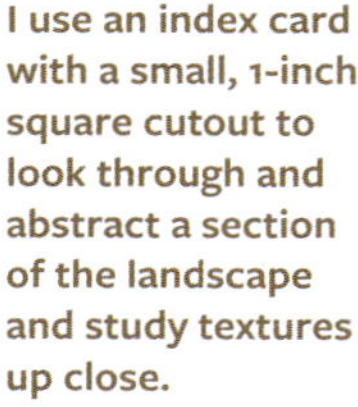

I use an index card with a small, 1-inch square cutout to look through and abstract a section of the landscape and study textures up close.

Reflection

Did you try out different drawing implements like pencil and pen? Which ones did you enjoy using? Why? Based on that reflection, is there something else you want to try?

I enjoy using pencil and pen for different purposes. Pencil can be great for figuring out proportions, making adjustments, and working in layers. When I want my sketch to be quick and gestural I will usually begin with pen. I prefer clean pen lines that don't smudge in my sketchbook, so I usually go over my pencil with a pen during sketching. That is my preference, and I encourage you to figure out what works for you. Some artists love to start their sketches with a light blue colored pencil. People practice field sketching with all different drawing and painting materials, including colored pencils, oil paint, pastels, ink, etc. Each has its advantages and disadvantages. Pay attention to and reflect on what you enjoy. There is no right or wrong way.

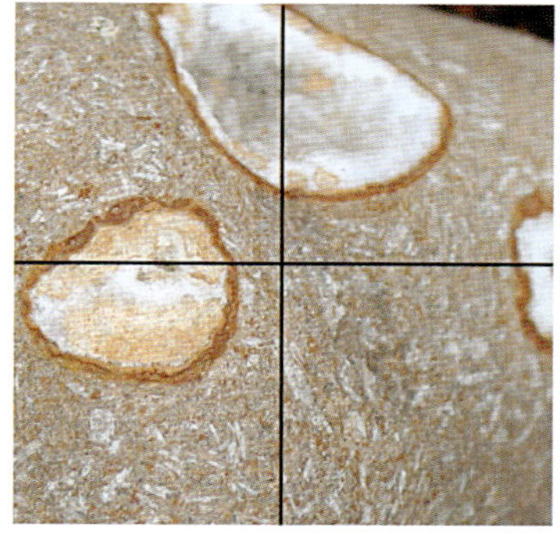

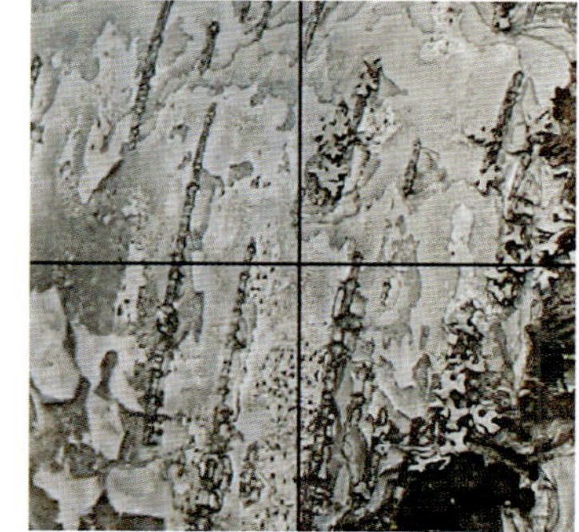

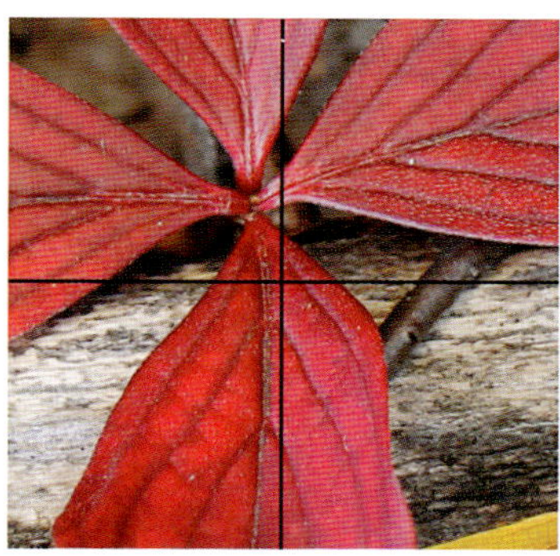

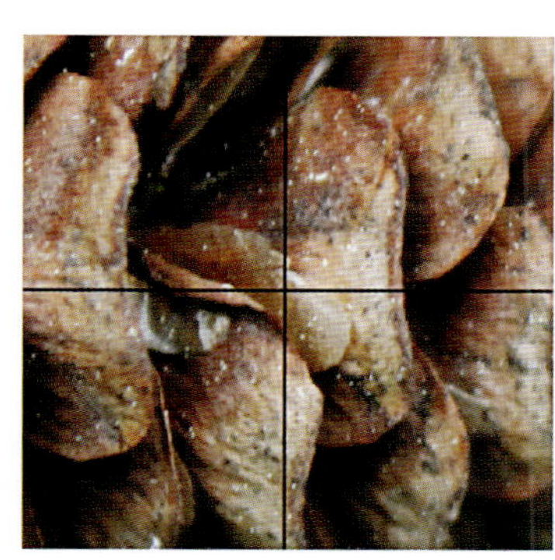

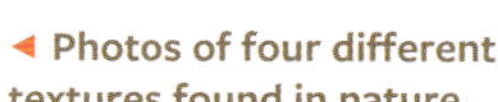

◀ Photos of four different textures found in nature

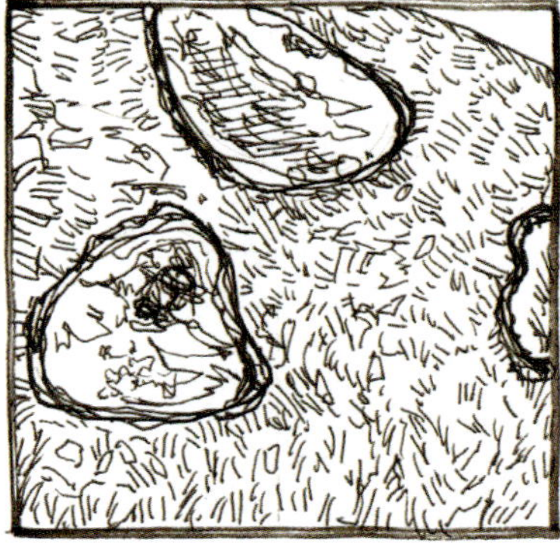

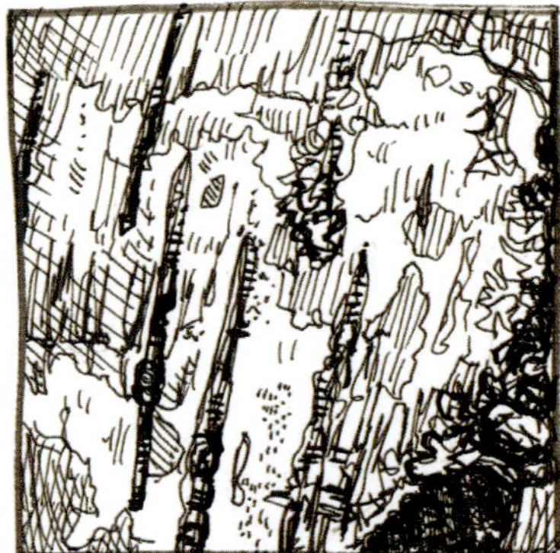

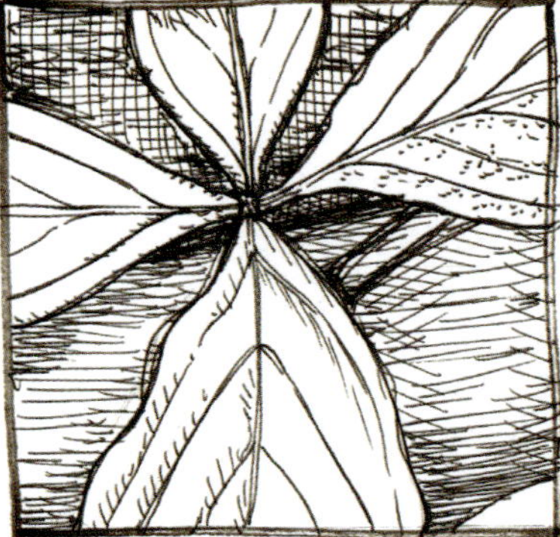

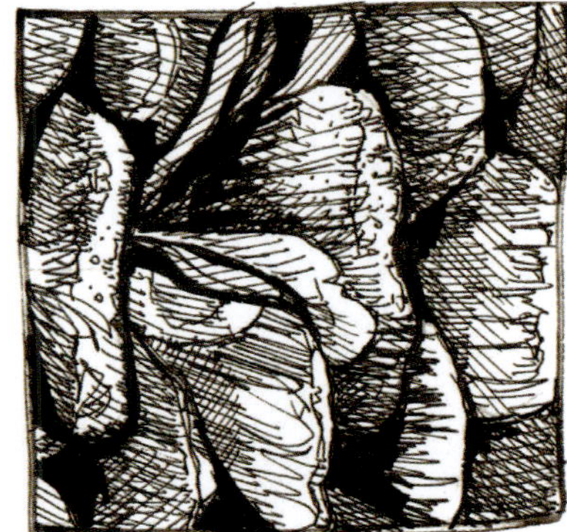

▶ Ink drawings exploring the textures from the photo references

Watercolor Basics for Sketching

One way to open your eyes is to ask yourself, "What if I had never seen this before? What if I knew I would never see it again?"

—RACHEL CARSON

Watercolor is a great medium to bring into the field because it is portable and you can use it to fill space quickly, adding color and value. It has a beautiful transparent quality that captures the light of the paper and the feeling of life from the natural world. Suspended in water, the pigment can sometimes move when it dries, capturing a dynamic and improvisational quality. However, it can also be applied with control and precision. We will begin by learning some techniques for working with watercolor paint. Like drawing, watercolor painting takes practice, but with time, a painter gains more control and can decide when to make a precise mark and when to let the medium do some of the work.

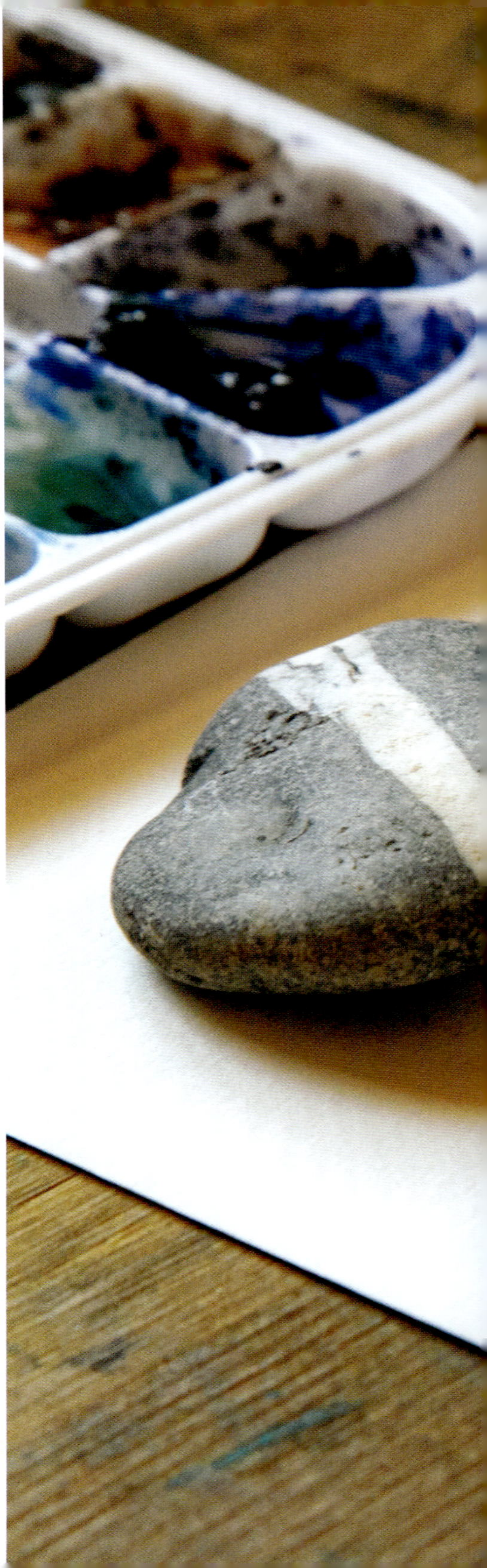

▸ Painting a rock with watercolor.

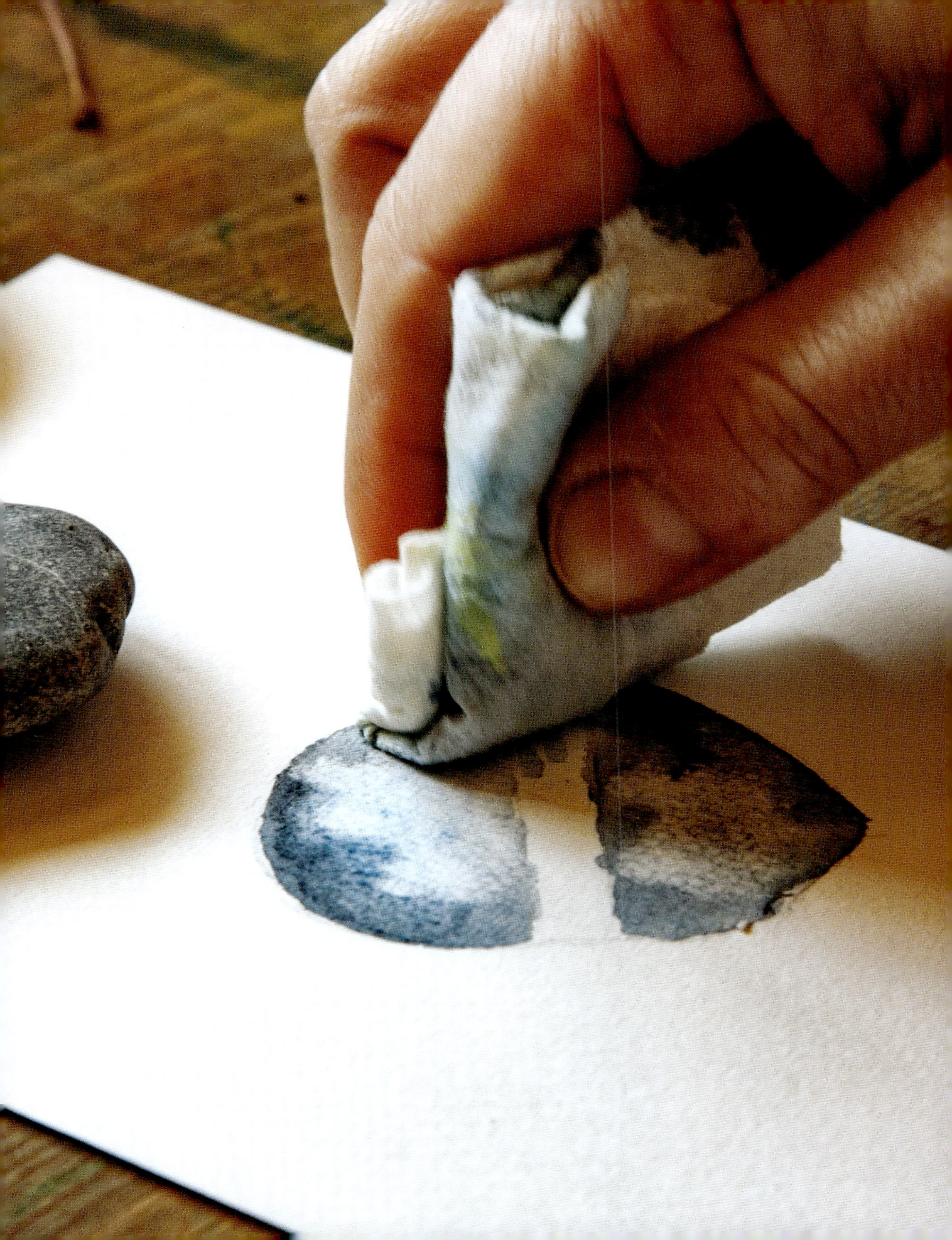

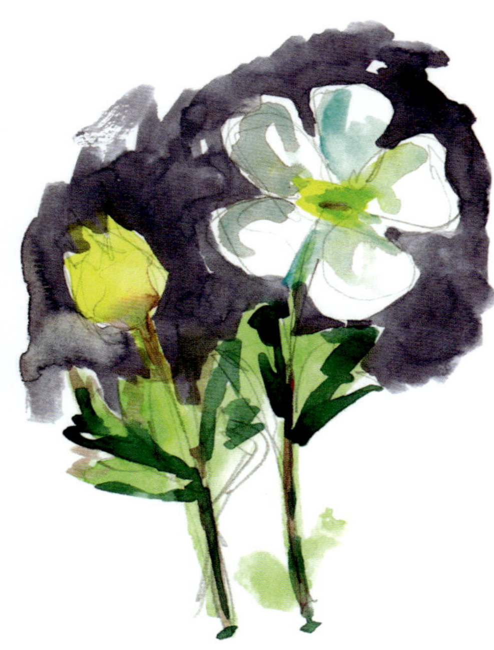

This sketch is made with a loose gesture approach. The watercolor is applied wet-in-wet, so it bleeds where the washes touch each other. Sketching this way gives the artist less control but can infuse the artwork with a sense of life.

MAKING A WASH

A wash is a way of applying watercolor to paper in one layer. In a flat wash, the pigment is applied evenly, and in a graded wash, the pigment goes from dark to light.

You can work on wet or dry paper. To work on damp paper, apply a thin layer of clean water with your brush to the surface you plan to paint. Wetting the paper first will help the pigment spread more easily but might give you less control. To work with dry paper, apply your paint mixed with water directly to the surface. I recommend experimenting with wet and dry paper and deciding your preference. The humidity and climate of your location will also change how the water and paper behave, so it might be worth changing up what you are doing if you are sketching somewhere very dry or humid.

AMOUNT OF WATER

More water mixed with paint will create a lighter wash, and less water makes a darker wash with more concentrated pigment. When you mix the concentration of paint that you want, you will need to get the right amount of paint loaded on your brush. You want your mixture wet enough that it flows easily onto the paper. The wash should not be dry and sticky, but also not so wet that it puddles and flows everywhere. I often dab my brush on a paper towel or cotton cloth to keep the moisture amount just right.

If you use a traditional brush, you will also need a water container to dampen it and clean it off between layers.

If you are using a water brush with water in the barrel, you might need to squeeze it gently to get the water flowing. Once the bristles are wet, they should wick the water out on their own, but you will still need to clean and dab them on a towel from time to time to control the amount of water.

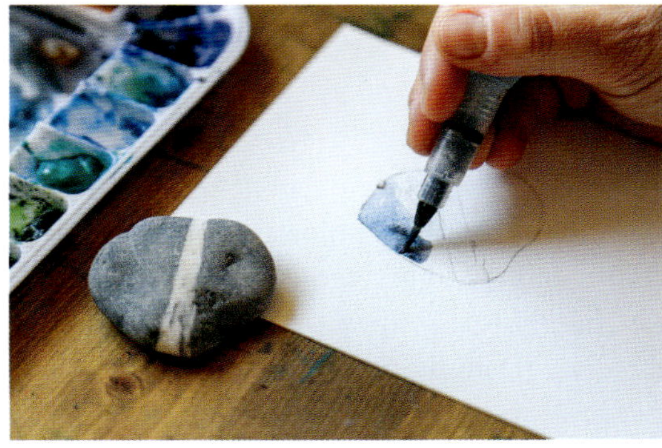

Once the subject is sketched with pencil, start painting along the edge and then pull the color towards the middle.

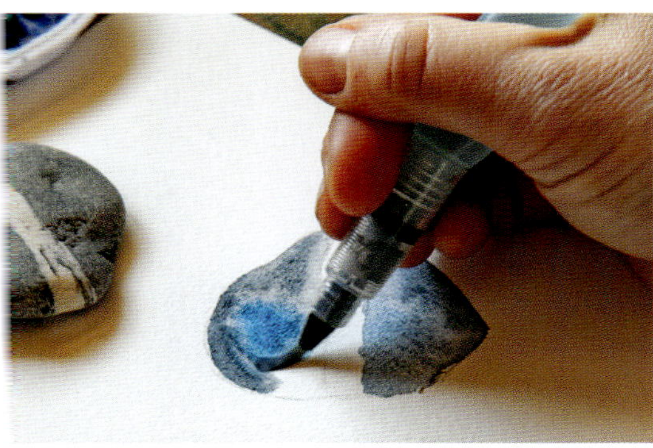

Add in other colors, such as blue with gray, in a wet-in-wet approach so the colors blend together.

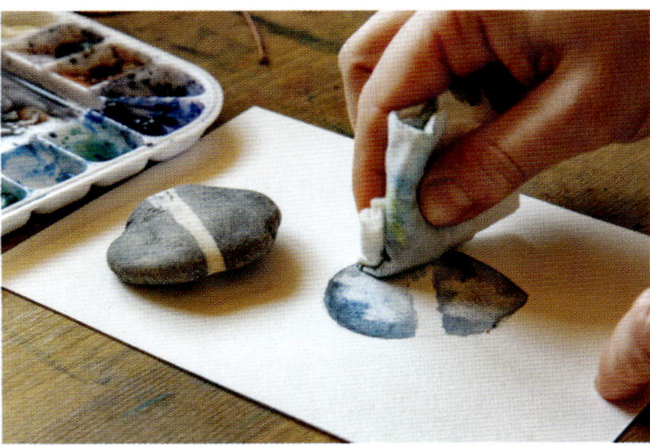

Dab up the wash with a towel to lighten it or remove it.

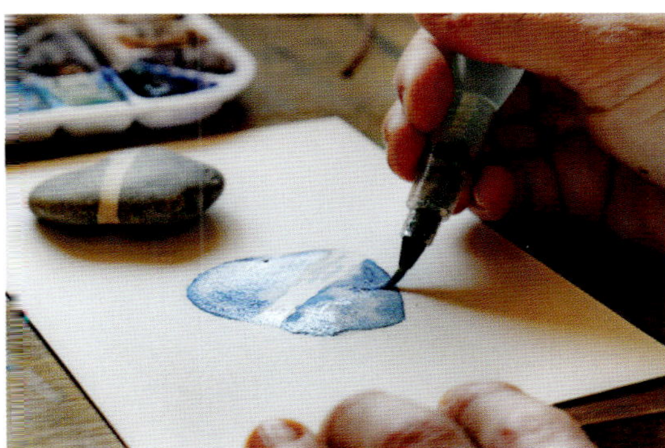

Add in a second wash to deepen the colors in some areas. Because watercolor is transparent, the first layer will shine through.

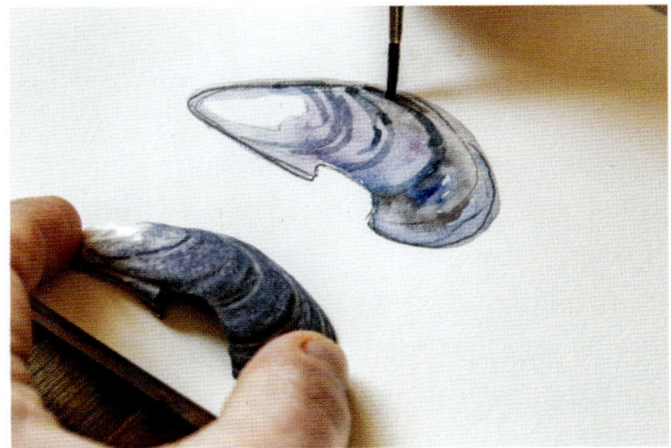

Painting a mussel shell with watercolor. Once the first, looser wash is dry, you can come back on top with another layer of line and detail.

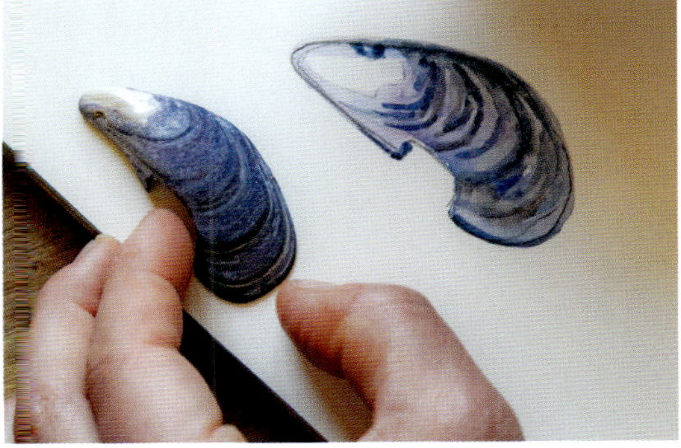

Adding more lines and detail with a small brush in the second wash

TYPES OF WASHES AND MARKS

FLAT: To create a flat wash, decide what shape you will fill with color. Mix up the color and value of paint you want to use and try to get enough mixed to fill the whole shape. (This takes practice, but you'll get better at it.) Mix a desired amount with water in a separate area to have the right consistency, even if you are using a color straight out of the pan or tube. Begin painting on one edge of your shape, carefully filling it with your mixed paint. You should have one damp edge where there is a bead of paint. Load your brush with more paint from your mix and work that bead and the wet edge to fill the shape. Leave it alone once a wash starts to dry because it can get blotchy if it is messed with. Once you fill the shape, pick up any extra paint with the tip of your brush. Don't stress if your wash isn't perfect. It takes practice. The imperfections that happen in our art-making are the signs that what we create is made by a person, not a machine. Few things in nature are perfectly even.

Flat wash

Graded wash

GRADED: A graded wash goes from dark to light. Begin the same way we started the flat wash, filling your shape with paint along one edge, starting on the side that you want to be darker. Instead of returning to your paint mixture for more, clean and wipe off your brush and refill it with clean water. Continue to paint across the shape using water instead of paint. This should help the pigment spread but get lighter as you go. This is an essential technique for softening edges that we will use when we want a layer to have a hard line on one side and then fade out on the other (which often happens with shadows).

Two-color wash

TWO-COLOR: This is the same as the graded wash, but instead of going from one color to the white of the paper with transparent water, the wash will go from one color to another. Begin by mixing up the two colors you want to use. Start on one side and create a graded wash. Clean and wipe off your brush. Start on the other side of your shape with the second color. Where the two colors meet in the middle, you can use the brush to blend them.

WET-IN-WET: This technique allows the paint to flow freely on a damp surface. With a clean brush, wet the shape you want to fill with clean water. Next, drop pigment into the wet area with a loaded brush and watch the paint spread and mix. Add dots, lines, and shapes. You don't have much control over where the paint goes, but the results can be beautiful.

GLAZING: Once a wash is dry, you can layer another wash on top. Since watercolor is transparent, the color from the wash underneath will show through.

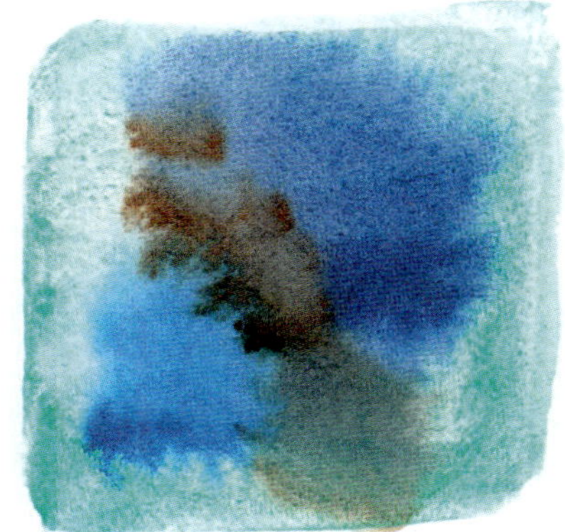

Wet-in-wet wash

Glazing

Sometimes water does weird things, and pigment will move to the edge of a wet section. This irregular pattern with hard edges is called a bloom.

MARK-MAKING: You can also use your brush, like a pencil, to draw lines and marks. You will get a thicker line if you push down with more pressure. You will get a fine line if you use the tip of the brush with very little pressure. Play around and experiment with this.

VALUE SCALES WITH WATERCOLOR: Practice making a value scale using watercolor to create five different values from light to dark. The white of the paper can be the lightest value. Vary the amount of water to make different concentrations of paint (remember that more water makes a lighter wash), and use glazing to layer multiple washes and get darker values.

▼ Lines and marks

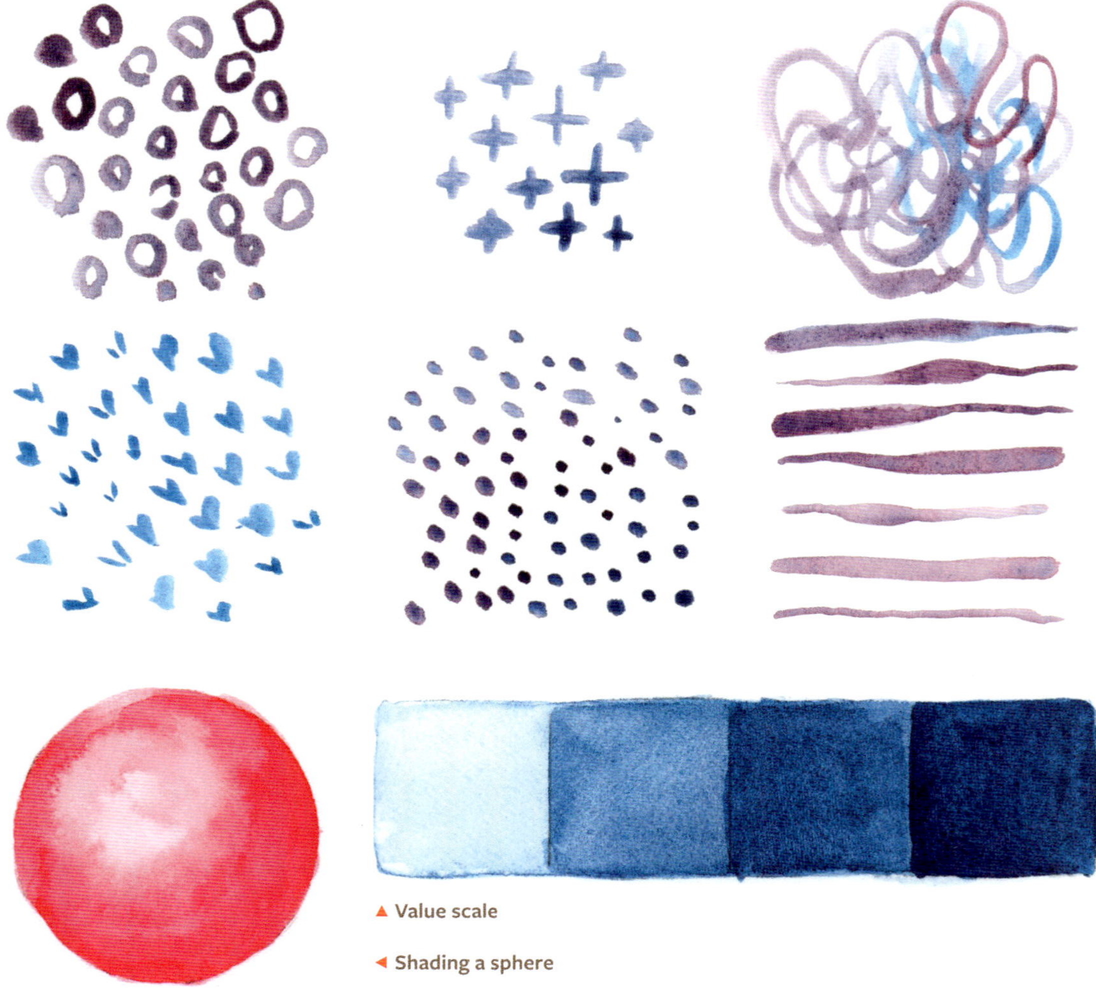

▲ Value scale

◀ Shading a sphere

LAYERING SHAPES

Practice these techniques by drawing a scribbly shape on watercolor paper and filling it with washes of different colors. Where the colors overlap, they will blend. If the washes are dry, you will get a glazing effect. If the washes are wet, you will get a wet-in-wet blending effect. You can also use mark-making in some areas. Practice layering washes and marks, experiment, and see what happens when you layer different colors on top of each other.

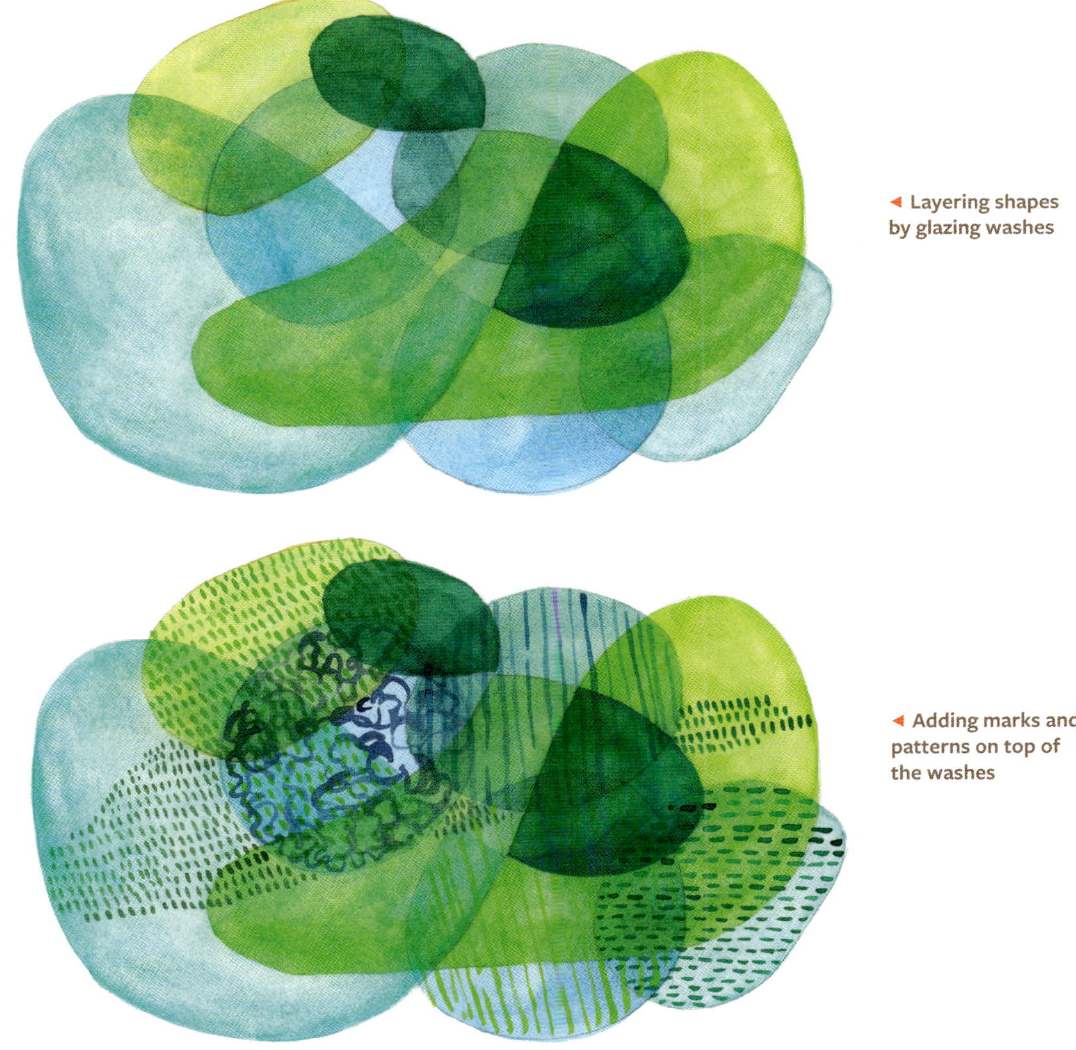

◂ **Layering shapes by glazing washes**

◂ **Adding marks and patterns on top of the washes**

FINDING NEGATIVE SPACE WITH A FLAT WASH

Sometimes, when sketching, it is hard to "see" the exact shape of the subject. It can be helpful to look at the shape of the space around the subject, called the negative space. I use a square window cut in an index card to abstract my subject so I can see the edges, then draw the space around the subject. In the photo examples, I look at the shapes around the flowers and the leaves. Where the flowers or the leaves overlap, I treat them as one shape because that is the space filled with plants, or the positive space. Once I had my negative shapes drawn out in pencil, I used a flat wash to fill them.

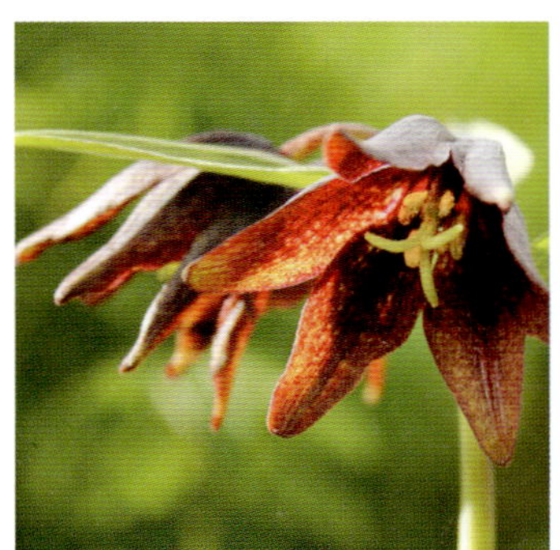

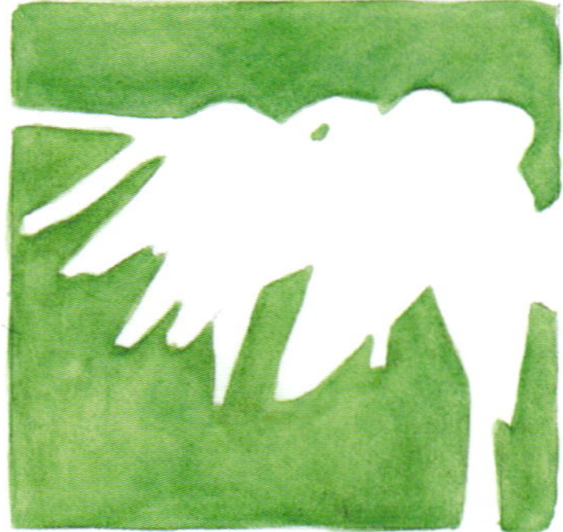

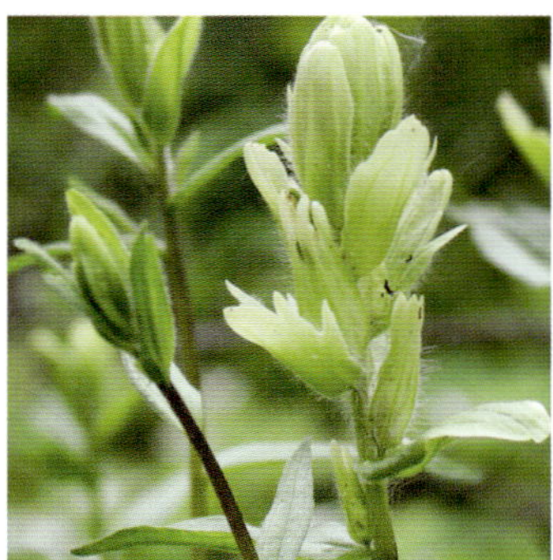

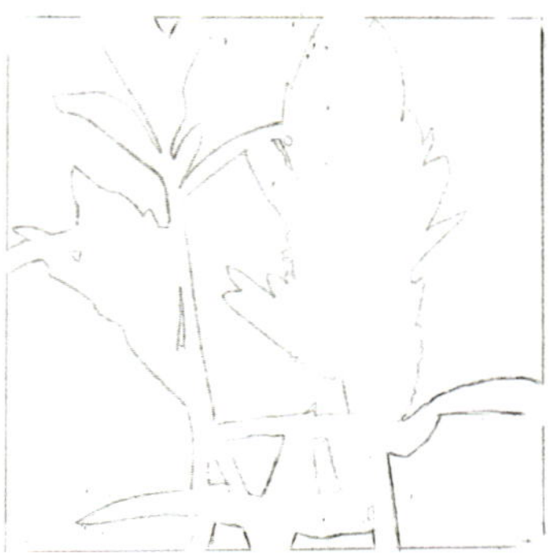

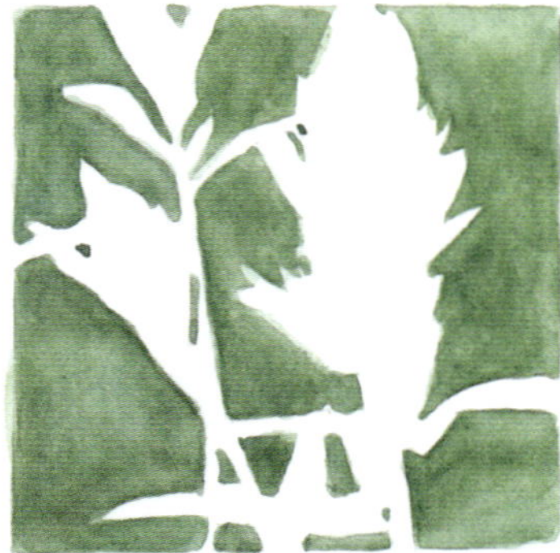

Use these photo references of a cholate lily and paintbrush flower to draw and paint the negative space.

Draw the negative space, or the area around the plants, with pencil line.

Fill the negative space with a flat wash.

Project 5

PAINT A FLAT LEAF WITH WATERCOLOR

Combine drawing and layering multiple watercolor washes to sketch this relatively flat subject of a leaf.

MATERIALS: a pencil, watercolor paper, and watercolors

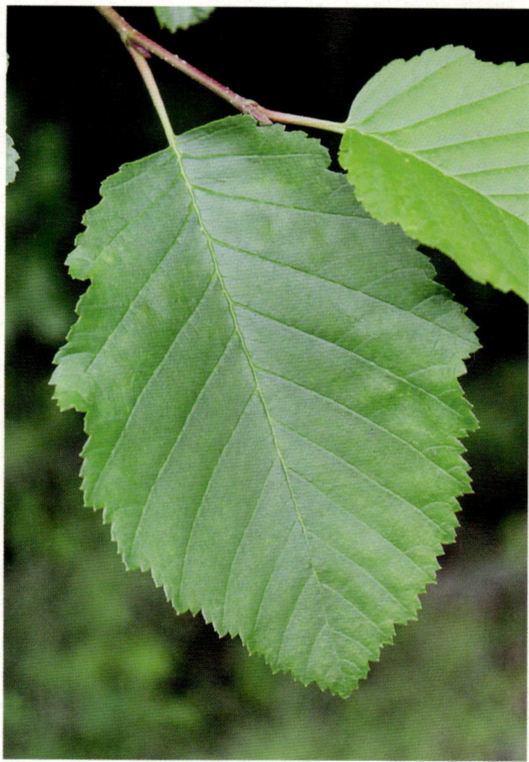

▲ This is the leaf from an alder tree. It is mostly flat, but I noticed some ridges and shadows on the surface along the veins. It is a bright spring green and shiny in some places. Where the two leaves overlap, I decided to sketch just the main leaf and use the information I had in the photo to draw what was underneath the other leaf.

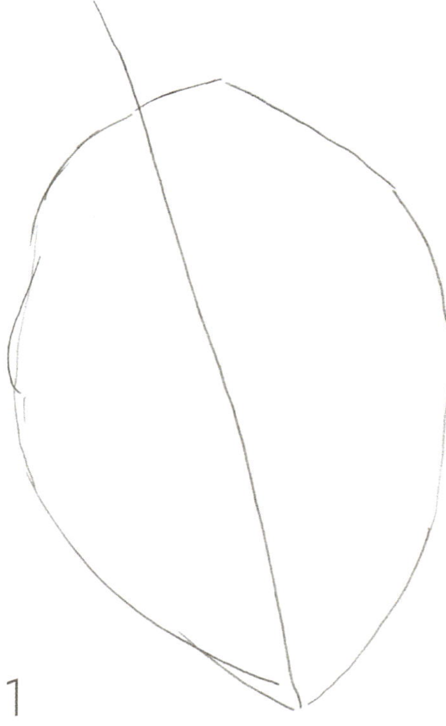

STEP 1: Start sketching the outline and main shapes. Begin by drawing the center rib vein of the leaf and then sketch a simple outline of the leaf shape in pencil. It is easiest to focus on general shapes first and then figure out the details of the jagged leaf margin later.

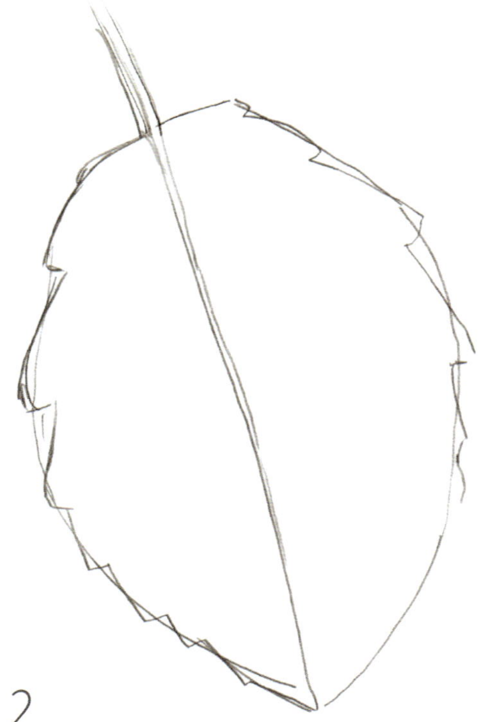
2

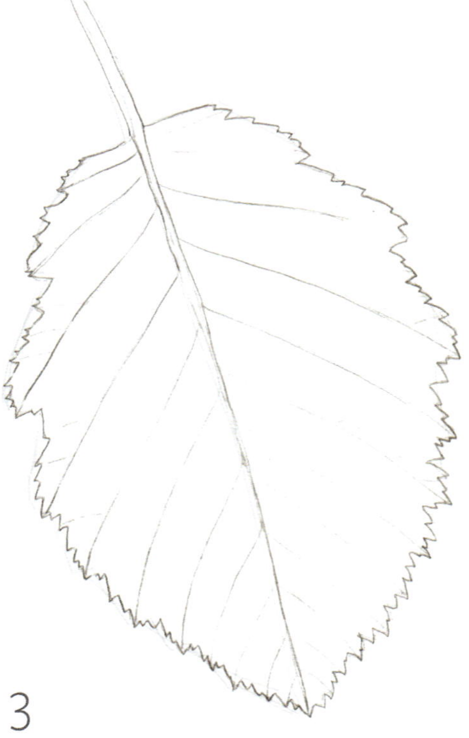
3

STEP 2: Refine the basic lines. Add some thickness to the main vein and some of the leaf's main jagged shapes. The margin of the leaf is toothed, but there are also some more prominent points.

STEP 3: Refine the sketch again. Once you have a basic shape, draw over the first line to add the texture and detail of the leaf margin. Sketch in the central veins of the leaf and anything else you want to capture before we move on to paint.

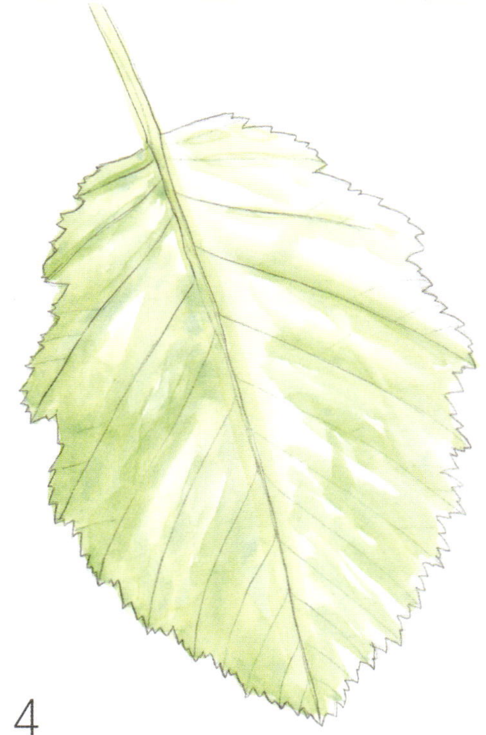

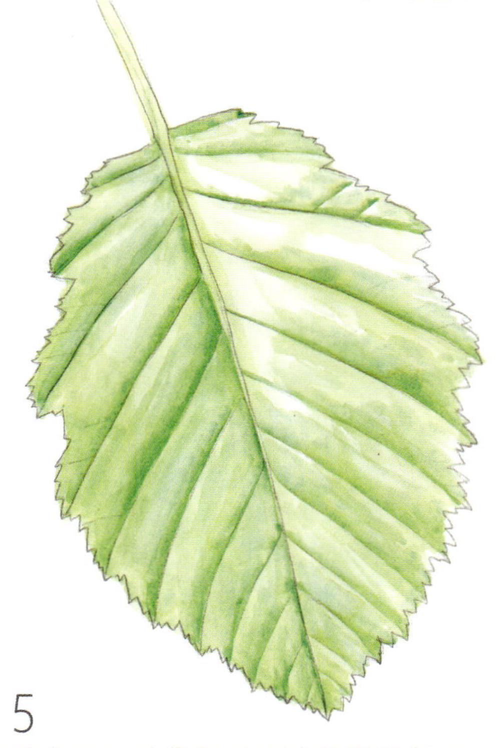

STEP 4: With watercolor, we want to save some white paper to make our subject glow, so we begin with a light wash. I almost always work from light to dark and build up a series of layers of washes. I mixed a light yellow-green with Cobalt Teal Blue and Hansa Yellow Light. I painted loosely, using a lot of water and leaving some white areas to capture where I noticed the most yellow-green.

STEP 5: Paint in light green along the veins using a series of graded washes, starting with a more concentrated wash along the vein edge and getting lighter towards the middle of each section. I continued this pattern for each vein of the whole leaf, indicating light from above and casting a shadow on the area above each vein.

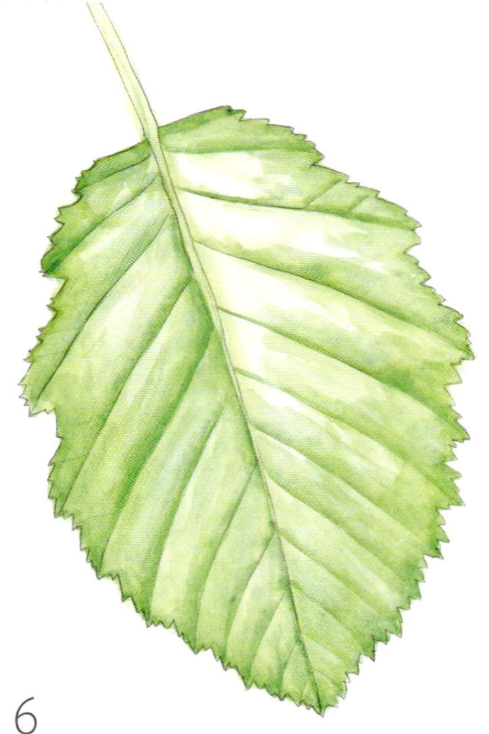

6

7

STEP 6: Add a wash along the edge of the leaf to define the margin. With the same medium-light green, carefully paint along the leaf margin, leaving a sharp edge to define the outer shape of the leaf. Lighten the wash while working towards the middle of the leaf so the wash blends in.

STEP 7: Add some shadows to create dimension. Mix a violet with Ultramarine Blue and Quinacridone Magenta. Use this as a graded wash, like in Step 5, to deepen the shadows along the top part of the veins.

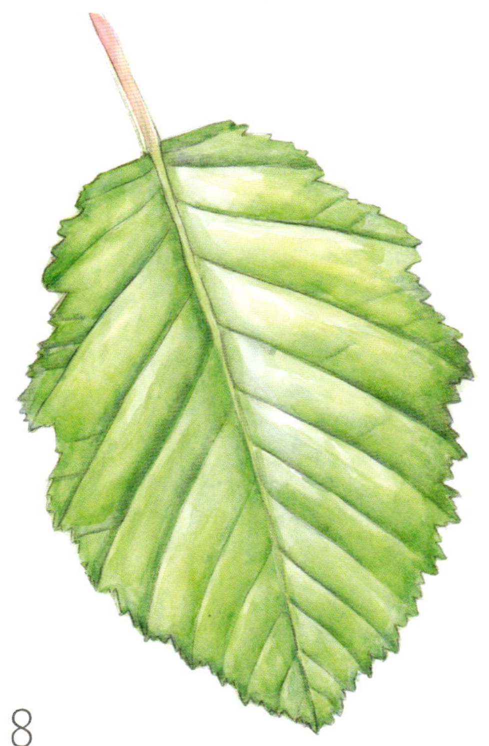

8

9

STEP 8: To increase the overall vibrancy of the leaf, I mixed a warm yellow-green as a more yellow mid-tone. I applied this across the leaf in the mid-tone areas, leaving some highlights on the right side of the central vein. I noticed the leaf stem was a bit reddish, so I added a wash of Quinacridone Magenta to it.

STEP 9: Deepen the colors in some areas and add any last details to make the sketch pop. I sharpened the edge of the leaf (margin) with a pencil to go over places where I painted outside of the lines. I also mixed a deeper green with Cobalt Teal Blue and Quinacridone Gold and deepened some of the shadows. If this was a botanical illustration, we could spend a lot more time drawing in each vein and bump, but since we are making a sketch, some looser marks give a general idea of the surface of an alder leaf.

Project 6

MONOCHROMATIC SHELL WITH BLUE AND BROWN

Paint a shell working with two colors (Burnt Sienna and Ultramarine Blue). Simplifying the color scheme to two colors and working with a grayscale image reference helps focus on value and shading. Burt Sienna is a warmer color that will appear to come forward in space. Ultramarine Blue is a cool color that makes things seem farther away or in shadow. Blended, the two colors make a neutral gray.

MATERIALS: a pencil, watercolor paper, and watercolors (Ultramarine Blue and Burnt Sienna)

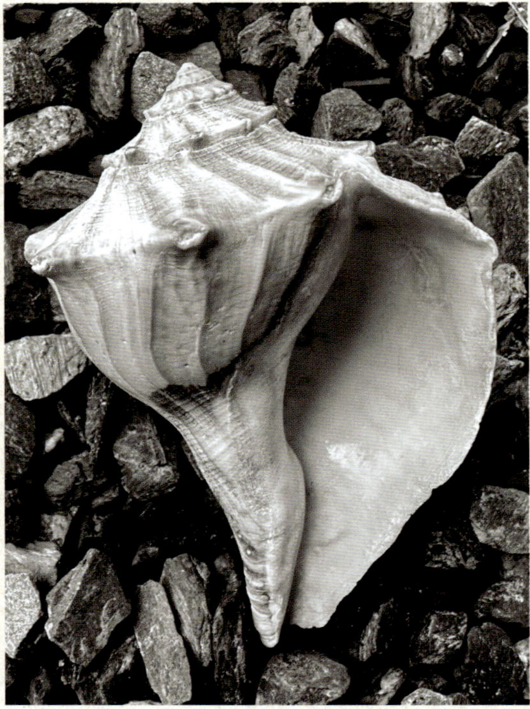

▲ Shells are a great subject to study because they often have exciting patterns and a distinct sculptural form.

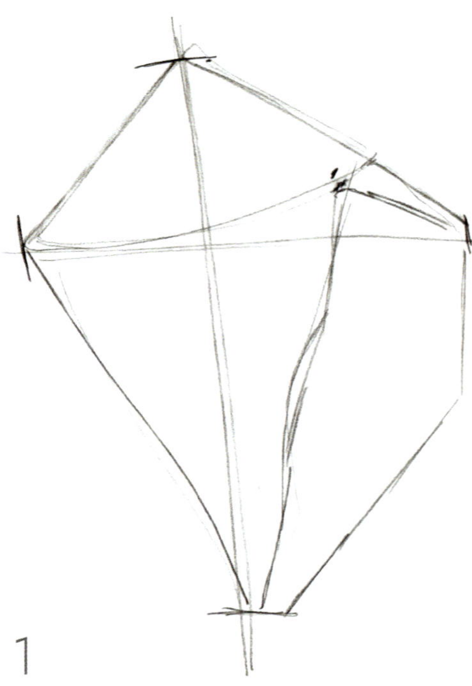

STEP 1: Begin with a rough outline, drawing the framework for the sketch lightly with a pencil. Mark hashes on the top, bottom, left, and right to indicate how big the drawing will be. Draw the main lines and angles of the subject. Simplify curves to straight lines and measure the angles to mark out the space the shell will take up on the paper.

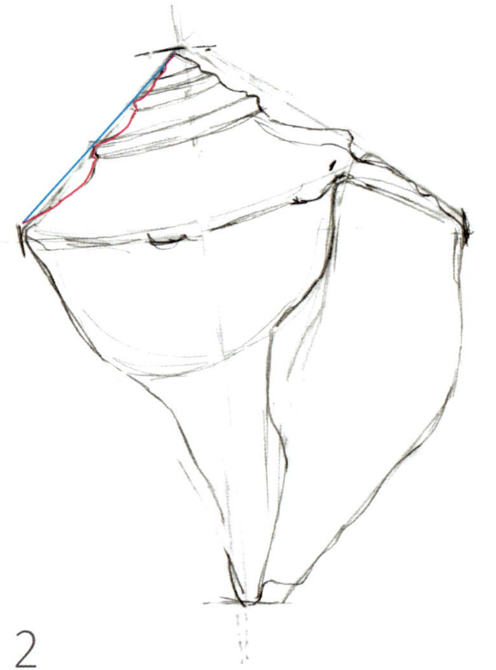

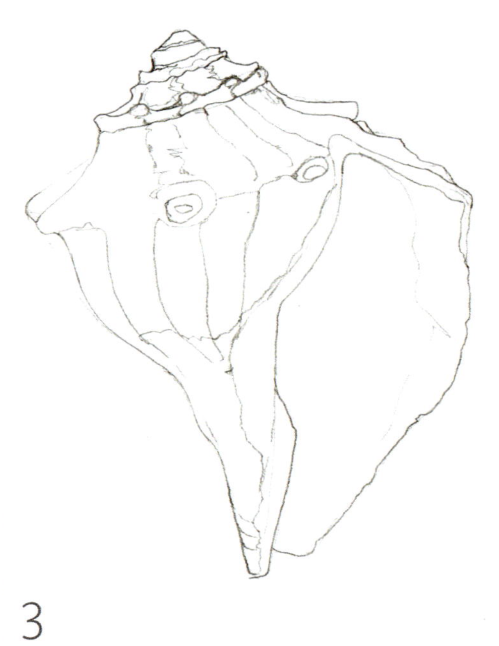

STEP 2: Refine the sketch by comparing the contours of the subject against the straight lines. Note the negative space between the blue and the magenta lines on the upper left ridge of the shell. Looking at the negative space and the shape around the subject can help visualize the shape of the shell's contours. Repeat this process around the shell.

STEP 3: Erase any extra lines, lighten any lines that are too dark, and refine lines from the previous steps. Fill in the contours of the interior of the shell that are important to the form and add some details and textures.

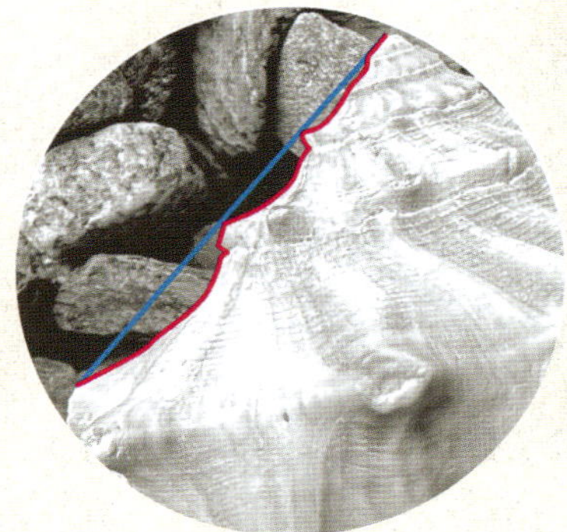

◂ **There is negative space between the blue and pink lines.**

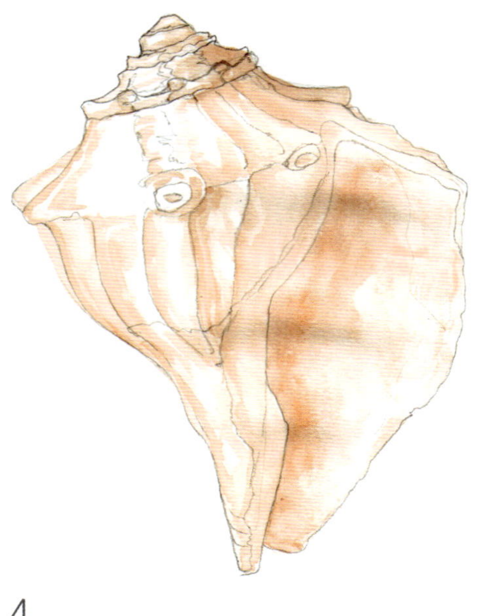

4

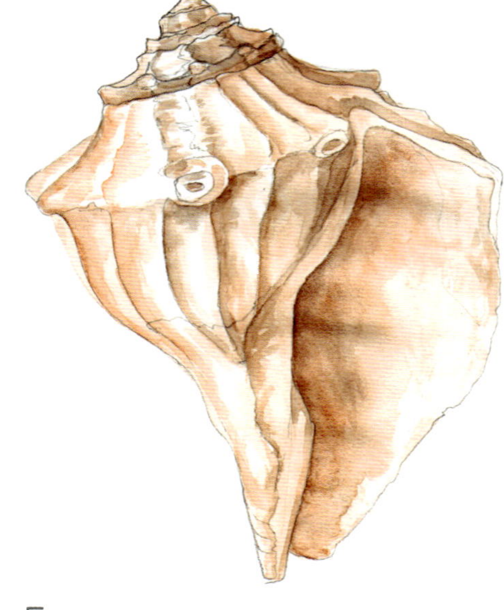

5

STEP 4: Begin painting. Mix a value scale working with the brown and the blue. Notice that the blue shades might be helpful in darks and shadows. To make the lightest wash, mix brown with water to create a light, warm brown. Adding more water to the paint makes it lighter in value. Observe the subject and notice the location of the lightest values. Paint around these areas to preserve the light of the paper. With watercolor, the lightest value is usually the paper itself. Use the light brown wash to paint in the mid-tone and shadow areas, painting around the light areas. Let the first wash dry.

STEP 5: Mix a darker brown by mixing more brown with less water and adding a tiny bit of blue. Paint in the mid-tones and shadows with this wash. Make sure to leave some white and light brown areas to preserve the light values. Pay attention to the way the shadows can help define the form. Making the right side of the shell darker helps the subject appear round. The roundness of the shadow in the shell aperture (opening to the inside of the shell) helps show its shape.

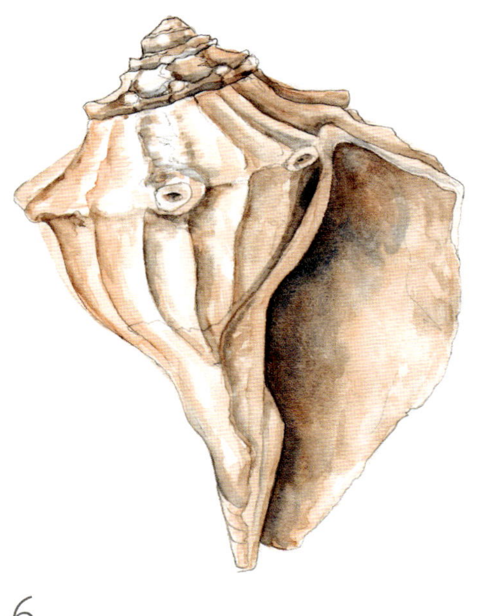

6

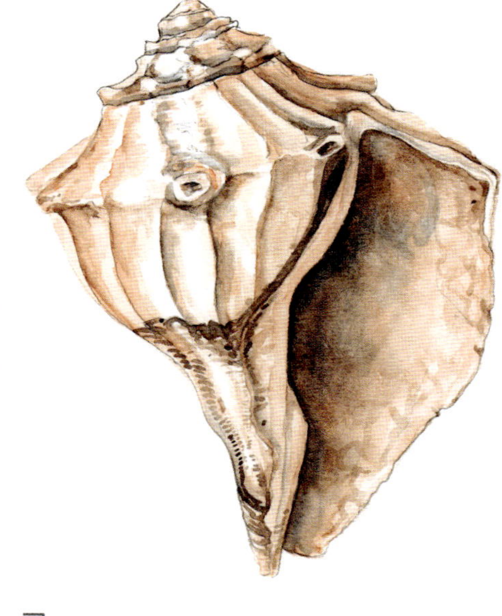

7

STEP 6: Mix blue and brown equally to create a medium-dark gray, which you can use to paint in the shadows and darkest tones.

STEP 7: Use the range of colors that you've mixed to paint some of the details of the shell. I painted some of the shell markings dark brown-gray and added some brown markings to the aperture.

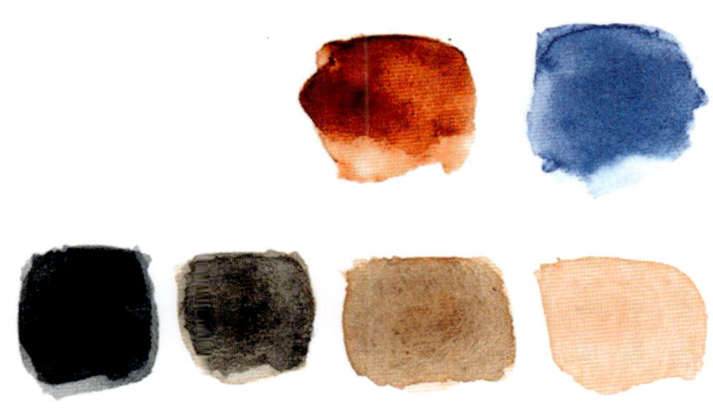

► **Burnt Sienna and Ultramarine Blue mix together to make a series of browns and grays.**

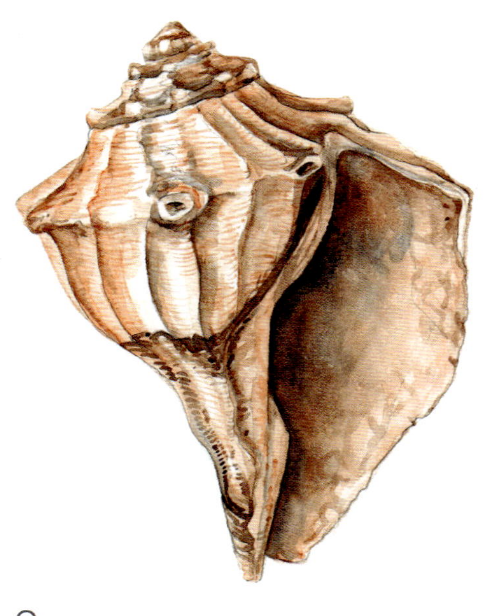

8

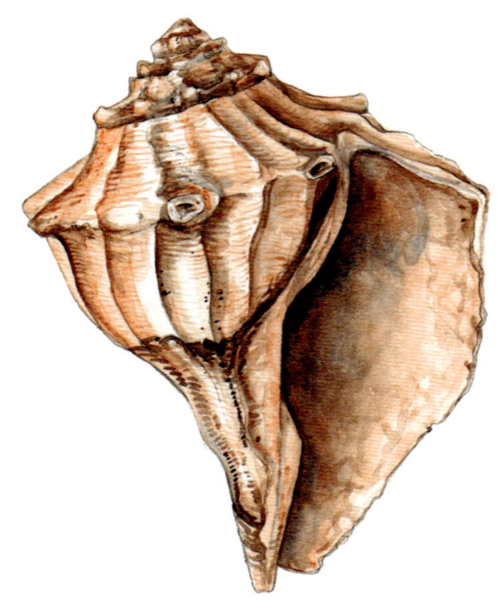

9

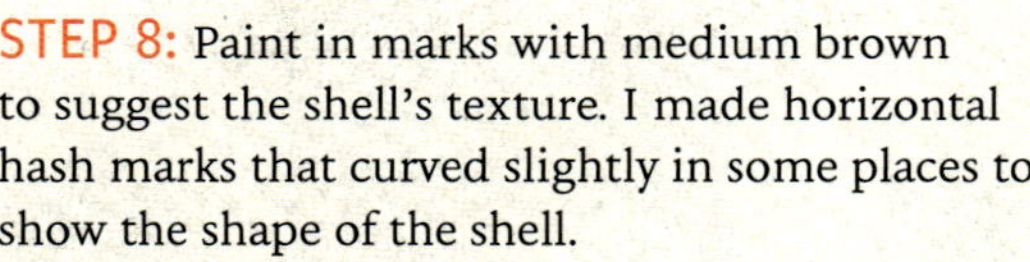

STEP 8: Paint in marks with medium brown to suggest the shell's texture. I made horizontal hash marks that curved slightly in some places to show the shape of the shell.

STEP 9: Add a few high-contrast details to the middle part of the shell. Having dark darks and light lights next to each other makes this part appear to pop forward, adding to the illusion of three-dimensional space. Likewise, soften any details that have too much contrast along the edges of the shell. This can be done with a slightly damp brush. Run it lightly on the spot you want to lift and blot with a paper towel.

FERRY SKETCHING

One early winter, I took the ferry from Bellingham, Washington, to Alaska, about a three-day trip. The winter nights were long, but the days were beautiful as we slowly traveled up the inside passage, passing cobbled beaches, mossy ledges, deep forests, tiny villages, and endless gray waves. Without phone and internet service, I had time to sketch and think. I pondered some of the prompts I shared in this book and reflected on my visual vocabulary and how I like to make art. Not what I might be good at, but what I genuinely enjoy doing.

I enjoy drawing because the practice of putting lines on paper is a meditation that allows me to forget myself, focus on my subject, and be intimately present. I also love the spontaneous feeling of watercolor, working in layers that reveal the process as the work builds. I enjoy the balance and tension between drawing and watercolor.

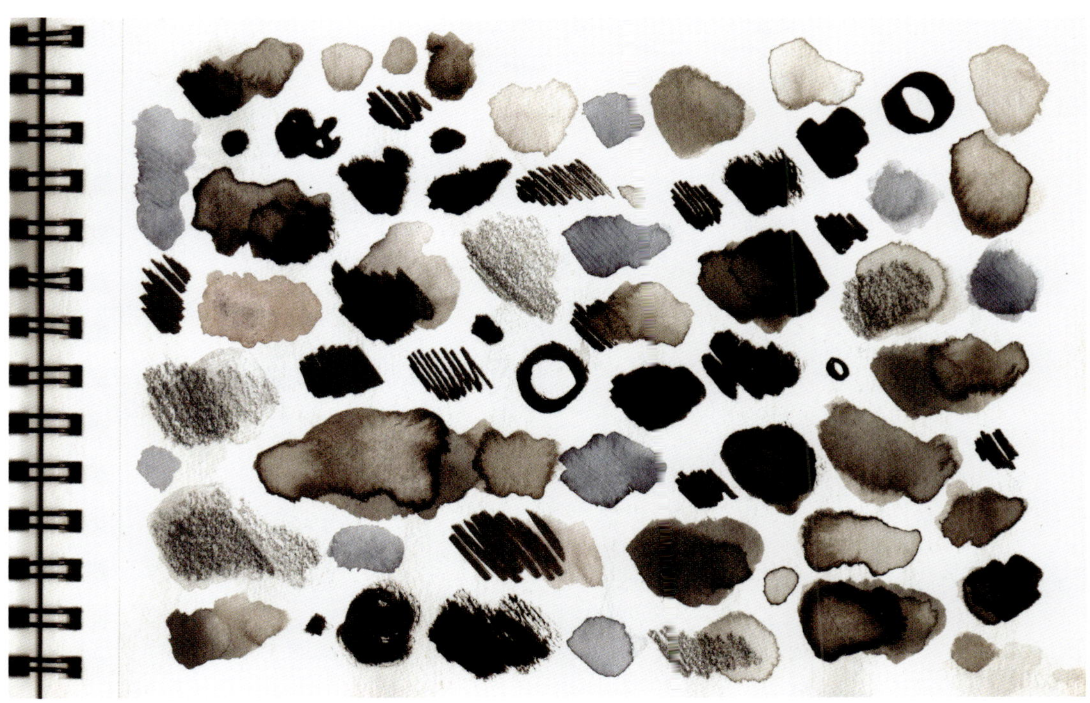

Exploring mark-making and visual vocabulary by layering different media to explore transparency and texture

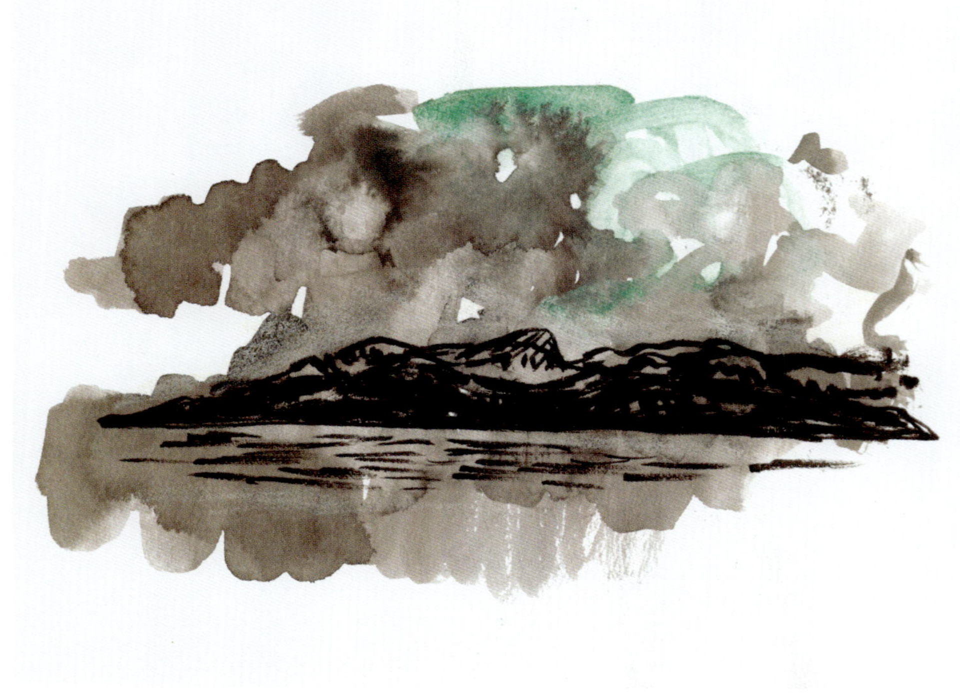

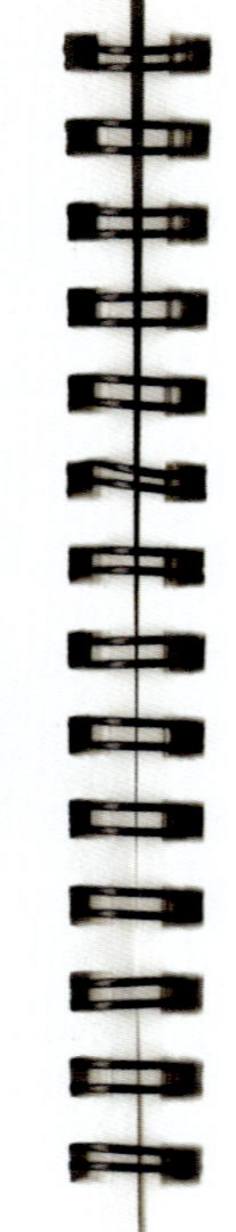

On the ferry, after exploring mark-making for a few pages, I started a series of sketches from the moving boat to practice my newly defined visual vocabulary. Sometimes I make work that is precise, but I also change it up and sketch with a looser style that is more of a gestural response to my surroundings. Sketching from a moving vehicle is fun because it forces you to respond to the world moving around you, to capture snippets here and there that form an overall impression, not a precise location or moment in time.

I made a series of fifteen little sketches capturing bits of the landscape we passed. To begin, I made some loose watercolor washes based on the colors and moods I saw outside the window. Once they dried, I added layers of drawing on top with a brush pen and colored pencil. Not every sketch was a success, but making the series was a great experience. It felt better because I responded to what I enjoy doing with my body and what art feels good to me.

Reflection

Expand your visual vocabulary to include watercolor. As you paint, pay attention to what feels comfortable to you. What feels challenging? What is interesting or pleasing to look at? The combination of what feels fun to make and what is interesting to look at can become your personal visual vocabulary.

◄ **Landscape sketches made from the ferry with ink, watercolor, and colored pencil, layering drawing materials on top of loose wet-in-wet washes**

Using Color to Build Up Texture and Form

You are not copying nature, but responding to nature in full awareness, to the way nature expresses itself in that object.

—FREDERICK FRANCK

Now that you know some ways to apply watercolor to paper, we will dive deeper into working with color. Color has value depending on the pigment and the saturation, so keep in mind everything we have practiced in previous chapters. Everyone experiences color differently, and what I see as blue-violet might look different to you. Color is relative, and the placement of one color next to another can change how we perceive it. As a younger

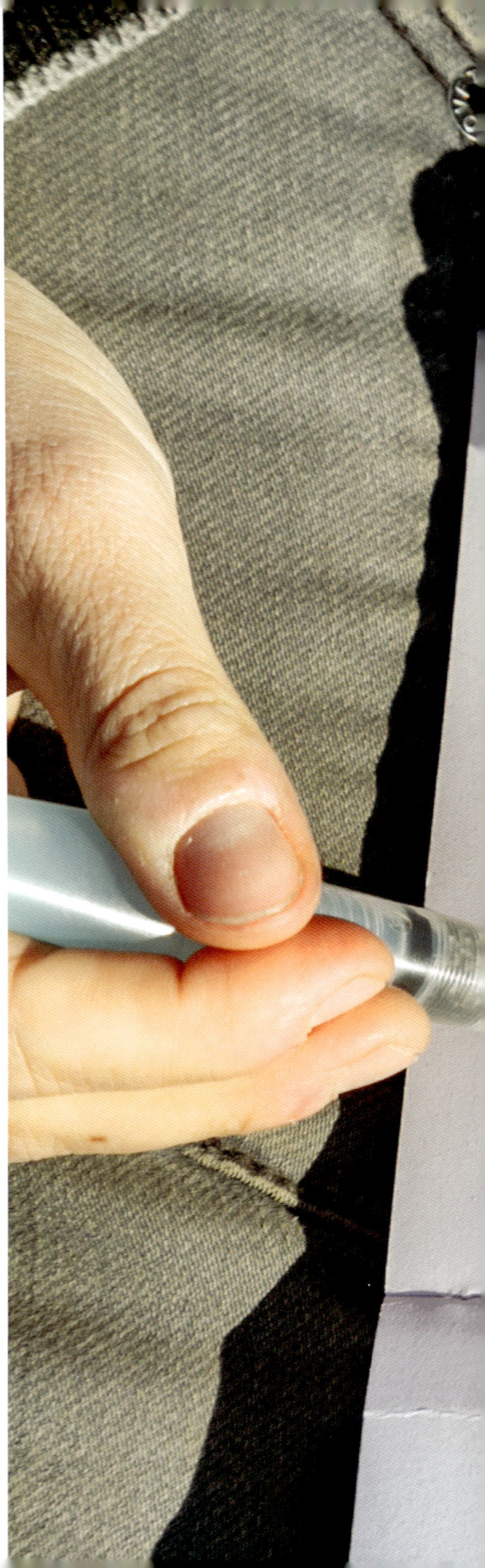

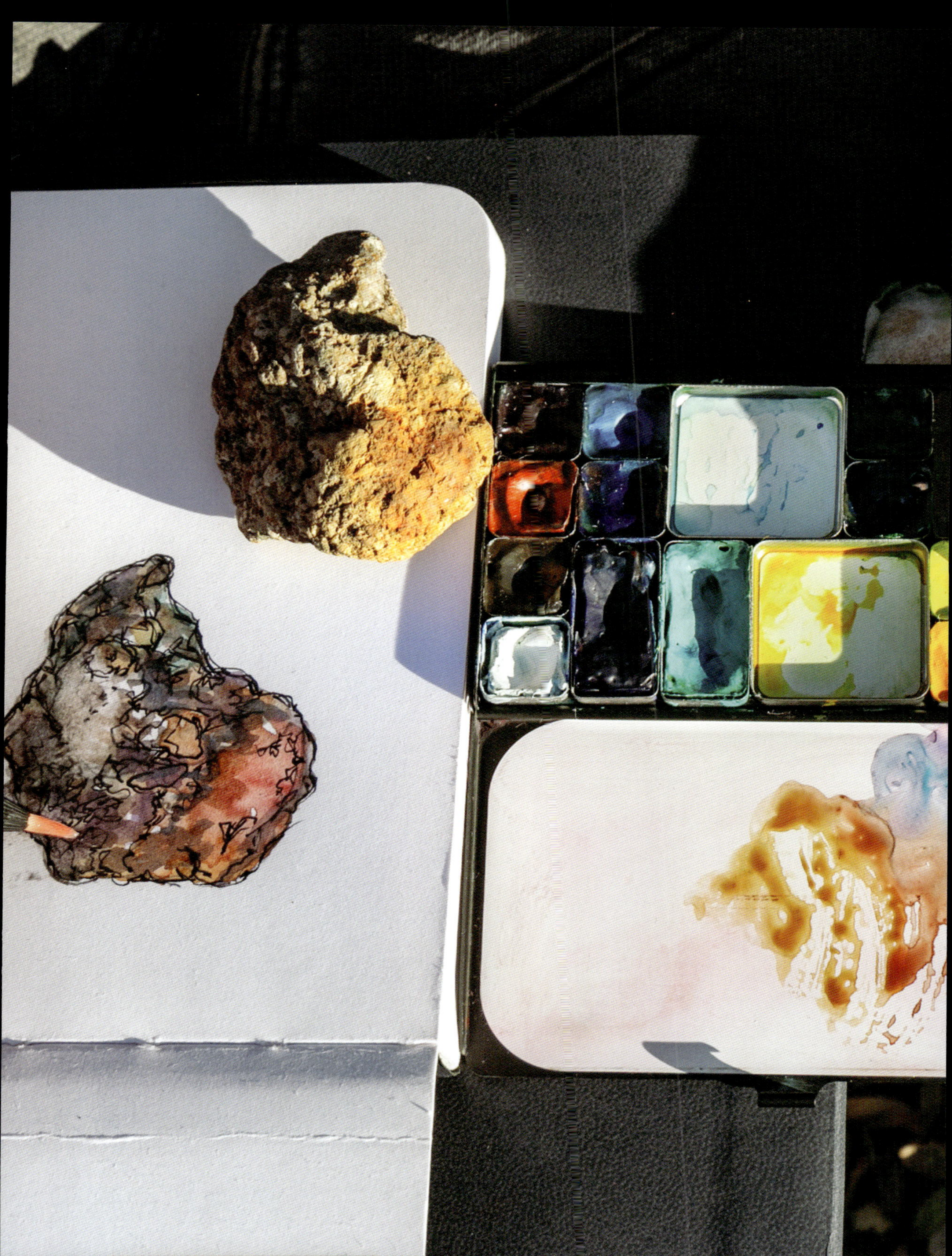

artist, I used to stress about getting an exact color match, but I've learned to relax and play more with my colors. Learning to mix accurate colors is still important, but I'd also like to extend permission to play and have fun.

An excellent place to start is to get to know the colors in your palette and how they might fit into a color wheel. The color wheel is a circular arrangement of colors organized by their relationships to one another.

THE COLOR WHEEL

PRIMARY COLORS: Cyan (or bright blue), yellow, and magenta (we are sometimes taught that red is a primary color, but magenta is most accurate). Theoretically, you can use these three colors to make any other color. Primary colors are equally spaced apart on the color wheel. If you mix all the primary colors together in equal amounts, you should get black.

SECONDARY COLORS: These are in between the primary colors, made of two primary colors mixed. For example, magenta and cyan make violet. The secondary colors are violet, orange, and green.

TERTIARY COLORS: These are in between the secondary and primary colors, including blue-violet, red-violet, yellow-green, blue-green, red-orange, and yellow-orange.

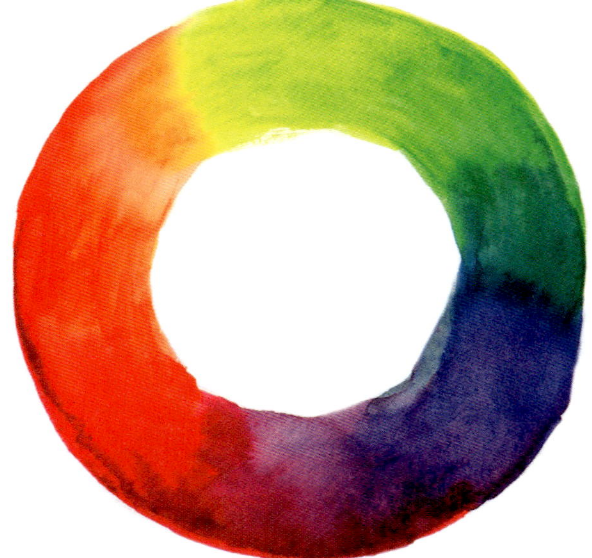

Color wheel with watercolor

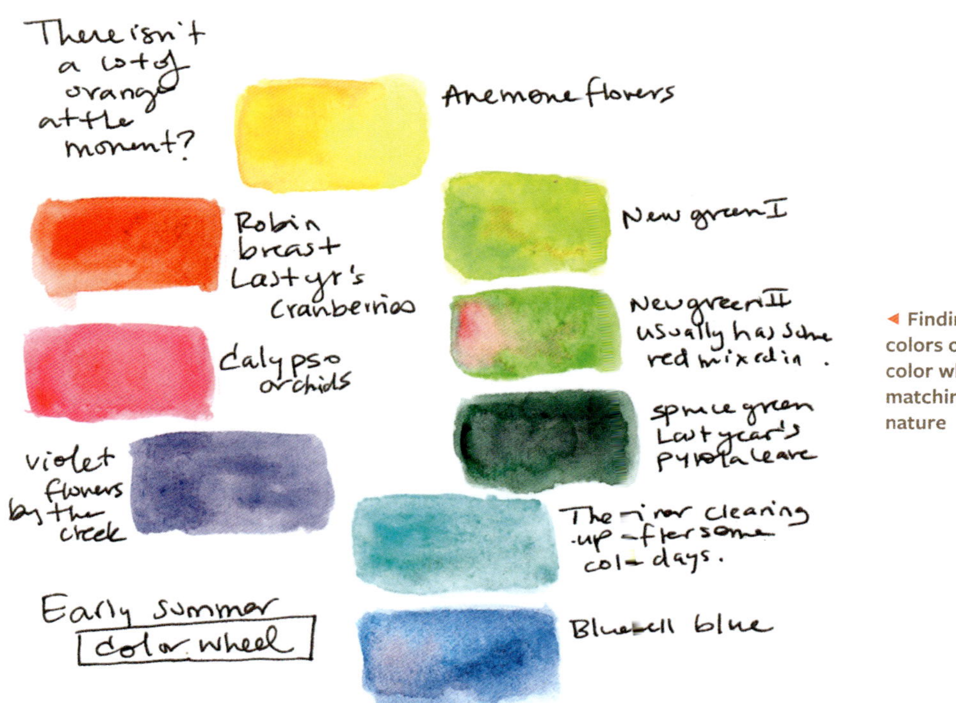

◀ Finding the colors of the color wheel and matching them in nature

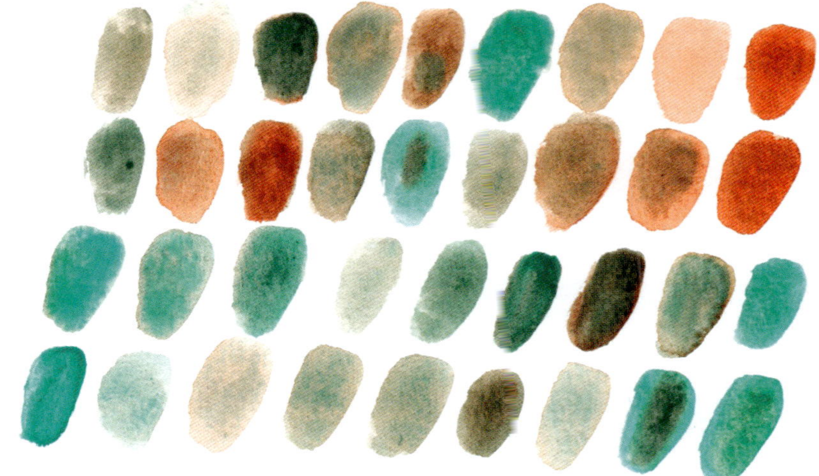

▶ Color swatches made by mixing Cobalt Teal Blue with Burnt Sienna

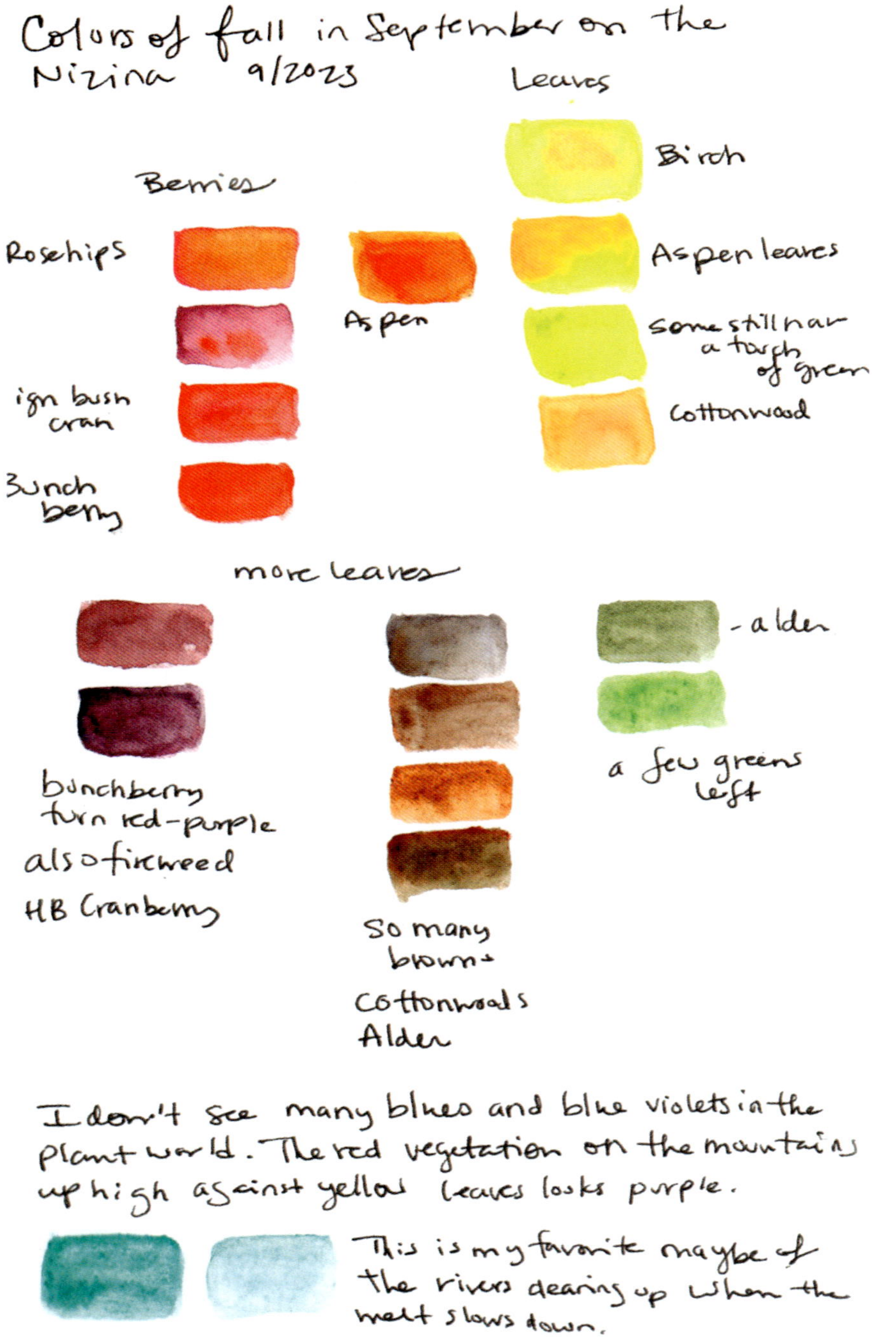

Mixing reds, yellows, violets, browns, greens, and a few blues based on the colors I observed in the fall landscape

Colors of fall in September on the Nizina 9/2023

Berries

Rosehips

Aspen

ign bush cran

Bunch berry

Leaves

Birch

Aspen leaves

some still have a touch of green

Cottonwood

more leaves

bunchberry turn red-purple

also fireweed

HB Cranberry

So many browns

Cottonwoods

Alder

- alder

a few greens left

I don't see many blues and blue violets in the plant world. The red vegetation on the mountains up high against yellow leaves looks purple.

This is my favorite maybe of the rivers clearing up when the melt slows down.

ANALOGOUS COLORS: These colors are close to each other on the color wheel, such as magenta, red-violet, and violet. These colors tend to be easy to mix and feel harmonious together.

COMPLEMENTARY COLORS: These colors are opposite on the color wheel, for example, red and green or yellow-orange and blue-violet. These colors have a lot of opposing energy and tend to make each other pop forward. If you mix complementary colors, you will get brown or black. This is useful to know if you want to dim the brightness of a color.

WARM AND COOL COLORS

Colors are also often described in terms of temperature. Cool colors include blues, violets, and greens. Warm colors include reds, oranges, and yellows. Warm colors appear to come forward in space, whereas cool colors read as farther away. Shadows tend to be cool colors.

The materials section reviews different kinds of blues, reds, and yellows. This is because each color can have a warm or cool bias. A warm blue is more violet, like Ultramarine Blue, and a cool blue is greener, like Phthalo Blue. You will get a brighter violet if you mix Ultramarine Blue with magenta than if you mix a cool-biased blue (like Phthalo Blue) with magenta.

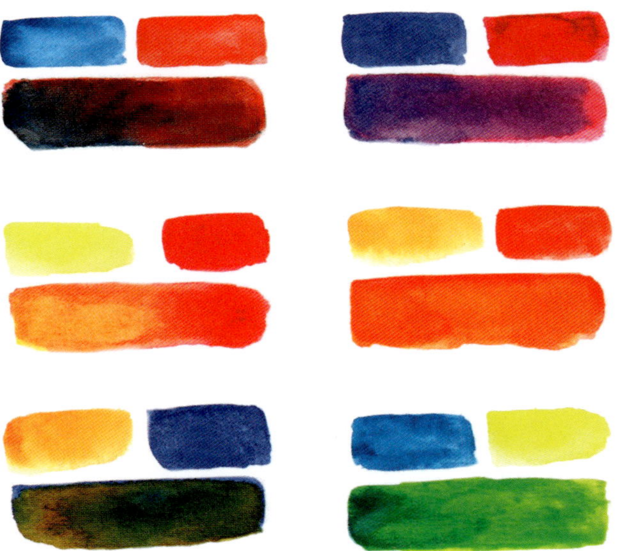

Examples of mixing warm and cool primary colors and getting bright or dull secondary colors as a result.

MIXING MUTED SECONDARY COLORS:
(left column, top to bottom)
cool blue (Phthalo Blue) + warm red (Pyrrol Scarlet)
cool yellow (Hansa Yellow Light) + cool red (Quinacridone Rose)
warm yellow (New Gamboge) + warm blue (Ultramarine Blue)

MIXING BRIGHT SECONDARY COLORS:
(right column, top to bottom)
warm blue (Ultramarine Blue) + cool red (Quinacridone Rose)
warm yellow (New Gamboge) + warm red (Pyrrol Scarlet)
cool blue (Phthalo Blue) + cool yellow (Hansa Yellow Light)

MIXING NEUTRALS

Bright colors can be fun but are not always accurate to nature. Placing a bright color next to a neutral color can make the bright color feel more intense since color is relative. Neutrals and grays are also crucial for making things recede into the distance and for describing shadows. To mix neutrals, you can combine two complementary colors. Experiment with them all, see which grays and browns you get with which colors in your palette, and what appeals to you. You can also mix blues and browns to get some rich grays. You will get a different gray depending on the warmth of the blue and brown, as well as the granulation of the pigment. Some combinations (such as Ultramarine Blue and Raw Umber) will separate as the wash dries. This can be beautiful and works for subjects with varied textures.

MIXING NEUTRAL COLORS:
Burnt Sienna + Indanthrone Blue
Raw Umber + Ultramarine Blue
Burnt Sienna + Cobalt Teal
Cobalt Teal + Quinacridone Rose
Phthalo Teal + Quinacridone Rose
Carbazole Violet + Quinacridone Gold
Sap Green + Quinacridone Rose

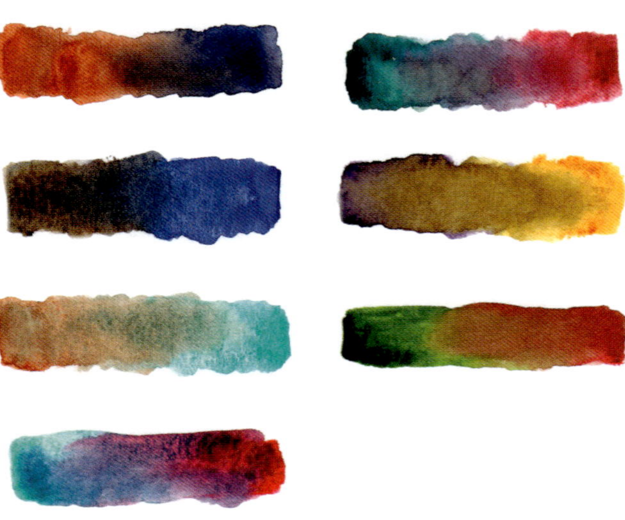

MIXING GREENS

We often see green in the natural world, and knowing how to mix many shades is vital. I keep a few greens in my palette for convenience, but I love mixing my greens from the variety of blues and yellows I also have. Sometimes, I observe a bright and fresh green, such as a new leaf, but often, natural greens are more muted. I will usually add some red, magenta, purple, blue, or brown to match the color of these neutral greens.

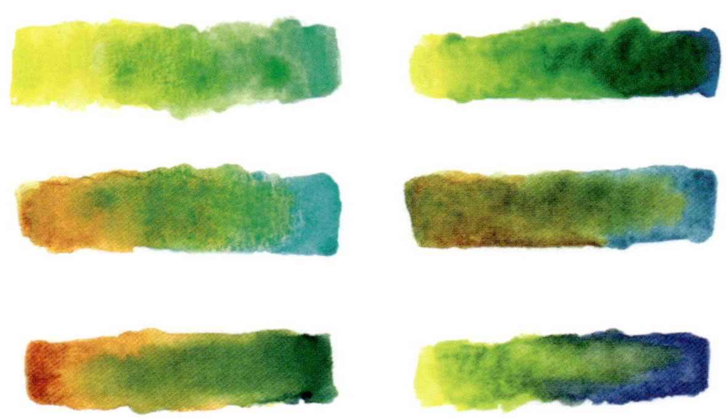

MIXING GREENS WITH DIFFERENT YELLOWS AND BLUES:
Hansa Yellow Light + Cobalt Teal
Quinacridone Gold + Cobalt Teal
Quinacridone Gold + Phthalo Teal
Hansa Yellow Light + Phthalo Blue
Quinacridone Gold + Cerulean Blue
Hansa Yellow Light + Ultramarine Blue

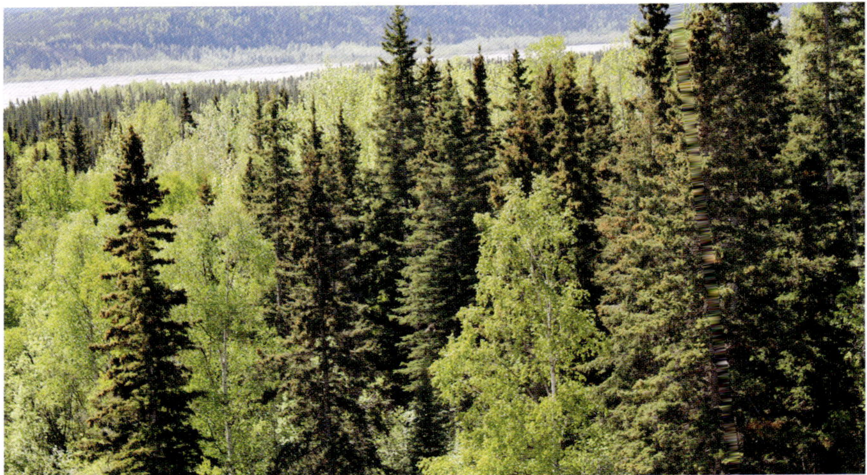

Look at all the different greens in this photo of a hillside in spring. How would you mix the colors that you observe? Practice mixing various shades of green.

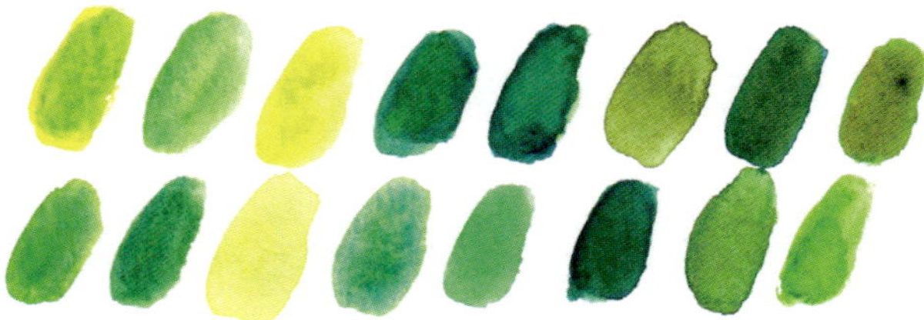

ANEMONE FLOWER

Use negative space and layering color to capture this yellow flower on paper.

MATERIALS: a pencil, a white gel pen, watercolor paper, and watercolors

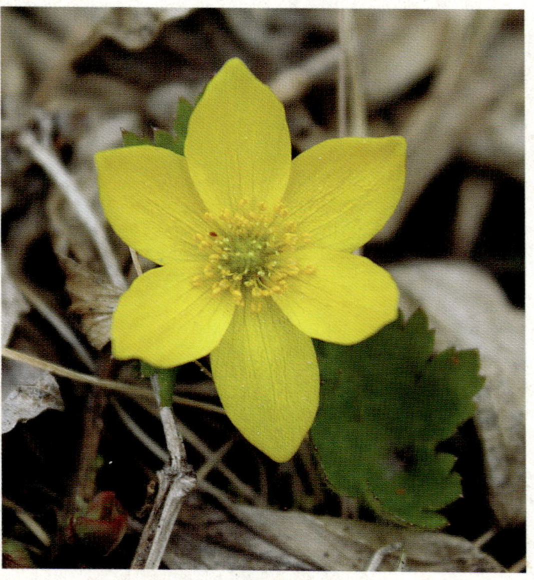

▲ **Growing out of the newly melted snow, anemone flowers are some of the first blooms I see in the spring. The yellow structures are sepals, not petals.**

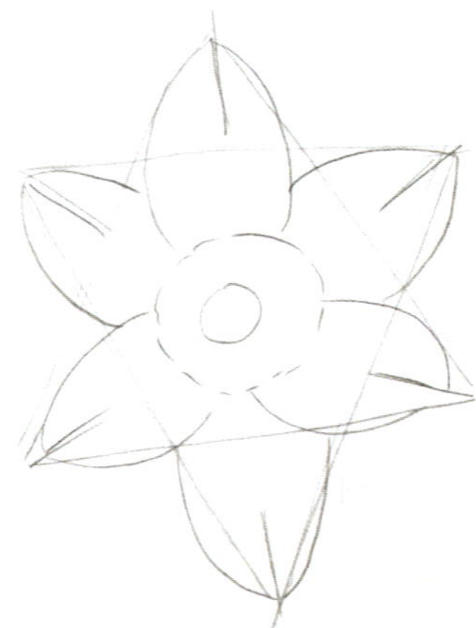

1

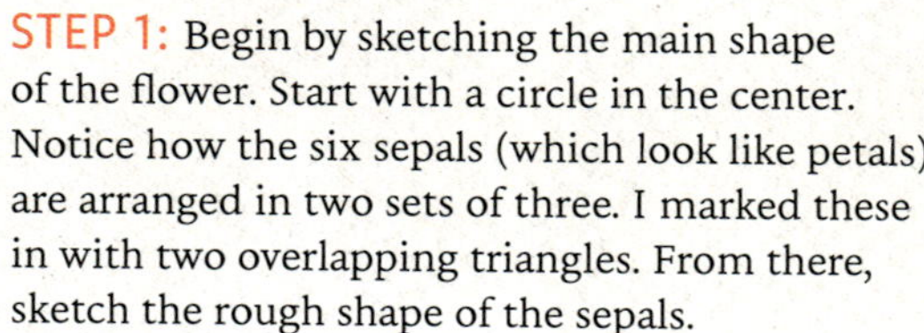

STEP 1: Begin by sketching the main shape of the flower. Start with a circle in the center. Notice how the six sepals (which look like petals) are arranged in two sets of three. I marked these in with two overlapping triangles. From there, sketch the rough shape of the sepals.

STEP 2: Go over and refine your sketch from the first step, fixing the shapes of the sepals, adding in the edge of the leaf shape, and adding detail to the center of the flower.

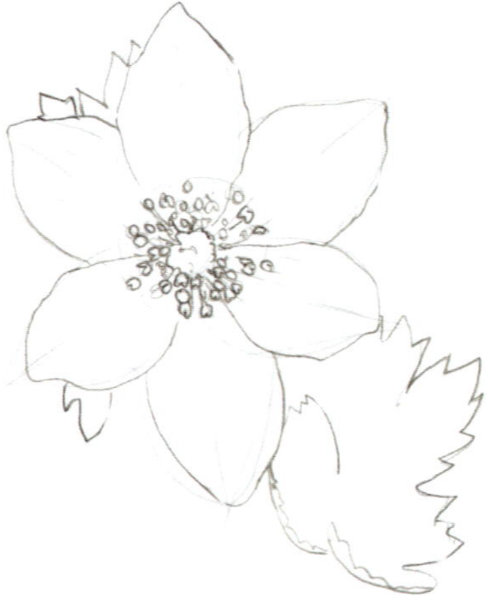

2

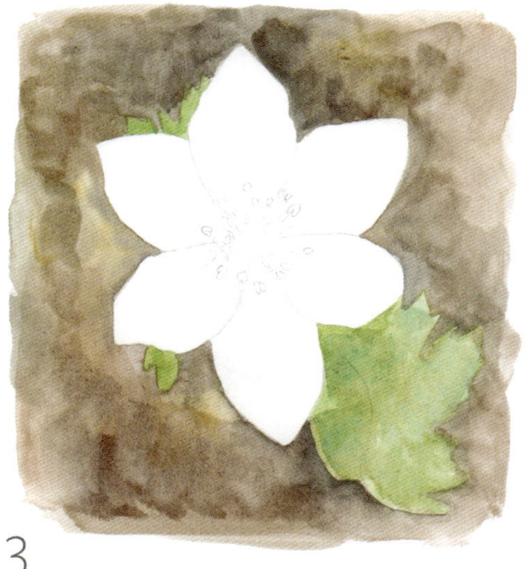

3

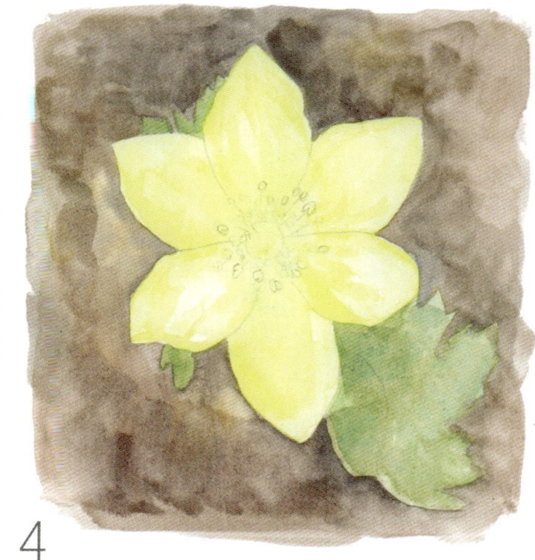

4

STEP 3: Since the flower is light in value compared to the background, focus on the negative space or the space around the flower, and paint the background first. I mixed Burnt Sienna, Raw Umber, Ultramarine Blue, and Quinacridone Gold to create a wet-in-wet wash. For the leaves, I mixed Cobalt Teal Blue and Quinacridone Gold. Let the background dry.

STEP 4: Paint the flower sepals with a light wash of a cool lemon yellow, such as Hansa Yellow Light.

STEP 5: Mix warmer yellows, such as New Gamboge and Quinacridone Gold, to get a deeper yellow, which will build up some shadows and texture in the flower petals.

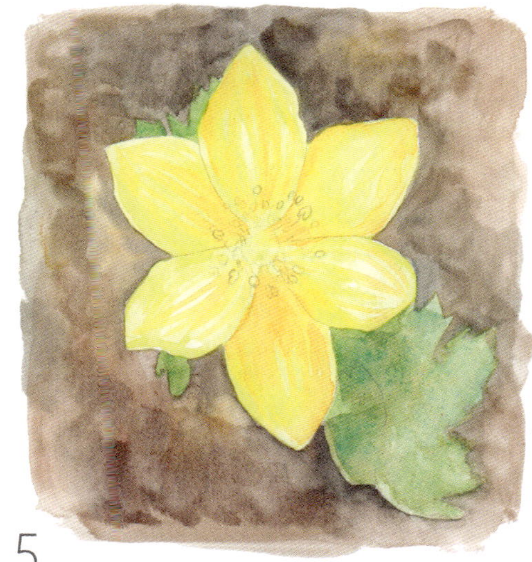

5

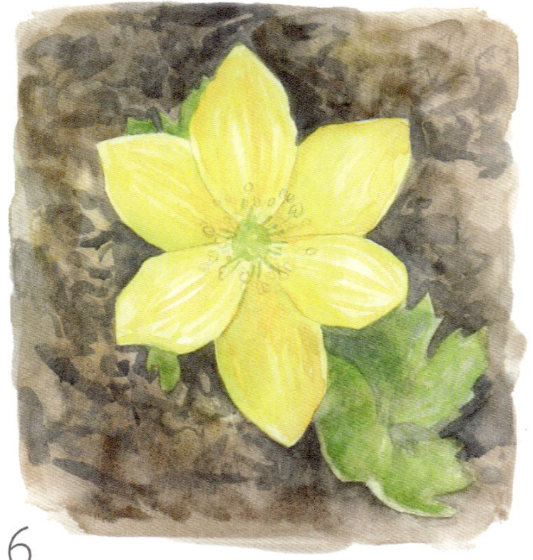

6

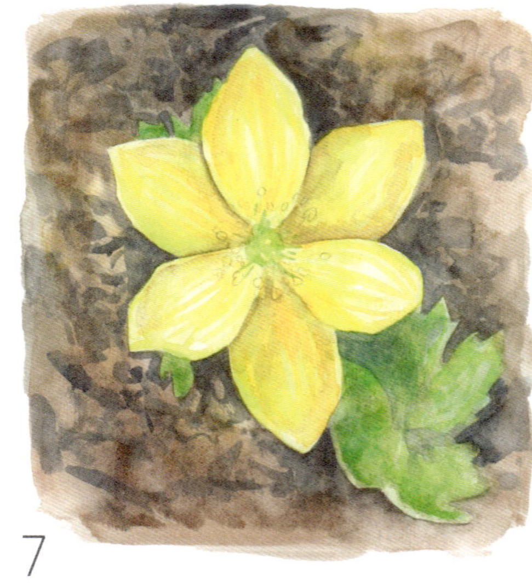

7

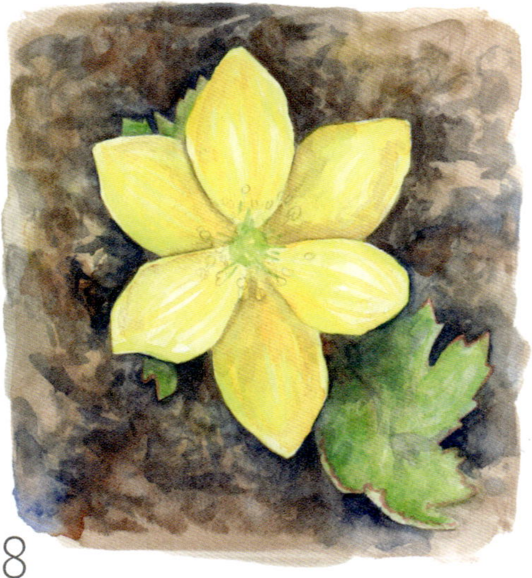

8

STEP 6: Use a light wash of Ultramarine Blue to add shadows and texture to the background. I added some shadows around the flower to create some contrast and to help the flower pop forward.

STEP 7: Mix a bright green with a cool blue and a cool yellow, such as Cerulean Blue and Hansa Yellow Light. Add that green to the middle of the flower to touch up some of the leaves, and mix it with water to lighten and add a very pale wash to some of the petals.

STEP 8: Mix violet with Ultramarine Blue and Quinacridone Rose to add shadows along the edges of the flower and to each sepal. This helps separate the sepals in the second row from the layer on top.

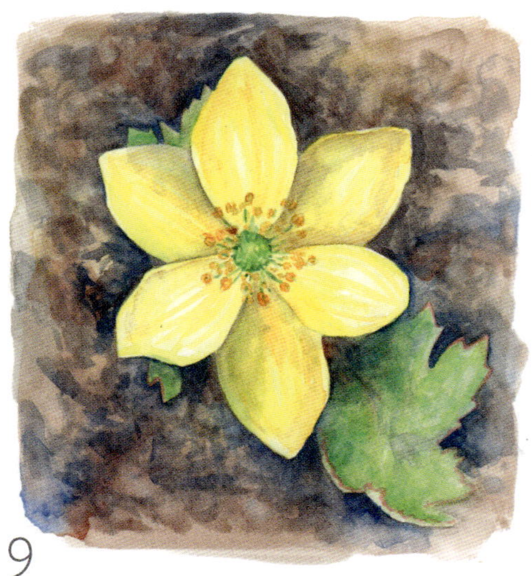

9

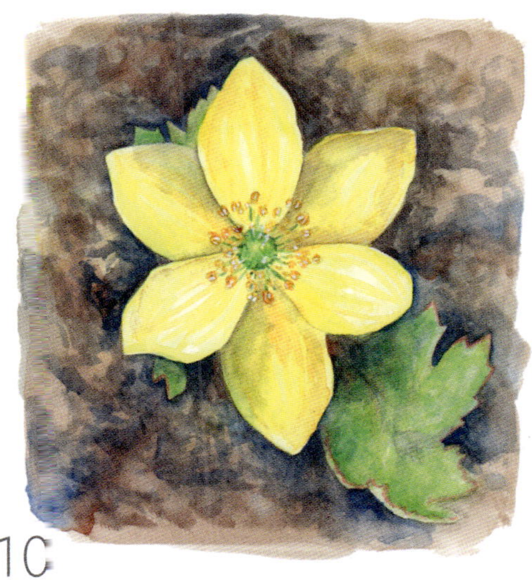

10

STEP 9: Using bright, cool green paint and a tiny brush, carefully paint the pistil in the middle of the flower. Paint the stamens (the structures around the pistil) with a fine brush and dark yellow.

STEP 10: Once the paint is dry, add some white pen or gouache to help the stamens and the pistil stand out.

Sketching a Whole Plant

I made this pencil sketch of a rhodiola plant growing in the alpine near the Juneau Icefield. I started by simplifying the flowers on top and sketching a bowl shape. I made little lines and arrows for each of the succulent leaves. This step helped provide an outline that I could refine to create the more finished pencil sketch on the right.

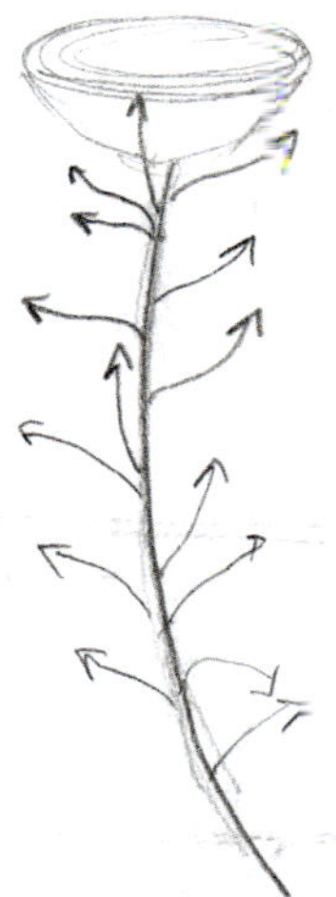

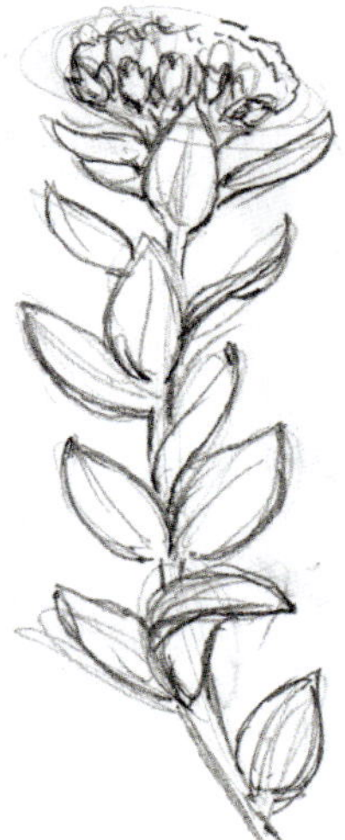

Project 8

WATERCOLOR AND PENCIL BOTANICAL STUDY OF LUPINE

Use color, value, and selective detail to make this sketch of an entire plant come together. We will practice using lighter values for the parts that are farther away and add extra details to make some leaves and flowers pop forward. This project is more complicated than some of the others. It can feel challenging to draw a whole plant with so many little parts, but we will break it down and use the pencil and the drawing skills we've practiced to create a map. As you go, add notes and observations and pay attention to what feels good to you.

MATERIALS: a pencil, watercolor paper, and watercolors

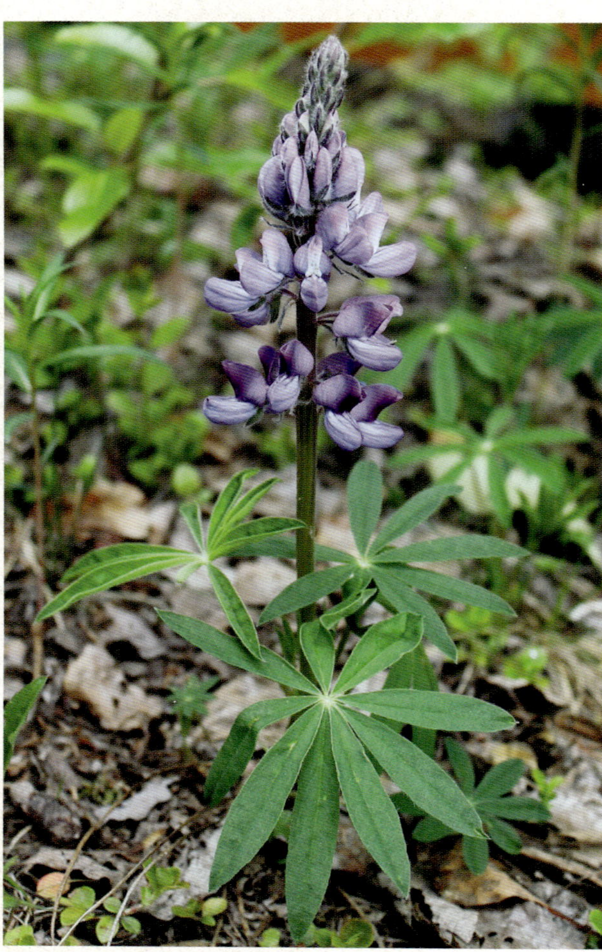

Lupine flowers are pretty common in Alaska. They can grow in areas with relatively poor soil. As part of the pea family, they have nodules on their roots to fix nitrogen. Their seedpods look like hairy peas but are poisonous.

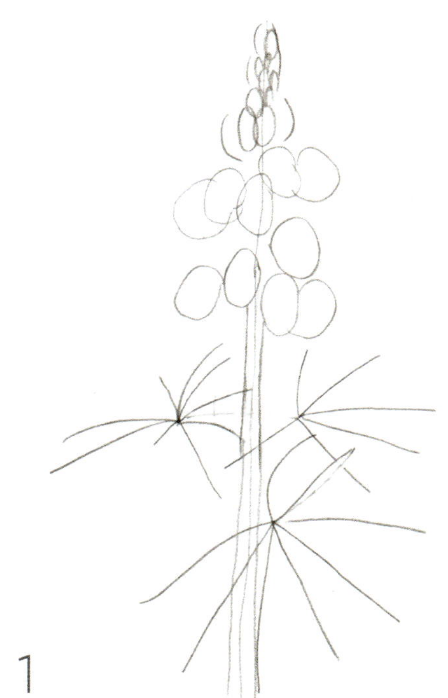

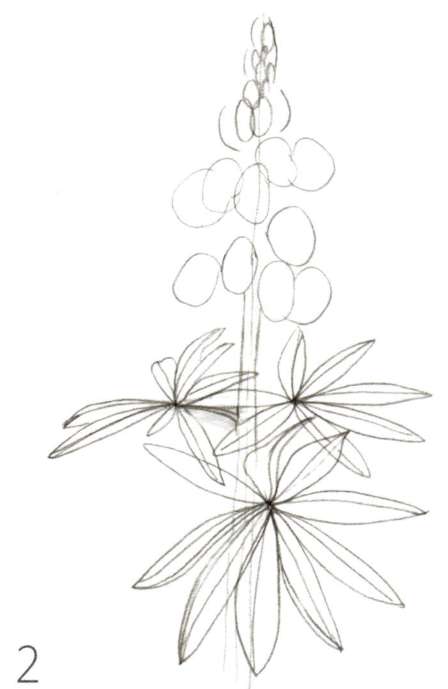

STEP 1: Begin with a sketch of the plant's "skeleton" to map out your drawing. I started with the stem and then added lines to show where the compound leaves would go, using the middle vein as my main reference. I drew oval shapes to show where the flowers would go.

STEP 2: Once you have a "map" from the previous step, refine the shapes, erasing where needed. Using the middle vein of each leaf, sketch in the margins or edges of the leaves. Instead of worrying about overlapping leaves, draw them on top of each other and erase the ones that are behind overlapping edges in a later step.

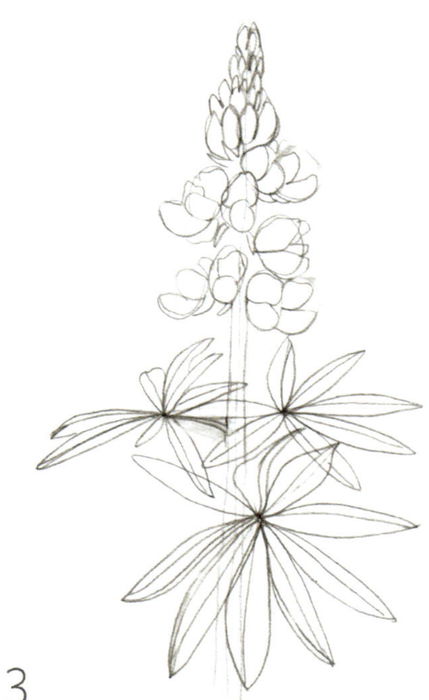

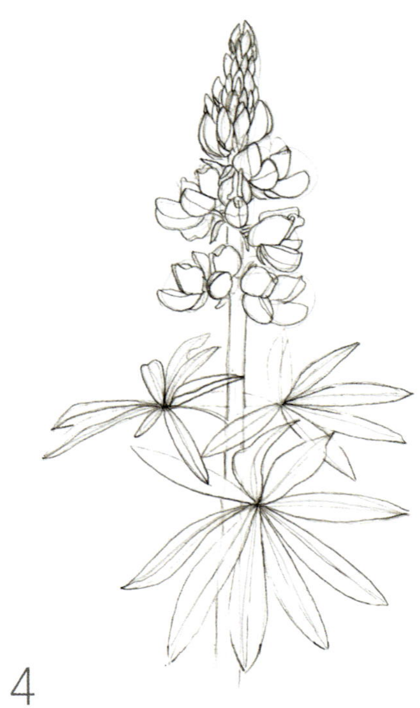

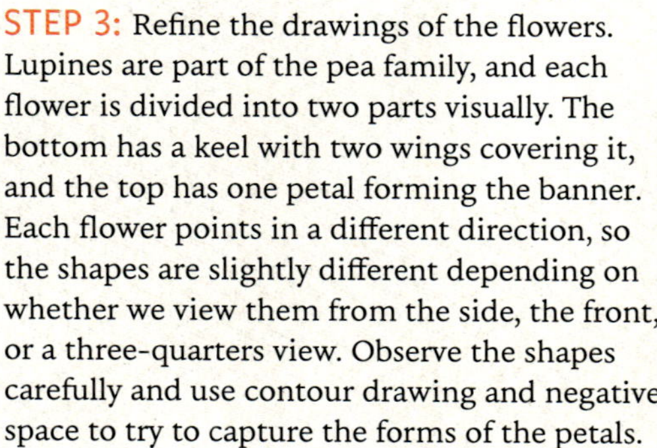

STEP 3: Refine the drawings of the flowers. Lupines are part of the pea family, and each flower is divided into two parts visually. The bottom has a keel with two wings covering it, and the top has one petal forming the banner. Each flower points in a different direction, so the shapes are slightly different depending on whether we view them from the side, the front, or a three-quarters view. Observe the shapes carefully and use contour drawing and negative space to try to capture the forms of the petals.

STEP 4: Continue refining the drawing, erasing unnecessary marks, further defining the shapes of the flowers and leaves, and adding details that will be important in the painting process. For example, I didn't add the spots on the banner petals, but I drew in the sepals and stems on the flowers.

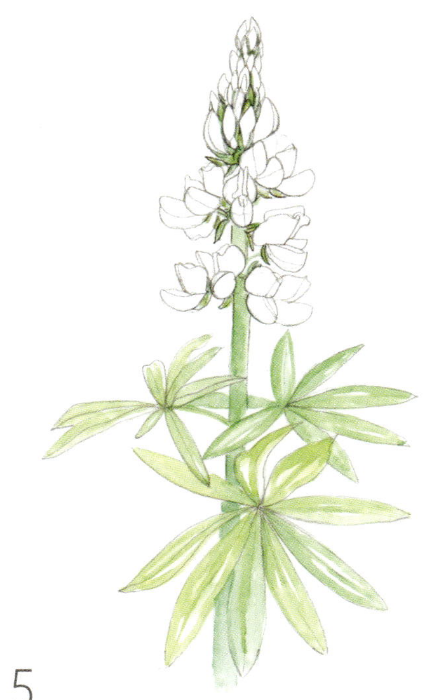

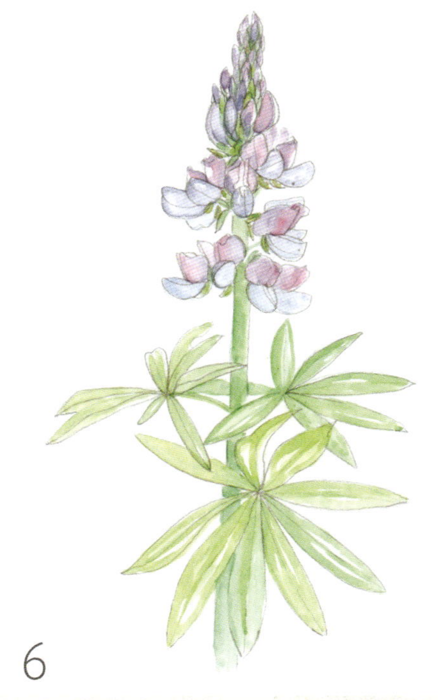

STEP 5: Mix two greens: a warm green with more yellow and a bluer, cool green. Use these greens in a light wash to paint the leaves and stems. Put the more yellow tones on the leaves that you want to come forward, since warm colors pop forward, and add cool green elsewhere, as well as on the stem.

STEP 6: Mix a warm violet (with more magenta) and a cool violet (that is bluer) using Ultramarine Blue and Quinacridone Rose. Paint a series of light washes to color in the flowers. I noticed that the top part of the flower is often a more magenta color while the bottom part is bluer.

STEP 7: Once your first layers of watercolor are dry, add pencil shading on top. Use the pencil to sharpen up some of the edges of the shapes and add shading to some of the parts of flowers behind where two petals overlap. The gray of the graphite will dull the color to make this part recede.

STEP 8: Add more layers of watercolor to build up the shadows and shapes. Putting the most contrast on the flowers and leaves will make them appear closest to the viewer and help them stand out from the background. I added some magenta to the stem, more blues and green shadows to the leaves, and pops of magenta and purple to the flowers. Once that was dry, I added white gouache to places where I wanted the white to come forward.

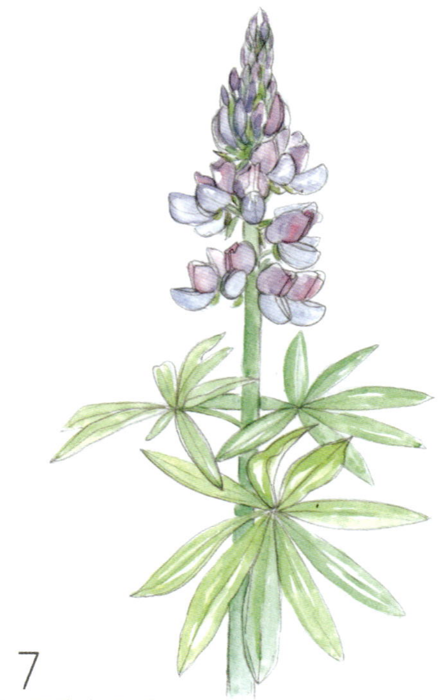

7

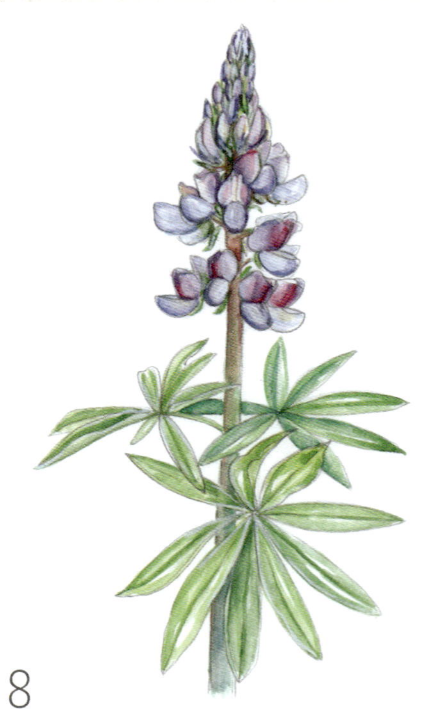

8

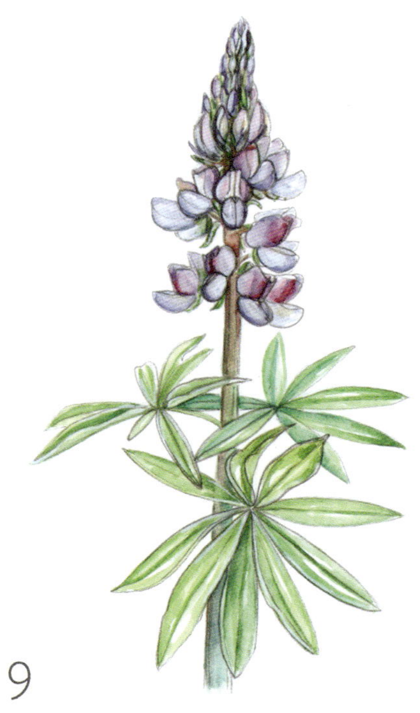

9

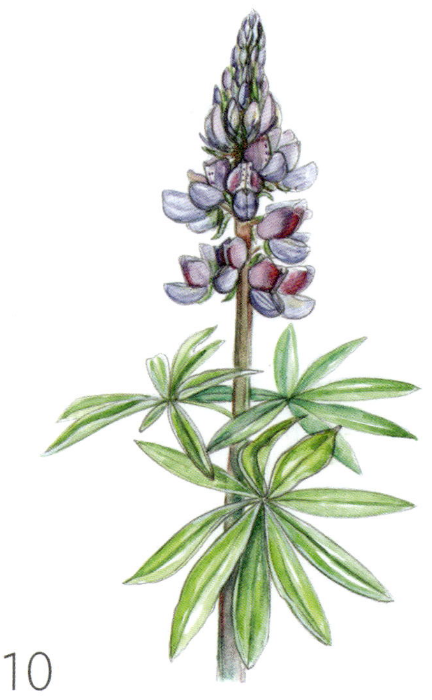

10

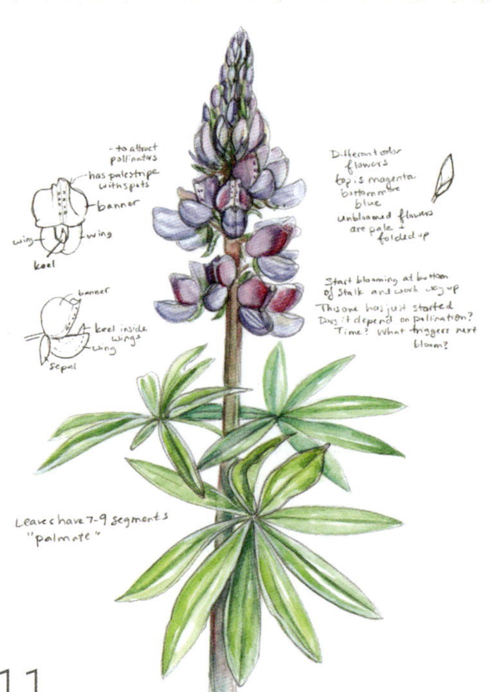

11

STEP 9: Once the watercolor is dry, sharpen the shapes again with pencil, especially with the flowers in the front.

STEP 10: Add a few details to the parts that you want to pop forward. I added some dots to the top banner petals, lines on the wing petals, and deepened some of the shadows on the leaves.

STEP 11: Add in a few notes and diagrams. Explain the shape of the flowers and leaves and what else you noticed and wondered while sketching.

COLOR DIARY

We will go into more methods of mixing different colors throughout the examples in this book, but a fun way to practice is to make sketchbook entries that are focused entirely on color.

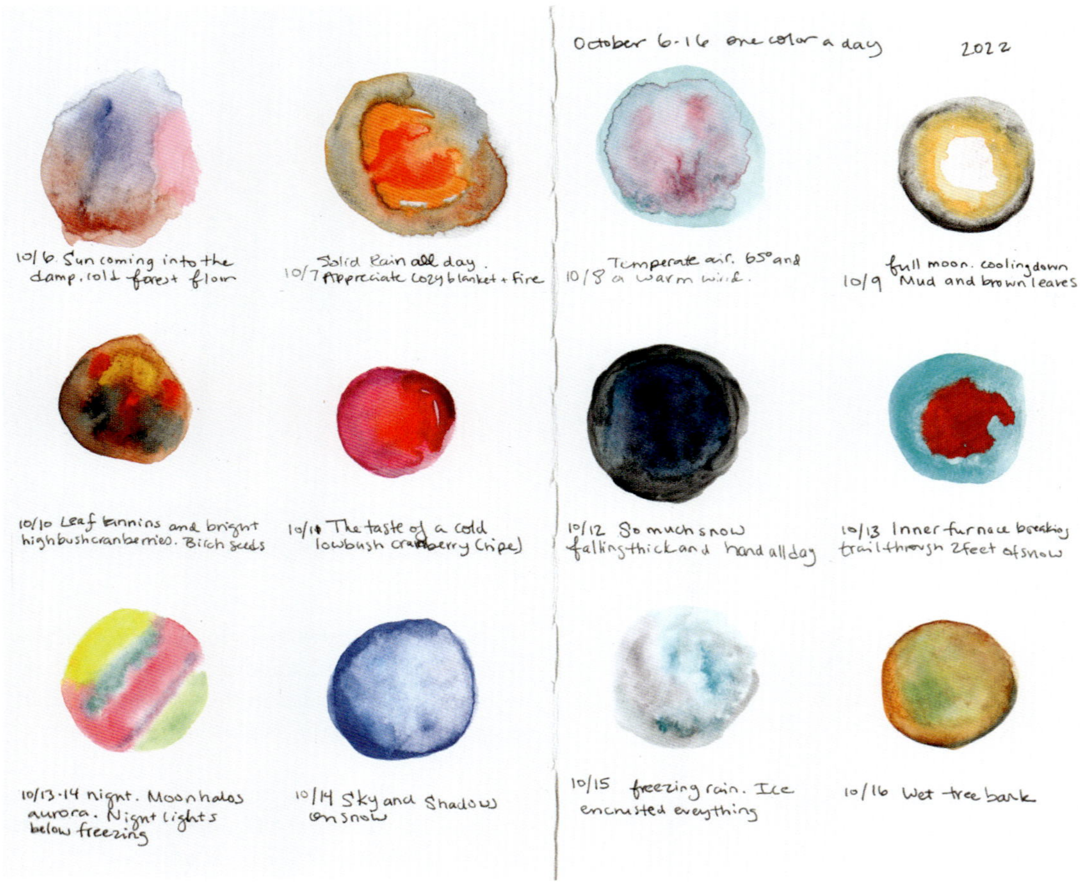

This page records one set of colors that I observed each day. I liked experimenting and seeing how the pigments interacted. I started by focusing on the colors I observed but then expanded my color diary to include other senses and how I felt.

COLOR WHEEL OF PLACE

Instead of sketching a whole landscape, sometimes I like to make a series of swatches or a pie chart of the different colors I observe in a place. This leaves me with other memories, but they are just as rich. This pair of color studies was painted one day apart in the fall, before and after an early snowstorm.

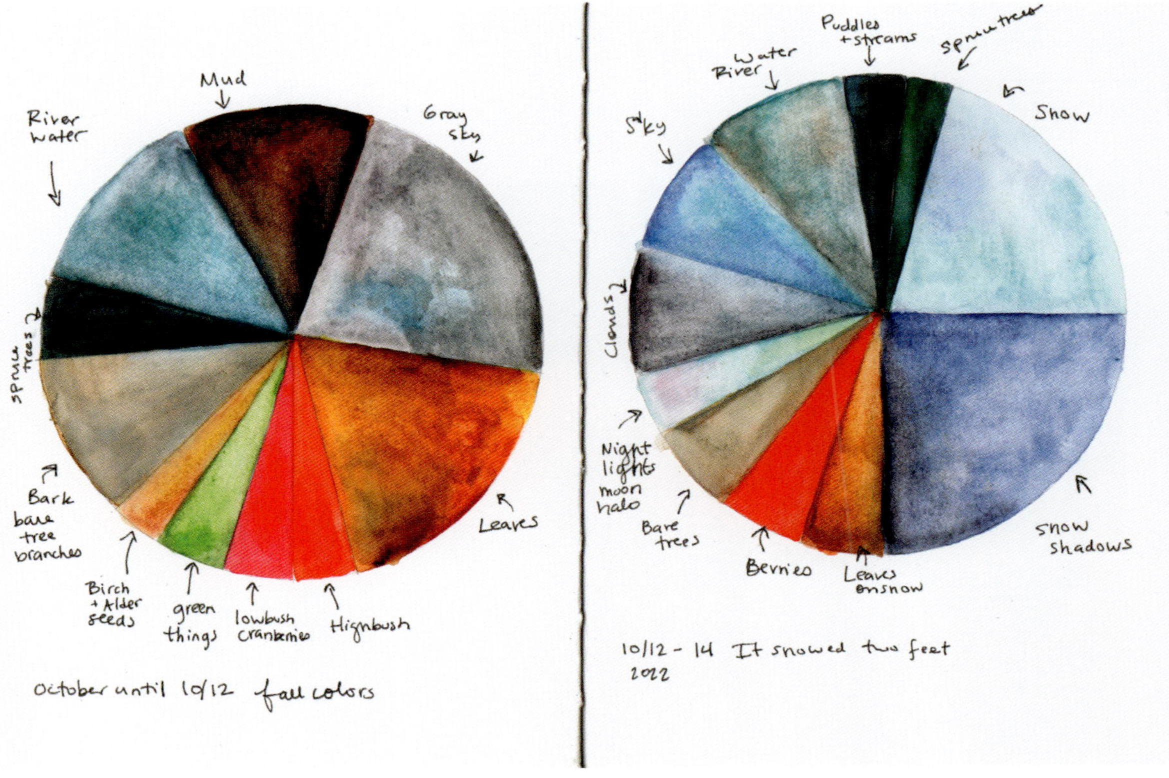

Instead of sketching a whole landscape, sometimes I like to make a series of swatches or a pie chart of the different colors I observe in a place. This leaves me with other memories, but they are just as rich. This pair of color studies was painted one day apart in the fall, before and after an early snowstorm.

Project 9

FALL LEAVES WITH COMPLEMENTARY COLORS WITH FIREWEED

Red and green are complementary colors so mixing them together makes brown. Painting a subject with both of those colors can be tricky, but putting contrasting complementary colors next to each other makes them pop, which is one reason why autumn leaves are so beautiful.

MATERIALS: a pencil, a gray marker, watercolor paper, and watercolors

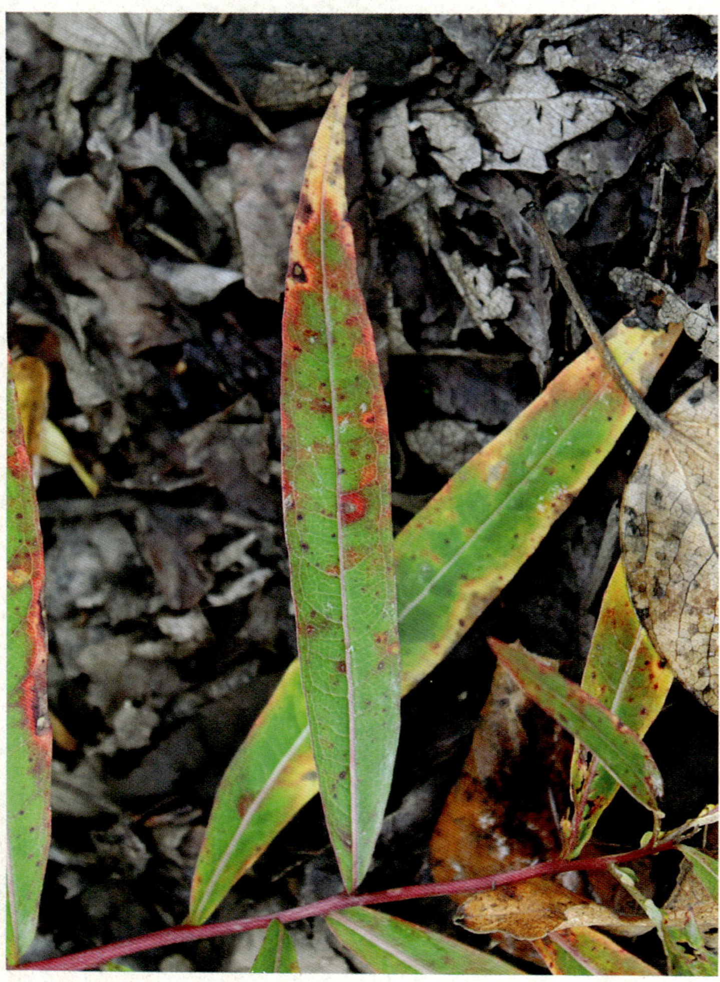

Fireweed is a flowering plant common all over Alaska. The flowers are beautiful magenta in the summer, but my favorite time of year is when the leaves turn red, purple, and yellow in the fall.

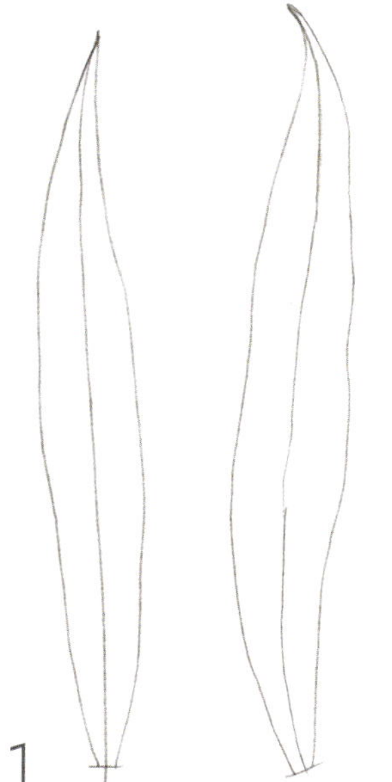

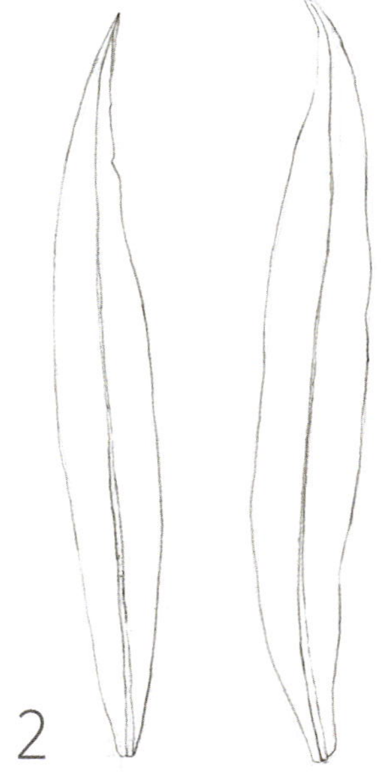

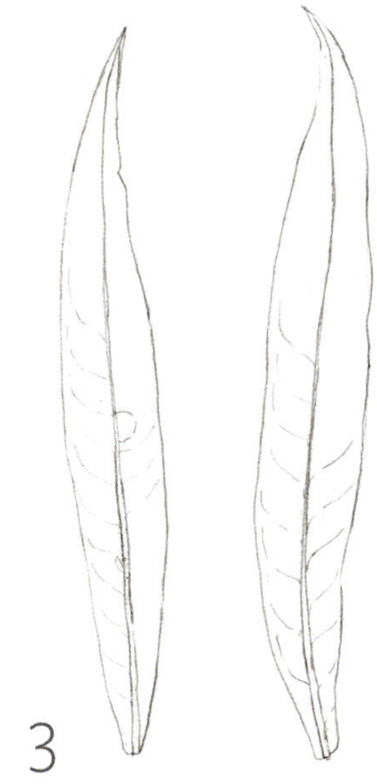

STEP 1: The photo reference shows two leaves crossing each other attached to a stem, but I want to paint the two leaves next to each other on a white background so that I can focus on painting the colors and patterns and not the structure of the plant. It takes a bit of imagination to fill in the missing part of the covered leaf, but we can work from observation of what we can see to make that up. Begin by sketching the general shape of each leaf. I started with the middle vein and then drew in the margin.

STEP 2: Draw the thickness of the center vein. Refine the margins as needed. I noticed that the leaf on the left has a small notch in the top right margin, which I added.

STEP 3: Lightly draw in some of the other veins and essential markings on the leaves.

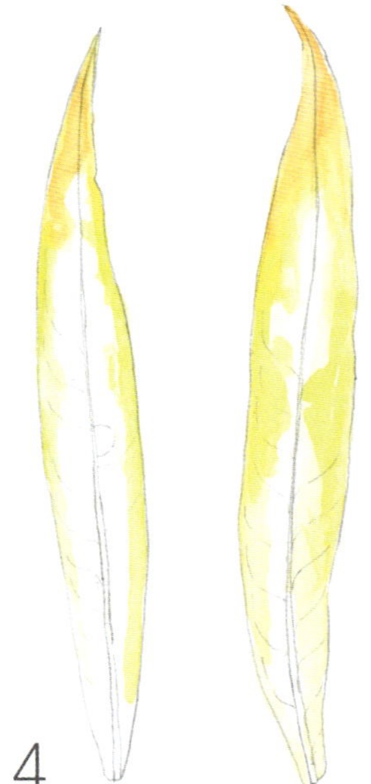

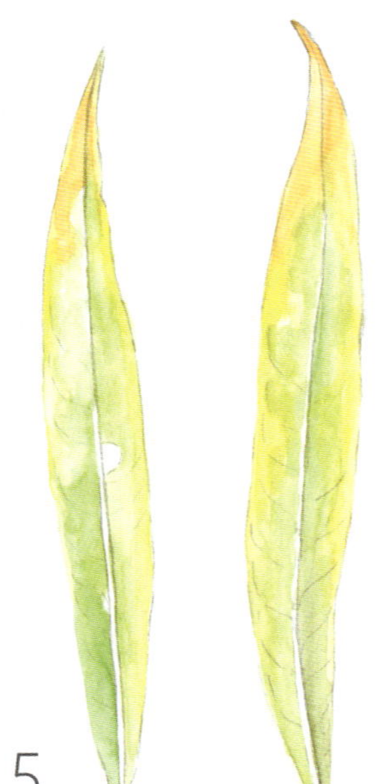

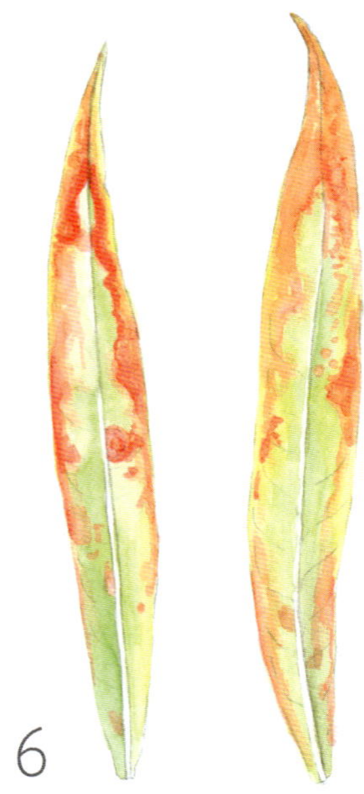

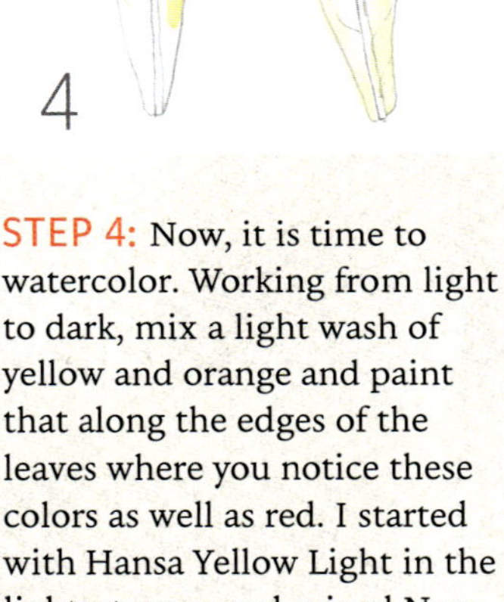

STEP 4: Now, it is time to watercolor. Working from light to dark, mix a light wash of yellow and orange and paint that along the edges of the leaves where you notice these colors as well as red. I started with Hansa Yellow Light in the lightest areas and mixed New Gamboge and Pyrrol Scarlet to make orange.

STEP 5: Make a light yellow-green wash and fill that in the middle of the leaf. Soften the edges with a graded wash where the green joins the yellow so the colors blend. Green and red are complementary colors and will make brown when mixed together. Since yellow is between green and red on the color wheel, we can use yellow as a bridge where the two colors meet. I mixed a pale green with Cerulean Blue and Hansa Yellow Light.

STEP 6: Mix some reds and oranges and apply them to where you notice them on the leaves. Layering the reds over the yellow will make it slightly more orange since the watercolor is transparent. Layering the red in some small areas over the light green will let some red dots sit on top because the red is darker. It is essential to do this before the green gets too dark.

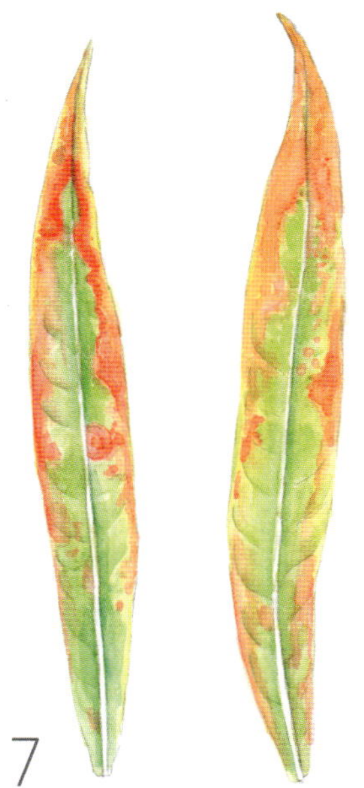

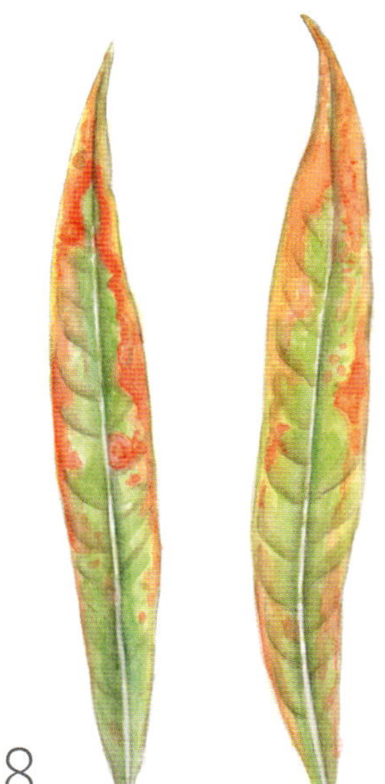

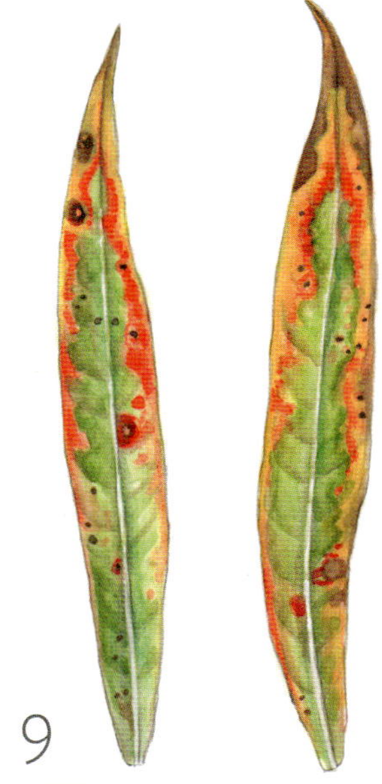

STEP 7: Go back to the greens and add a layer of green to define the veins, especially along the middle vein where the greens are deeper. I try to keep the middle vein pale by not painting on top of it, but you can always go back at the end with a white pen or a thin line of white gouache to lighten the area.

STEP 8: Use a gray marker to add shadows along the veins. If the pen is water-soluble, you should be able to soften the edges on one side of the shadow with a watercolor brush and water. I keep a hard edge next to each vein to indicate its linear form and soften the edge as the shadow moves toward the space between the two veins. If you don't have a gray marker you can also do this step with watercolor.

STEP 9: Add brown spots and marks for some final details. Once you add these darks, you can increase the saturation of some other leaf areas. I added a bit more red and green to some places I wanted to look darker.

DAILY DIARY

A few years after I made the series of sketches from the Alaskan ferry, I wanted to revisit my visual vocabulary development to create a small daily practice. I asked myself what parts of sketching were fun and easy to do so that there would be a low barrier to entry. I also wanted an interesting practice that I'd be curious enough to repeat day after day.

I settled on a "daily diary" of sorts where each day I sketched and wrote on a 5 x 7 inch piece of watercolor paper. I changed around the order of operations, but I would consistently follow three steps: 1) write the date and a title, which eventually became a whole sentence, 2) paint a wet-in-wet watercolor wash, and 3) make a contour drawing with one continuous line. The process takes under 10 minutes, except for waiting for the watercolor to dry. I enjoy experimenting with how watercolor pigments interact with water and each other. Occasionally, I build in little spots of negative space where the white paper shows through. Sometimes, my drawing matches up with the paint; sometimes, it does not, but it creates its own poetry. I appreciate the way the writing adds an element of ritual and reflection.

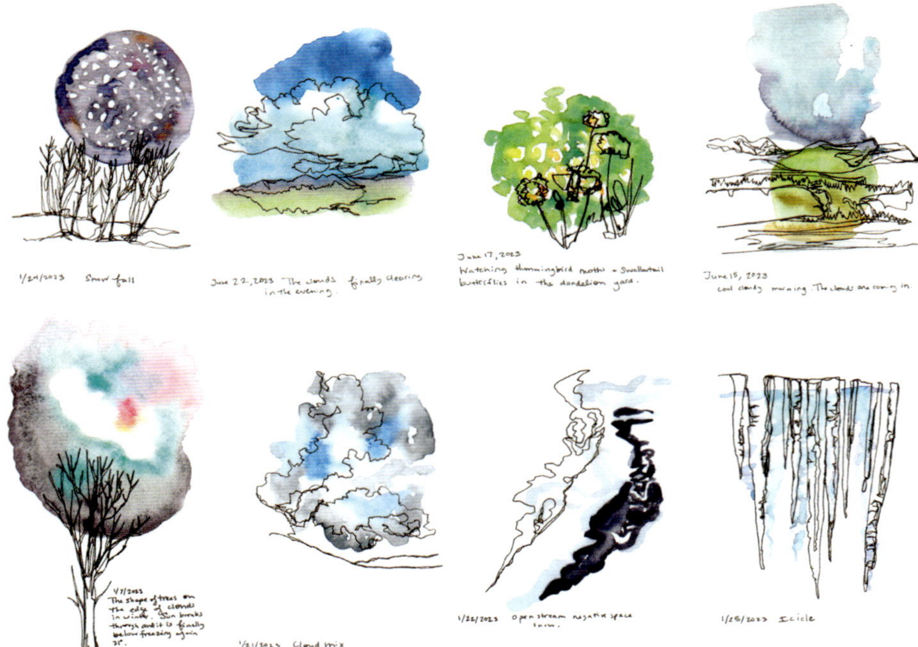

Daily diary pages made by writing the date and one sentence, making a wet-in-wet watercolor painting, and a contour drawing

FOCUSING ON TEXTURE

As with pen, it is a good exercise to practice rendering surface textures with watercolor. Focus on the abstract square and ignore the whole shape. I practiced layering washes, making different marks, and mixing colors to recreate the textures in the photos and to build my visual vocabulary with watercolor.

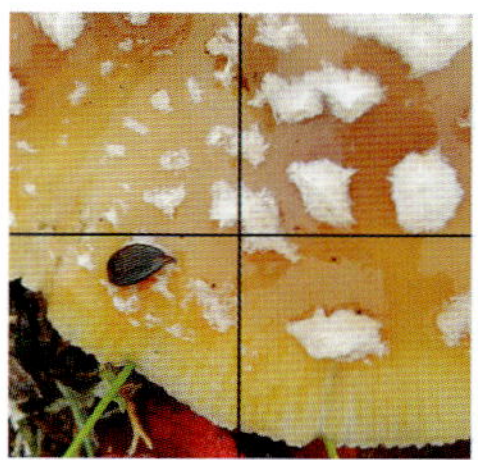
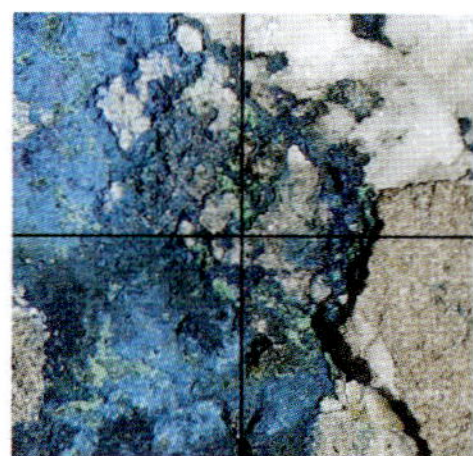
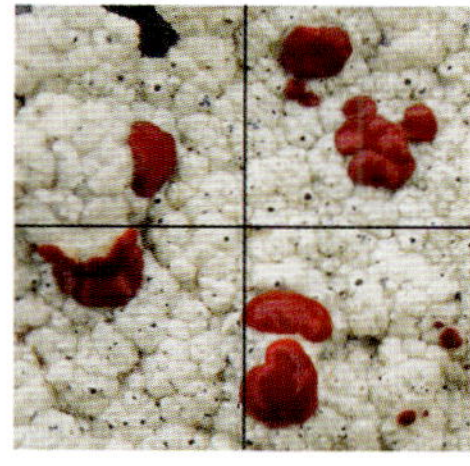
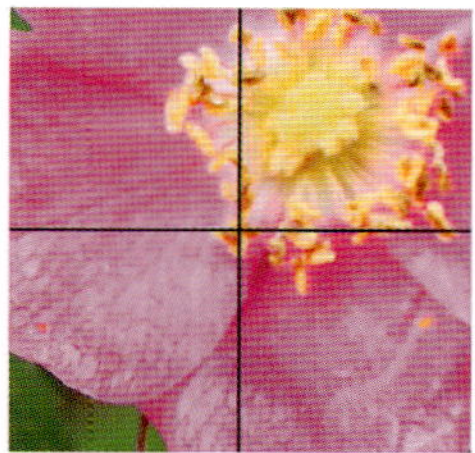

Photos of textures in nature. You can use the grid to help sketch the shapes.

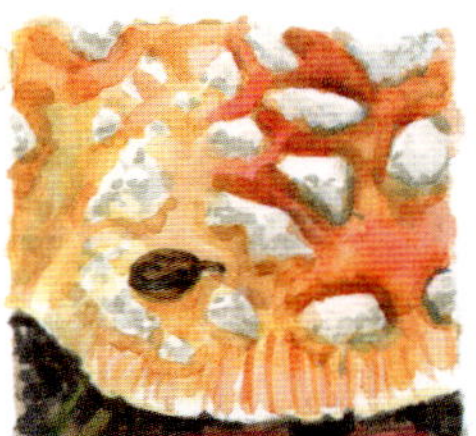
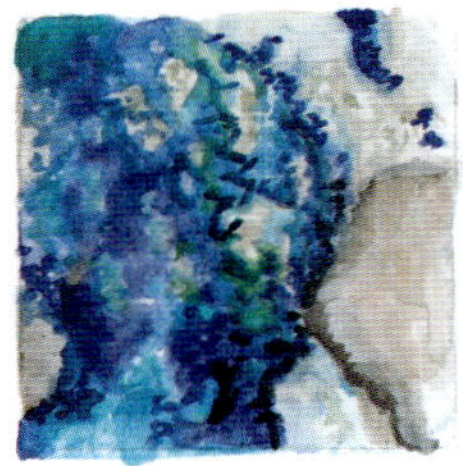
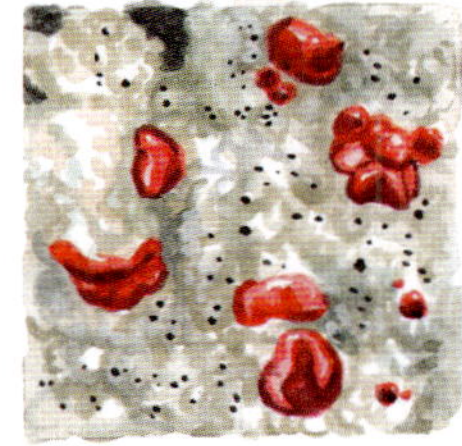
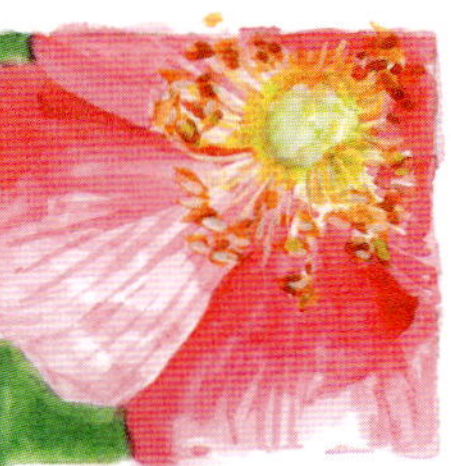

Watercolor studies from the textures in the photos

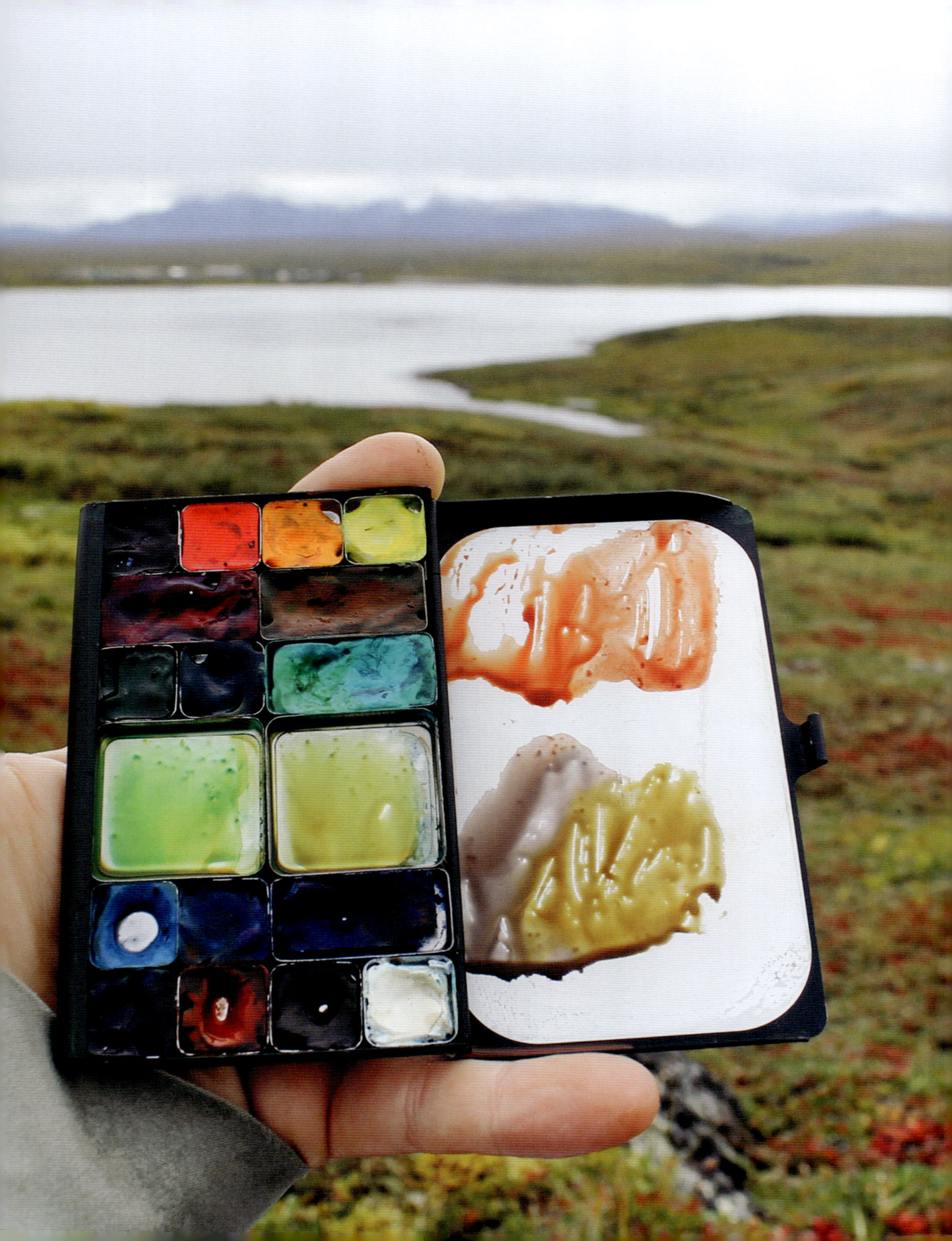

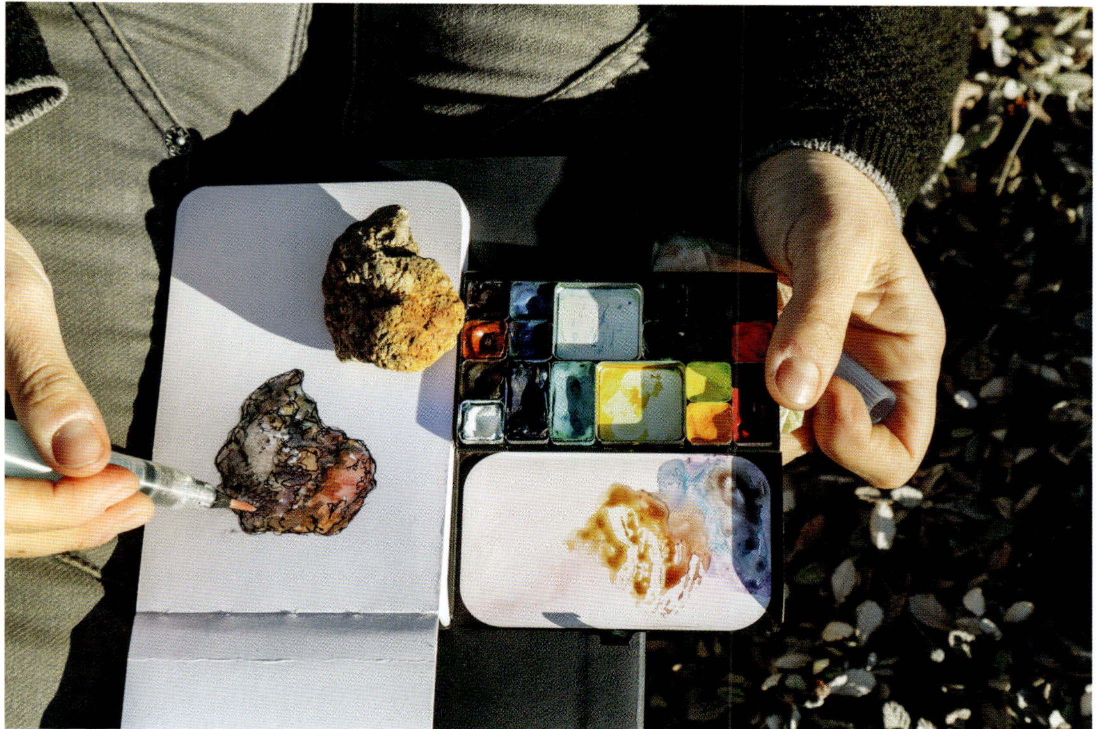

I use wet-in-wet color mixing and abstract the texture of the rock to paint it in my sketchbook.

Reflection

Swatch out all the colors in your palette. Which two are you most drawn to? Why? Practice mixing swatches with those two colors and see how they interact at different levels. Sometimes, this can yield surprising results. What would you name the other colors that you mixed?

◀ Mixing colors of the arctic tundra in fall at Toolik Lake

Putting It Together and Mixing Media

Drawing takes time. A line has time in it.

—DAVID HOCKNEY

Different media can achieve various effects, and my favorite way to work in the field is to combine materials, working with each to its strength to sketch more quickly. The materials that I use the most for sketching are watercolor and pen. A small watercolor set and a pen are easy to carry almost anywhere. I enjoy the result and the process of working with watercolor and pen, but I love mixing things up depending on the situation, and I encourage you to figure out what works for you.

For my process, I like to begin with a pencil. Pencil is an excellent way to get a page mapped out, but it smudges in a finished sketch. I usually only use a pencil for the first stages and for "thinking" on paper, and then

▸ Sketching at the edge of the Root Glacier

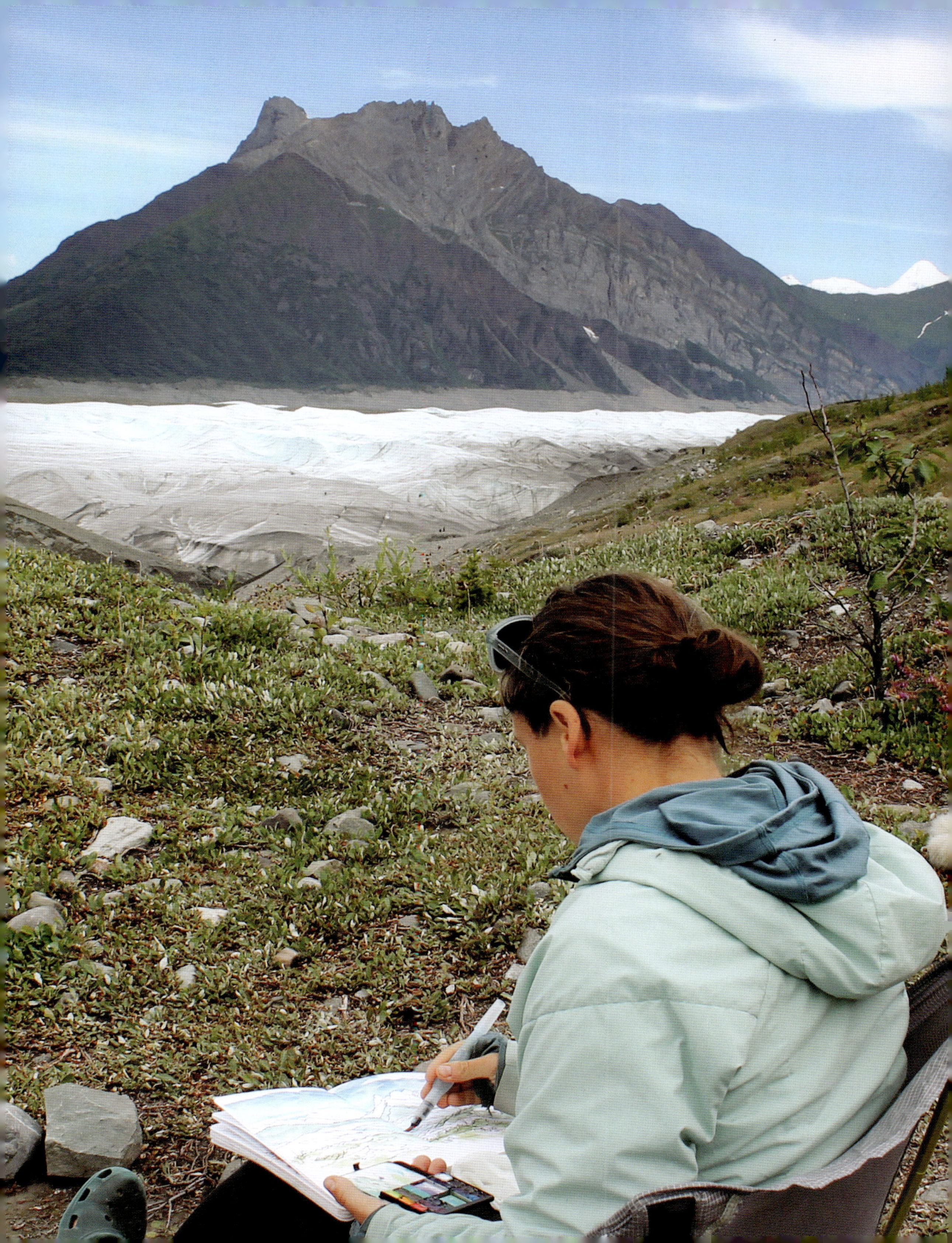

I draw over my pencil with a pen. Pen creates a sharp, crisp, permanent line. Brush pens can create more expressive lines. I like the contrast I get quickly by incorporating pen into my work. I also enjoy the meditative process of drawing and how the pen leaves records of those thought lines on paper.

Watercolor can fill space quickly with a series of washes. Because it moves on its own, it can also capture transparency and the feeling of things living, for example, by working wet-in-wet. Watercolor can also be precise when I use brush control to make specific marks and to fill in shapes.

Sometimes, I'll use other materials. Colored pencils can add texture and detail and don't need to dry like watercolor. They can also be layered over watercolor to achieve more depth. Gouache can be used to add light values at the end of a sketch or achieve a chalky finish or bloom.

MIXED-MEDIA COMBINATIONS

WATERCOLOR AND PENCIL: Graphite smudges and is semi-water-soluble, so it can blend with watercolor, creating a subtle effect. Pencil can be soft and smeary, which can be nice for building up values and rounded forms.

WATERCOLOR AND PEN: Pens can create exact lines, and watercolor fills the paper quickly. Sometimes, I draw with a pen first and then color in my drawing with watercolor, like in a coloring book. Sometimes, I start with watercolor and add ink towards the end of the process to deepen values and sharpen shapes.

WATERCOLOR AND COLORED PENCIL: Colored pencil is wax- or oil-based and will resist a watercolor wash. Layering colored pencils with watercolor works well to build up texture. Colored pencil also sits on top of the paper and can be added later once a watercolor sketch is dry. If I want to achieve more depth of color, I might add some colored pencil on top of a watercolor sketch. It can be fun to use watercolor and colored pencils on mid-toned paper, where you can work on both light and dark values.

PEN AND COLORED PENCIL: When I don't have time for paint to dry, I might make a quick sketch with a brush pen and then add some colored pencil on top. Adding the colored pencil on top of the black pen allows me to work in some lighter values in places.

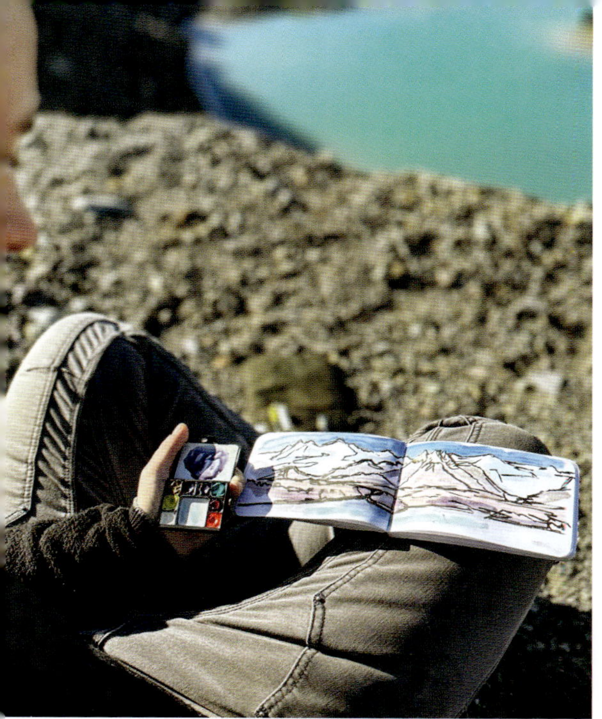

Working with a brush pen and a simple watercolor set with a limited eight-color palette is a quick way to create a sketch with a lot of character.

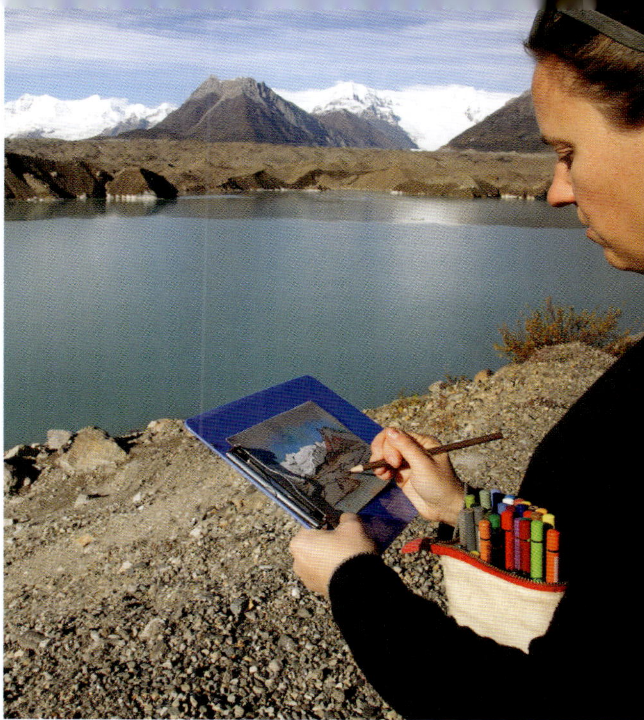

Different strategies for working in the glacial landscape include working with colored pencils on toned paper to capture light and dark values. One advantage of working with colored pencils is that you don't need to wait for them to dry.

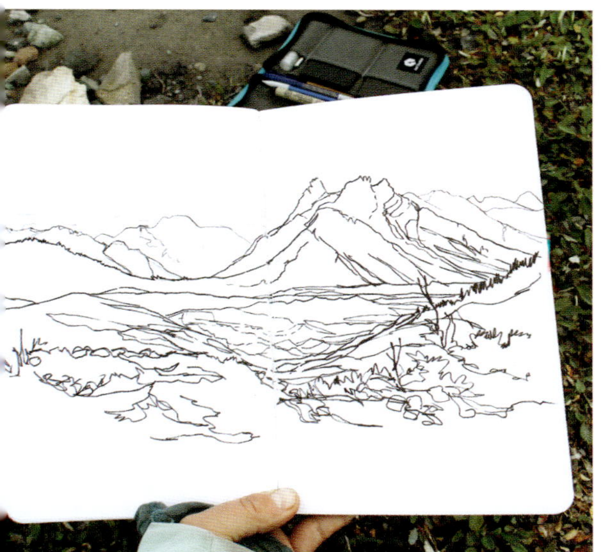

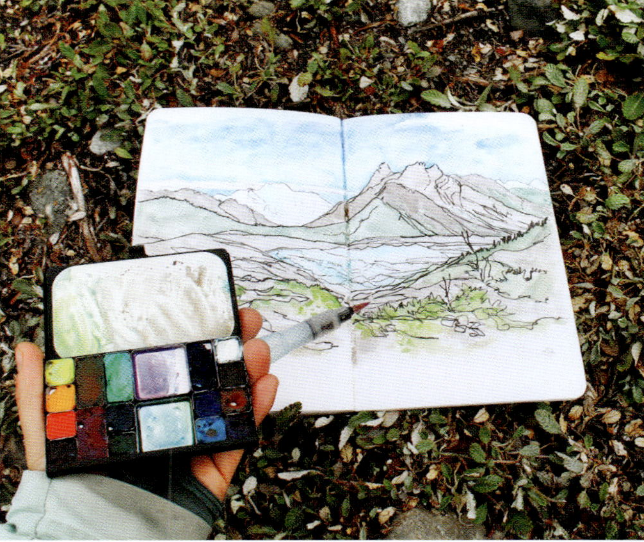

Sketching with brush pen and watercolor. Brush pens create a quick coloring book with expressive lines. Watercolor fills the space quickly and builds up vibrant layers of color.

FINDING A MOMENT FOR A QUICK SKETCH

A few summers ago, I was working as an instructor on a backcountry field semester for college students in the Wrangell Mountains near where I live. Our group was out on a three-week backpacking trip, and one morning, we were supposed to get resupplied with food by a tiny bush plane on a backcountry tundra strip. We camped in a large fosse, a narrow depression between the edge of a retreating glacier and the wall of its valley. This fosse has a towering wall of rock on one side over which I could see a triangle-shaped peak with hanging glaciers. I sat in my tent and watched the sun warming the colors across the valley.

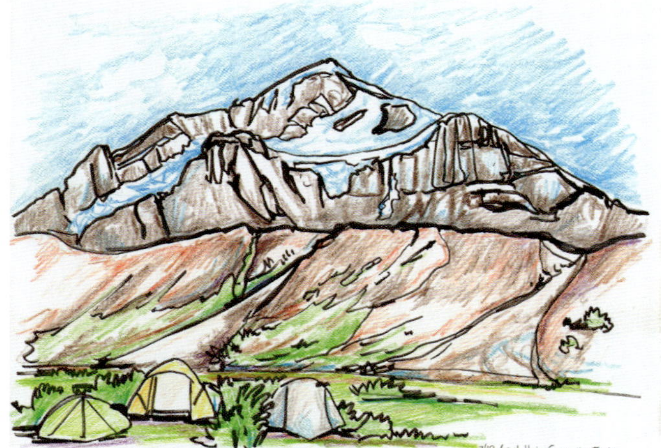

▶ Brush pen and colored pencil sketch done while waiting for the resupply plane

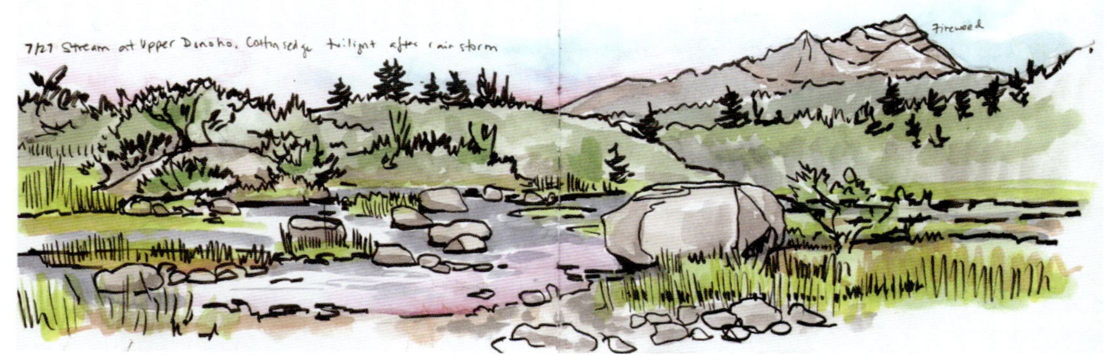

▲ More approaches for fast sketching using mixed media. This was a quick gesture sketch at sunset using a brush pen and watercolor.

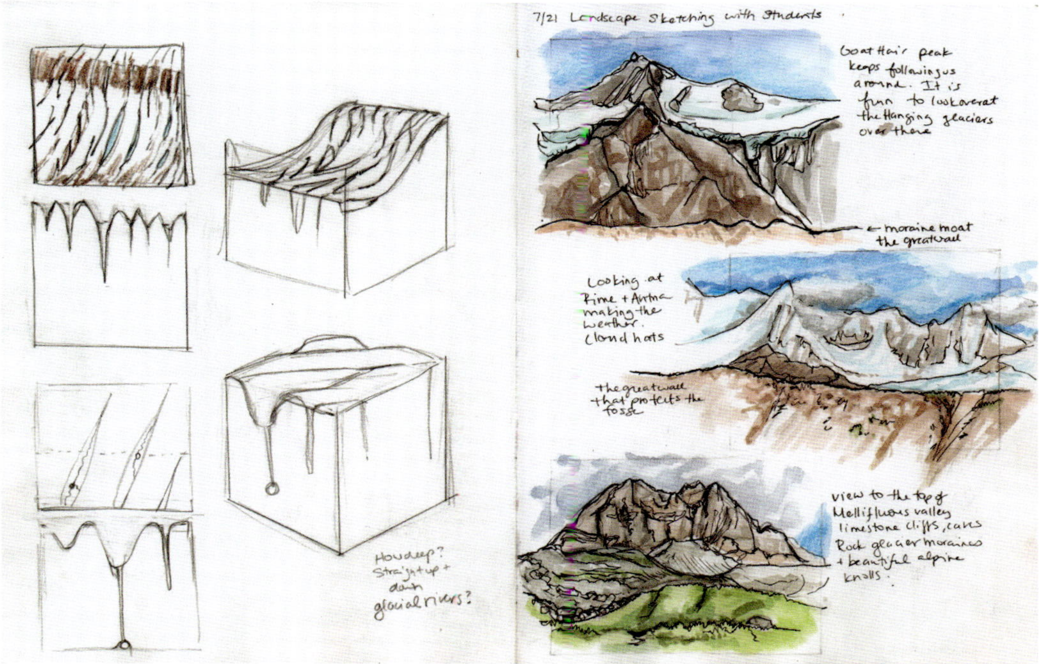

Sometimes, it is nice to make a series of small thumbnail sketches instead of one big drawing. On the left page, I sketched some views of different surfaces of a glacier, looking inside as well as at the surface, with pencil and colored pencil. On the right, I sketched some of the surrounding glacial valleys with pencil, pen, and watercolor.

I knew I had a few minutes before the plane got there, and then I'd have to drop everything to help unload. It was such a beautiful and crisp morning that I wanted to make a sketch, but I didn't want to wait for watercolor to dry or have to smear my half-finished painting by closing my book. I decided to sketch quickly with my brush pen to at least capture something.

I moved my pen across the landscape, starting with the beautiful mountain in the background to the moraine wall and some of our tents in the foreground. The plane wasn't there yet, so I added some blue with colored pencils to the brilliant sky that greeted us that morning. I kept the pencils and colors moving down my page. I carved in some blue on the glacier ice. My rocks got warmer, redder, and more orange as my pencil traveled closer to the bottom of the page to help distinguish the moraine from the mountain. And the bright greens and colors of the tents made the foreground pop. It was quick work, but I could close my book when I saw the plane coming. No smudging. An hour or so later, the light was different, and it was time to leave for a hike, but I was happy that I had captured that sliver of peaceful morning.

ADDING WHITE BACK IN

You might want to add white back into your sketch towards the end of the process. With watercolor, we try to work from light to dark and save the white of the paper so that it can shine through the sketch. A sketch might get darker than intended, and it is crucial to add some light values back in at the end. Sometimes, I don't have the patience to paint around every highlight in my subject, and it feels better to add those light areas later. Some textures and subjects present a chalky or waxy bloom or highlight best captured by layering white or light values at the end of the process on top of a darker wash. There are several ways to add white back into your sketch, and it is a good idea to try them out and see which work for you. None of them look the same as saving the white of the paper, but they can be effective.

WHITE GEL PEN can be great for drawing small details like the vein of a leaf or stars in the sky. You can paint over the pen gently with watercolor to get a lighter color, for example, light yellow veins on a dark green leaf. You can also add color on top of the white pen with colored pencil or watercolor paint.

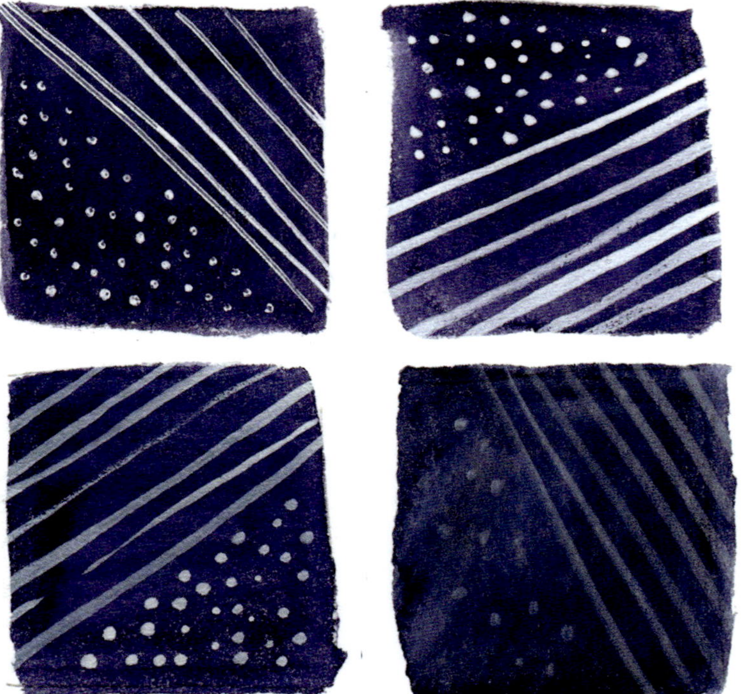

I painted a dark violet wash with watercolor and added white with different media on top when the wash dried. I used a white gel pen, Bleedproof White, white gouache, and a white colored pencil.

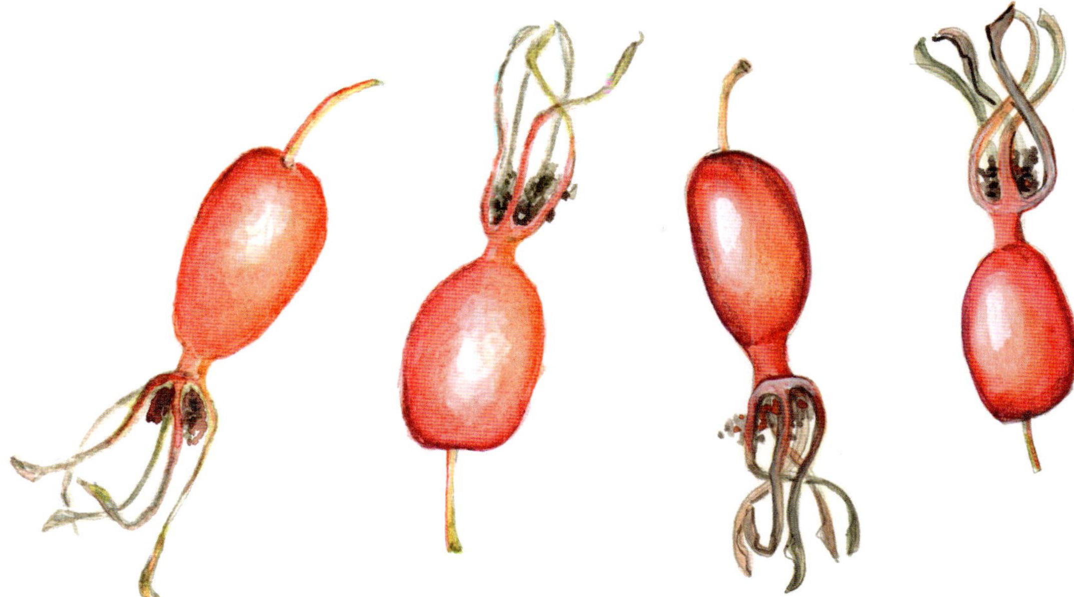

When I painted the two rose hips on the left, I saved the highlight with the white of the paper, working around that area with watercolor paint. For the two rose hips on the right, I added a highlight at the end using opaque white paint. The highlights have a different color and feel. The highlight from the paper on the left glows more from the inside of the painting and preserves some of the warmth of the paper. The highlights on the right feel cooler in color and chalkier, which can work well for some subjects.

I use **BLEEDPROOF WHITE AND A SMALL ROUND BRUSH** or **WHITE GOUACHE** to paint white on top of watercolor. I put gouache in my travel palette instead of white watercolor paint. I also keep a jar of Bleedproof White in my studio so that I can use it at my desk once I get home from sketching in the field. I appreciate the variety of line quality I can get with a brush and the chalky texture of the opaque white paint.

WHITE COLORED PENCIL is more transparent but also works well for lightening values, mainly when used on top of a dark wash. It has the waxy feel of a blueberry skin.

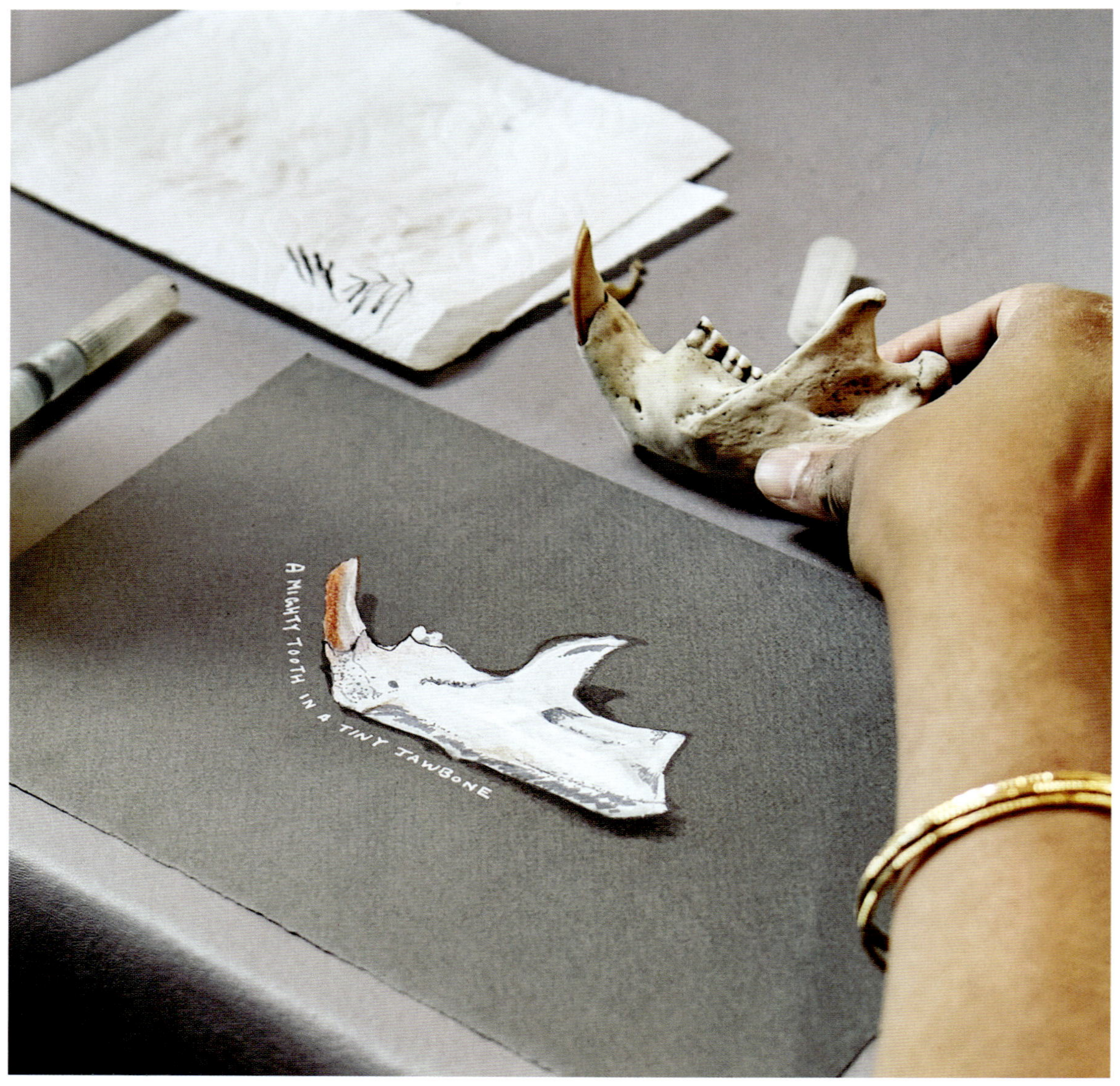

This sketch was a group project from a workshop where many students worked together to create one drawing. We used Bleedproof White and white gel pen to help the light-toned beaver jawbone stand out against a dark background. Watercolor and black ink were also added on top.

Project 10

HUMMINGBIRD MOTH WITH PEN AND WATERCOLOR

This sketch uses pen and linework to help make the moth, the main subject, stand out from the background.

MATERIALS: a pencil, a pen, watercolor paper, and watercolors

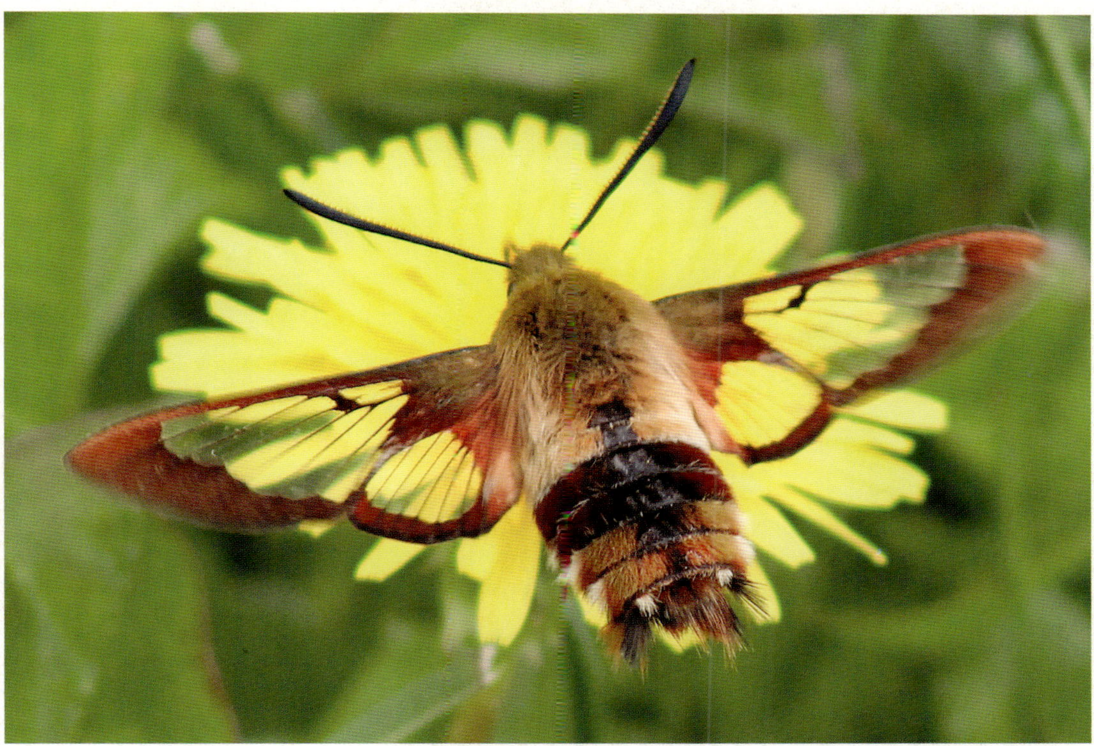

The first time I saw a hummingbird moth, I thought it was a bird, but then I noticed it was silent and not humming. I realized it was a moth disguised to look like a hummingbird! The wings have transparent windows, making them look like a hummingbird's blurry wings, moving fast. Their bodies are furry, with tufts on the end of the abdomen that mimic a bird's tail. When you look closely, you can see that they are moth-shaped and don't have bills but fly from flower to flower to suck nectar with their long, curled tongues.

Project 10

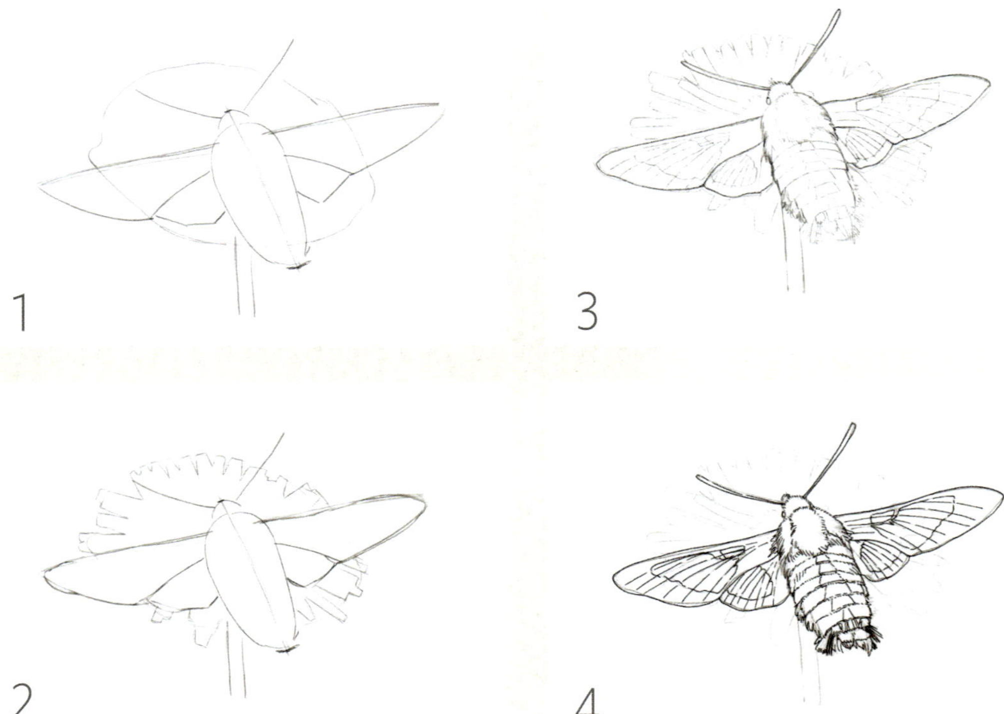

STEP 1: Lightly sketch the general shapes of the dandelion flower and the moth with a pencil. I drew an oval for the dandelion and used it to reference where the moth would go. I began the moth sketch by measuring and drawing the angle of the line of symmetry down the middle of the moth. From there, I sketched an oval for the body, measured the angles of the wings and antennae, and drew straight lines to rough in those shapes.

STEP 2: Refine the shapes and lines from the previous step. I added the jagged edge of the dandelion petals (these are called ligules in this compound flower) and refined the shapes of the moth wings to show the more curved form, using straight lines as guides.

STEP 3: Add in the main segments of the body and the veins in the wings. Include the main areas of patterning in different colors, such as the trapezoid shapes on each section of the abdomen and the clear panels in the wings. Lighten and refine the drawing, using a kneaded eraser to lighten the pencil marks and a sharp pencil to go over lines in places.

STEP 4: Draw over the moth with a pen. I traced my pencil drawing with a 05 pen, but I added little lines to indicate where the moth is furry and used some broken, dashed lines on the wings where the veins are somewhat transparent.

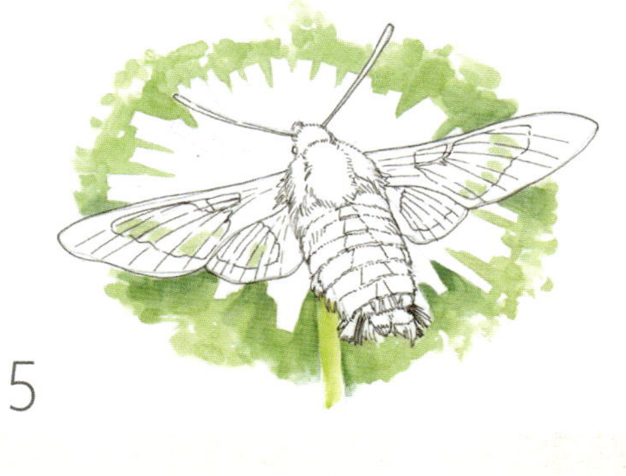

5

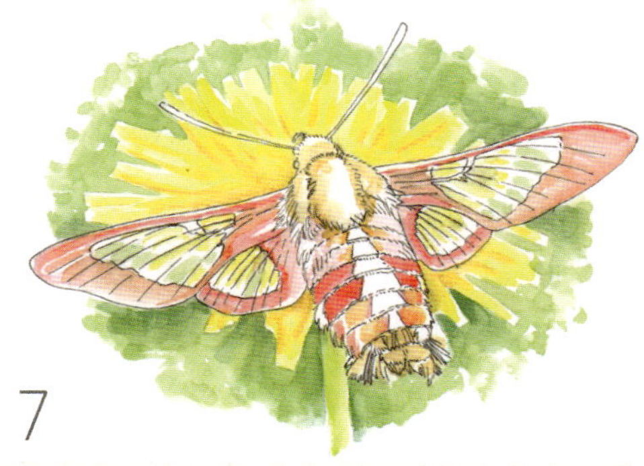

7

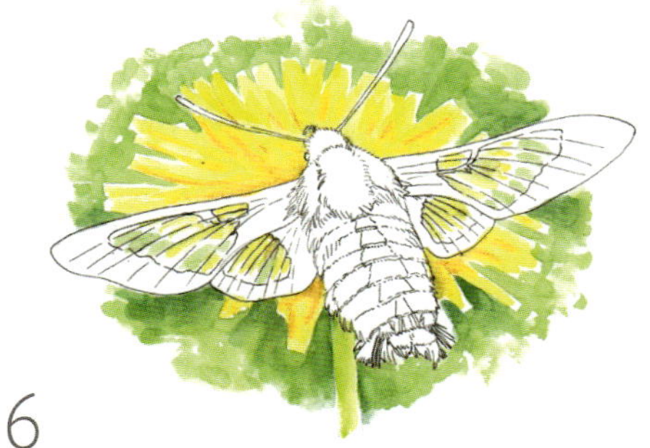

6

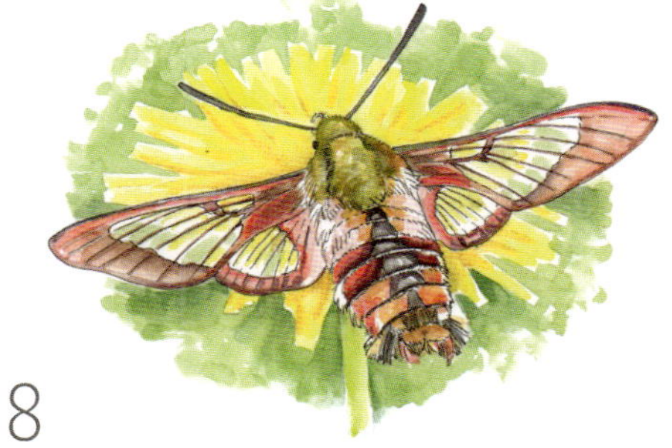

8

STEP 5: Paint the negative space around the dandelion flower with green. I mixed Sap Green with some Cobalt Teal Blue and Quinacridone Gold. Include some spots that show through the transparent sections of the wing. To keep the focus on the moth and the flower, I used a faded splotchy edge on the border by lightening the green wash with water. To create variety, I added a bit more blue to the green underneath the dandelion and more yellow to the green that would be the flower's stem.

STEP 6: Use a cool yellow and a warm yellow to paint in the dandelion flower. Use the darker warm yellow to define the direction and shape of the ligules and petals where they overlap.

STEP 7: Paint the moth in light colors. Start with a wash of golden brown (I used Quinacridone Gold and Burnt Sienna), then mix up a dusty rose color for the wings and parts of the body (I mixed Quinacridone Gold, Quinacridone Rose, and a tiny bit of Pyrrol Scarlet).

STEP 8: Once the wash from the previous step is dry, add another layer of mid-tones. I added green to the head and thorax, purple-gray along the wings and abdomen, and gray to the trapezoid segments. To make gray, I mixed Burnt Umber and Indanthrone Blue, with a little bit of Quinacridone Rose where I wanted it to be more violet.

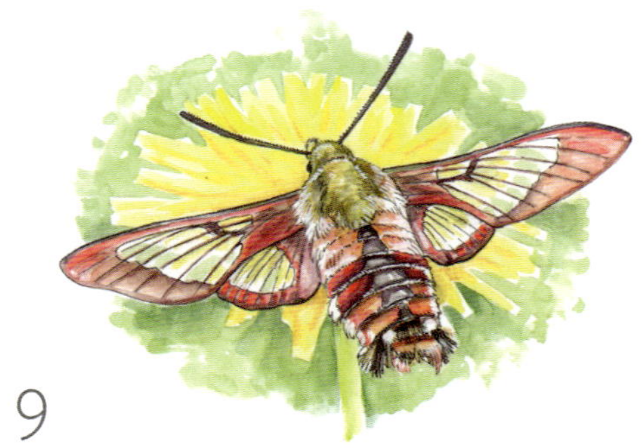

9

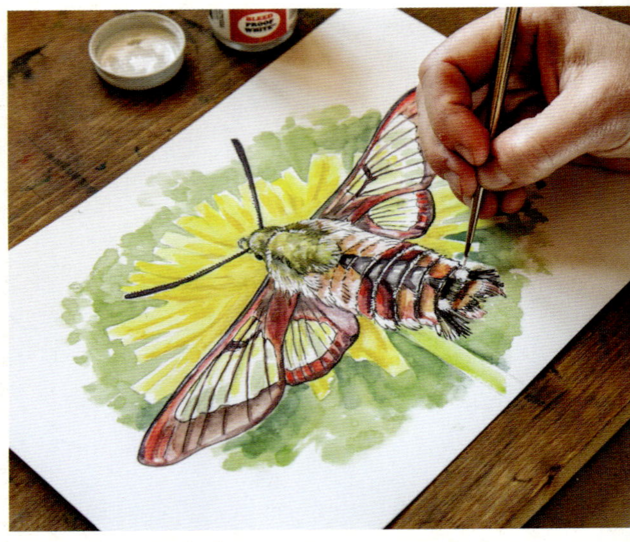

Adding details at the end using Bleedproof White and a fine brush

STEP 9: Go over the moth again with a pen to sharpen some shapes and add texture. I added the texture along the inside of the antennae, the eye, and the tongue, which you can barely see along the top edges of the head. I also drew in a bit more texture for the fur. I added a few pops of color, such as maroon, in some sections of the abdomen and the wings to make those stand out. Finally, I used a white pen or gouache to add some highlights where the moth's fur reflected light and to define some of the lighter patches on the abdomen. You can also lighten some sections of the clear panels of the wings if they get too dark.

CREATING MORE TEXTURES WITH WATERCOLOR

Watercolor can be fun to work with because it can create many different effects and textures. Here are a few more techniques to get different watercolor results. Many of these require stepping back, letting go of control, and letting the media surprise you.

PLASTIC WRAP: Once you have a damp watercolor wash on paper, try pressing in some bubble wrap or plastic wrap on top and then remove it. The watercolor will cling to the plastic and dry in an interesting texture.

WAX RESIST: Use a wax resist before painting by drawing on paper with colored pencil, crayon, oil pastel, or by rubbing over wax paper. The wax or oil will repel the watercolor, leaving lighter lines. The softer the drawing implement, the stronger the resist seems to work, but you will get a smudgy line.

SALT: Salt repels water and can create beautiful crystalline textures in a wash. Try to sprinkle some salt on top of a damp, half-dry wash. Let the wash dry and scrape the salt away. This is a bit of an experiment, and you don't always have much control. I find that big flecks of salt work better than tiny grains.

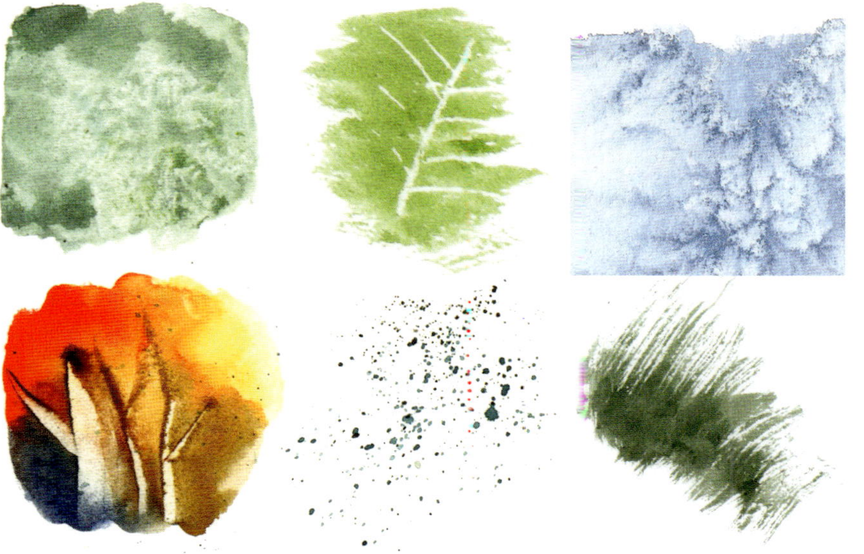

Creating different effects with watercolor using plastic wrap, wax resist, and salt. You can also create effects by scraping back in with a card, splattering paint, and using a dry brush.

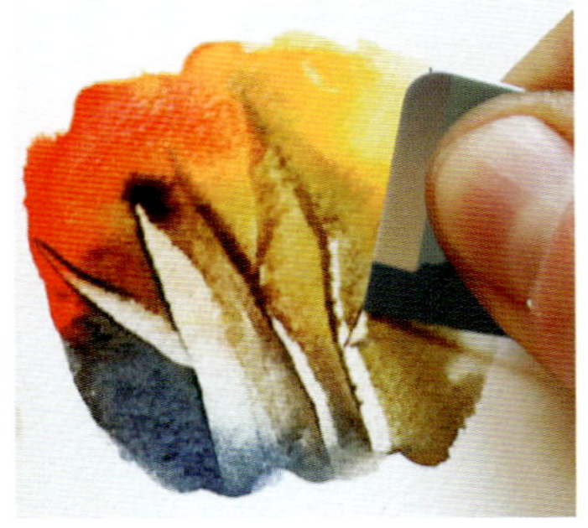

Scraping

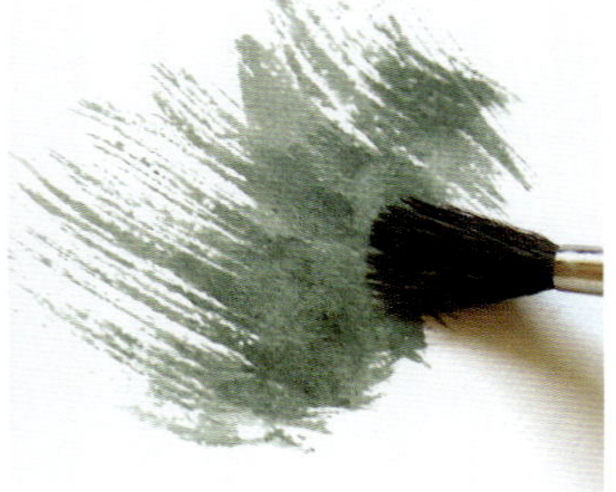

Dry Brush

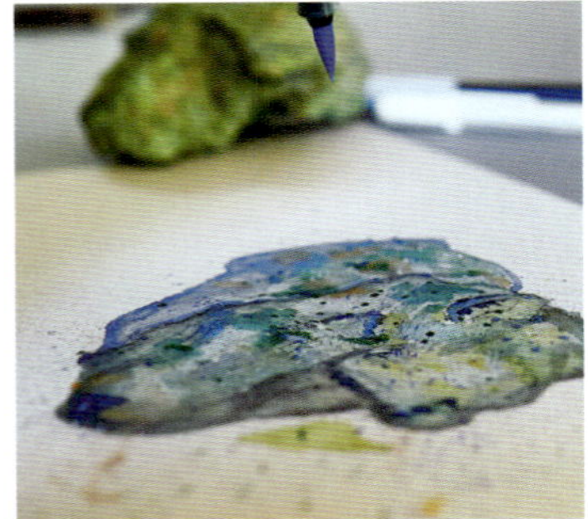

Adding splatter texture to a sketch of a rock during a sketching workshop

PLASTIC CARD SCRAPER: Cut up an old plastic card and use it as a scraper to scratch the watercolor from a damp area. This can be used to add lighter-colored tree trunks, blades of grass, or leaf veins.

DRY BRUSH: Use a dry brush and damp paint, so that the bristles on the brush are separate and don't form a sharp point, and scrape the brush across the paper. With less water, the bristles will stay separate, leaving textured marks on the paper. This works well for grass or water.

SPLATTER: Load a paintbrush with watercolor paint, and instead of applying it to the paper, tap it with a pencil an inch or so away from the page to splatter the paint onto your paper. If you don't want the splatter to hit a particular area, you can cover the section of the page with scrap paper.

Reflection

Since this chapter is about using different media and materials, consider what materials you like working with. What materials do you like using to create various textures and effects? How can you use media together to get your desired result quickly? What is fun to use?

What is the most accessible tool that you've tried so far? Could you try starting your sketch with that? What materials are frustrating? Is the frustration because you need more practice or something else? What materials would you put in your smallest and most basic sketch kit, and what materials might you add to your sketch later when you return home?

▶ This gesture sketch shows two spruce trees on a snowy day. I used pen, watercolor, and white and blue splatter painting to capture the effect of the weather.

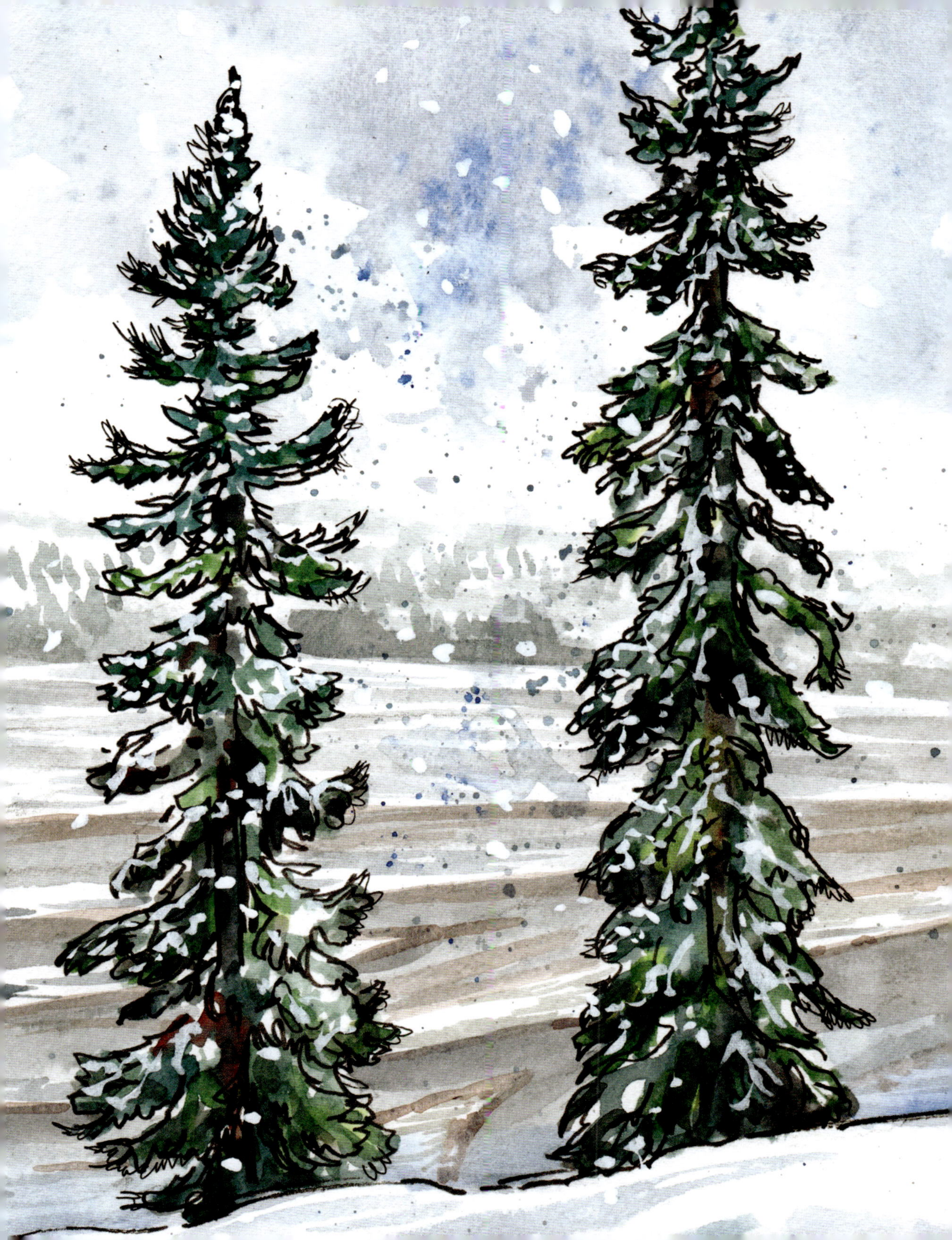

Project 11

SKETCHING ROUND SUBJECTS: ROCKS

Use a salt-effect watercolor wash layered with colored pencil to create a textured surface for the rocks, then add shading to help define the forms.

MATERIALS: colored pencils, a pencil, salt, watercolor paper, and watercolors

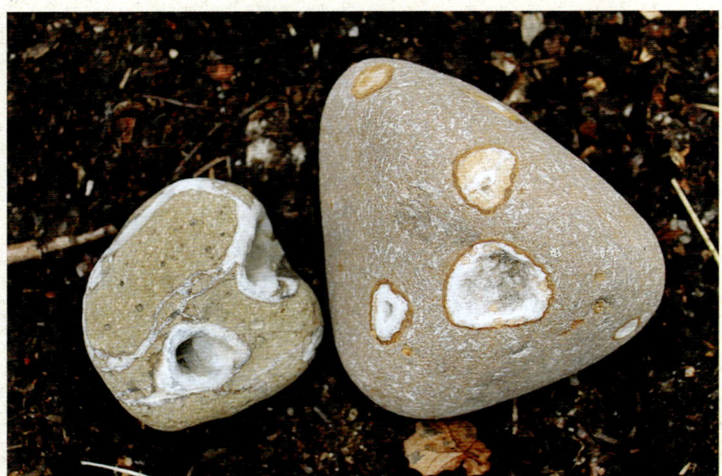

These rocks come from an area with a lot of volcanic activity. Some rocks have air pockets inside, which can fill with crystals and other interesting textures if water seeps in and leaves behind a residue of minerals.

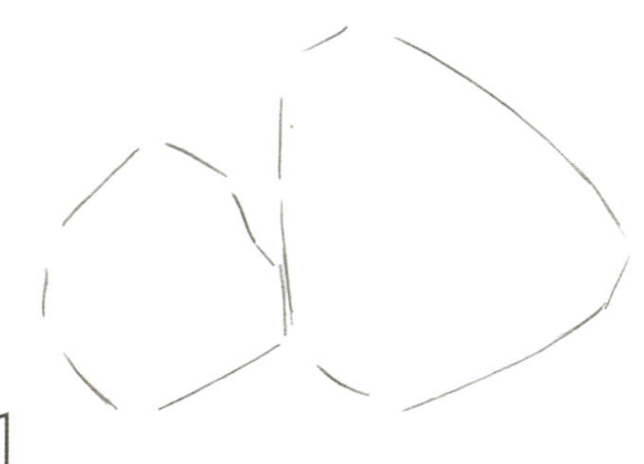

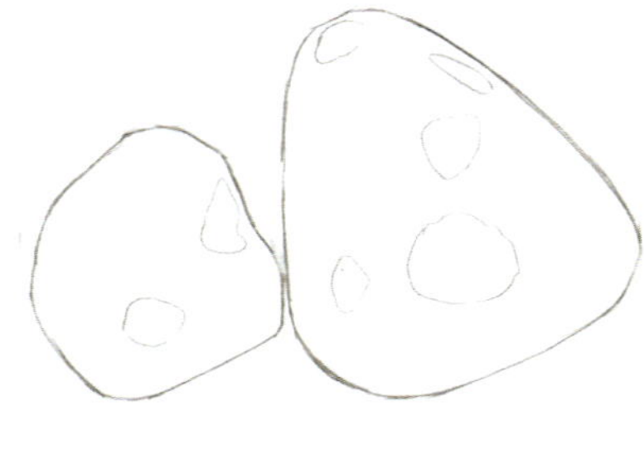

STEP 1: Mark the main shape of the rocks with a pencil, using straight lines. You can also use your pencil to measure the angle of the edges.

STEP 2: Refine the straight lines from the previous step to make curves to define the outer edges of the rock shapes. Start marking the main sections of patterns on the rocks' surfaces.

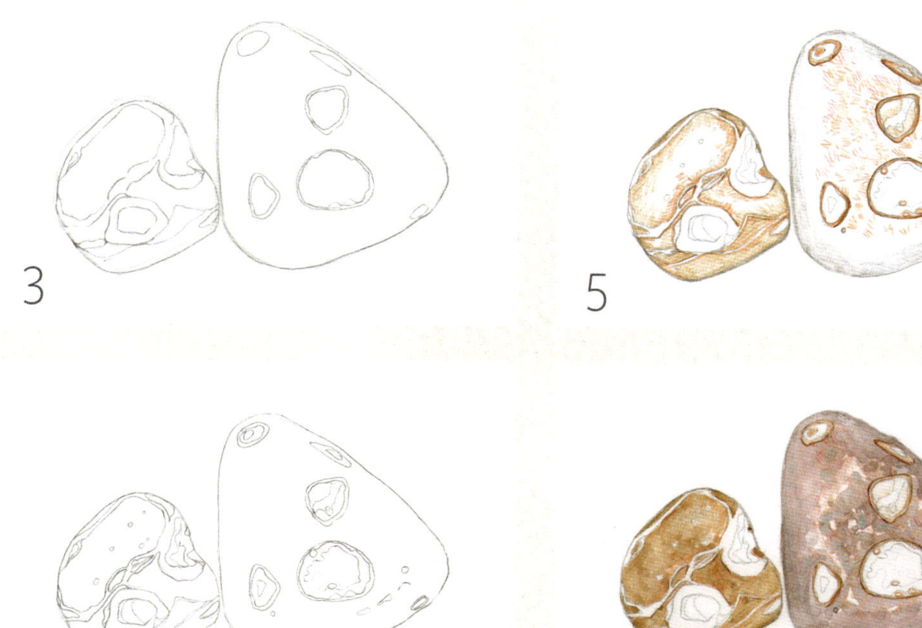

STEP 3: Add more information to mark out the patterns on the rocks' surfaces, including some of the veins and the crystallization shape.

STEP 4: Lighten your drawing with a kneaded eraser and refine any lines that need correction. Add any other essential details and marks.

STEP 5: Use a layer of colored pencil to create a wax resist under the watercolor we will add next. I used two browns and a gray colored pencil to add some surface texture. I also used the reddish-brown to define the ring around some of the round crystal structures. The colored pencil helped get these sharp, fine lines.

STEP 6: Add a wash of watercolor. I used a reddish brown with Quinacridone Gold and Burnt Sienna for the rock on the left. For the rock on the right, I mixed Cobalt Teal Blue, Burnt Sienna, and a bit of Quinacridone Rose. The Cobalt Teal Blue separated to create a granulating wash that enhanced the texture. Try adding salt on top of the wash at this stage to get further granulation and texture. Either way, let the wash dry well before continuing. If using salt, brush that off your sketch once everything is dry.

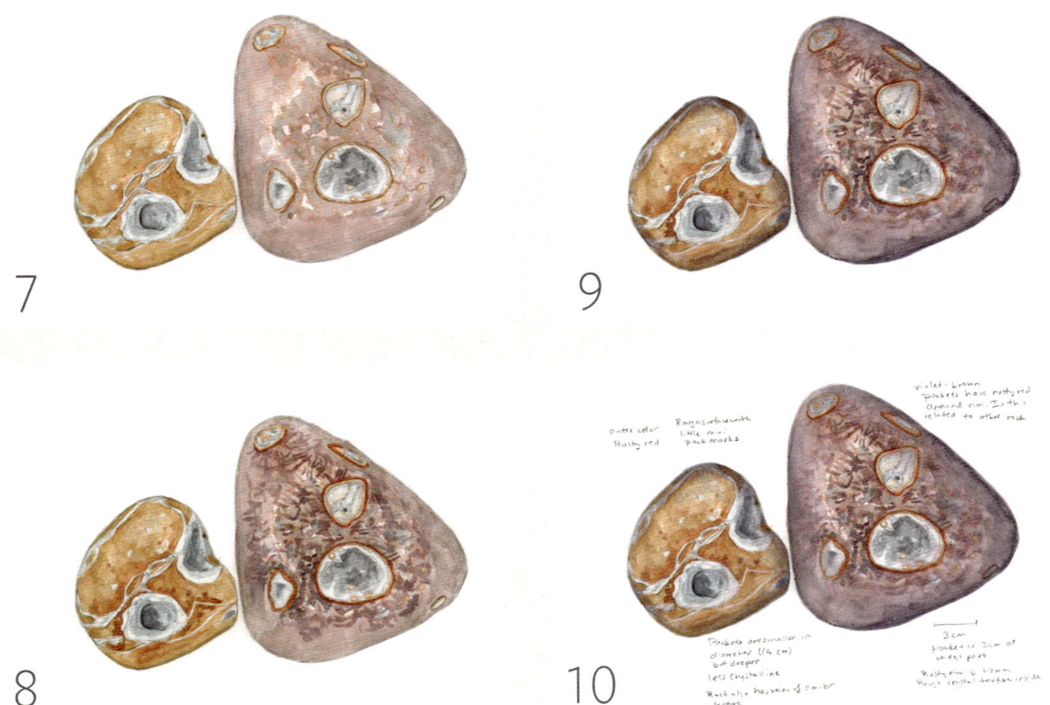

STEP 7: Using different shades of light gray, paint in the light sections of the rock where the crystal pockets are. Pay attention to the shape of the shadows and where it is darker or lighter. I mixed a gray with Burnt Sienna and Cobalt Teal Blue, adding some magenta where I wanted it to be more violet.

STEP 8: We see the most texture in the area between the highlight and the shadow. The rocks are both lopsided organic round shapes so it is helpful to imagine how you would shade a sphere and adapt that to these forms. Adding more texture, detail, and contrast to this area will help it appear to come forward in space. Paint or draw in more texture on the top of the rocks using the tip of the watercolor brush to make fine marks or by using colored pencils.

STEP 9: With a gray, add some shadows to indicate the roundness of the rock. I used the same Cobalt Teal Blue, Raw Sienna, and Quinacridone Rose to make a violet-gray and paint a graded wash along the edges of the rock, ensuring this was deepest on the right side of the rock that is in shadow. As I softened the edge of the shadow towards the inside of the rock, the wash lifted some of the texture from the last step, which worked well to create a round form. You can dab the highlight area with a clean paper towel to remove some paint.

STEP 10: Add some notes comparing the two rocks. What is similar, and what is different? I added a few notes about the color of the rocks and the size and texture of the lighter colored, crystal-like pockets.

Project 12

ADDING IN WHITE AND BLACK INK: BLACK MOREL MUSHROOM

The black morel is a tricky subject because the cap is dark in pigment but also has a complicated form with pits and ridges. We will use shadows and add some white background to build up this structure.

MATERIALS: a pen, a pencil, white ink or gouache, watercolor paper, and watercolors

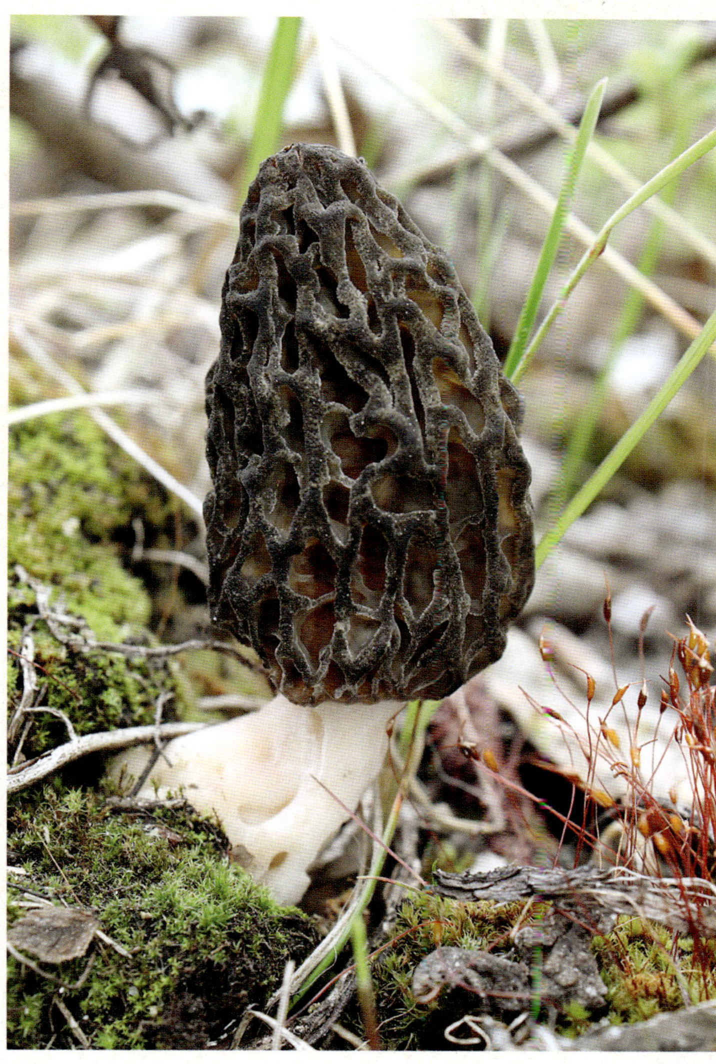

Morel mushrooms tend to grow after a fire or disturbance. They are delicious if you know how to recognize them. We get some black morels growing on our yard's edge each spring.

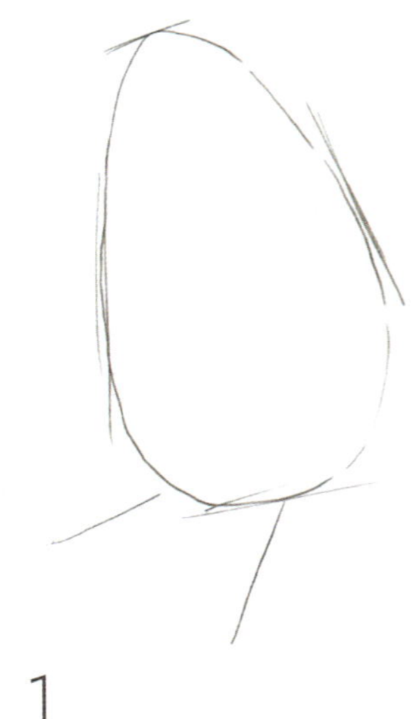

1

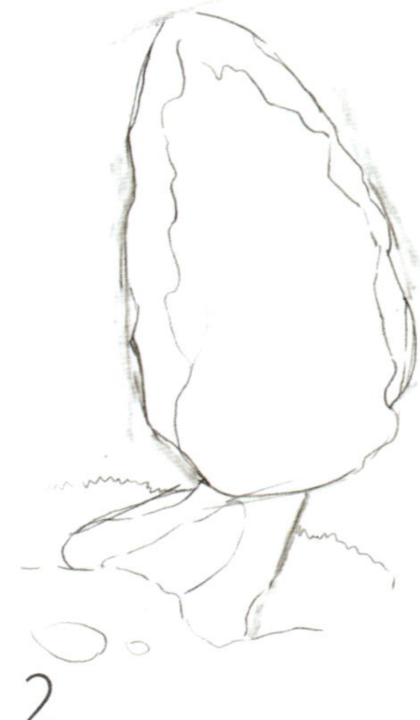

2

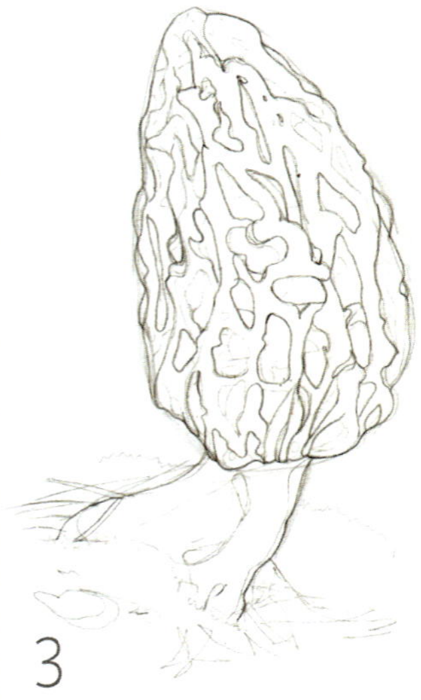

3

STEP 1: Lightly sketch in a rough outline of the main shapes you notice. I drew an oval for the mushroom's cap and two lines for the stem.

STEP 2: Refine the shapes from the previous step. I noticed that the cap is pointy on top and that the stem is slightly curved. I also added some texture to the ground.

STEP 3: Add the texture and describe how the morel cap is made of pits and ridges. Start drawing one shape at a time, noticing how each is connected to the next. This doesn't have to copy the pattern in the photo perfectly; instead, it should reflect the general pattern of how a morel cap is formed. Refine and lighten the drawing with a kneaded eraser as you work.

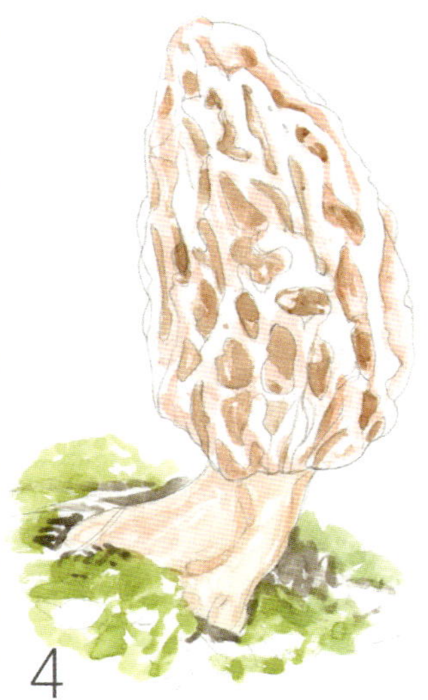

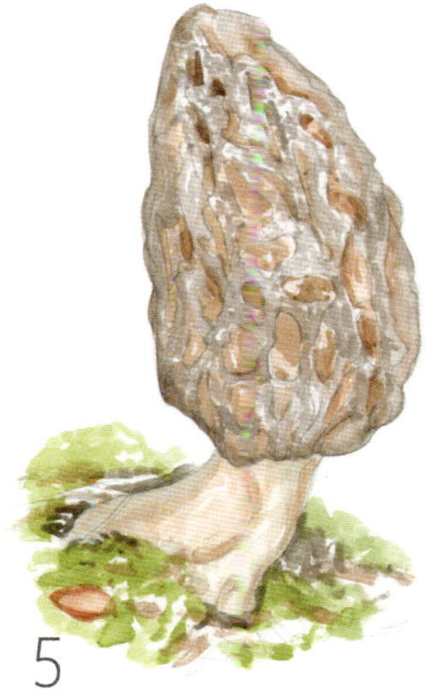

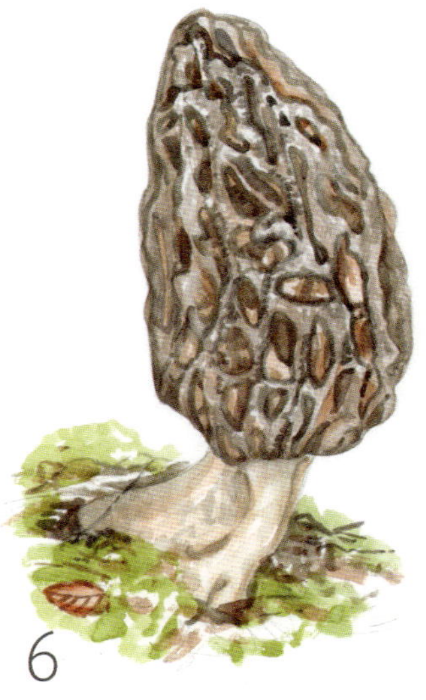

STEP 4: Begin painting with watercolor, working from light to dark. I started with a warm brown wash of watered-down Burnt Sienna. I also painted in some of the green and brown for the ground. I added some darker browns in the pits of the morel cap using Raw Umber.

STEP 5: I mixed a darker brown with Raw Umber and Ultramarine Blue. I will use this color for the black parts of the mushroom. The morel cap is complicated to capture because the raised sections of the cap are darker in pigment than the pitted sections, but the pits are also in shadow, which makes them appear darker. I use different browns to distinguish these sections. I also mixed a light gray to add shadows to the mushroom stalk and added a few Burnt Sienna details to the ground to show some leaves.

STEP 6: Add more blue-brown to the rings around the pits to help define those shapes. When I looked closely, I noticed that the stalk was slightly pitted, so I added some marks to indicate this texture.

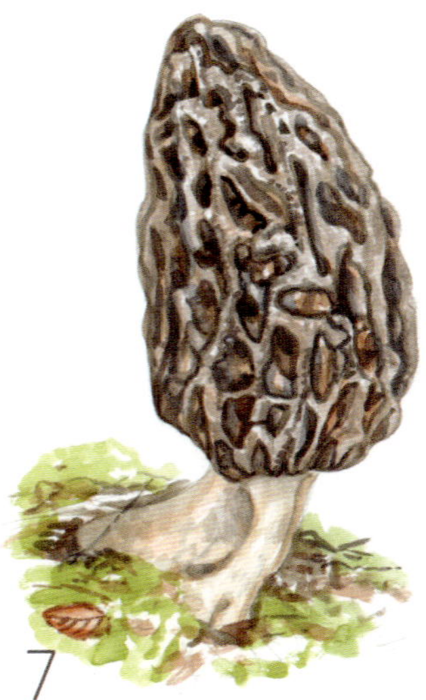

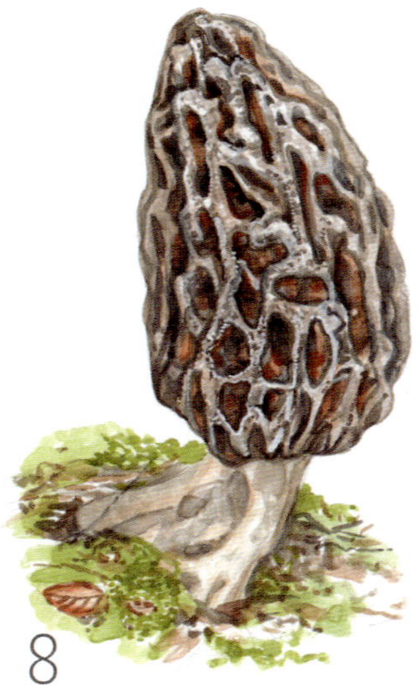

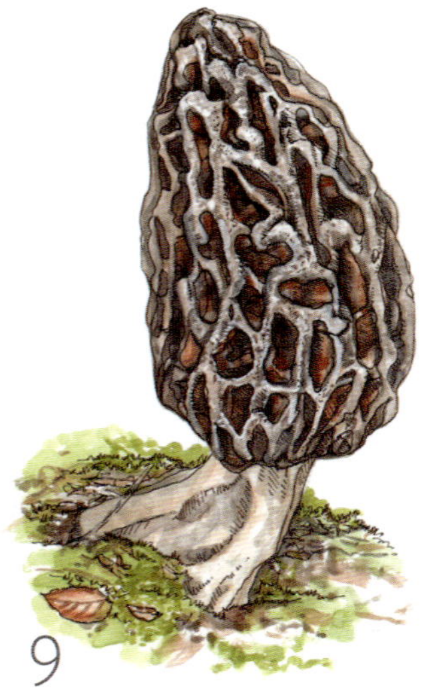

STEP 7: Continue to build the darks. Remember that the biggest range of values will be in the middle of the mushroom cap (the part closest to the viewer). Add more shadows to the pits and further define the ridges.

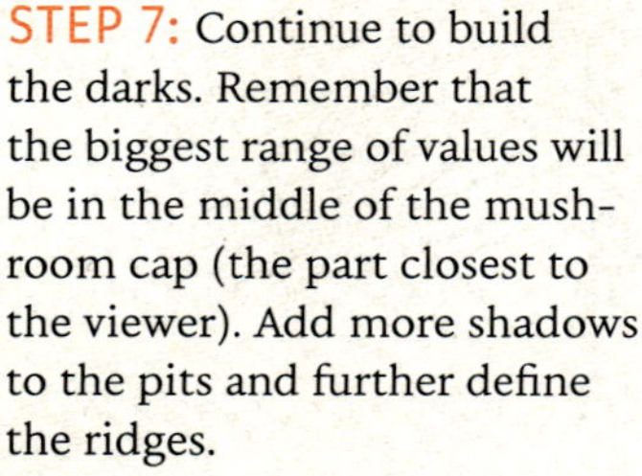

STEP 8: Continue to build contrast and texture in the mushroom cap. I added Burnt Sienna to the pits so that they captured a sense of light shining through them. I also deepened some of the shadows one more time. I finally added some opaque white to the ridges in the cap to capture some of the shine there and the sense that they are raised.

STEP 9: I decided to add a pen at the end of this sketch to define the mushroom's form and add more contrast. I tried to use the most pen in the places where I wanted light against dark to make the middle of the mushroom come forward. I also added some texture with pen to the moss and duff around the mushroom, so that the whole sketch felt like it had a similar treatment. I wanted the mushroom to feel like it was growing from the ground.

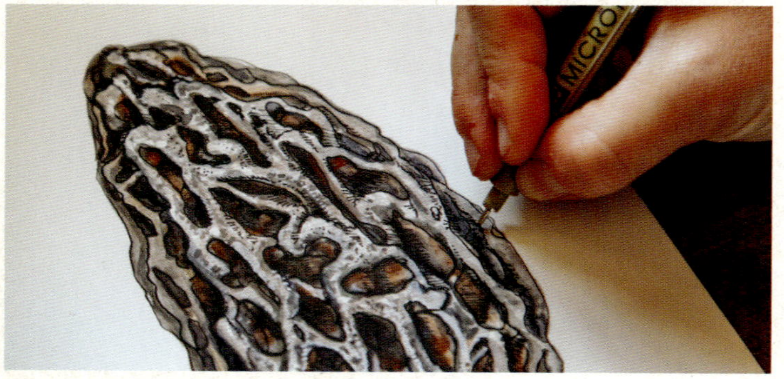

◂ **Adding some ink with a fine pen at the end of the sketch helps build contrast and detail in select areas.**

BUILDING UP TEXTURE WITH COLORED PENCIL AND WATERCOLOR: ROBIN'S NEST

Explore and build up the textures of the nest with watercolor, colored pencil, and pen.

MATERIALS: colored pencils, a pencil, a pen, watercolor paper, and watercolors

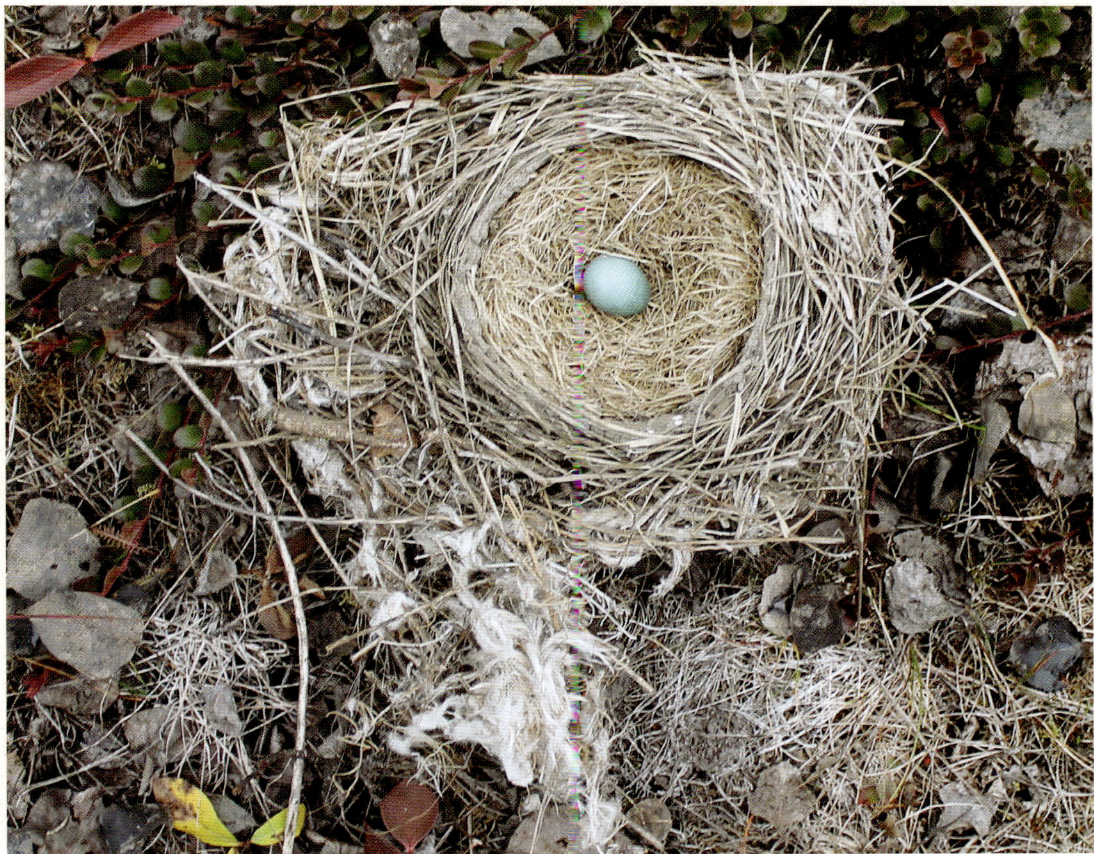

Each summer, American Robins build a nest in the eave of our cabin, and it is a treat to watch them incubate, hatch, and raise their babies. I have learned so much about how they build nests by sketching them and looking closely at their materials' different textures. The nest is built of an outer ring of rough vegetation: fireweed stems, horsetail, some sticks, and strong grasses. Inside the vegetation is a cup of mud lined with fine, dried grass. This nest I collected one year had one egg that never hatched.

Project 13

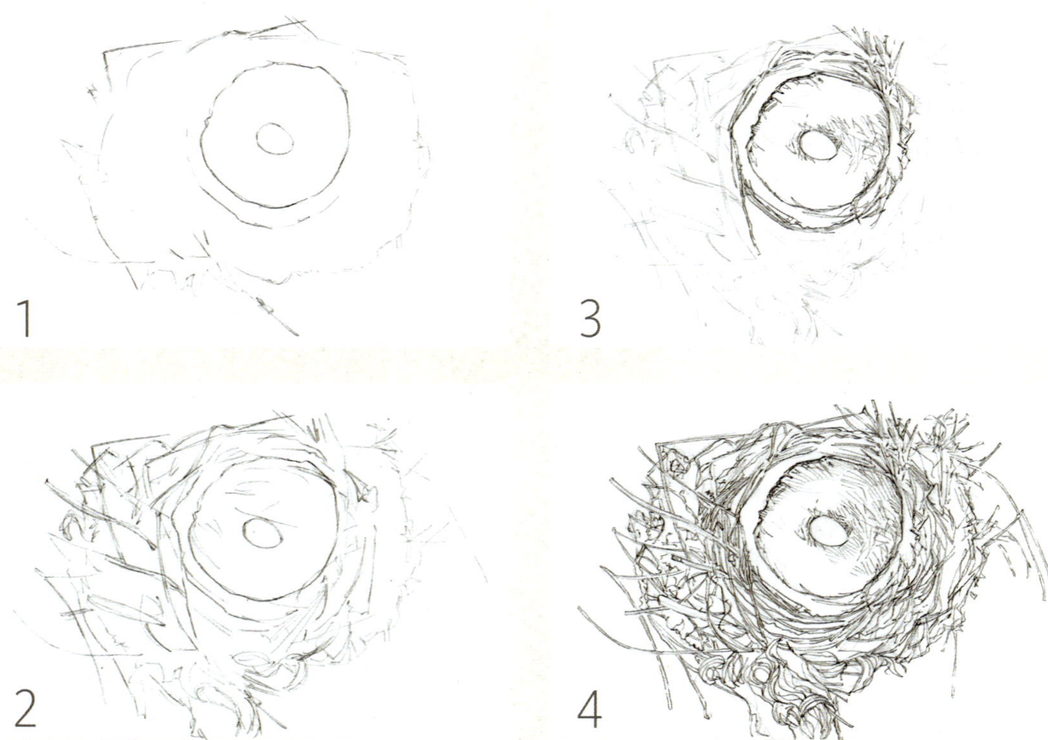

STEP 1: In pencil, lightly sketch the main shapes of the nest. I began by drawing the circle shape for the main cup, then added the egg because I thought it was important to the drawing. I also added some rough lines for the outside margin of the nest.

STEP 2: Add more lines with a pencil to mark in some of the directions of the grasses and vegetation that make up the nest, especially in the outer cup, which is roughly constructed and has a lot of texture.

STEP 3: Go over the pencil drawing with pen. Begin with the cup of the nest, which is made of mud and lined with grass. Notice the different textures that support the structure and use marks to help define the materials.

STEP 4: Add pen to show the vegetation that makes up the outside structure. This part is built of dried fireweed flower stalks, small twigs, horsetail, and some other materials. The material is rougher and stiffer and appears messy, though it provides an essential base for the cup of the nest. Not every stalk has to be accurate, but it is important to capture the crisscrossing vegetation and how it is weaved together and looser along the edges. What else do you notice as you draw?

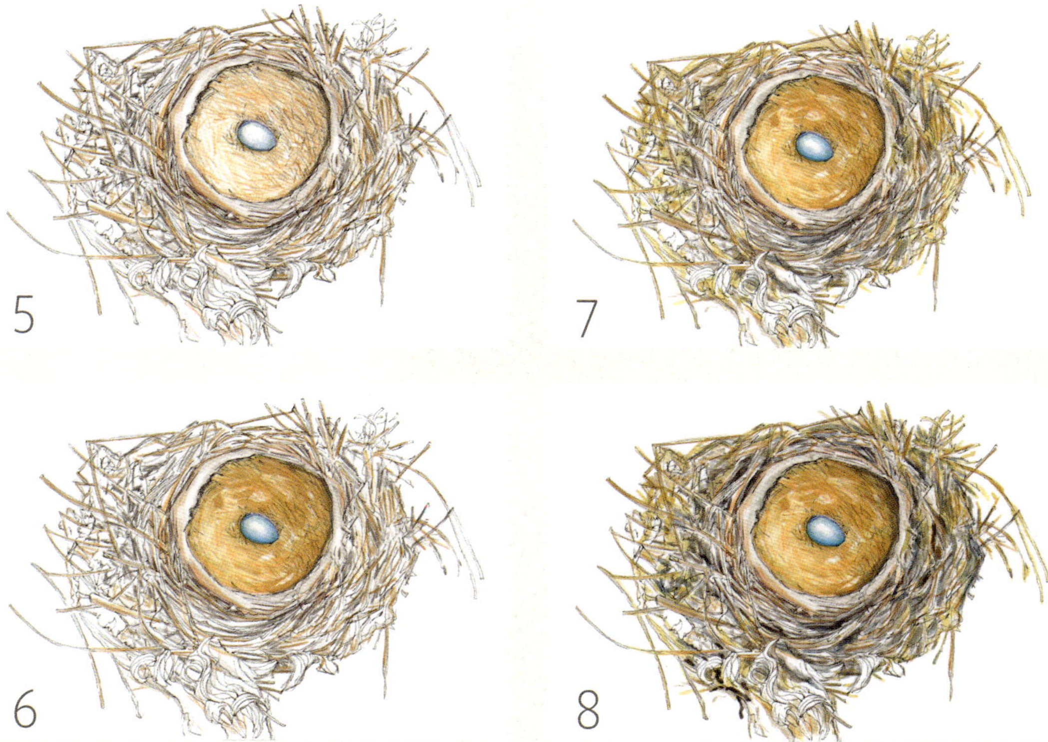

STEP 5: Since the nest is made up of many linear structures of different stems and grasses, I used colored pencil lines to get a wax resist that would stand out from the watercolor and add to the textured effect. I used some light browns, ochers, and grays to define some of the texture, showing the soft grass in the cup and the rough lines that support the outside of the nest.

STEP 6: Now we are ready to add watercolor. Mix colors that are slightly different from the colored pencil so that the pencil will stand out, and apply in strokes and washes. I started with the cup of the nest. I used a desaturated, graded wash of Phthalo Blue for the egg. I mixed Quinacridone Gold and Burnt Sienna for the grass in the cup.

STEP 7: I painted the outside of the nest using Burnt Sienna, Cerulean Blue, and Ultramarine Blue to make a purplish brown. I mixed Quinacridone Gold and Burnt Sienna for the grassy bits. I used brushstrokes to define the texture, to keep some light values, and to fill in the space. I wanted to make sure that the cup, the grass of the lining, and the outside are visually distinct.

STEP 8: The last step is to add some shadows to the nest as a whole, to bring it together and further define its form. I mixed Raw Umber and Ultramarine Blue to make a blue-gray and painted some shadow layers with graded washes along the inside of the cup and, in some places, deep divots around the overlapping vegetation.

Animals and Moving Subjects

Curiosity is not a trait you are born with. It is a skill that you can develop and refine with practice. It is more essential than any drawing trick or tool and can make a nature journal burst to life.

—JOHN MUIR LAWS

Observing animals in the landscape is a unique and exciting experience, but they can be hard to capture because they might move or leave the scene. However, you can learn much about animals by watching them closely and trying to capture them on

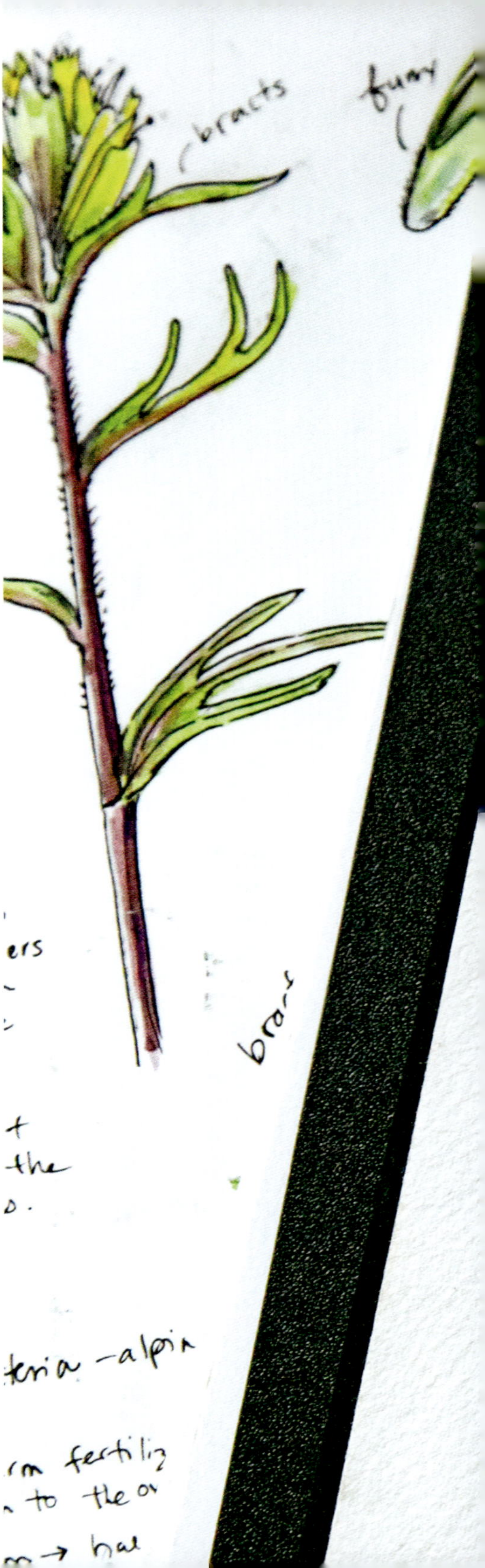

▶ I sketched these sandpipers, looking through my binoculars while sitting on the mud flats in Cordova, Alaska. Cordova hosts a shorebird festival every spring, when the shorebirds migrate through in the thousands. The sandpipers were moving quickly and scurrying around, probing at the mud. There were so many, and they repeated similar behaviors, so I could work on several sketches at once and revisit each drawing from time to time. These sketches are simple lines and circles but took a lot of concentration and observation.

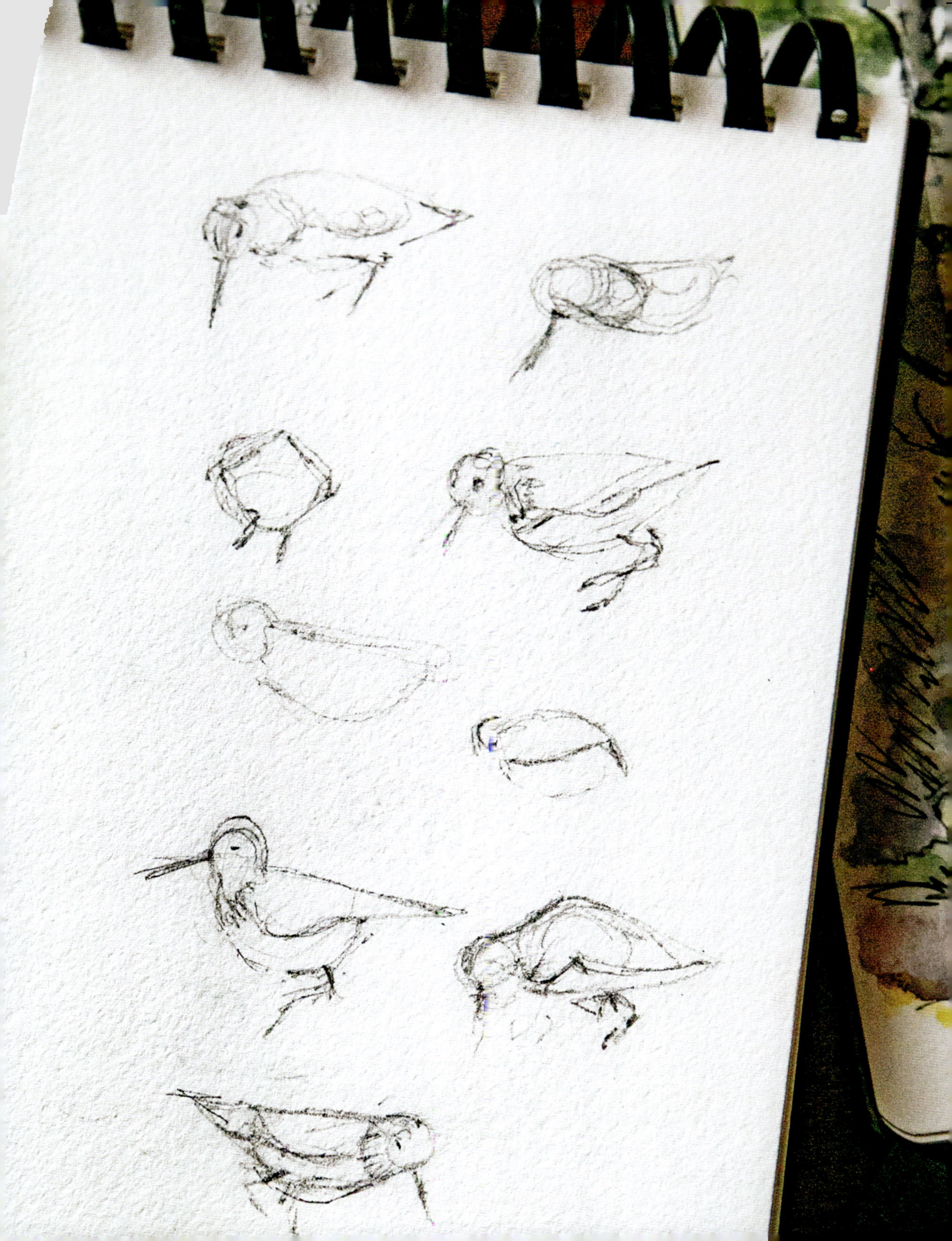

paper. This chapter will review gesture sketching and seeing the forms and structures that make up an animal, as well as how to sketch different textures like feathers and fur.

When sketching an animal, I will often start with a gesture sketch of lines and circles to make up the main chunks of the body. It is helpful to understand different animal anatomy and imagine the skeleton underneath the skin, scales, fur, and feathers. Most animals have a body plan similar to that of humans, but their bones are elongated and fused depending on what they need to survive.

I often imagine and feel different animal skeletons by relating them to my body, which helps me remember their anatomy. Once I visualize the skeleton in my mind, I think of the muscles that layer over top of that, and then the fur, feathers, and layers of skin and fat that layer over and attach to the muscles.

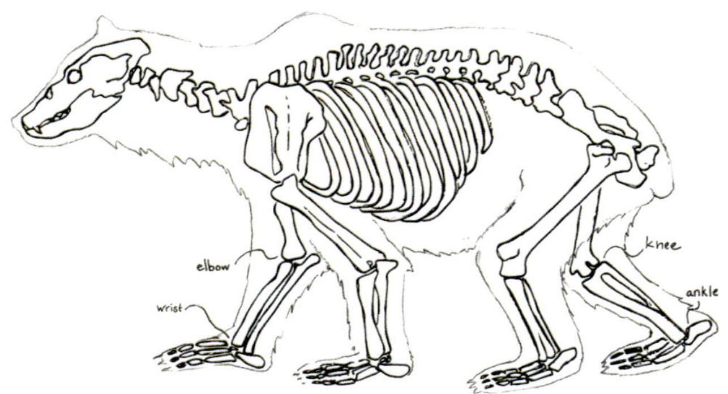

◀ Plantigrade animals like weasels and bears walk on all four legs but walk on their heels like humans.

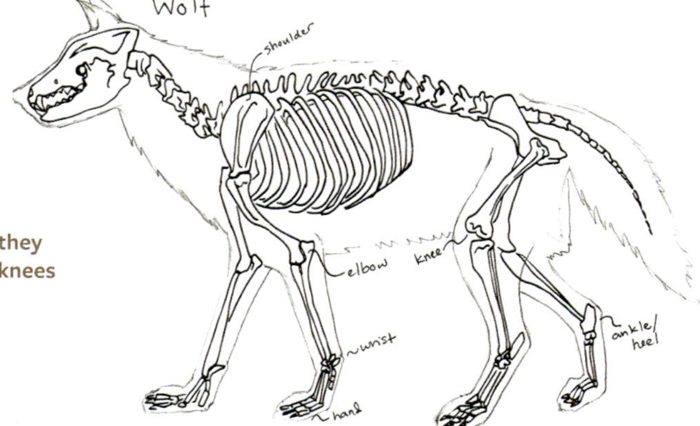

▶ Canines and felines walk on their toes, so they have elongated ankles and their elbows and knees are closer to their main body than humans.

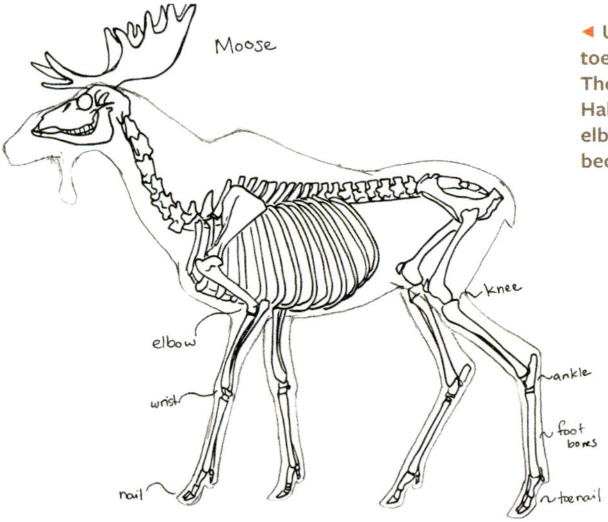

◀ Ungulates like deer, caribou, and moose walk on their toenails; thus, their ankles and feet are even more elongated. Their knees and elbows are part of the main body shape. Halfway down the leg, where we would have a knee or an elbow, they have a wrist or an ankle; that is important to note because it bends in the opposite direction.

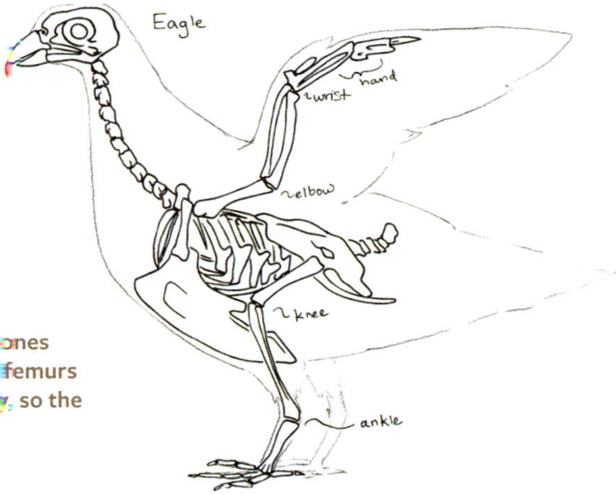

▶ Bird skeletons have adapted to be light, so many of their bones are fused. Their arms form the structure of their wings. Bird femurs are relatively short, with the knee tucked in close to the body, so the main hinge we see on the bird leg is the ankle.

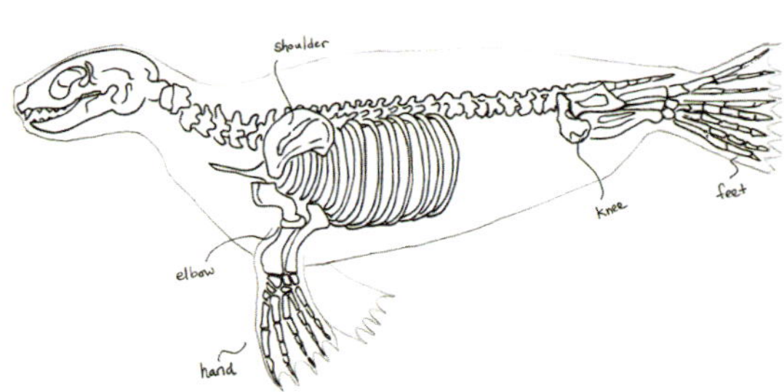

Aquatic mammals like seals have adapted their hands to have long fingers for front flippers. Their feet are their back fins, and their short leg bones make up part of their tail.

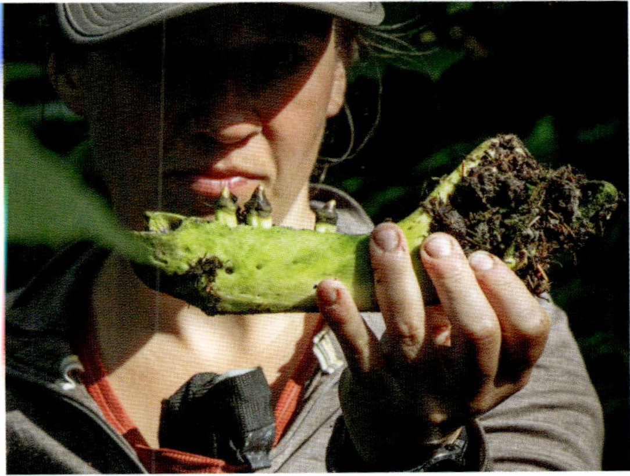

Finding and studying animal bones is a great way to learn more about anatomy. I found this jawbone on the beach, and even though it was old and mossy, it was cool to look closely at the pointed teeth.

GESTURE SKETCHING ANIMALS

Sometimes, when you see a moving animal, it starts in one position, moves to another, and then returns to the first position. I find it helpful to make a series of quick gesture sketches to capture moving animals' different poses quickly. All of the sketches you start might not get finished, but you can gather information as it is available and return to a sketch if the animal repeats a pose. It is also helpful to practice working quickly from photos (you can even set a timer) to prepare for sketching moving animals.

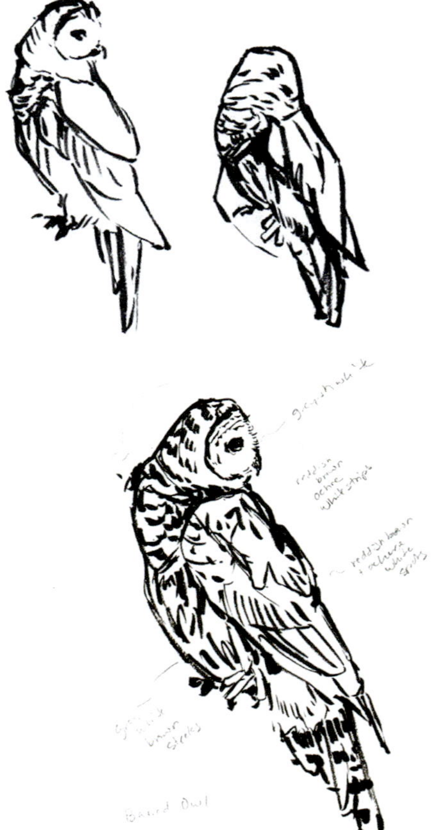

I was able to work with this live Barred Owl who visited a class from a raptor rehabilitation center. I started with a pencil and sketched the main shapes and patterns with a brush pen. I added a few notes about behavior and patterns when the owl moved and I wanted to watch it.

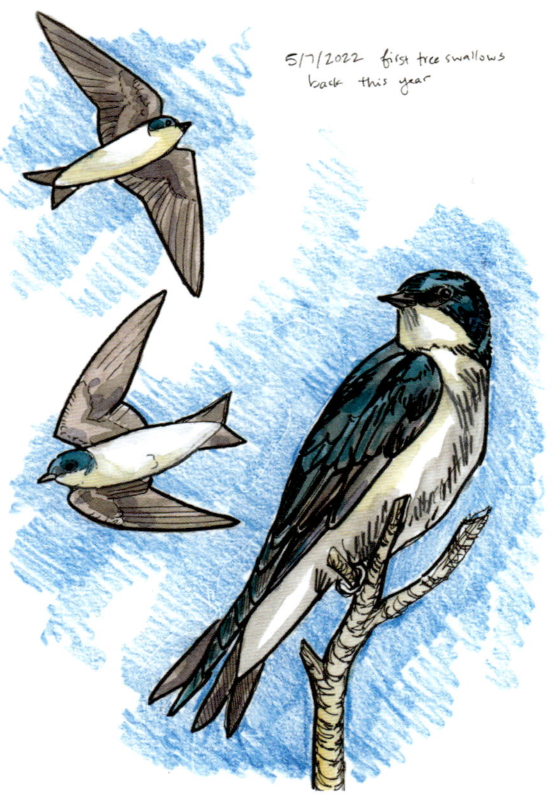

I was able to finish these gesture sketches of tree swallows hanging out in my yard with colored pencil and watercolor.

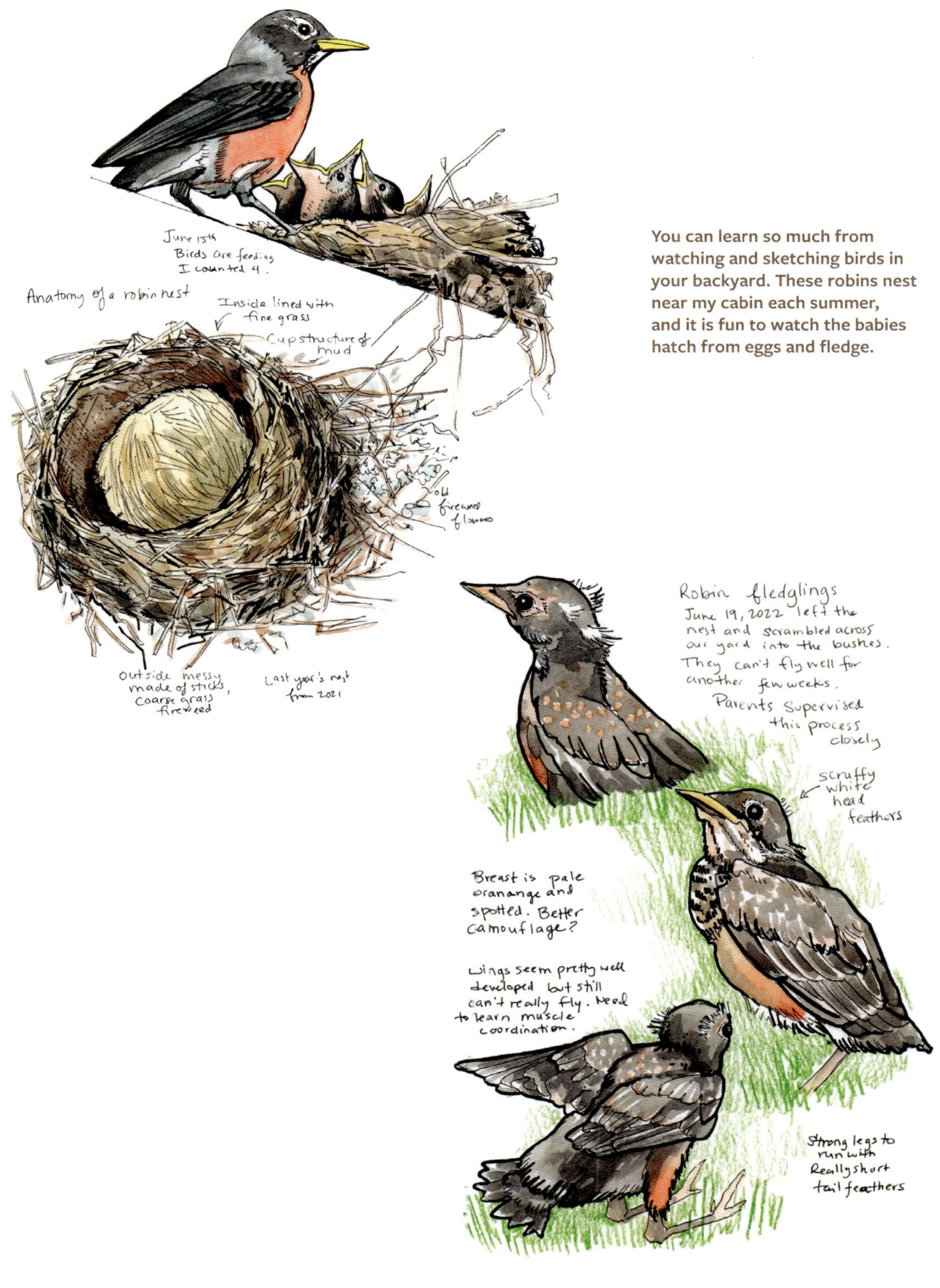

You can learn so much from watching and sketching birds in your backyard. These robins nest near my cabin each summer, and it is fun to watch the babies hatch from eggs and fledge.

Project 14

GESTURE SKETCHING ANIMALS: MOOSE

We can practice gesture sketching, working from the three positions I observed and photographed. We'll begin by blocking in the main shapes and figuring out how to fit three positions on the paper. Then, we will work quickly with a gray marker, pen, and watercolor.

MATERIALS: a pencil, a gray pen, a brush pen, watercolor paper, and watercolors

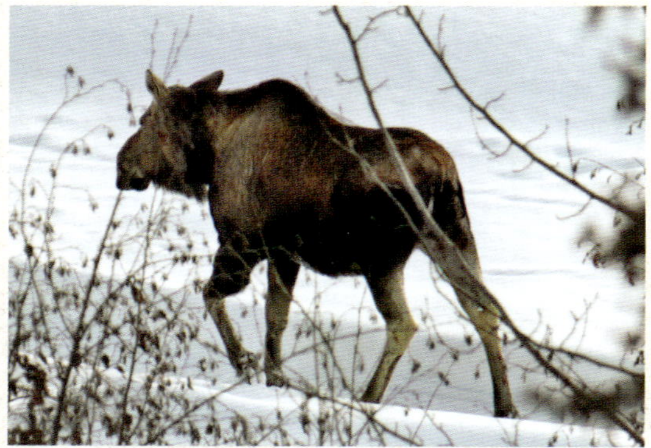

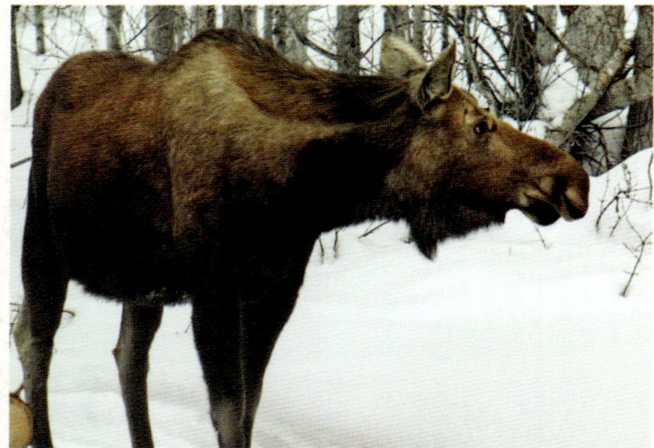

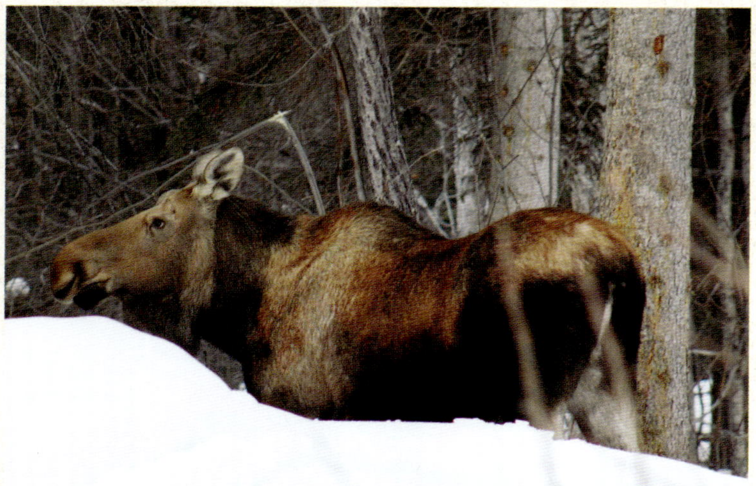

Moose are the largest ungulates in the deer family. They walk on their toenails, and their long legs help them navigate through deep snow. In Alaska, we see moose quite frequently, especially along trails in the winter.

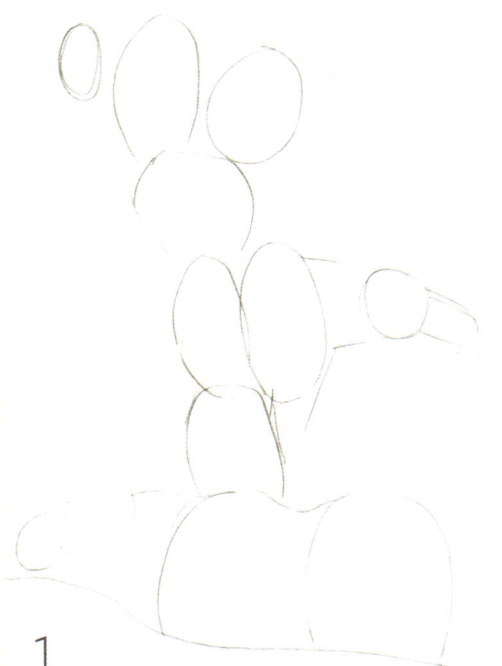

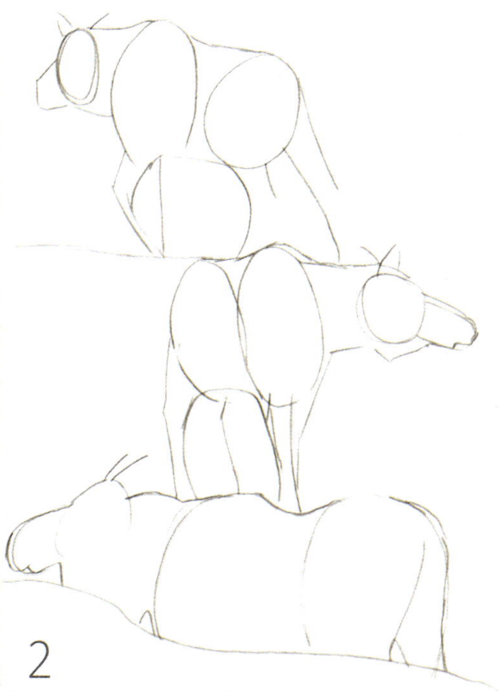

STEP 1: To start a gesture sketch, use a pencil and mark out the main body shapes with ovals for the hips, the shoulders, the head, and the negative space under the legs. I decided to arrange the three views vertically on the paper, which gives the sense that this is one encounter with a moving animal.

STEP 2: Connect the shapes from the previous step to show more of the animal. Use lines and angles to show the back and neck. Measure and mark the angles of the legs. Think about the skeleton of a moose. Moose are ungulates and walk on their toenails, so their wrists and ankles are elongated compared to ours. Their elbows and knees are much higher, quite close to the main part of their body.

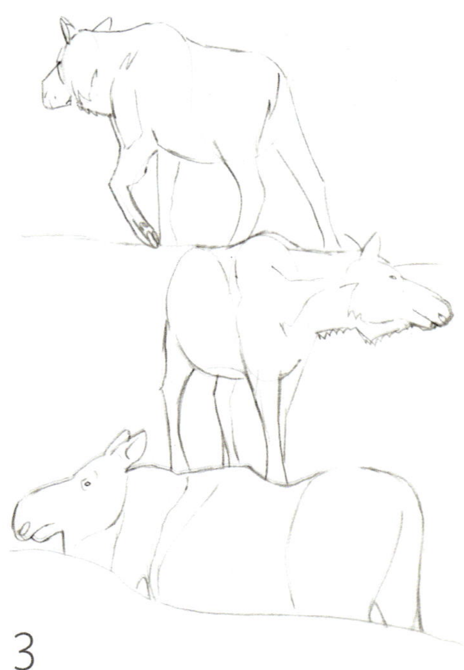

3

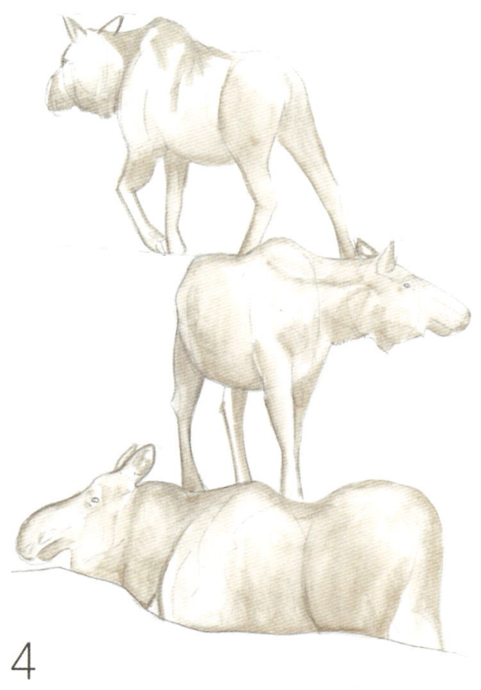

4

STEP 3: Add in more details. Draw where you notice important muscle groups indicated by changes in the fur and shadows. Refine the lines from previous steps and draw in the rest of the legs. Add in the eyes and the essential details on the face, such as the nose and the ears. You can use your pencil to measure some of the critical angles of the face and ears and erase these lines later. Next, add some fur and any other changes in coloration. Since I have three sketches on one page, I note where the animals overlap and pretend that the one on the bottom of the page is closest to the viewer and the one on top is the farthest away. This helps make sense of the page even though it is the same moose sketched three times.

STEP 4: To add volume and value quickly, I used a gray marker and a water brush to dissolve the ink and soften the edges to sketch in some of the shadows. I made sure to leave some areas light so there is a range of values.

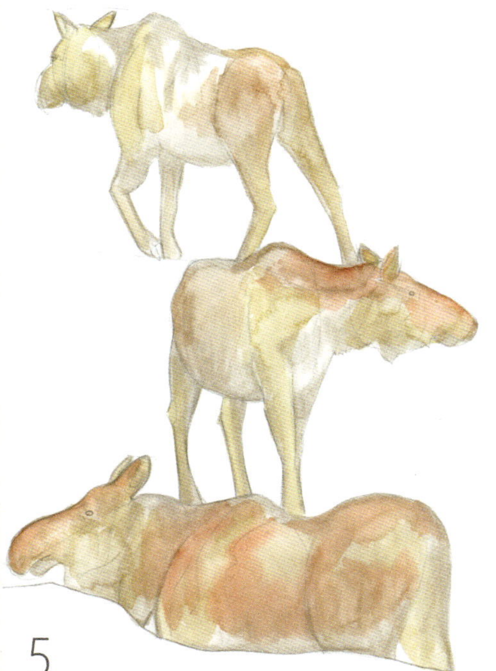

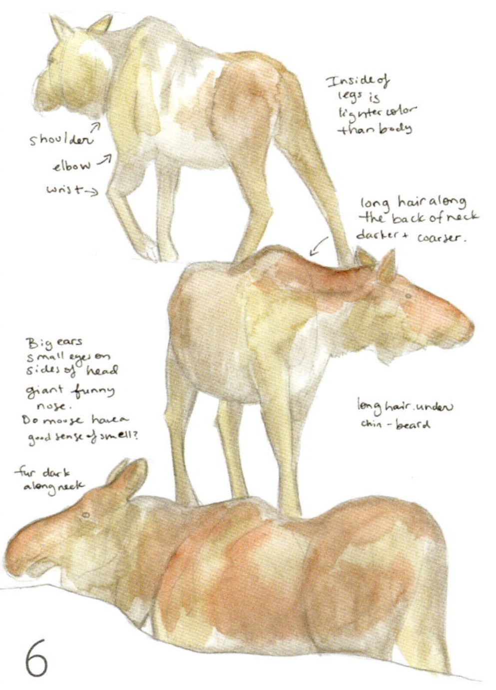

STEP 5: Add some brown tones with watercolor by mixing different browns and yellows and painting over the gray marker. The marker does most of the work with value and shadow, so this step is mostly about adding the color of the fur. Where the fur is reddish brown, I used Burnt Sienna. Where the fur is tanner, I used Buff Titanium with a bit of Raw Umber.

STEP 6: While you wait for the water to dry, add a few notes about what you notice and any questions you have. Write down information that you might use later to finish the sketch.

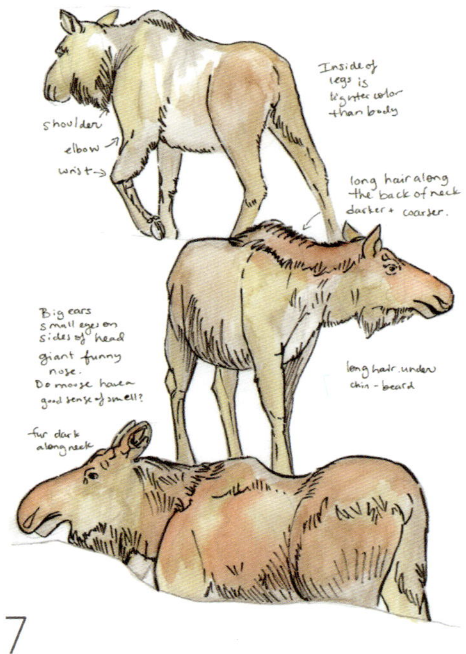

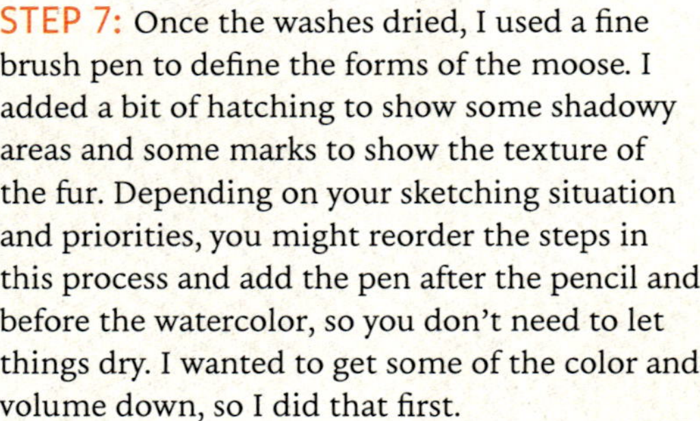

7

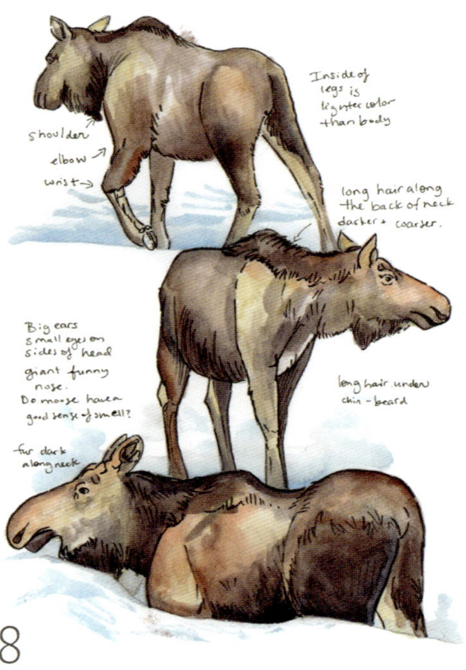

8

STEP 7: Once the washes dried, I used a fine brush pen to define the forms of the moose. I added a bit of hatching to show some shadowy areas and some marks to show the texture of the fur. Depending on your sketching situation and priorities, you might reorder the steps in this process and add the pen after the pencil and before the watercolor, so you don't need to let things dry. I wanted to get some of the color and volume down, so I did that first.

STEP 8: Once the pen is dry, maybe later in the day, sketch from memory and the information you got down on paper to add more shadows and details with watercolor. I added some purple, gray, and brown for the shadow areas and put some blue to show the shadows in the snow and to add depth. Review your notes and see if you have more questions.

Project 15

STUDYING ANATOMY WITH AN OWL SKULL

Use negative space and shading with watercolor to study the structure of the owl skull.

MATERIALS: a pencil, watercolor paper, and watercolors

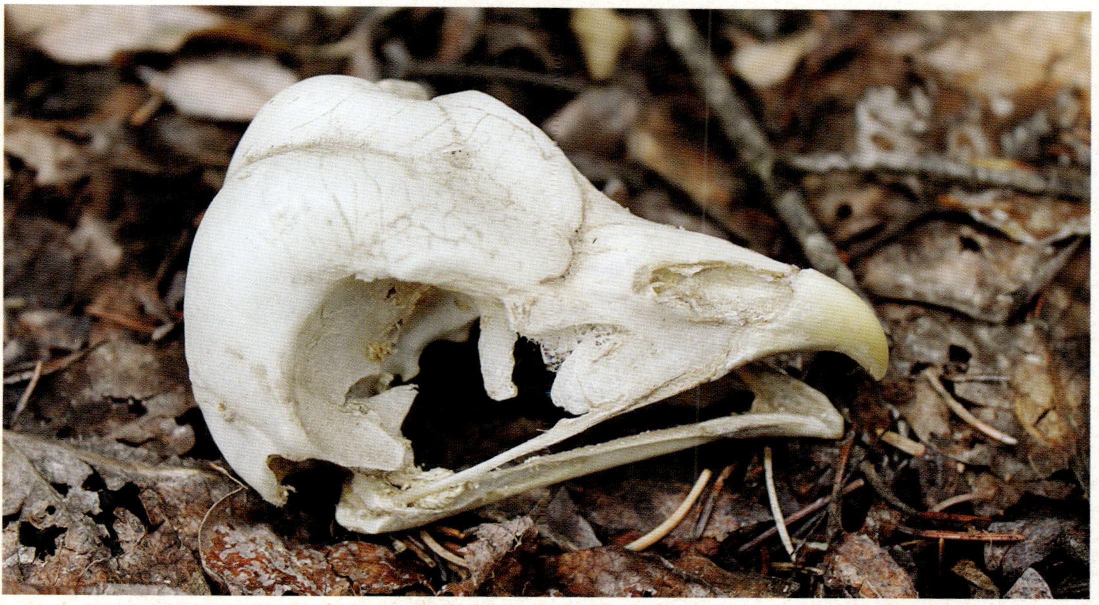

When sketching an animal, it is helpful to have some knowledge of the anatomy and skeleton. Sketching skulls, bones, and articulated skeletons can help you better understand what is happening beneath the feathers and fur. This is the skull of a Great Gray Owl.

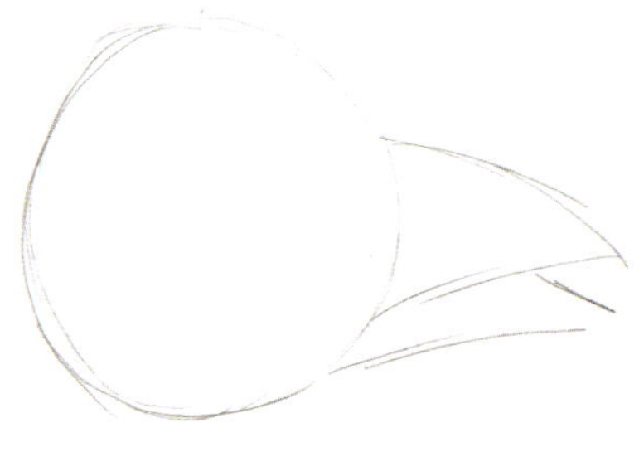

STEP 1: Begin by noticing and sketching the basic shapes of the skull. I drew an oval for the braincase area and some triangles for the bill.

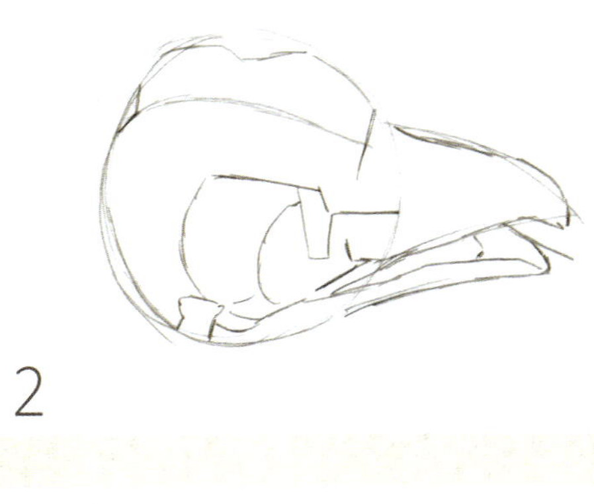
2

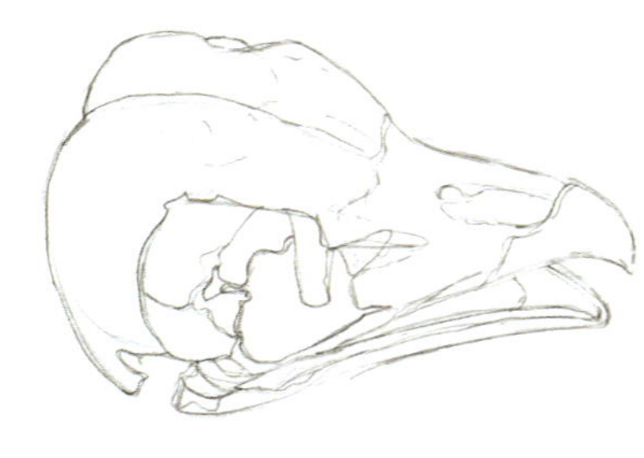
4

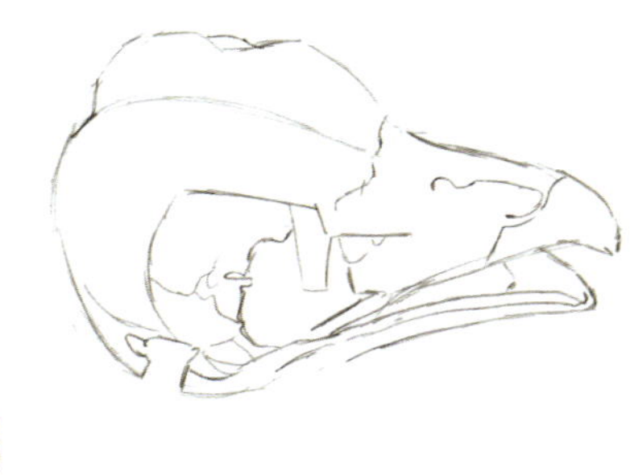
3

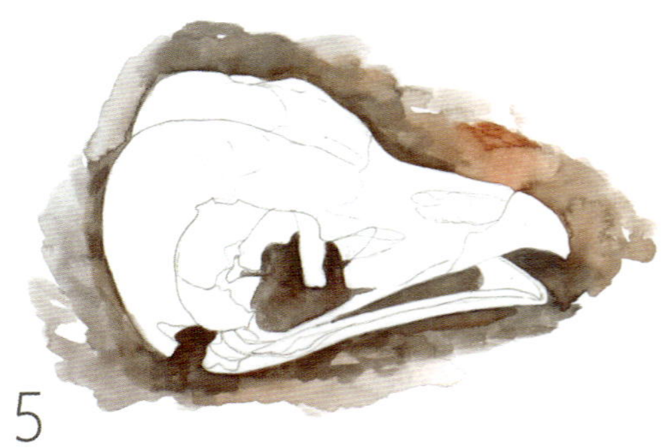
5

STEP 2: Refine the shapes by measuring and drawing lines and curves. Continue to focus on the big picture and the primary forms, not the details.

STEP 3: Continue refining the shapes, now looking at the details, contours, and negative spaces of the skull.

STEP 4: Refine your sketch from the previous step by blotting your pencil with a kneaded eraser and redrawing lines where you want them. Add in some of the details on the surface of the skull.

STEP 5: Since the skull is almost white and the background is dark, we can begin painting in the negative space with a series of browns, letting the warm and cool browns (Burnt Sienna and Raw Umber) mix with a wet wash but keeping the outline of the skull sharp.

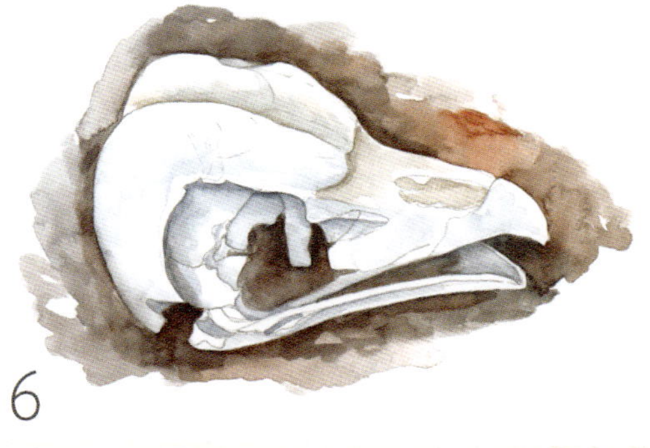

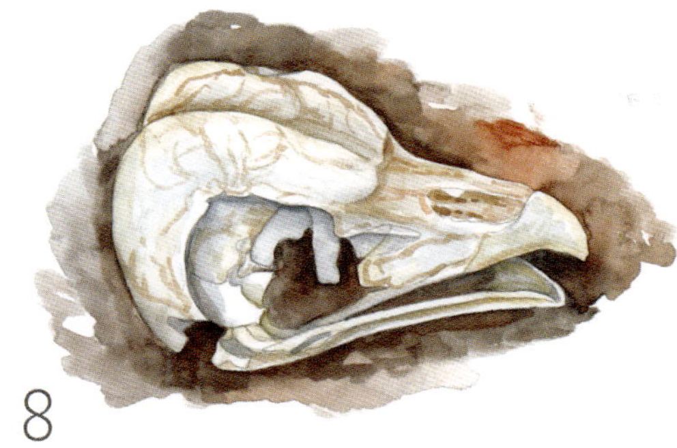

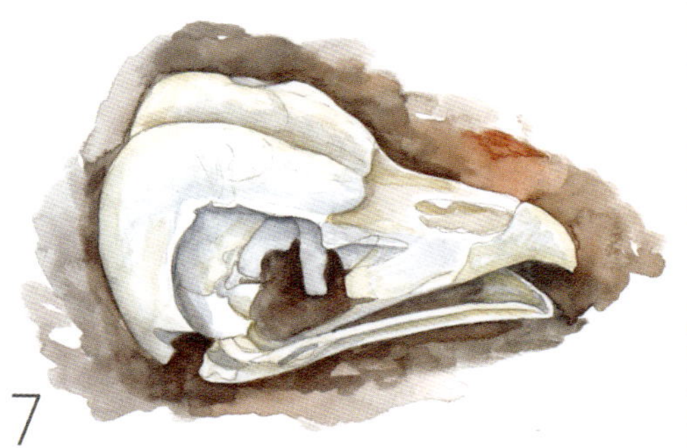

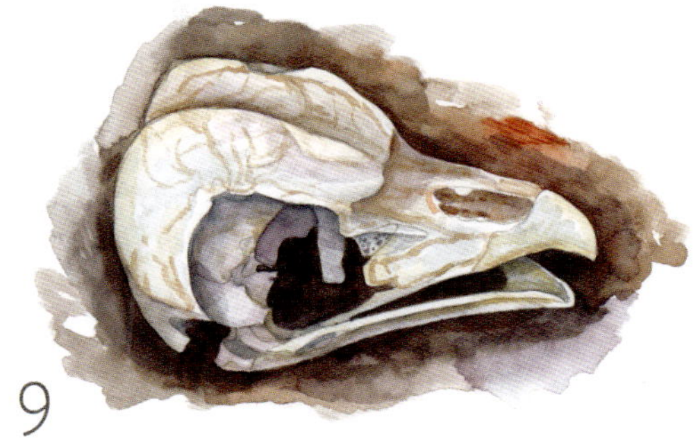

STEP 6: Once the background is dry, mix some brown and violet-blue together in a light gray wash to paint some of the shadows of the skull. I used watered-down Indanthrone Blue mixed with a little bit of Burnt Sienna.

STEP 7: The skull is white, but much of it is a warm ivory color. I mixed Buff Titanium with some browns. I used this light ocher color and painted some of the areas with warmer tones. I tried to leave some white on the paper for the areas of the highlight in the middle of the skull.

STEP 8: Paint in some of the skull's texture using pale, watered-down paint, a fine brush, and a delicate touch. Remember, you can always go darker if you want. I painted in some wavy lines and dots to show some of the skull's surface texture.

STEP 9: Add another layer of shadows to help the whole sketch come together. I used a light wash of shadow violet from Indanthrone Blue, Burnt Sienna, and Quinacridone Rose to deepen the area around the skull and to round out the shadows on the skull itself. I also added some small final areas of detail, such as the holes inside the beak.

Project 16

CAPTURING FUR: RED SQUIRREL

Fur and feathers are attached to the skin, which is laid over the muscle, which is laid over the top of the skeleton. It is helpful to think of an animal from the inside out, beginning with the bone structure and noticing how the feathers or fur are grouped in different muscle masses over the skeleton.

MATERIALS: a pencil, watercolor paper, and watercolors

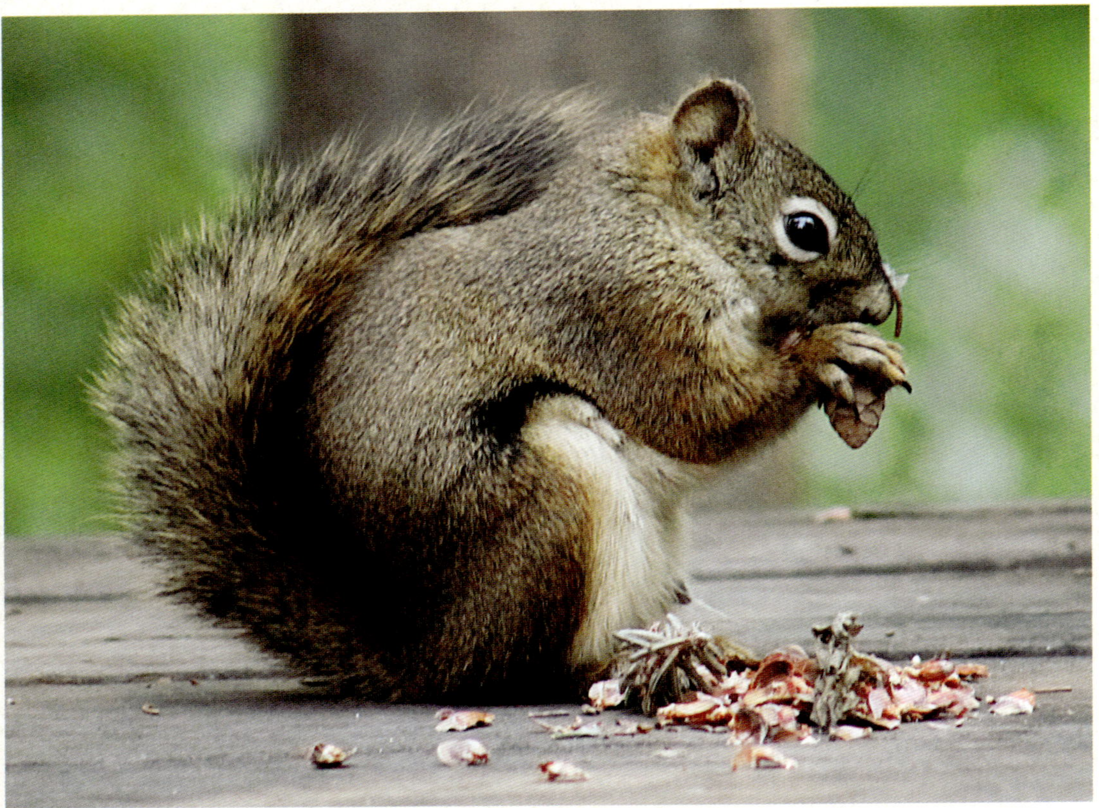

Red squirrels are common in Alaska and are active year-round. I took this photo at a picnic table in a park and was glad the squirrel was more interested in eating their favorite food, seeds from spruce cones, instead of my snack.

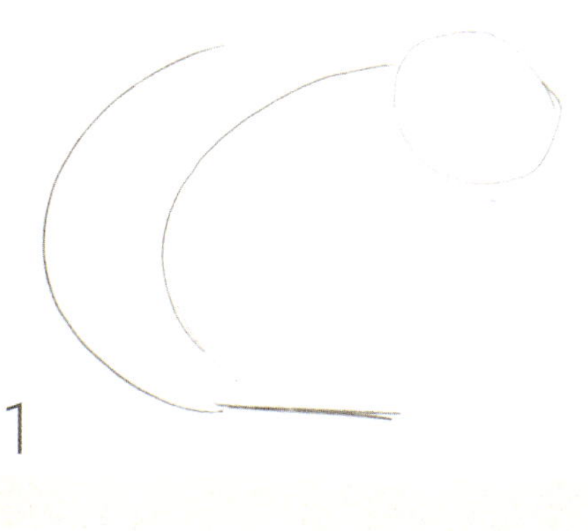

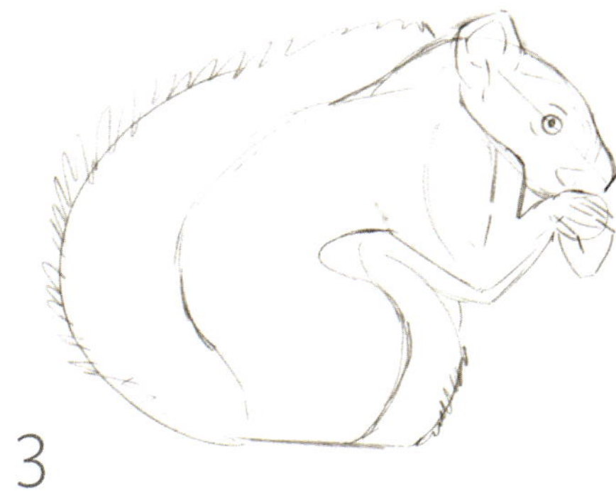

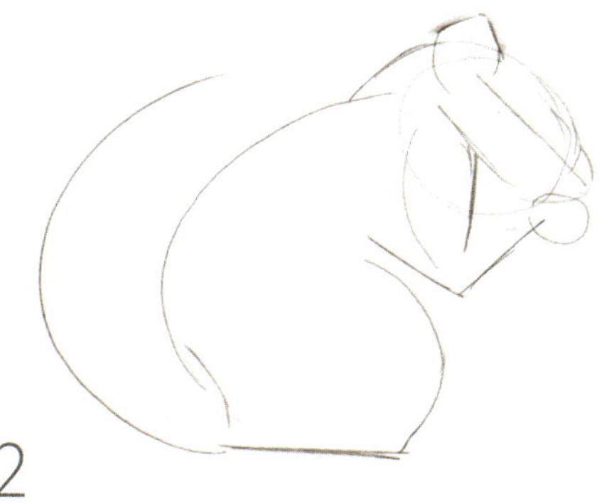

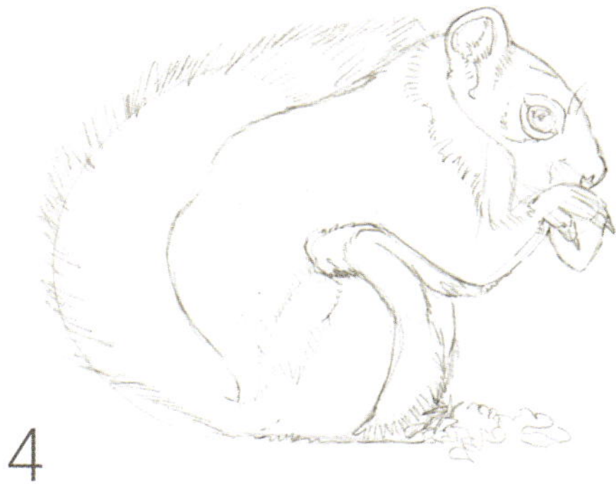

STEP 1: Sketch the main shapes of the body: a circle for the head, a curved line along the spine and tail, and a straight line at the bottom where the squirrel is sitting on the table.

STEP 2: Add more anatomy for the face and limbs. I noticed that I made the head too big, so I refined the shape of that circle and added some space for the ear and the nose. I also measured a straight line from the ear to the nose to measure where the eye should go. I drew some lines to show where the arm is and a circle where the squirrel's hand is holding the cone it is eating.

STEP 3: Add the eye on top of your guideline from the previous step. Add more details in the face and body and some fur texture. Continue using simple lines rather than focusing on the details. I also measured and drew lines for the three fingers that are visible.

STEP 4: Refine the sketch from Step 3 by lightening the drawing with a kneaded eraser and redrawing the critical lines with a bit more finesse and detail. Now that the main shapes are marked out, pay attention to the textures and shapes that the fur makes—for example, marking out the little black stripe of fur on the sides of the squirrel's belly or the shape of the ruff around its neck.

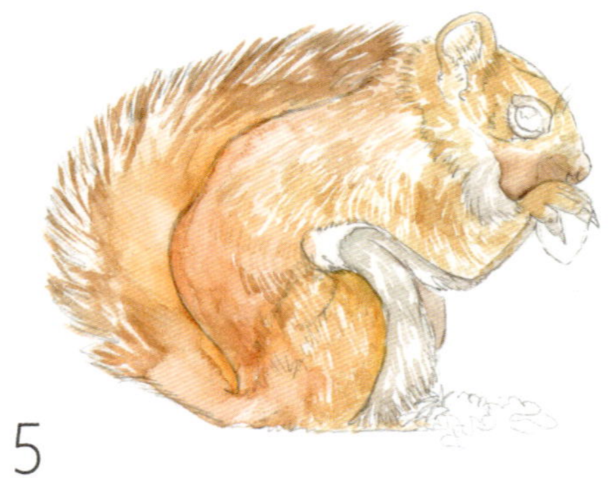

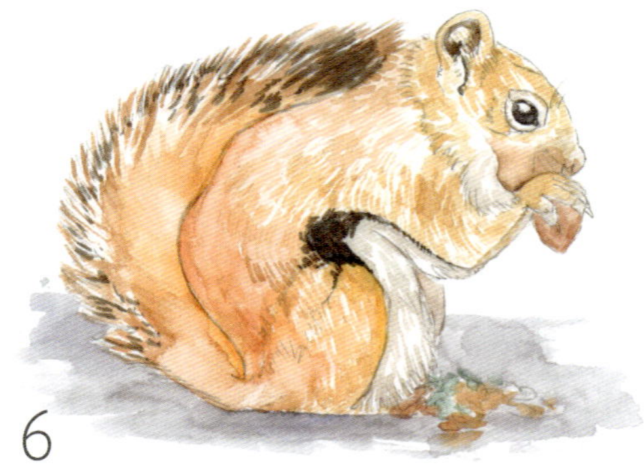

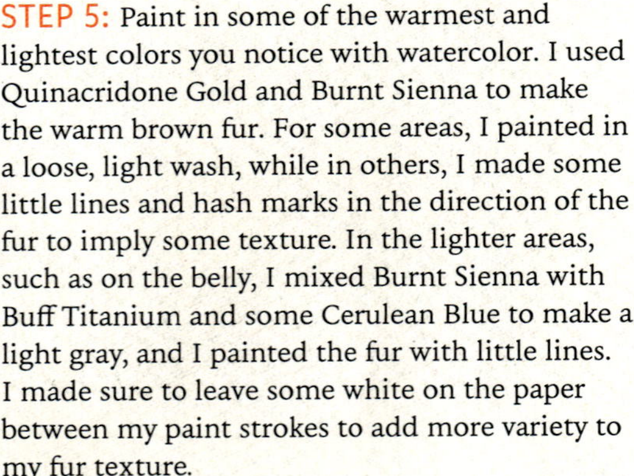

STEP 5: Paint in some of the warmest and lightest colors you notice with watercolor. I used Quinacridone Gold and Burnt Sienna to make the warm brown fur. For some areas, I painted in a loose, light wash, while in others, I made some little lines and hash marks in the direction of the fur to imply some texture. In the lighter areas, such as on the belly, I mixed Burnt Sienna with Buff Titanium and some Cerulean Blue to make a light gray, and I painted the fur with little lines. I made sure to leave some white on the paper between my paint strokes to add more variety to my fur texture.

STEP 6: Paint in some background to give the sketch a sense of place and that the squirrel is sitting on something. I added a violet-gray shadow and some greens and browns to show the squirrel is eating spruce cones. Once my wash from the previous step was dry, I mixed a darker brown with Indanthrone Blue and Burnt Umber and painted in some of the darker sections of fur, the eye, and the inside of the ear.

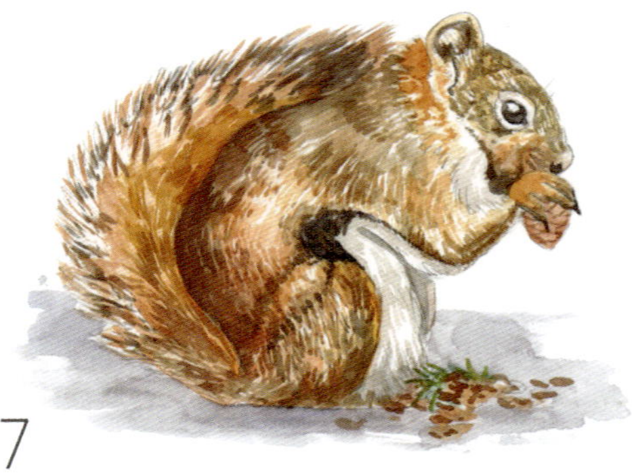

STEP 7: Mix some mid-tones for the squirrel. I used Burt Sienna, Raw Umber, and Quinacridone Gold to paint in more fur texture. I noticed how the fur along the tail next to the back and on top of the ruff is quite gold, whereas the fur on the back of the squirrel is more reddish. The colors change slightly depending on the shadow and how the light hits the fur. You can use the browns I mixed to add more texture to the spruce cones.

STEP 8: Mix a shadowy violet with Ultramarine Blue, Quinacridone Rose, and some Cobalt Teal Blue. This is quite purple, but it contrasts nicely with the orange of the fur and will dull down when layered on top. I painted some shadows where I noticed them along the top of the tail, the back, the lower parts of the squirrel, and under the chin.

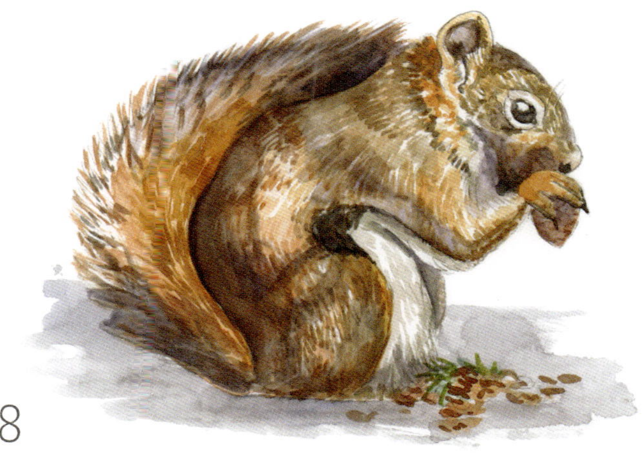

8

STEP 9: Add some final dark details. I mixed dark brown with Indanthrone Blue and Burnt Umber to add texture to the top of the tail and the hand and to define some details in the squirrel's face.

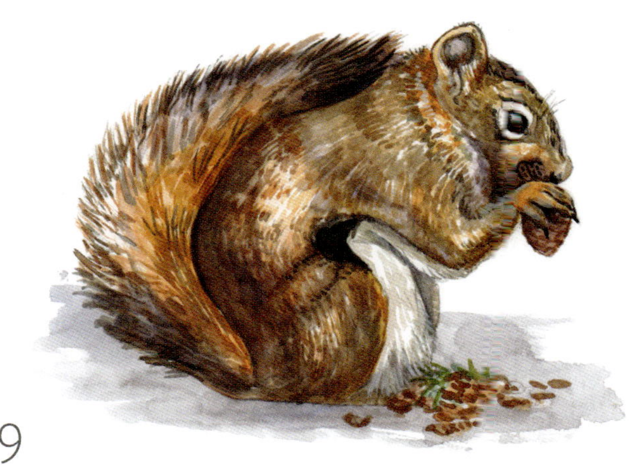

9

Project 17

IRIDESCENCE AND FEATHERS: RAVEN

Ravens are an excellent subject for studying iridescent feathers and capturing all the blues, purples, and greens that shine through their black feathers when they hit the light a certain way. This is also an excellent way to practice learning to notice and sketch the different feather groups and sketching birds in general. Birds that do different things have wings and bodies that are adapted to those tasks, but in general, they all have the same groups of feathers; they are just shaped differently.

MATERIALS: a pencil, fine and brush pens, watercolor paper, and watercolors

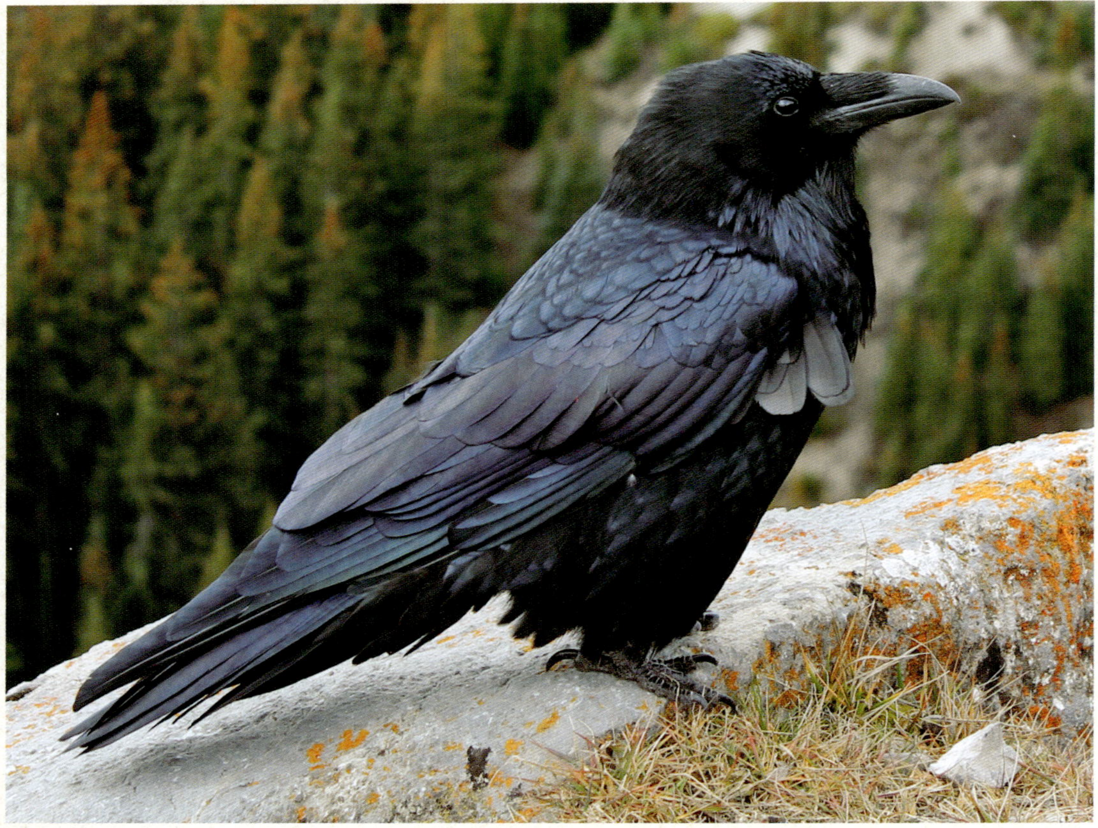

Ravens are intelligent and extraordinarily adaptable to different environments. They live in the hot desert and cold interior of Alaska all winter. I love seeing them play in thermals and perch up high in the mountains, like this one.

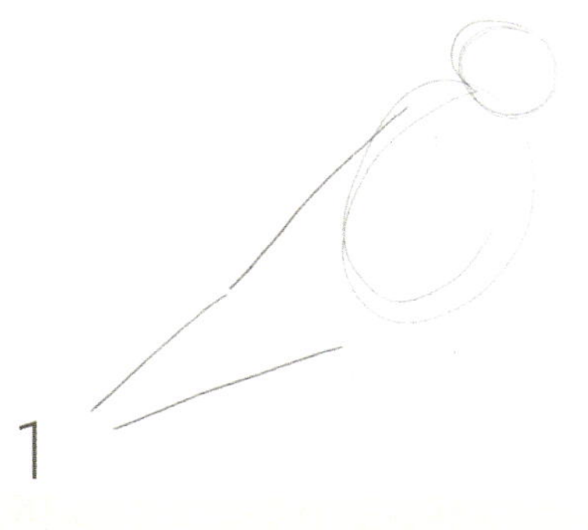

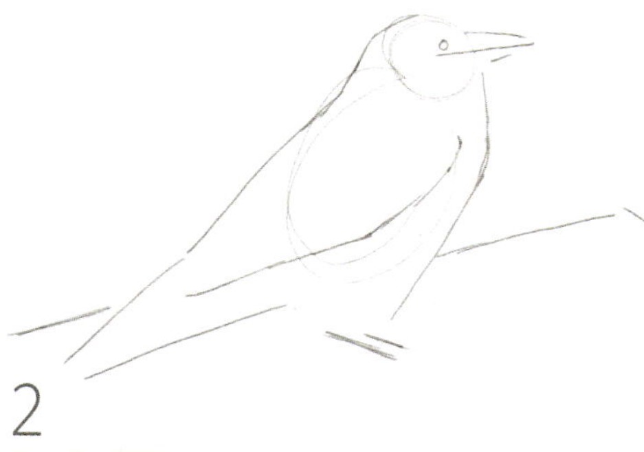

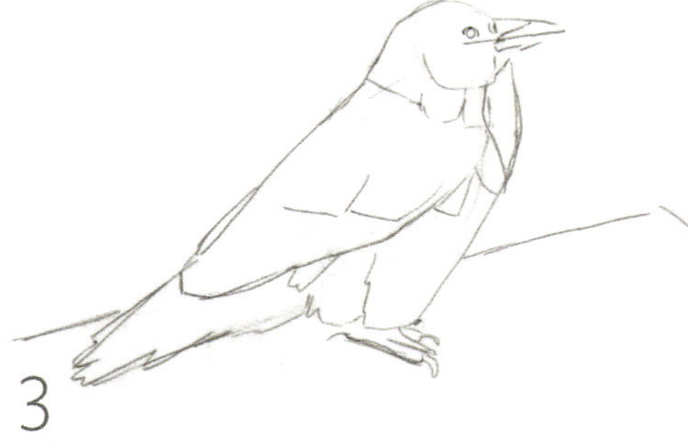

STEP 1: Begin by sketching out the main body parts you notice. I drew an oval for the main part of the body and a circle for the head. I measured the angle of the back with my pencil and then added the two angles for the tail, simplifying the shape into a kind of triangle.

STEP 2: Refine the shapes from the previous step. I added some straight lines around the head, measuring the angles with my pencil. I also drew a straight line for the bill and continued it through the inside of the head to help place the eye, which sits above this line. I also drew the outer shape of the beak, a few lines for the legs and feet, and started to sketch the outer margin of the folded wing.

STEP 3: When drawing birds, breaking down the feathers into groups is helpful. Look at the photo and notice where you see shadows. Feather groups are separated by the muscles they are attached to, so you'll often see clumps of feathers that seem to move together. There is a line of shadow around the cheek, and you can see how the feathers on the neck are slightly different in shape. The feathers in the wing are divided into groups as well: the primary flight feathers at the ends of the wing; the secondary and tertiary feathers that fill the wing closer to the body; the coverts that cover and support the flight feathers; the alula, which is a group where the thumb would be; and the scapula feathers that cover the shoulders. See if you can find groups of feathers in the wing and sketch them out, not worrying about each feather yet.

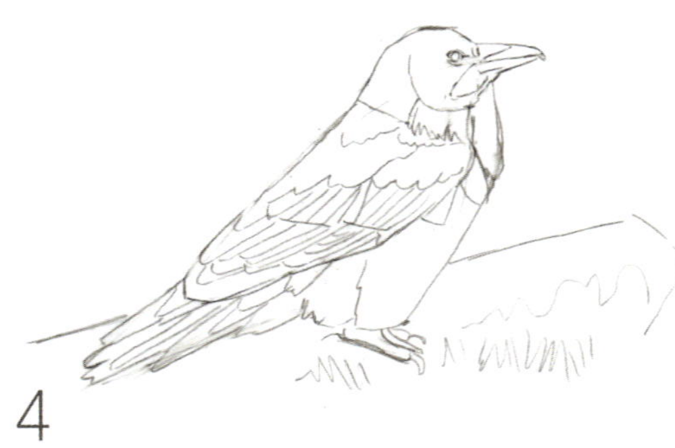
4

STEP 4: Now that the main feather groups are marked out, you can draw in some of the individual feathers. I drew lines for the ones I thought were most important on the wing and the tail and then generalized the feathers on the back and belly instead of drawing every single one. Putting the most detail in the wing parts close to the viewer will make them come forward in space. I also added some marks for the background where the grass overlaps the rock.

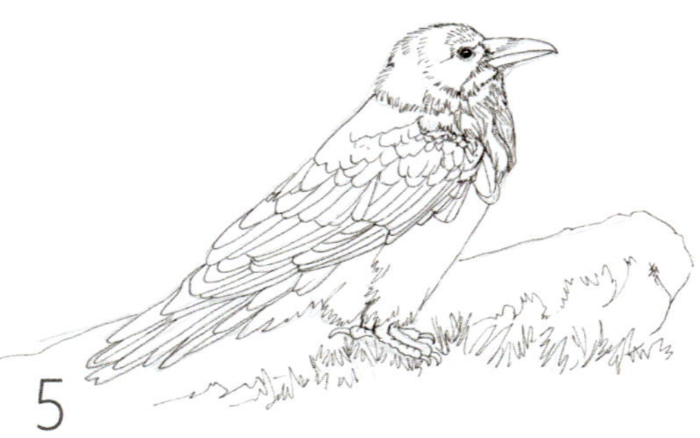
5

STEP 5: Go over your pencil sketch with a fine waterproof pen. I used fine lines, planning to thicken them in some areas after I added watercolor. I spent a lot of time sketching out the raven and its feathers, so I want that work to act as a guide or a kind of coloring book for my next steps, adding watercolor. I marked the important feathers and added some lines and textures to the areas I wanted to generalize.

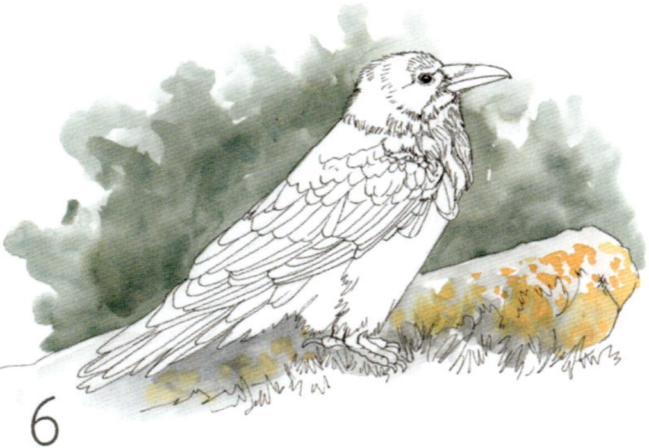
6

STEP 6: Add color by painting in a loose wash in the background. I mixed Ultramarine Blue, Cobalt Teal Blue, and Quinacridone Gold to make the blue-gray wash for the background. I also mixed gray and orange for the rock and let those two washes blur a bit while working wet-in-wet. I want the raven to be the focus of the sketch, so I kept these washes quite loose.

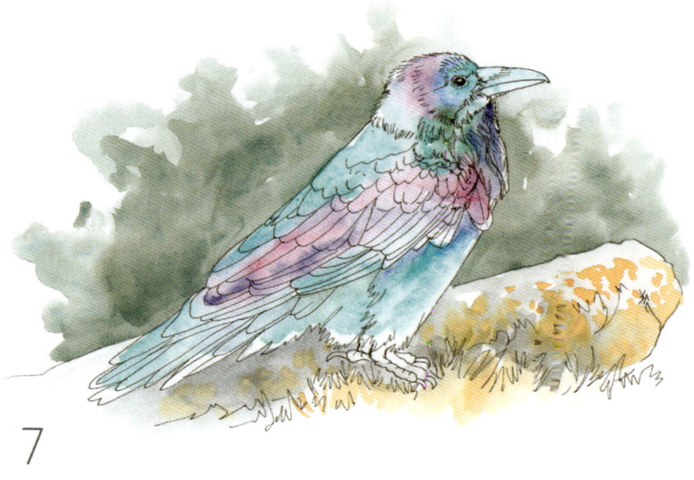

7

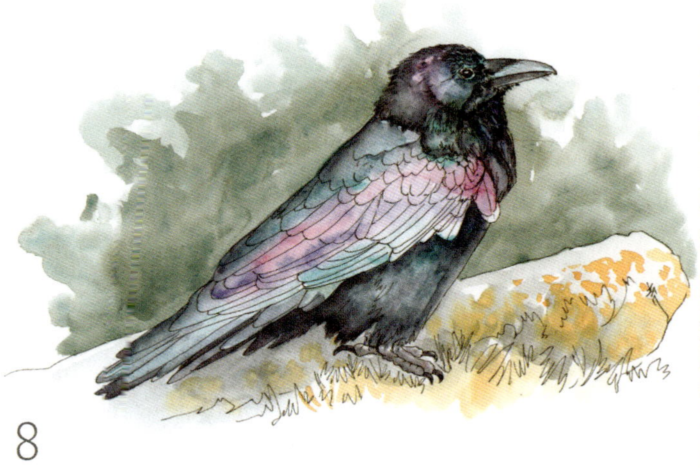

8

STEP 7: To achieve iridescence, I took note of the colors I saw underneath the black. We will work in layers with these colors first, and then we can add black or gray to the top. I noticed blue, purple, magenta, and green. I can create a gradient from green to magenta by mixing Phthalo Turquoise into Phthalo Blue into Cobalt Teal Blue into Ultramarine Blue into Quinacridone Rose, working wet-in-wet. Once I practiced this gradient, I applied it to the raven, working wet-in-wet so the colors blend but preserving areas of teal, magenta, and green in some areas. It is essential to let the wash dry before moving on.

STEP 8: Mix a blackish-gray color to layer on top of the rainbow-colored raven. I mixed Indanthrone Blue with Quinacridone Rose, Phthalo Turquoise, and Raw Umber. Paint this over the body, emphasizing the shadows and leaving light areas where the iridescent colors from the previous step can shine through.

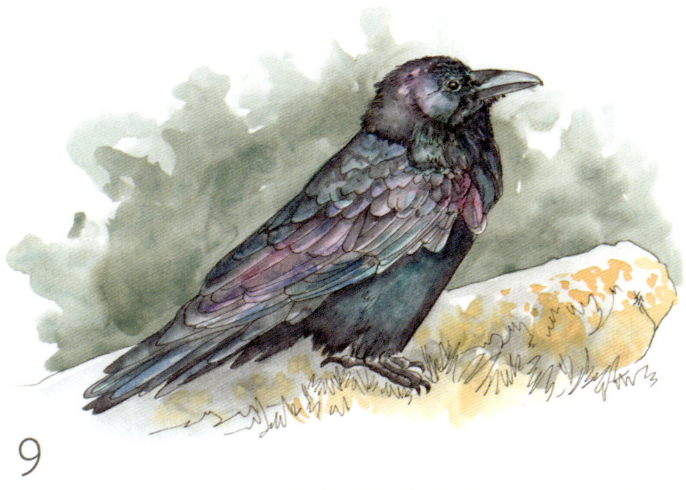

9

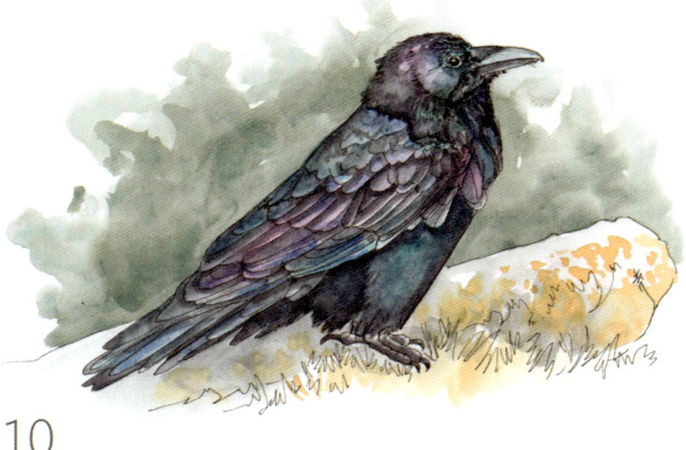

10

STEP 9: Continue painting the dark wash over the wing. For this section, I was careful to add the deepest shadow where the feathers overlap and then lighten my graded wash towards the outer edge of each feather.

STEP 10: Let the paint from the previous steps dry. There might be some color shift after the paint dries, which is normal. You can go over some areas again to deepen the values and make them darker, especially where you notice the feathers are blacker and less iridescent.

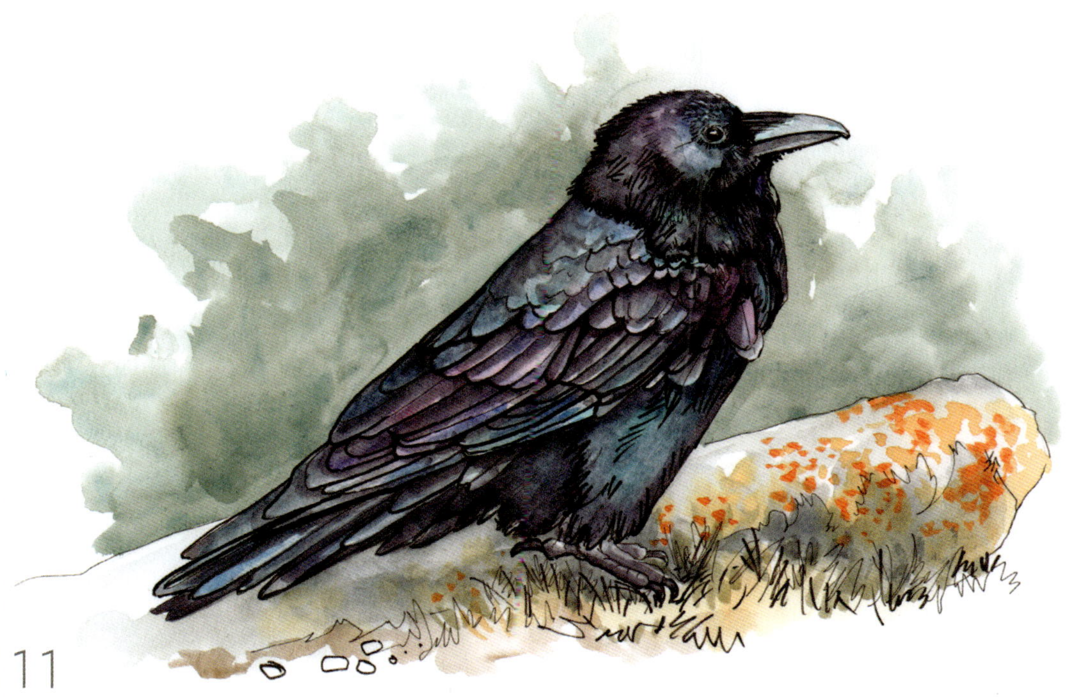

STEP 11: Add another layer of paint to the rock and grass where the raven is standing. When the paint is dry, go over the drawing with a fine brush pen to add more contrast and texture in some areas.

THE HUMMINGBIRD AT KAYAK ISLAND

On the southern tip of Kayak Island is Cape St. Elias, where an old lighthouse and a few buildings stand. We went into the lighthouse to watch the sunset over the Gulf of Alaska and found a small surprise in the light chamber room. At some point, a female Rufous Hummingbird got trapped in the glass room and sadly died there. Eastern Prince William Sound is about the northern extent of where this hummingbird migrates, though I rarely see them in the mountains where I live. Finding the tiny dead bird and seeing the iridescent body up close was sad and remarkable.

I made a simple pencil drawing in my waterproof notebook. The feathers on her back transition from green to orange, which is impressive to me as an artist, knowing that green and orange are nearly complementary colors. Her wings were so slender and tiny when folded. The proportion of the bill was about half the length of her body. The tail feathers went from reddish brown to green, ending with black and white patches. Maybe that is to help signal? Each feather is a work of art. The bird was only 3 inches long, including the bill and wings. It was a tiny, beautiful creature.

I wanted to sketch it because I rarely have an opportunity to see a hummingbird. I have learned so much from sketching dead animals, but I try to act with utmost respect for the gift that nature lent me for a while. Making a sketch is an act of respect, but it depends on the situation, and each case must be considered. I've also gotten more sensitive over time. Art can be an act of reciprocity, and sometimes, I leave a small drawing made with natural materials to thank nature for letting me sketch or gather something.

Reflection

Think about what information you like to include in your sketches beyond the drawings. Do you write the date or about the subject? Do you practice asking questions and develop your curiosity? Where can you expand your practice?

Remember to consider working with words, pictures, and numbers as well as the prompts: I notice . . . I wonder . . . It reminds me of . . .

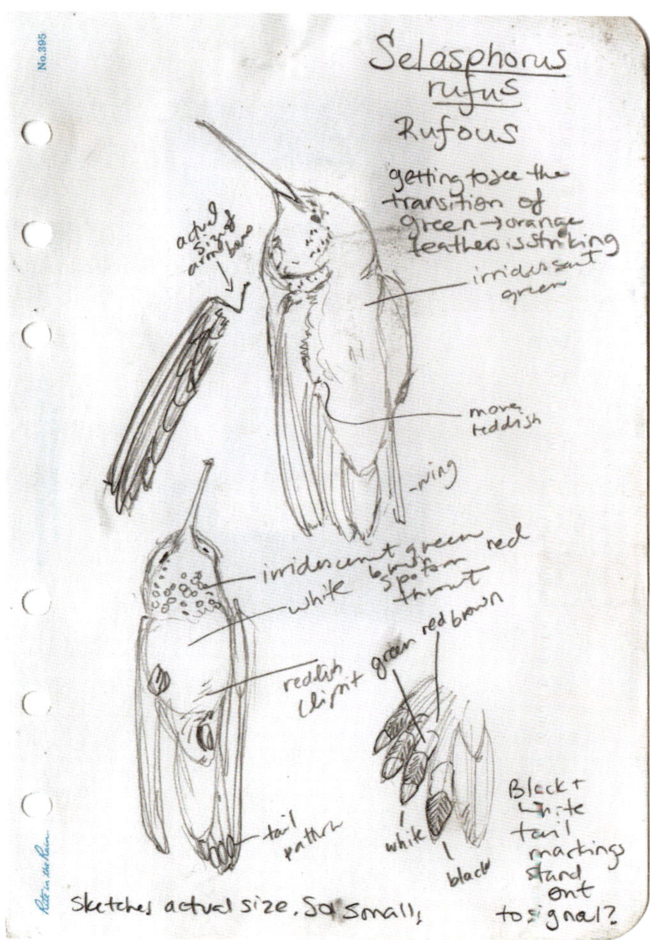

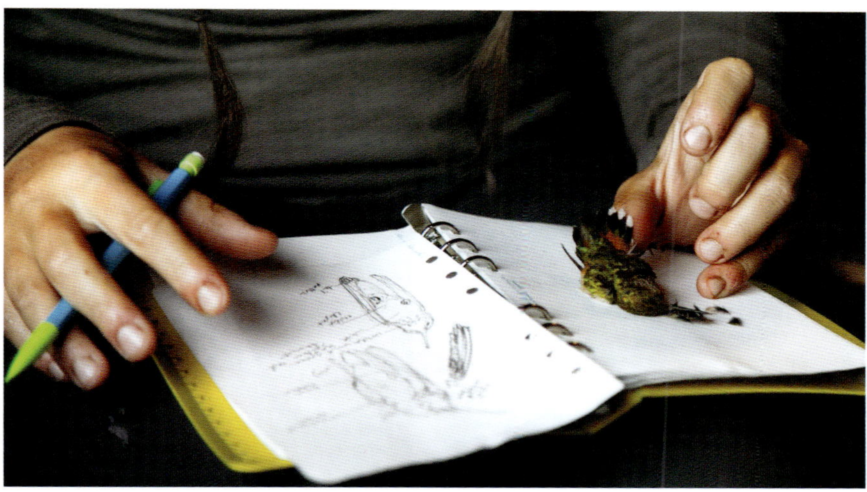

Sketching from a rare subject, a dead Rufous Hummingbird, with pencil in a waterproof sketchbook

Sketching Landscapes and Creating the Illusion of Space

If we opened people up, we'd find landscapes.

—AGNÈS VARDA

So far in this book, I've discussed how to render a subject to make it appear round or dimensional on a flat piece of paper and how to use selective detail and contrast in certain areas that you would like to emphasize.

When we sketch landscapes, we will continue to build these techniques on a larger scale in terms of what we

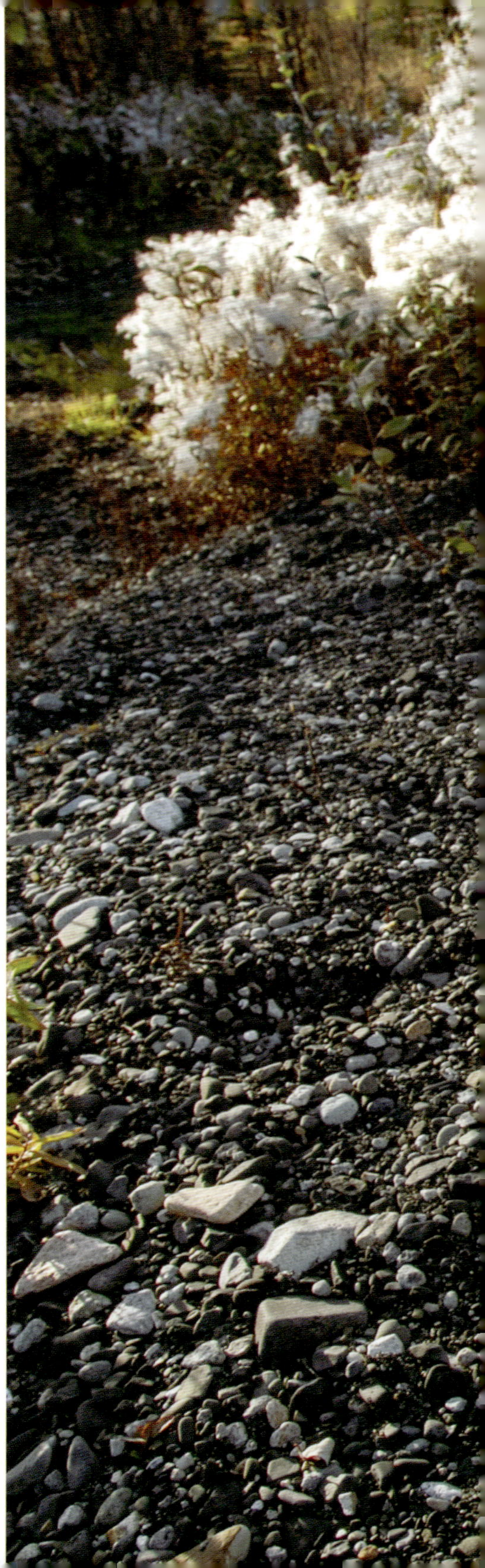

▸ **Enjoying the late-day light and the expressive fall colors of the Alaskan landscape with watercolor and sketchbook**

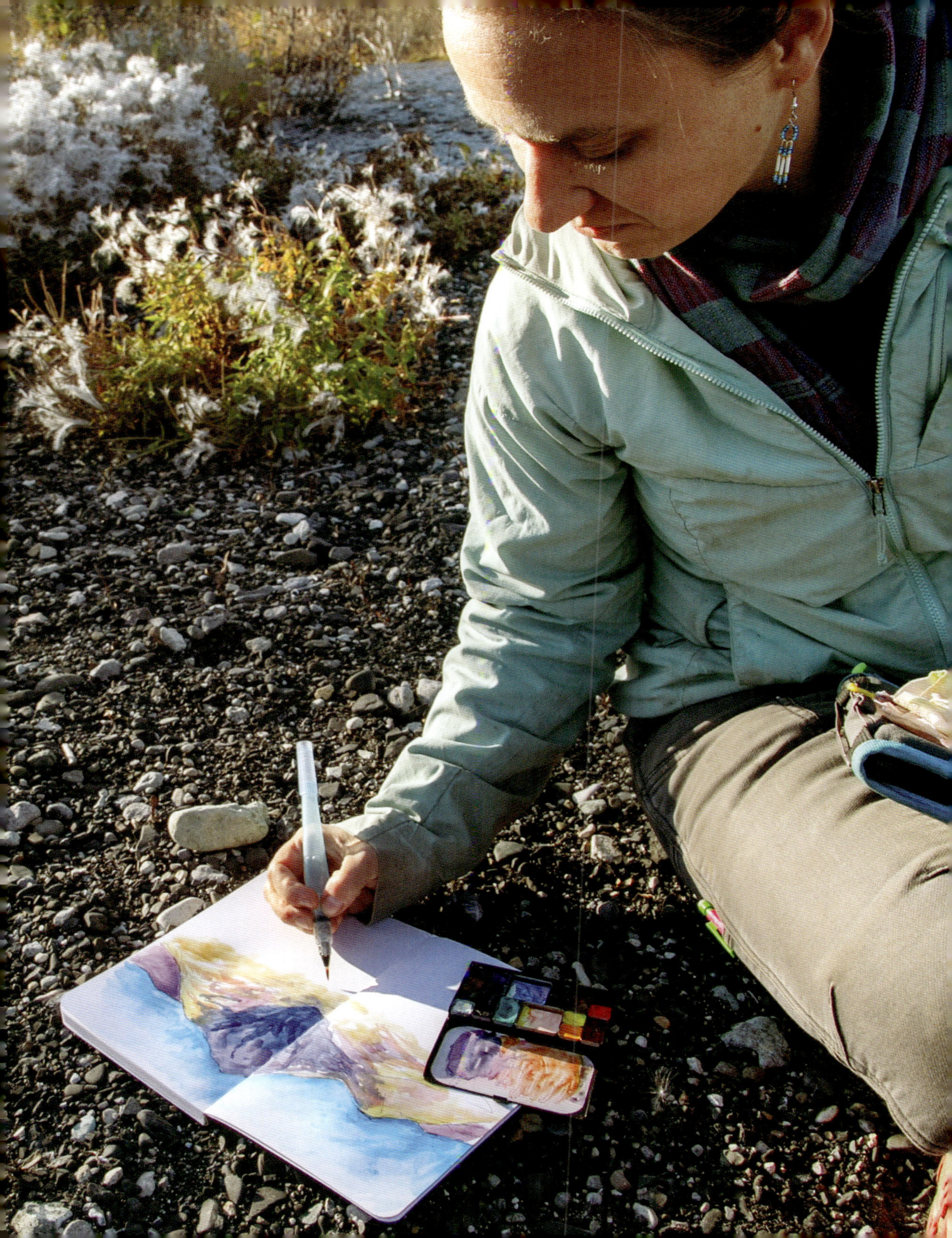

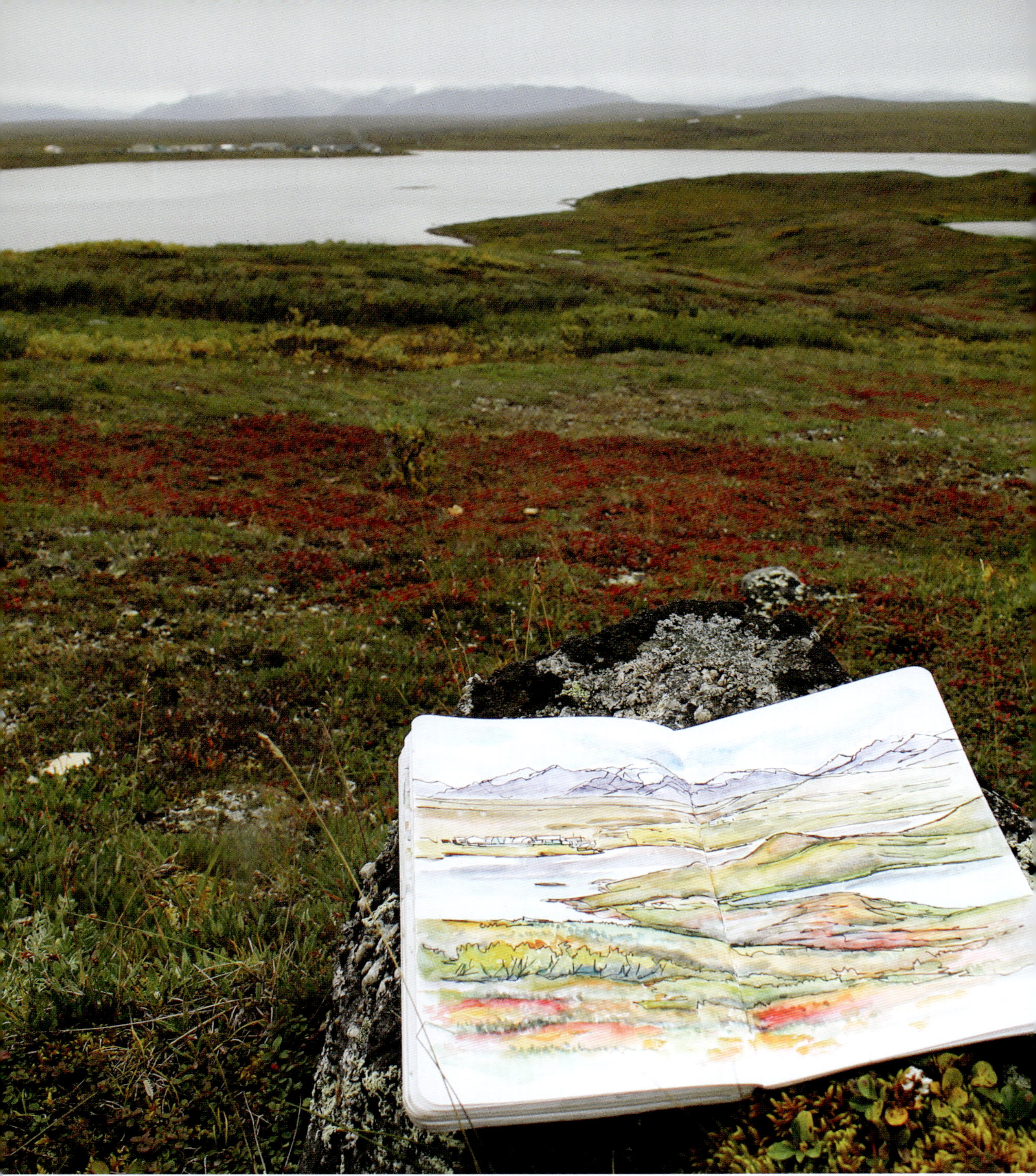

Sketching the fall colors on the arctic tundra at Toolik Lake. I noticed that the colors of vegetation in the fall are more vibrant in person than in photos, where they tend to mix together and make brown, so I tried to increase the saturation in my sketch to exaggerate this.

are trying to capture. The Alaskan landscape can be awe-inspiring, featuring the tallest mountains in North America, huge vistas with braided rivers, giant old-growth rain forests, and small trees growing at the edge their ecological range, overlooking the vast tundra. Sometimes, I find it overwhelming and choose to zoom in and study one plant or rock. Other times, I will focus on a series of texture studies or color swatches, tune into my senses, and draw what I smell or hear.

Certain techniques can make it easier to capture the complexity and grandeur of the landscape in a sketch. One is to make your sketch small, only a few inches by a few inches (4 x 6 or 2 x 3 inches), which will force you to simplify and pick which details are important. It is also essential to think through the rules of atmospheric perspective and decide how to work with them to emphasize the illusion of space.

CREATING THE ILLUSION OF SPACE AND USING PERSPECTIVE

Atmospheric perspective follows a series of guidelines in which things that are farther away appear smaller in size, closer to the horizon line, bluer or cooler in color, less saturated in color, and lighter in value. Closer things appear to have more contrast in value and color. For example, two saturated complementary colors, such as bright green and scarlet red, will have a lot of energy between them and will tend to pop forward. A detailed texture with a dark black on a white surface will also pop forward. A light gray-green and blue-green will feel more harmonious and can fit well into the background.

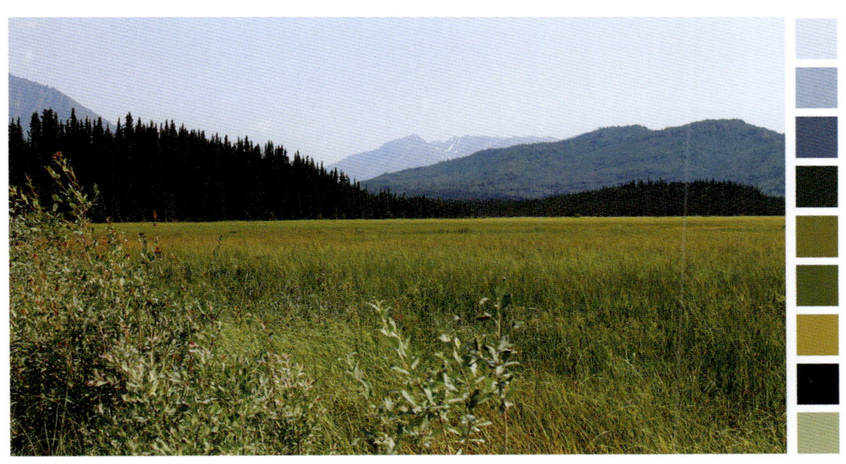

The color boxes on the right were picked directly from the landscape photo. Notice how the colors are bluer and lighter in the distance. The foreground colors have the most contrast and warmth.

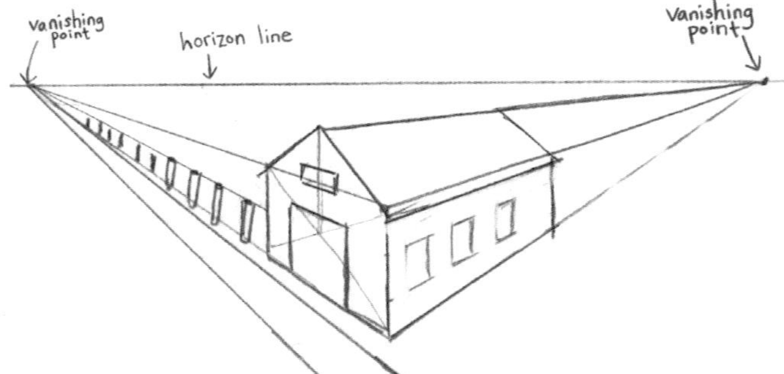

Simple sketch showing how linear perspective can be used to create the illusion of space. Parallel lines converge towards two vanishing points on the horizon line.

Things in the foreground also appear bigger, so if you want something to appear close, you can make it larger, maybe so large that it overlaps in front of another thing. Closer objects will be farther from the horizon line, so they will be placed at the bottom and the top of your page. Distant objects will be closer to the horizon line.

I remind myself that the landscape often breaks these guidelines. For example, giant white, glaciated mountains might be glowing in the distance, but I can play around with atmospheric perspective to help convey a sense of space. I could make those mountains bluer in color and make sure that they are comparatively small, while emphasizing the warm colors and contrast of the textures in the foreground.

Linear perspective is a tool that helps explain how straight lines converge towards the horizon line. It works best for linear objects like a straight road, a house, or a line of fence posts, but it can help us understand how things get smaller as they are closer to the horizon. The drawing in the example has two vanishing points on the left side and the right side of the horizon line. All straight lines going left or right converge on those points. Notice how the fence posts on the left side of the drawing get smaller as they get farther away.

STARTING A LANDSCAPE SKETCH

With landscapes especially, it is helpful to sit down and consider what you want to achieve and capture in the sketch. If I am feeling meditative and want to figure it out as I go, I may begin with a contour drawing. Sometimes, I want to capture specific shapes and patterns that I see, so I might use a grid to sketch these out. If I am more interested in capturing the changing colors or the way a tree is moving in the wind, I might use a looser gesture sketching approach.

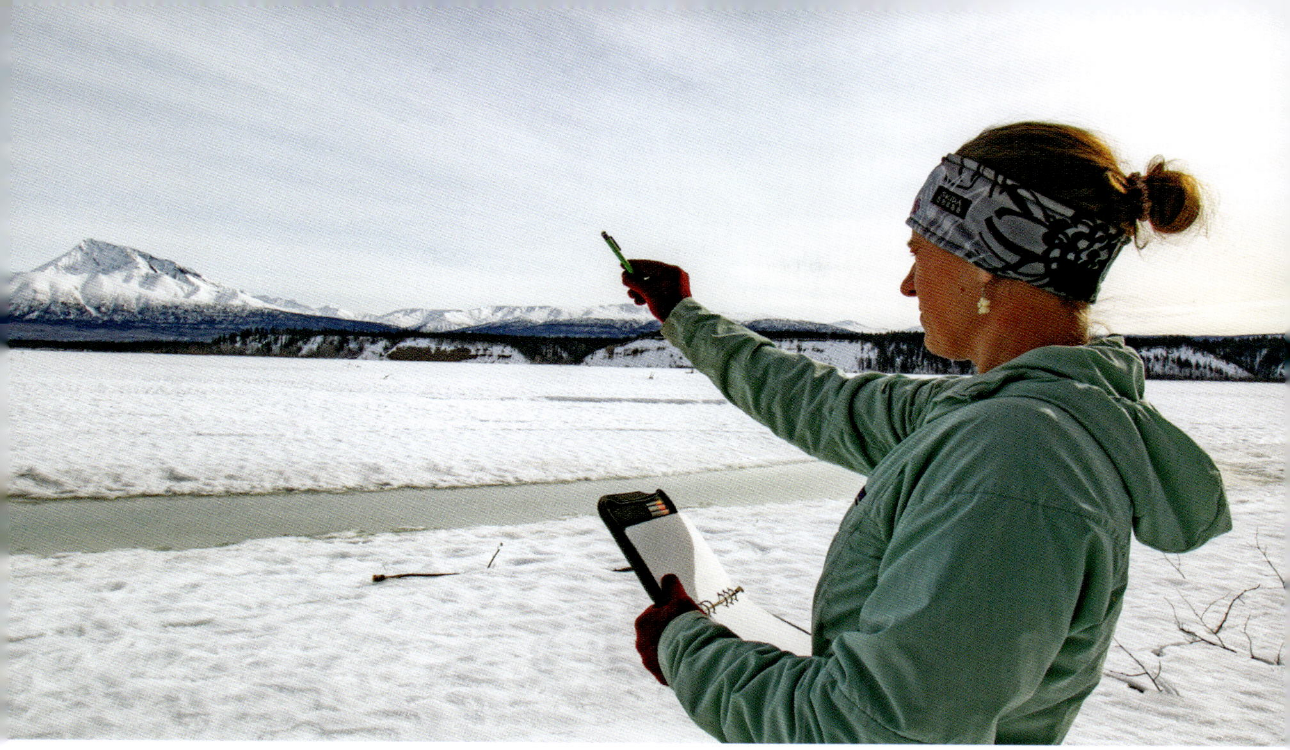

▲ Using a pencil to measure the angles of the mountains in the distance while setting up a landscape sketch. Getting the angles and proportions correct in the beginning helps the process go smoothly, though anything can be changed later on if needed.

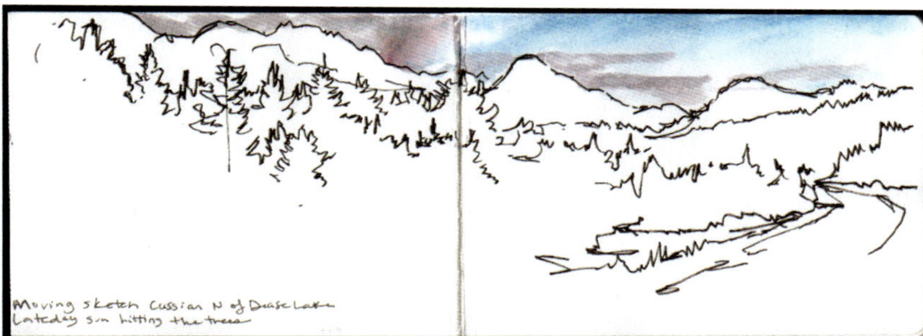

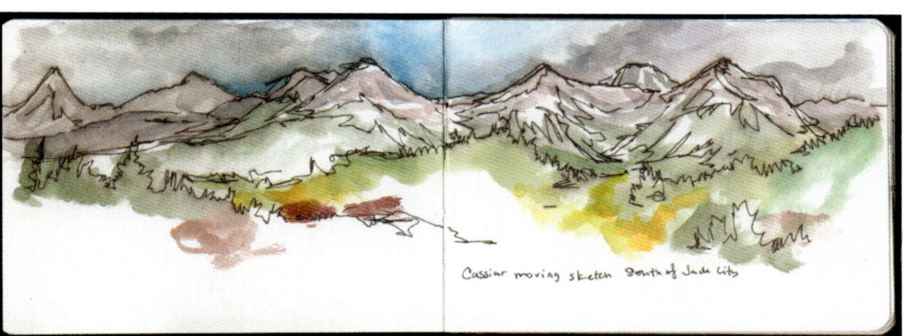

▲ When sketching a landscape, sometimes less is more. I made both of these sketches from the passenger seat of a moving car and only had the chance to sketch part of the scenes. They capture a sense of movement and depth with simple lines and shifts in color.

In addition to the general approach, it is helpful to think through composition, or how you will position things on the page. Looking through a small viewfinder can be helpful, such as a 1-inch square window cut into an index card. You must decide where the horizon line will go in your sketch. Sometimes, you cannot see the horizon because mountains, forests, or buildings may block it, but you can imagine the flat line that you would see if you were looking out over the ocean or a perfectly flat landscape. That line is the area that is the farthest away in your sketch. If you position the horizon line towards the top of your frame, the ground will dominate the sketch. If you position the horizon line towards the bottom of your page, the sky will dominate. We don't usually put anything right in the middle of the paper because it tends to make the composition less dynamic. Still, if you put the horizon line in the middle, it will make the sketch appear more balanced between the sky and the ground. In that situation, I would make the horizon line slightly off-center just to add some interest.

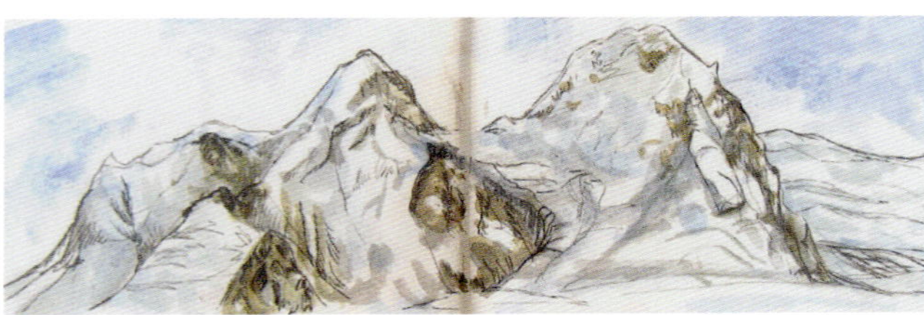

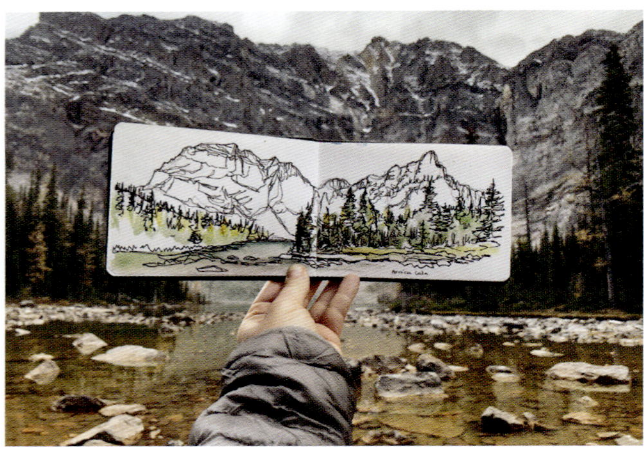

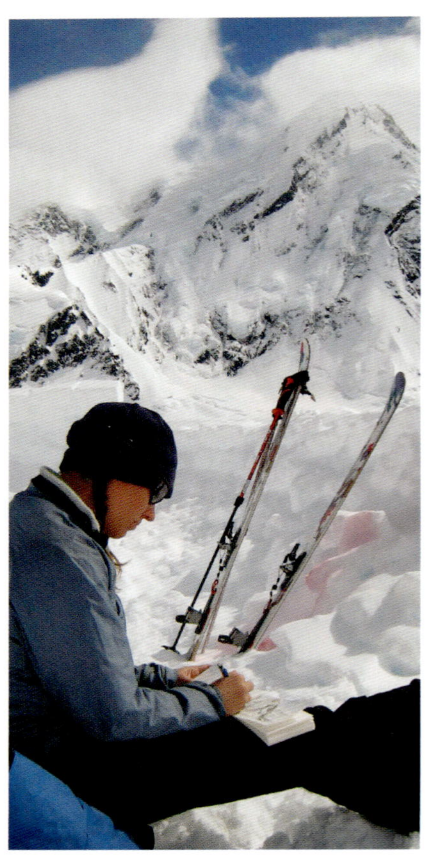

Both of these sketches were made in cold environments where I didn't have a lot of time to sit still. It was important to be able to work in more of a gestural style. In these circumstances, I often color in only a part of the sketch, such as the sky or the foreground, but not both.

Project 18

SKETCHING TREES

We will use a brush pen to build a gesture sketch of the tree while letting the background be washy and loose.

MATERIALS: a pencil, a pen, a brush pen, watercolor paper, and watercolors

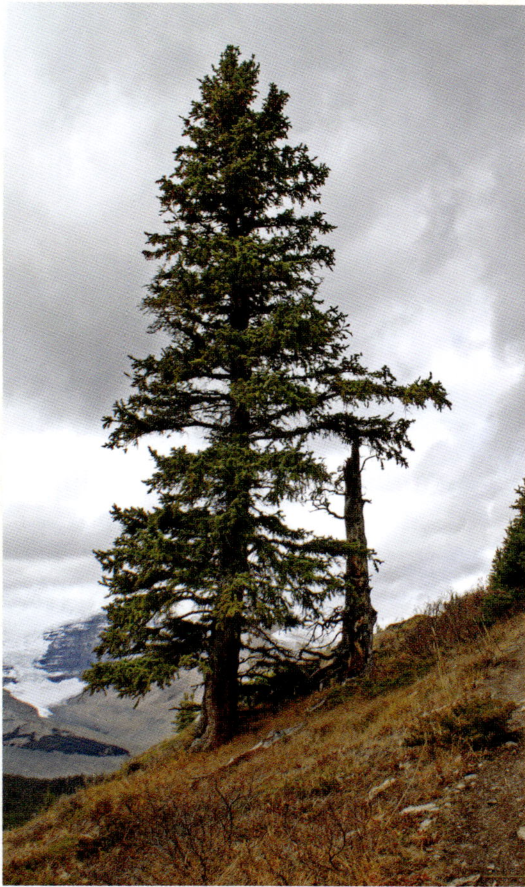

This pair of spruce trees was growing on an exposed hillside. One is almost dead but has a few living branches, and the other stands tall and blows in the wind.

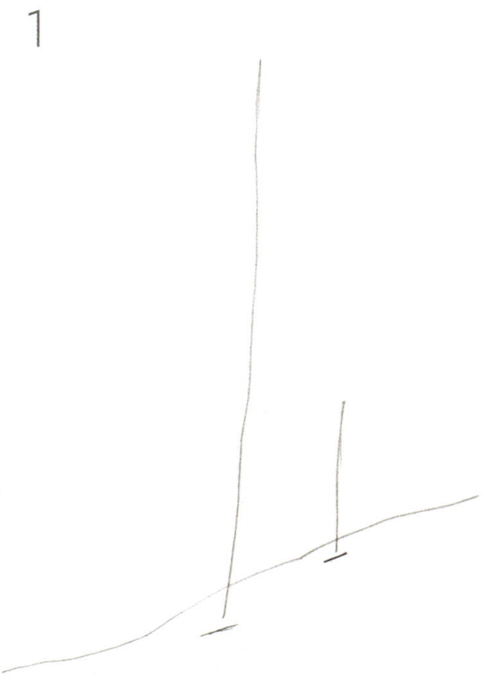

STEP 1: Begin by sketching the basic shapes lightly in pencil. I drew the line where the ground will go and two vertical lines for the trees. I marked where the base of the trees would go and roughly how tall on my paper they would be. I also noted that the dead tree on the right is about one-third the height of the main tree. I chose a composition looking up at the trees, with the ground and horizon line low on the paper. This gives the sense that the trees are growing into the sky, which emphasizes the exposure of their location on the hillside.

2

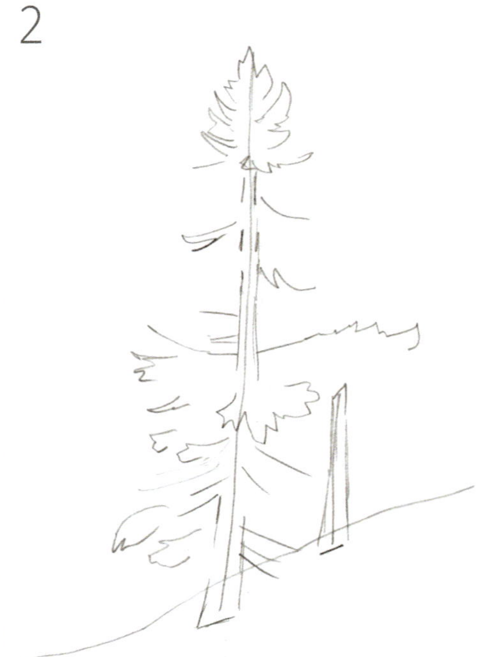

3

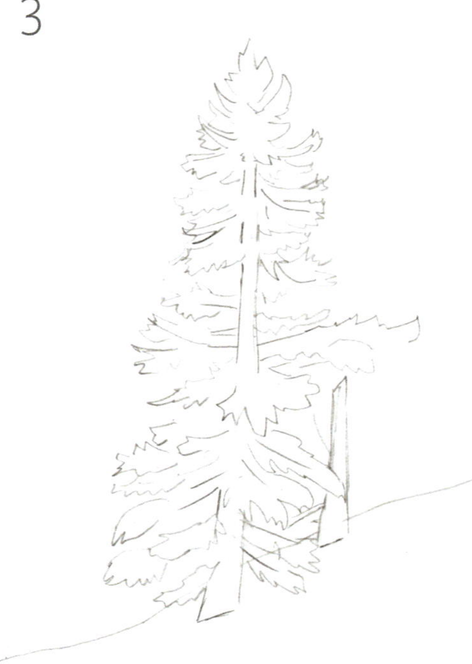

STEP 2: Begin sketching the main branches, limbs, and trunk edges. Where the branches are sparse, draw lines to indicate the main direction in which they are growing. Where there are more needles, I drew zigzag shapes to represent where the bulk of the vegetation will go.

STEP 3: Continue refining the shapes and drawing in the rest of the branches. Instead of drawing each branch, I grouped them where I noticed individual shapes.

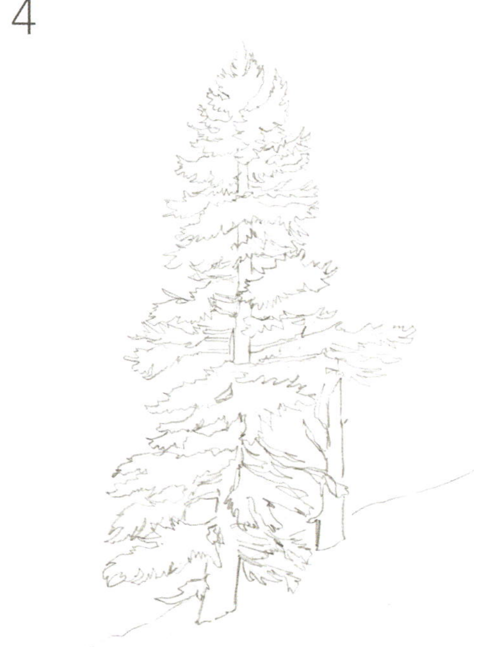

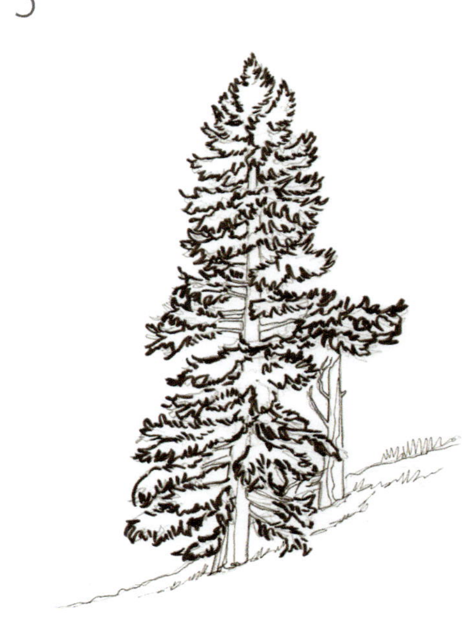

STEP 4: Now that we have drawn a basic map, lighten that sketch with a kneaded eraser and go over it again with a little bit more detail. Practice contour drawing to get the shapes of the boughs, and look to the negative space between branches to capture those shapes. Use the reference photo as a guide and inspiration, but it is OK if you also move or change some of the branches.

STEP 5: Add in pen. I used a fine pen to sketch the trunk, branches, and ground. Then, I used a brush pen to make more expressive marks where the branches and boughs go. I paid attention to my pencil sketch and the different directions the needles pointed as I sketched, changing the direction of my marks accordingly. I was not so interested in achieving precise accuracy as much as the general feeling and movement of the tree.

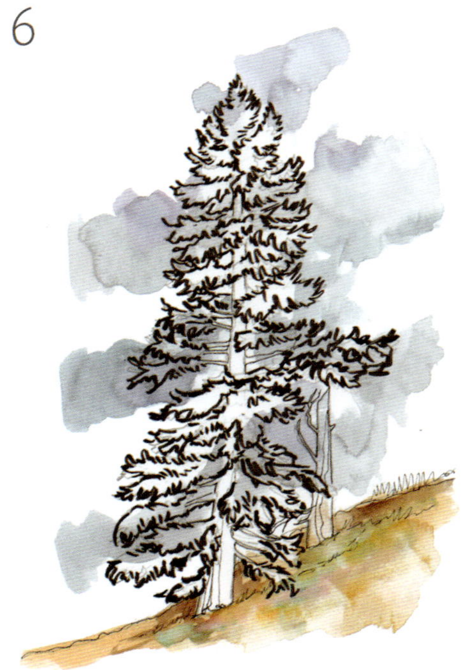

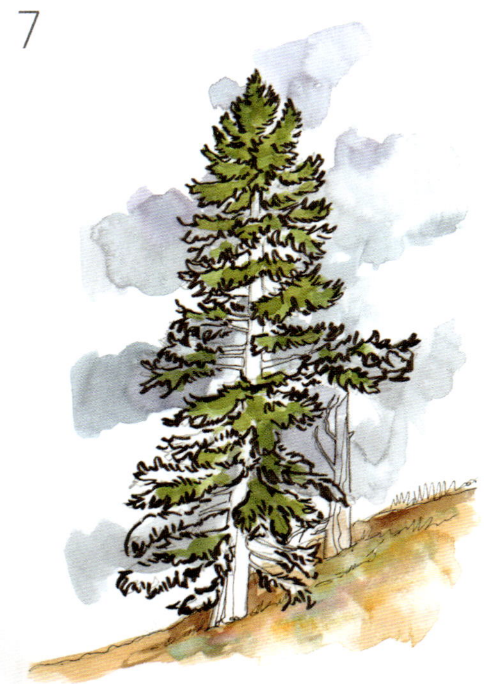

STEP 6: Use watercolor to paint in the background so that it is light and washy. I mixed Burnt Sienna, Quinacridone Gold, and a tiny bit of Quinacridone Rose and Cobalt Teal Blue for the ground and painted in a wash that was wet-in-wet. I wanted a light gray for the sky to get the feel of the cloudy day. Since the tree will be painted darker on top, you can paint right over the branches; you don't have to work around them. I used Cobalt Teal Blue, Ultramarine Blue, Quinacridone Rose, and Burnt Sienna for the background gray. I used a lot of water in both washes and let the pigments separate on the paper.

STEP 7: Once the background wash is dry, mix a warmer green for the tree's boughs. I mixed Sap Green with Quinacridone Gold and painted in some of the lighter branches.

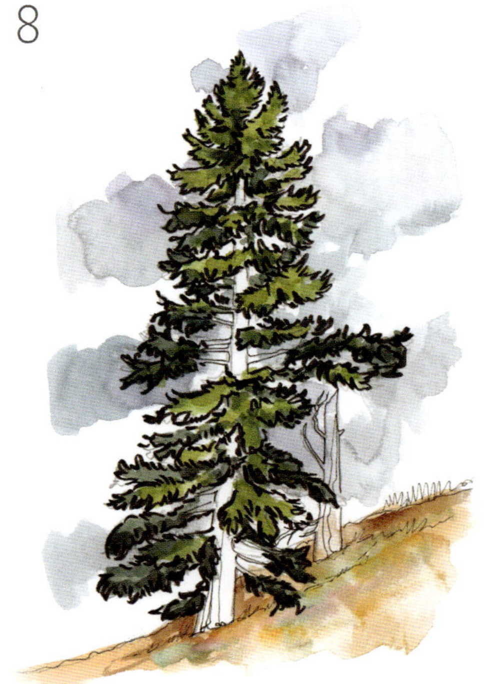

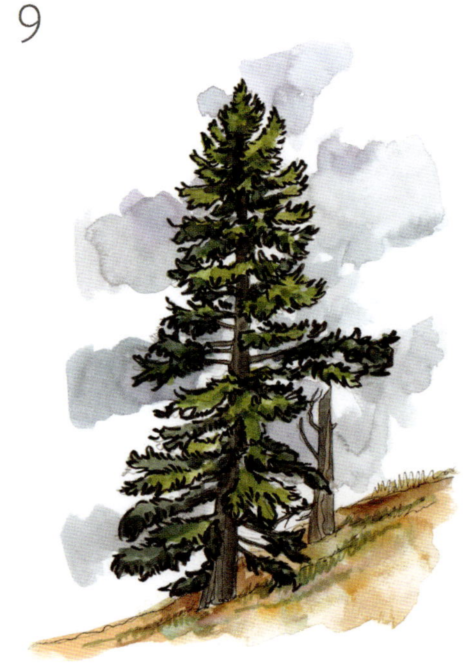

STEP 8: Add layers of shadows to contrast with the warmer green from the previous step. I mixed up a darker green with Sap Green and Indanthrone Blue and layered this over top of the lighter green to paint in some of the darker branches.

STEP 9: Bring the whole sketch together by adding some texture to the ground with the colors you've mixed for the trees. Finally, paint in the tree trunks. I mixed gray-brown with Burnt Sienna and Indanthrone Blue.

Project 19

COLOR AND SPACE: MEADOW

Consider how you can use atmospheric perspective to create the illusion of space. For example, you could make the mountains in the distance cooler and lighter in color and sketch the vegetation in the foreground with the most detail and contrast.

MATERIALS: a pencil, watercolor paper, and watercolors

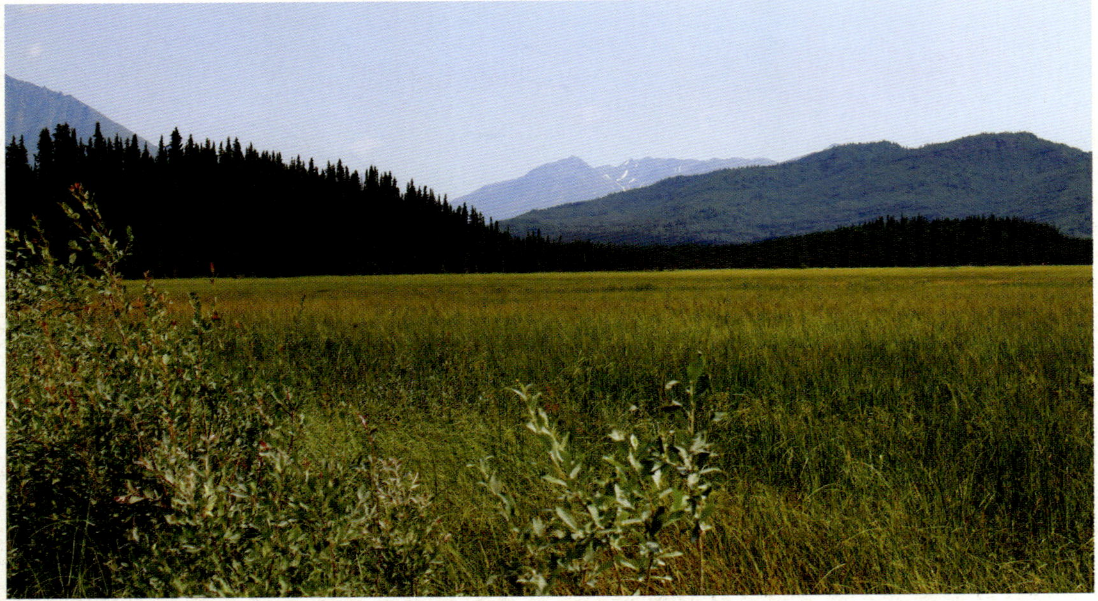

Use color, value, and detail to enhance the illusion of space in this relatively simple scene.

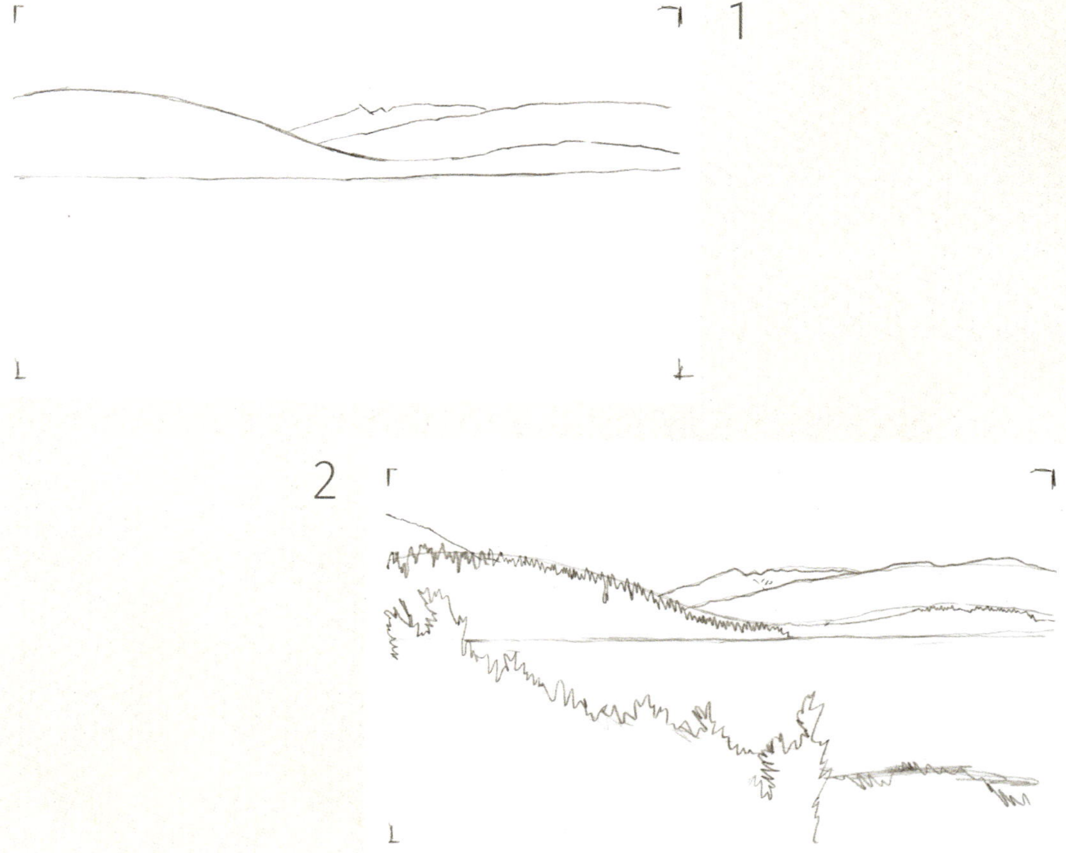

STEP 1: I wanted to make my sketch slightly smaller to force myself to simplify the landscape, so I began by marking the corners of my frame at roughly 4.5 x 7.5 inches. I decided to put my horizon line about two-thirds of the way up the paper and sketched the main shapes of the background. I started with the horizontal, nearly straight line on the far side of the meadow. Then, I sketched the hill of spruce trees and some basic shapes to mark in the mountains in the distance. Instead of drawing each tree, I generalized the shapes with curves and lines.

STEP 2: Continue working on the sketch. I added in some vegetation for the foreground, sketching in a squiggly line along the rough diagonal. I measured how high up in the background the vegetation starts and noticed it stops about two-thirds of the way across the page. I added the jagged edge of the spruce hill and refined the shapes of the mountains. On the lower right part of the image is a golden meadow wetland with some water between the grass, so I lightly marked in that shadow where the water is.

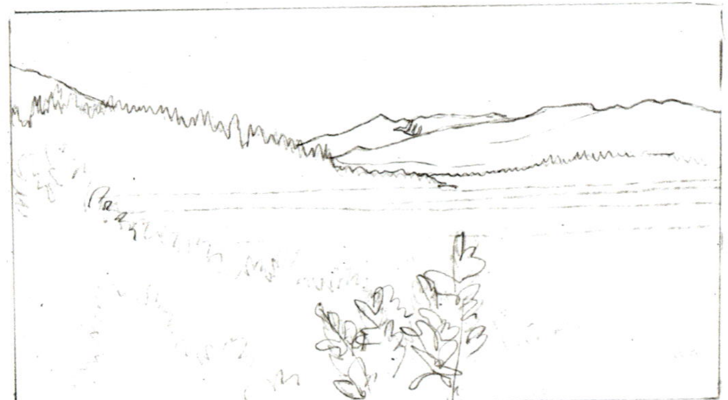

3

4

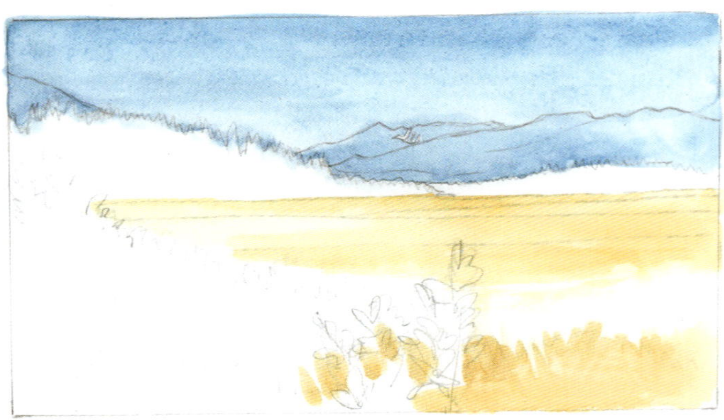

STEP 3: Lighten the lines from the previous step and refine the pencil drawing, adding more layers to the meadow wetland where you notice different colors. Clean up some of the scribbles in the foreground where the vegetation is if you find them distracting.

STEP 4: To get the feeling of space, I wanted to make sure the background is cool in hue to contrast with the gold and bright greens of the meadow and the willows in the foreground. Work from light to dark and build up transparent layers of watercolor. Start with the background and a light wash of Cerulean Blue painted over the sky and the distant mountains. Paint around and leave a few patches of snow on the distant mountain. You can also start painting in some of the foreground. I mixed Quinacridone Gold and water and painted in some of the golden-brown colors of the meadow.

5

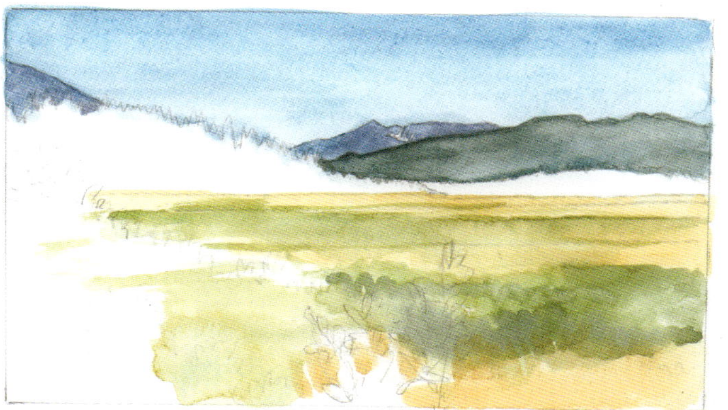

6

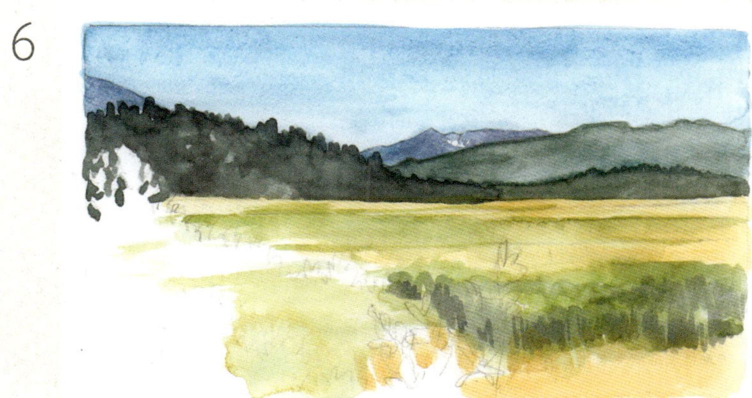

STEP 5: Continue to build in layers. To distinguish the mountains from the sky, I used Ultramarine Blue with a bit of magenta and painted the distant mountains with a glaze of light violet. I mixed that color with some Sap Green and painted the next forested range with that deep green. I also added some of the green to the area where I noticed deep shadows and water in the wetland. I painted some of the brighter green with Sap Green going over the layer of Quinacridone Gold. In each layer, the colors get warmer and more saturated, with bright greens and yellows.

STEP 6: Add some dark mid-tones. I mixed a darker green with Phthalo Turquoise, Sap Green, and a bit of Burnt Umber and painted the spruce trees on the far side of the meadow. I tried to keep my brush marks somewhat blotchy to give them some texture and to distinguish them from the smoother layers in the distance. I also added this deep color and some texture to the darker part of the meadow in the lower right. When the paint dried, I erased the pencil lines from my sketch.

7

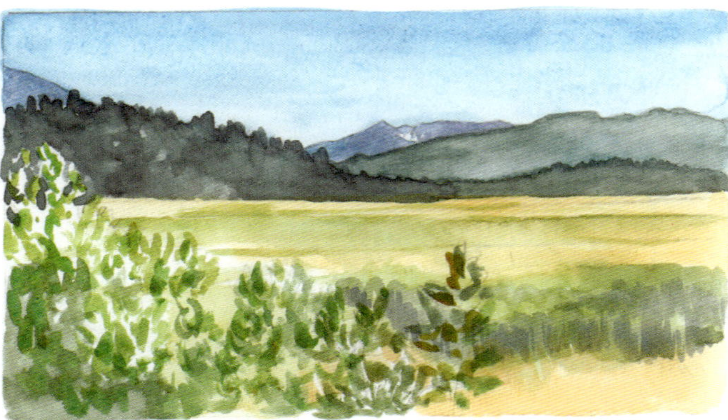

8

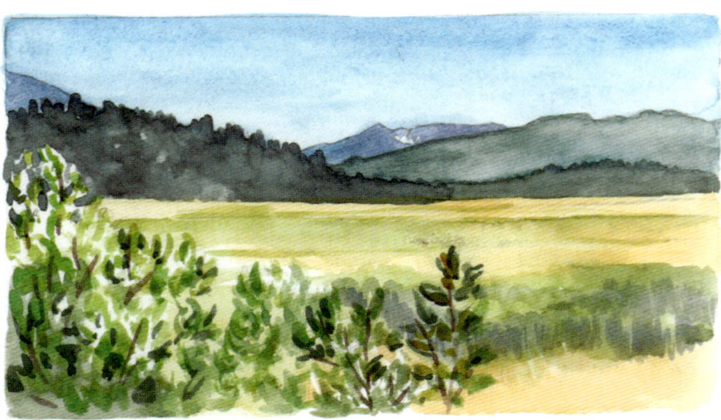

STEP 7: Paint some of the details in the foreground. To help this pop forward, retain some of the white of the paper for the highlights where the sun is hitting some leaves. Also, make sure to keep a good amount of contrast (light next to dark). I used a few different shades of green, mixing Sap Green with Cerulean Blue and Quinacridone Gold.

STEP 8: Add a few high-contrast details to finish the sketch. I added some shadows to the leaves in the foreground and branches to the willow bushes with some broken lines of Raw Umber.

Project 20

LANDSCAPE GESTURE SKETCH OF SUNSET AND LAKE

Work with brush pen and wet-in-wet watercolor to capture the colors and the reflection of a brief sunset over a lake.

MATERIALS: a pencil, a brush pen, watercolor paper, and watercolors

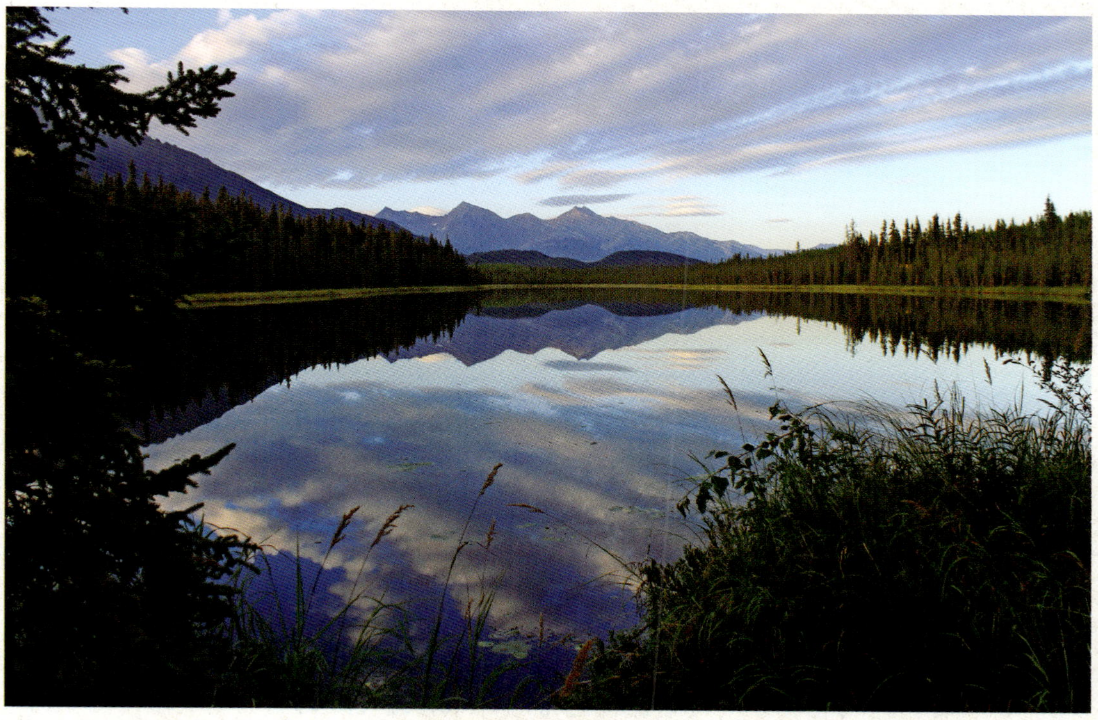

Since the colors in the sunset change quickly, we will use some approaches such as gesture sketching to try to make this sketch quickly.

STEP 1: I decided to focus my sketch on the lake and the sunset and ignore the silhouetted elements in the foreground (the spruce tree and the grass) for now. I can add those at the end with a brush pen or dark watercolor. I liked the balance between the sky and the reflection in the lake, so I put my horizon line and the far shore of the lake slightly off-center on my page. Sketch the main shapes in the landscape with a pencil. I started with the shoreline on the far side of the lake. Then I moved up and down from that reference line to sketch in the trees and the mountains. The reflection in the water mirrors what is seen above but is at a slightly different angle than the photo was taken. This is most noticeable when looking at the clouds, which we see from a different angle in the water than in the sky.

STEP 2: Roughly sketch the clouds in the sky. I focused on the main shape and direction of the clouds. Since this was a quick gesture sketch, I was not too worried about things being perfectly accurate, but I wanted to capture some of the essence of the colors in the sky.

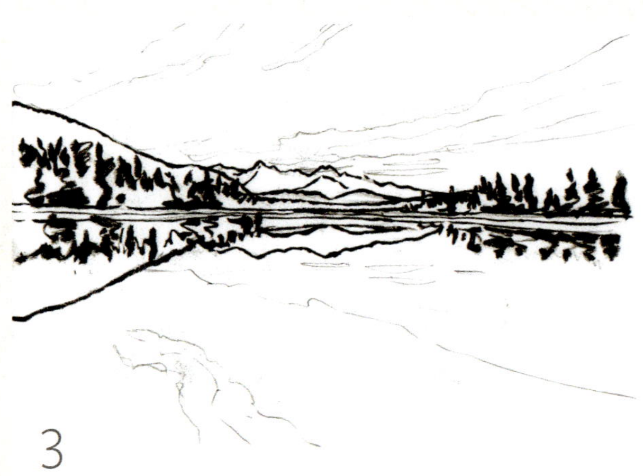

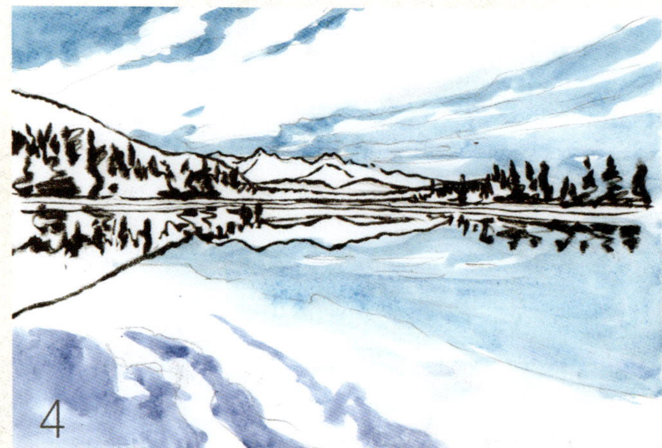

STEP 3: Draw over the land and trees using a brush pen. I used a bigger brush pen to get a variety of marks, using the thin tip and light pressure to get some fine lines on the mountains in the background and more pressure and directional marks to draw in the spruce trees on the lakeshore.

STEP 4: Make sure the ink dries from the previous step, then start painting some of the blue for the sky and its reflection. I used Cerulean Blue for the sky and painted around the placement of the clouds, paying attention to the negative space in the sky. I did the same on the bottom of the reflection but also used some Ultramarine Blue to deepen the blues at the bottom of the paper, since I noticed that the colors in the reflection were a bit deeper and cooler in color.

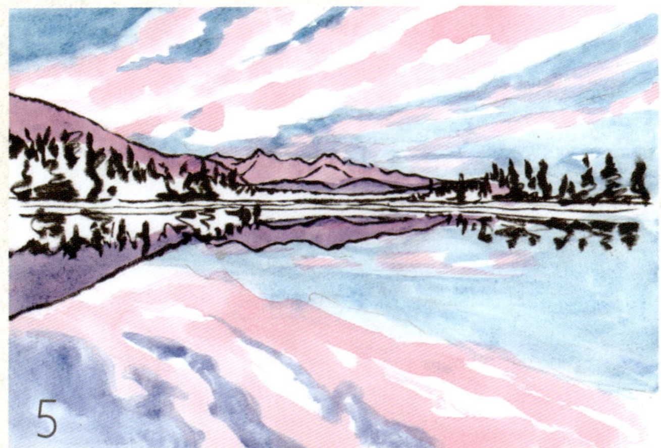

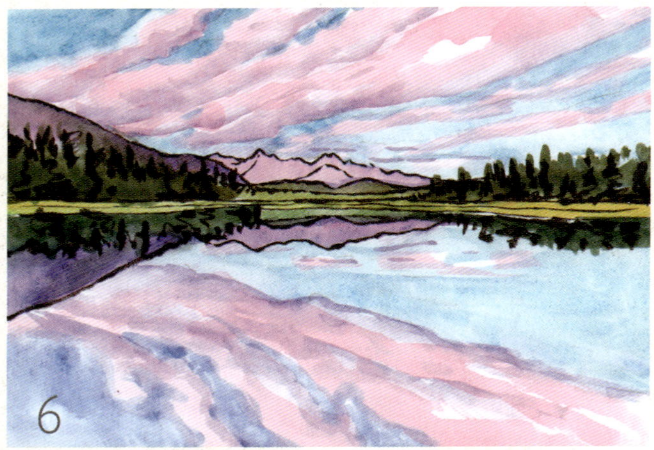

STEP 5: Add some pink to the sky. I mixed Quinacridone Rose with water and painted in some of the pink in the sky. I worked with a lot of water and let the pink overlap with the blue in some places to make violet tones. I also mixed Quinacridone Rose with Ultramarine Blue to make some violet washes for the mountains. I noticed that the hills closer to the lake are darker, and so is their reflection, so I used more blue in those areas.

STEP 6: Using the same violet from the previous step, add some shadows to the clouds in the sky and the sky reflection. Also, add some of the greens. I mixed Quinacridone Gold with Ultramarine Blue and Cerulean Blue to create some different greens for the land. I noticed that the green for the spruce trees is more purple, so I used the Ultramarine Blue and put more gold where the grass grows along the lakeshore.

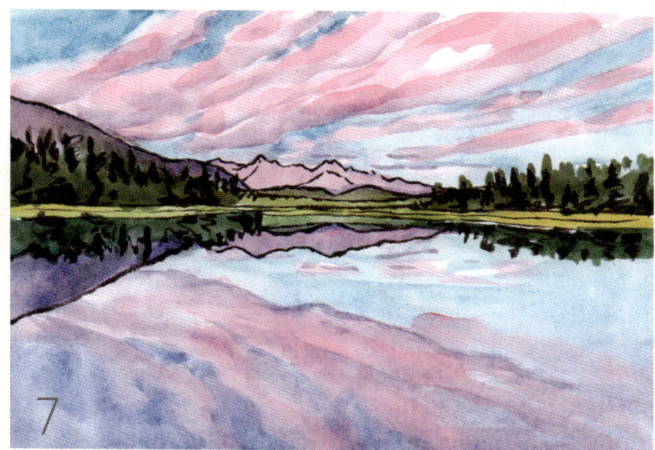

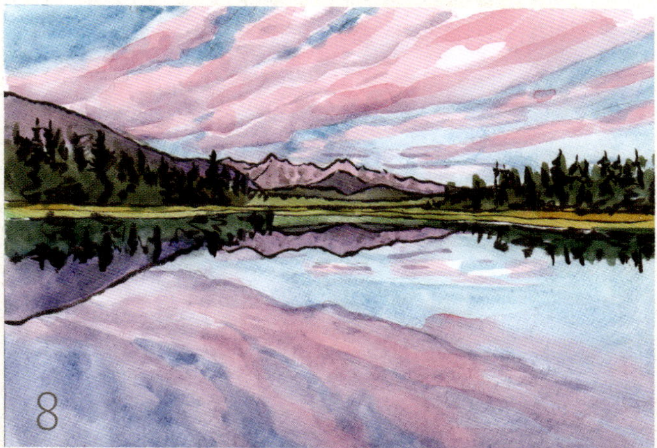

STEP 7: To add some texture and variation to the clouds in the sky, I added another layer of pink. I mixed Quinacridone Rose with a little bit of Ultramarine Blue. I also made a wash of Ultramarine Blue and glazed this along the reflection on the bottom of the page, creating a graded wash that gets lighter towards the shoreline. This deepened the color and shade of the reflection.

STEP 8: Include some last details by adding more pen to the spruce trees on the lakeshore. Mix a light brown to add some of the rocks in the mountains in the distance. I decided not to add the tree or the grass from the photo, but you can try that and see how it changes the sketch. My sketch exaggerates the pink colors from the photo. Still, I often find that photos tone these colors down from what I experience, so one thing I enjoy about sketching sunsets is getting to use the most vibrant colors to try to capture the experience.

Project 21

MEDITATIVE SKETCHING: K'ESUGI RIDGE

Use contour drawing to break down and feel your way through this complicated landscape of Denali, the tallest mountain in North America, as seen from a beautiful tundra on K'esugi Ridge.

MATERIALS: a pencil, a pen, watercolor paper, and watercolors

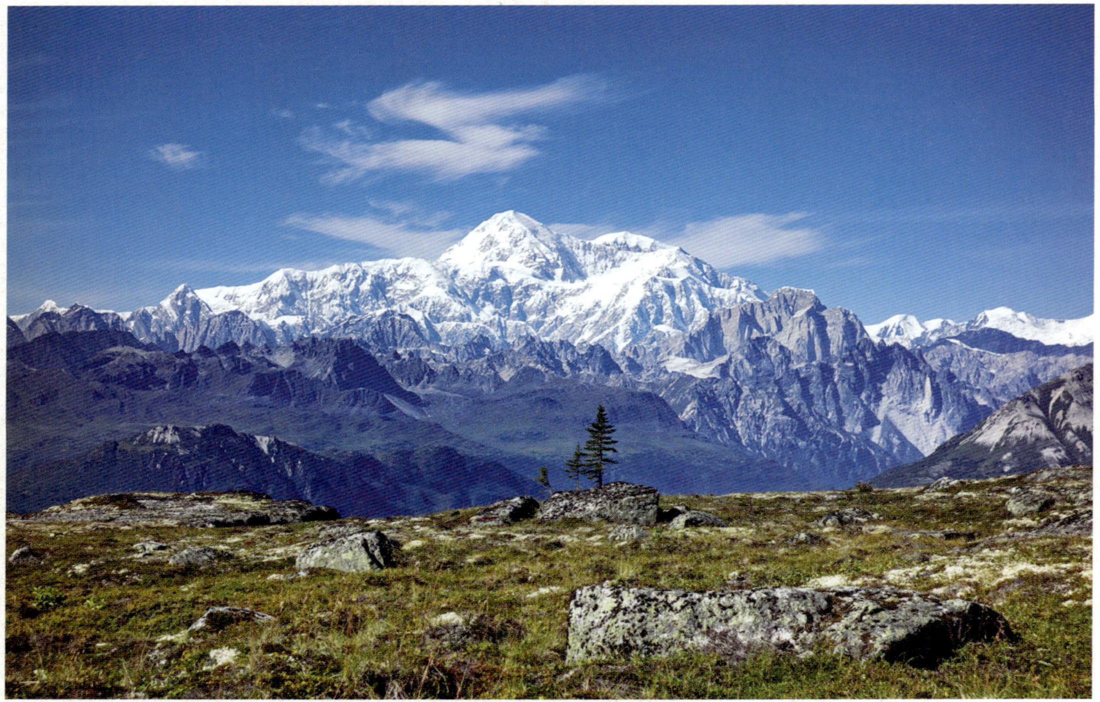

This view has many layers to the landscape and can feel overwhelming when we start looking closely at all the rock faces and glaciers, but we will use meditative sketching to try to break it down and enjoy the process.

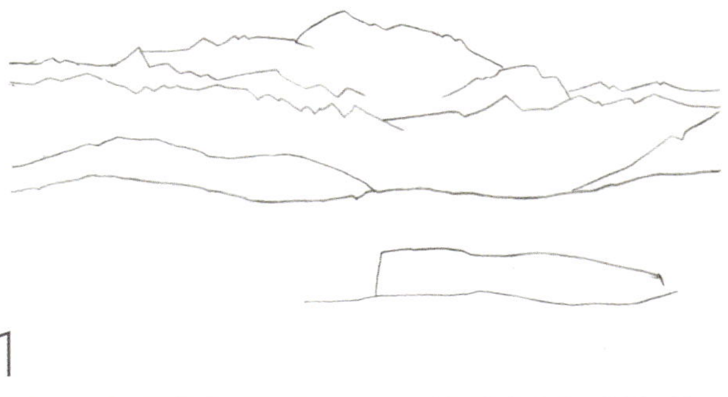

1

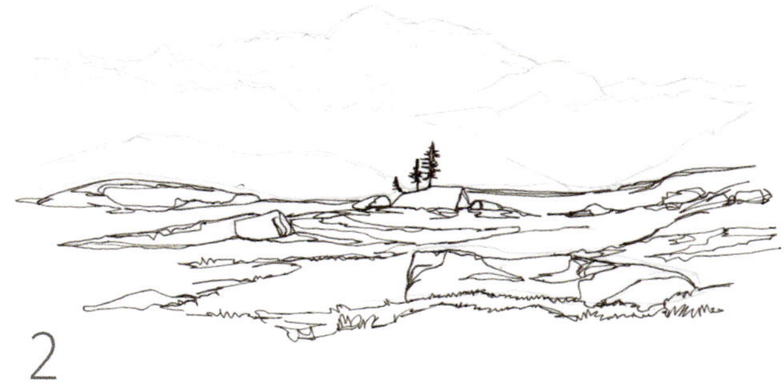

2

STEP 1: Squint your eyes at the landscape and separate things into a few different layers or strips. I see the white mountain, Denali, in the background and the bright green, rocky tundra ridge in the foreground. There are a series of vegetated and rocky ridges between the white mountain and the foreground, but when I squint my eyes, I can separate those into two chunks: the blue-green of the forested mountains and the light gray of the rock. I am going to ignore most of the shadows on the landscape so that I can focus on the structure and the layers. Because the landscape is quite complex, I started sketching some of these areas with pencil. You could skip this step and begin with a looser contour drawing without worrying about how accurate or precise your sketch is. Accuracy is only sometimes the main goal.

STEP 2: Return with a light pencil and add another layer of detail to the landscape. We can draw over this with a pen, so it is OK if it ends up being messy. Once you feel good about your pencil drawing (if you decide to make one), start the contour drawing in the foreground with a waterproof pen. Try to keep the pen moving slowly and draw lines to describe how different parts of the landscape are connected, drawing in some of the rocks, the clumps of vegetation, and the three small spruce trees in the middle.

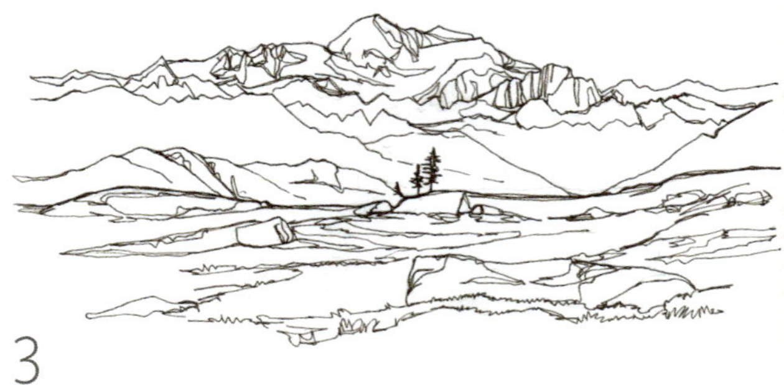

3

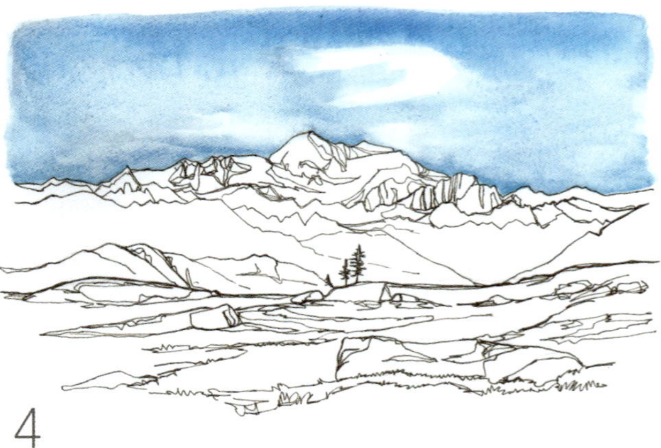

4

STEP 3: Use the same pen and contour drawing method to sketch in the mountains. I am most interested in the tundra in the foreground and the rocks and glaciers that are farthest away, so I decided to skip some of the details in the middle ground and sketch the main shapes of the different ridges. When I got to the last range of mountains and Denali, I added more lines and shapes using my pen to feel my way along the faces, sketching in the glacier's slope or steep, rocky cliffs. I call this meditative sketching because contour drawing is meditative for me.

Another tool for meditative drawing is to switch back and forth between line drawing and writing things down. You can write about the landscape, your feelings, or anything else.

STEP 4: Once the pen is dry, begin painting, starting with the lightest values farthest away. I used Cerulean Blue for the sky, leaving the wash lighter toward the horizon and working around one area where I wanted to include a cloud.

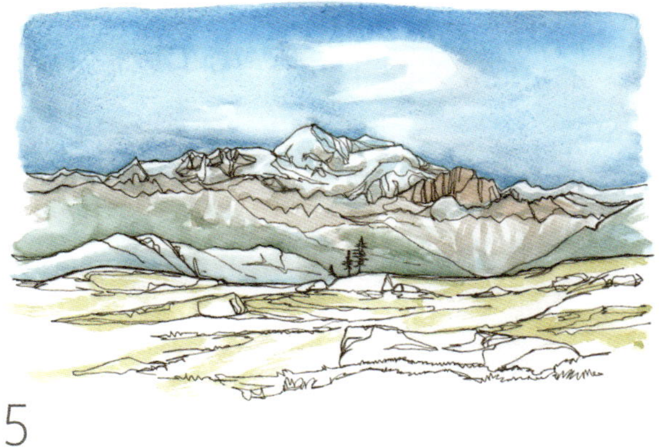

5

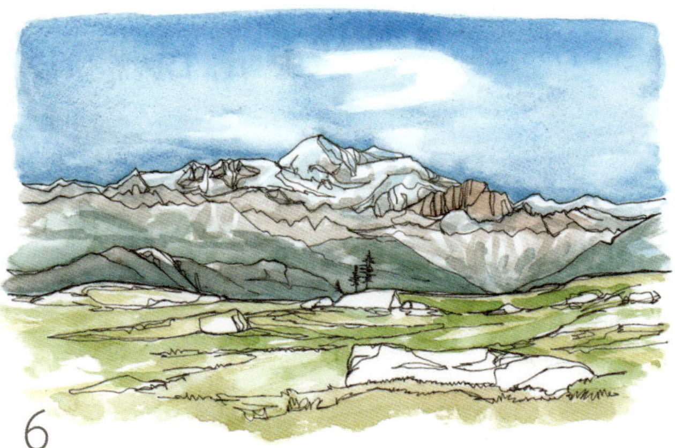

6

STEP 5: Color in the main areas of land, which we noticed when we were squinting our eyes at the landscape in the first step. Use some very light blue for the glaciers. I mixed Cerulean Blue and Burnt Sienna to get the brownish gray for the rocks. I added some Quinacridone Gold to that mixture to get the blue-gray for the mountains. I used Quinacridone Gold and Cerulean Blue to sketch in some bright green for the tundra in the foreground.

STEP 6: Now that the main sections of the landscape are defined, add more greens. I painted in more blue-green to the middle ground and some mid-tone greens using Sap Green for the tundra foreground. I want the greens that are close to be warmer and have more yellow in them so that they will feel brighter and pop forward from the blue-green in the middle ground.

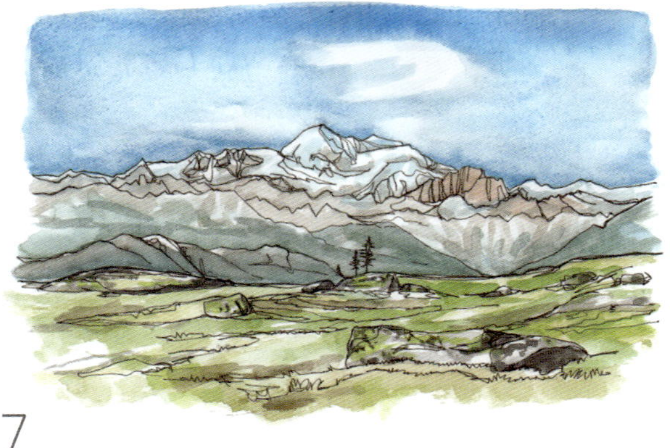

7

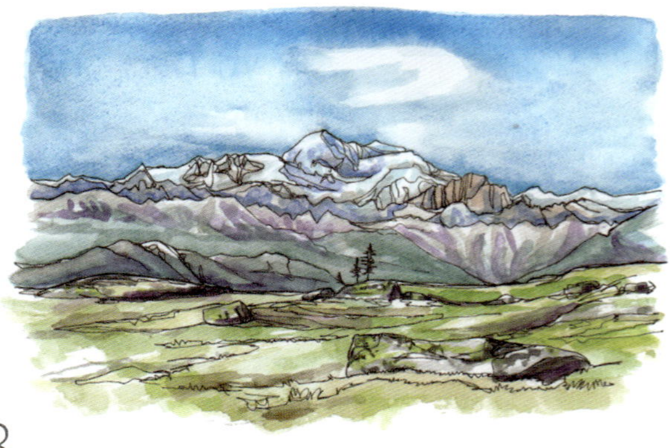

8

STEP 7: To add more detail and help the foreground pop forward, I painted some details and dark shadows. I mixed Indanthrone Blue and Burnt Umber to make a slate gray shadow color. I painted this where I noticed some shadows on the rocks, increasing the contrast in the foreground. I also painted some lichen and texture on the rocks. I lightened that wash with water and added in some shadows, showing how the tundra rolls.

STEP 8: The last step is to paint shadows across the landscape. I used Ultramarine Blue and Quinacridone Rose to make a violet for the foreground and the middle ground. In the background, I used Ultramarine Blue to cool the colors down and help things recede. The shadows separate the ridges from each other and help define which layer is in front.

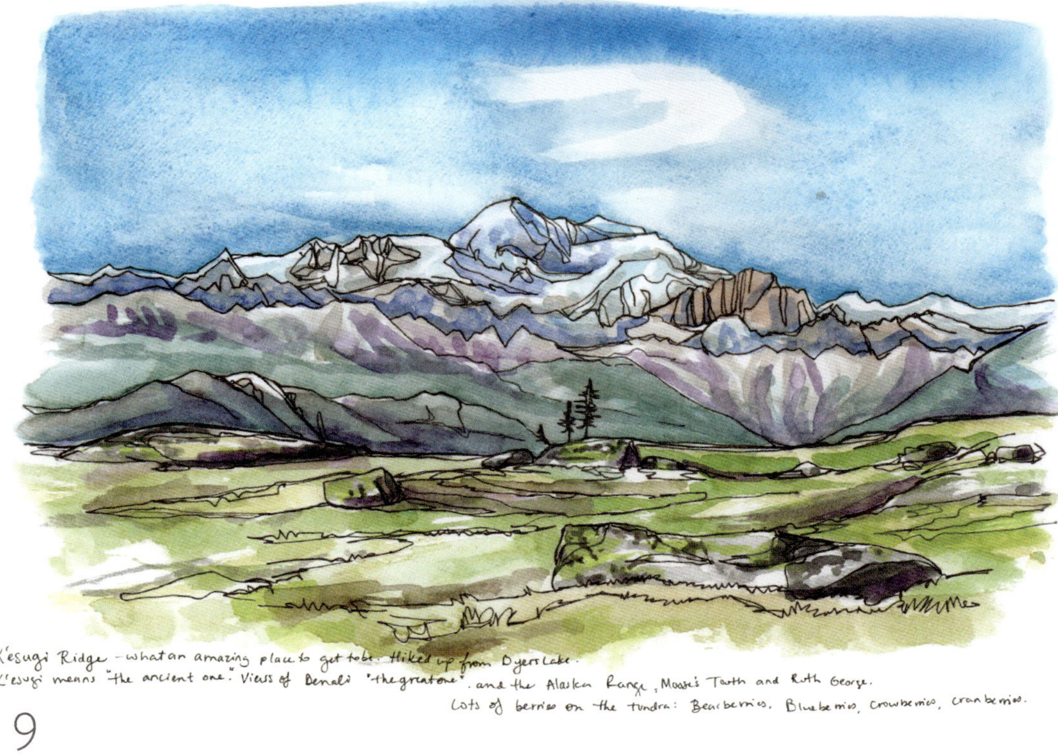

STEP 9: Add a few notes or a sentence or two about what you were thinking about while sketching. You can do this at any point in the sketching process and work back and forth between writing and drawing.

DEASE LAKE

Driving south through British Columbia on our way out of Alaska, we pulled off the Cassiar Highway down a rutted gravel road with a hairpin turn and a steep grade. There was a tree across the road, but we could skirt around it. We wondered if this was the right road and if it would deteriorate more. The whole Cassiar Highway felt that way. There is no center line and very few signs. Phone service was gone within the first 5 miles. In the first section, we drove through an extensive wildfire burn where there was scarcely a living thing. All the trees were charred, standing black sticks. The soil was black and red mud. We felt like we were entering a death zone. Looking back, we wish we had stopped to take in the apocalyptic landscape, but I think we were too unnerved.

Then, the landscape was filled with forest, and a series of green and rocky mountains came into view. It was late afternoon. No one was there. It was mid-October, and we were racing winter by driving south. Everyone else had left months ago. Down the dirt road, we got to a sign for "Sawmill Point," marking a user-maintained campground with six gravel spots with fire pits and picnic tables. There was no one there either. We were in a forest of giant hemlock and spruce trees leading out to the gray gravel shore of Dease Lake. The lake was long and skinny, with clear, gorgeous water and soft waves lapping against the rocks. It took us a while to decide if we wanted to stay there, just because the arrival felt so stark. Eventually, the place slowly welcomed us. We set up the tent. We let the dog wander.

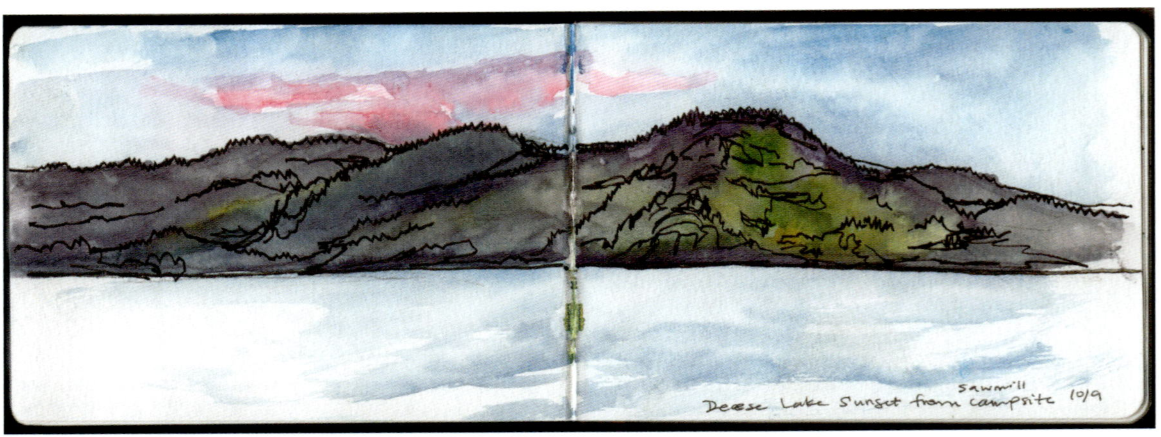

Sunset sketch made at Dease Lake with watercolor and pen

We settled into the loneliness there, and I took my sketchbook down the lakeshore. The sun was going down fast. I captured one magenta cloud resting on the ridgeline of the far shore before it disappeared. Across the lake, the ridge quickly fell into shadow, but you could see where a glacier traveled some lifetimes ago and where some aspens still hung onto their golden leaves between the evergreens and the cliffs. The sketch was quick. I worked with greens and purples in a wet wash where the shadows ran with their own life. It was getting cold and dark, but it allowed me to be there and take in a moment of change as the light went down.

Reflection

Review the landscape sketches from this chapter and the next and consider composition. How does moving the horizon line change how the sketch feels? What kind of composition are you most drawn to? Rework one of the photo references from this book to move things around and tell a different story.

10 More Approaches for Sketching Landscapes

A person can find anything if he takes the time—that is, if he can afford to look. And while he's looking, he's free, and he finds things he never expected.

—TOVE JANSSON

Alaska is a vast state with many different types of environments. Being farther north means the tree line is lower, and we can often see into the distance for miles and miles of jumbled rock, tundra ridges, and jagged mountains. In this chapter, we will go over a few more approaches to breaking down complicated vistas. One tool I use often is looking through a grid to help simplify a composition. Changing the scale

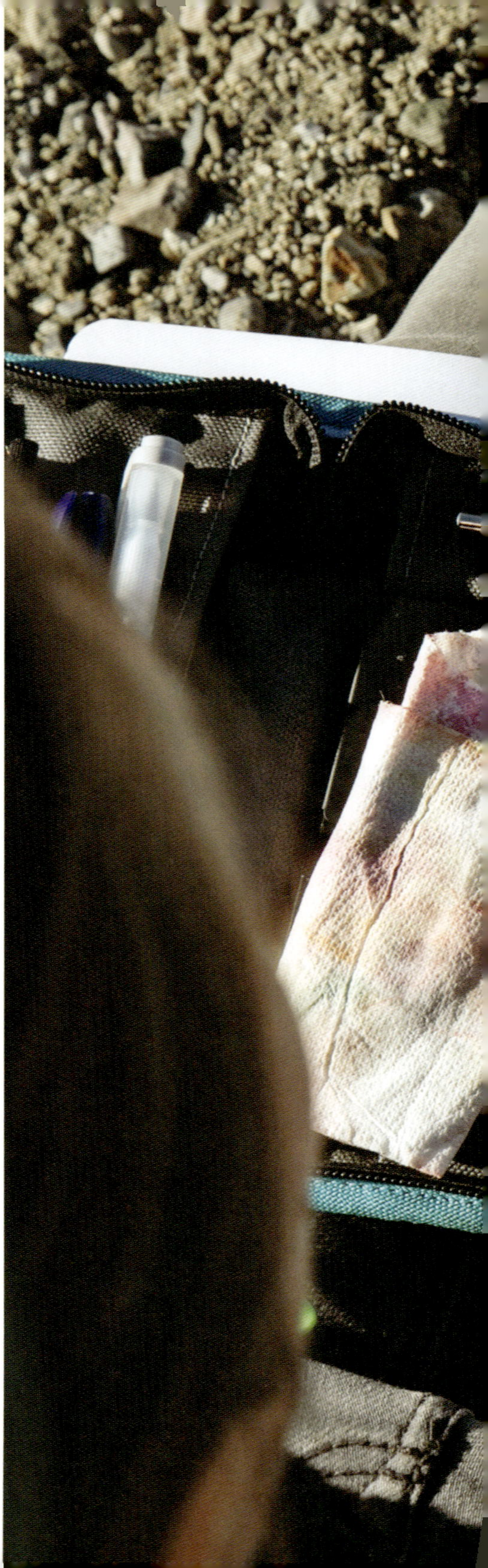

► You can see the grid lines on this sketchbook page that I used to draw the complicated overlapping mountains in the composition. Working with a grid helped me break things down, square by square.

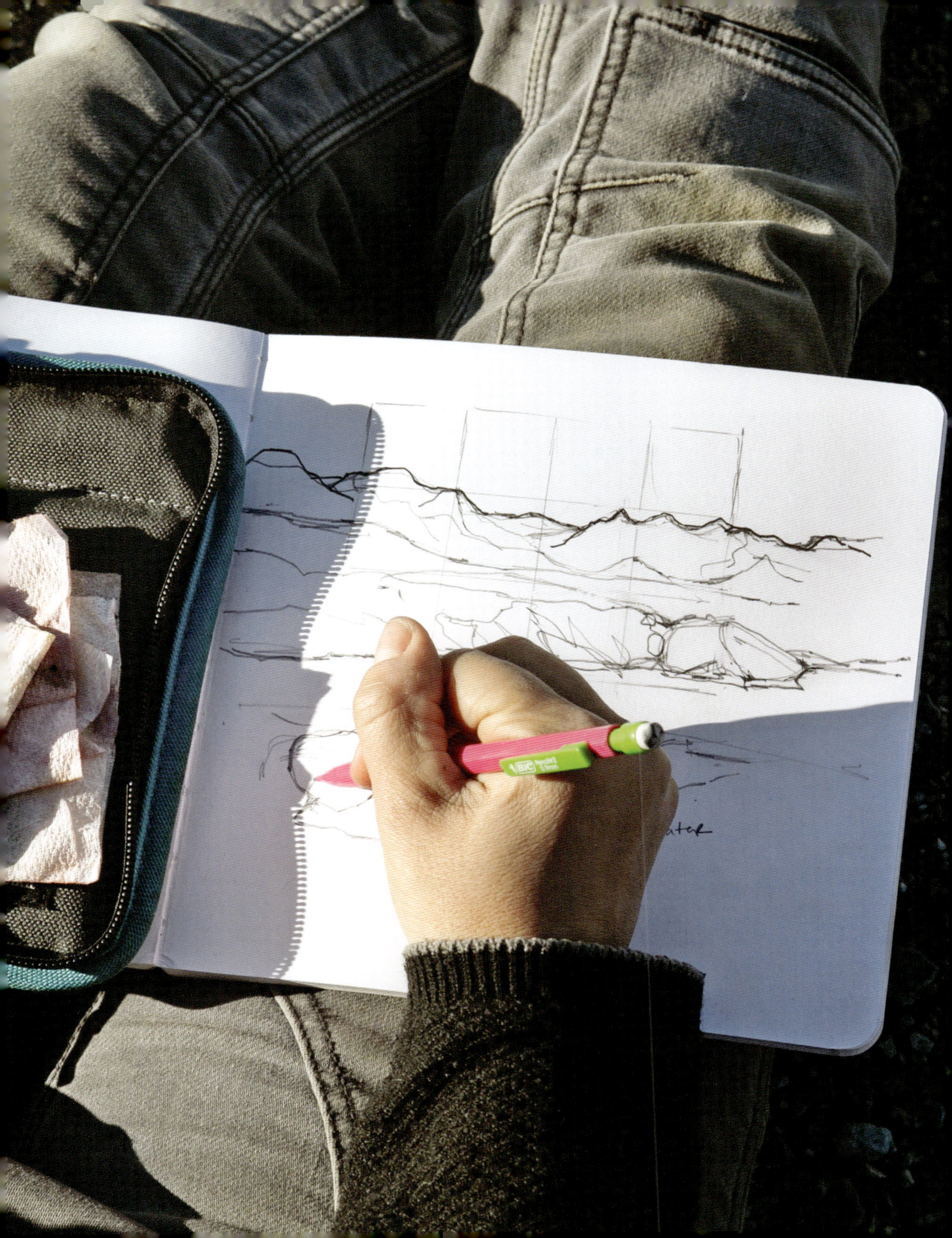
BIC

and emphasizing something small in the foreground can also be useful for creating a sense of focus. Another strategy is to use the color of the paper to help capture some of the information in a scene. Finally, we'll look at moving water and try to notice the shapes we see there. The projects in this chapter explore glaciers and arctic and alpine tundra, some of Alaska's most remarkable landscapes. I'm excited to take you along with me.

WORKING WITH A GRID

Using a grid to break down the landscape and transfer it with the correct scale and proportions can be helpful. Observing square by square can be easier than sketching the whole landscape at once. You can buy or make your grid by drawing or printing on transparent paper. To use a grid, look through your grid window and draw a grid of the same proportions in your sketchbook. The two grids can be different sizes; they are a great tool to enlarge a drawing, and I'll often use a grid to transfer a drawing for a mural. They are also great for sketching a small drawing. Looking through the grid window, match up one part of the grid with one part of the landscape so that you can hold the grid still while looking through it. I usually have the grid at arm's length to keep the distance stable and squint one eye, then I sketch square by square, using the grid lines for reference. When you go back to looking through the grid window, make sure to line it up in the same place and hold it at arm's length again. This takes some practice, but it does help! Continue to sketch the main elements square by square until you have enough information.

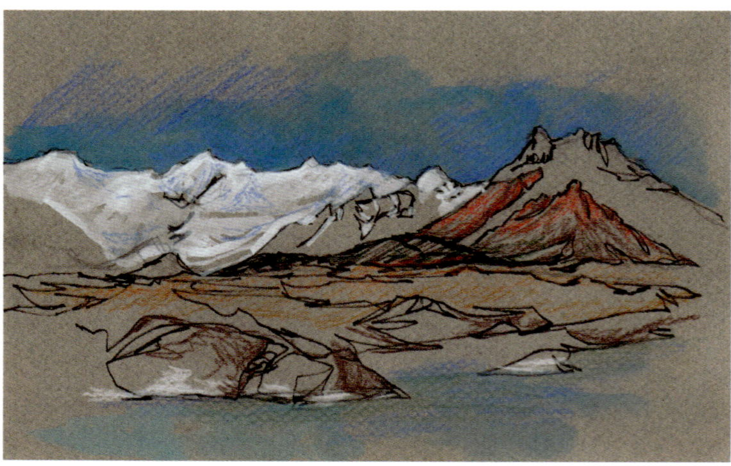

I sketched this view from the toe of the Kennicott Glacier on toned paper using white gouache, watercolor, and colored pencil.

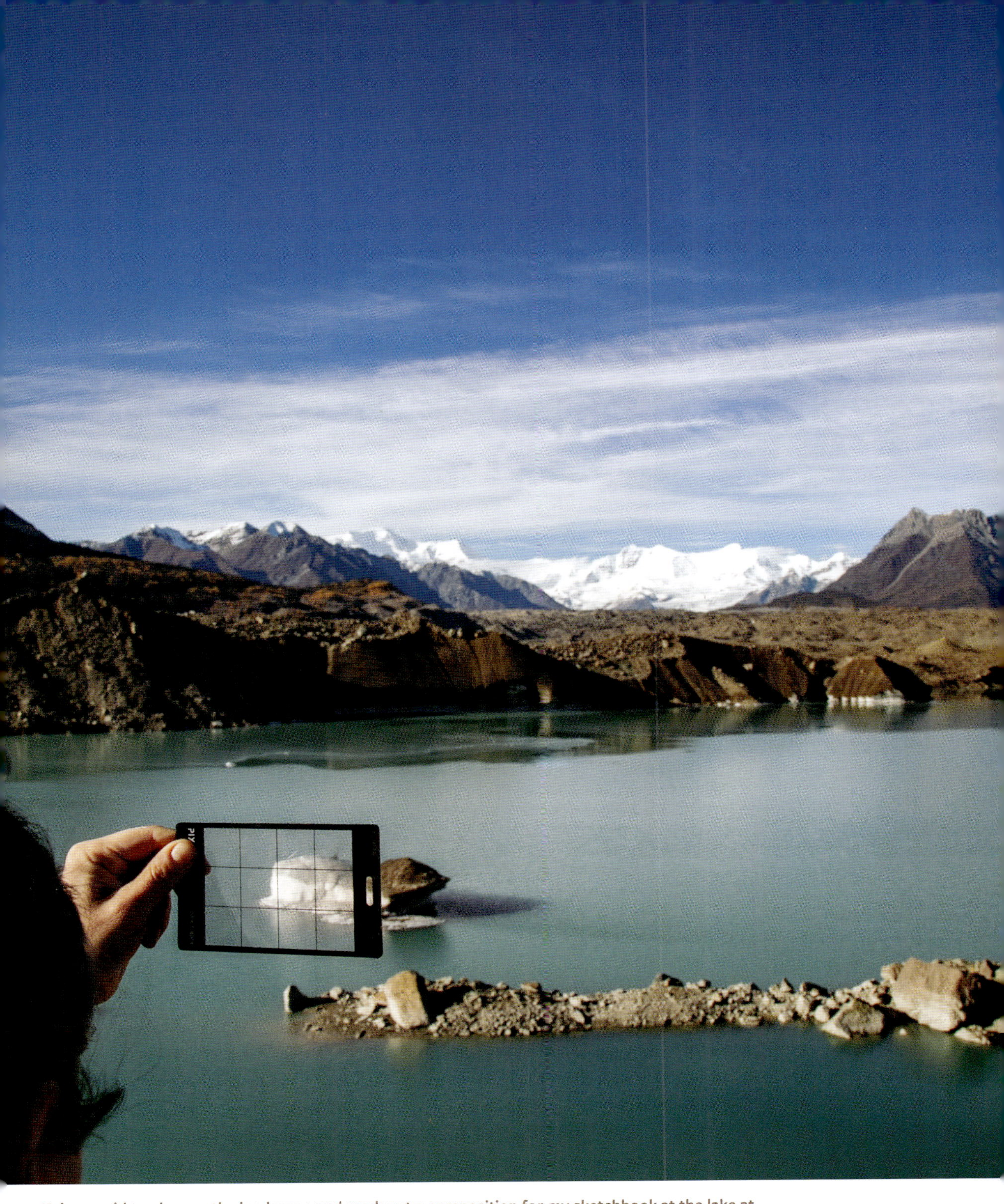

Using a grid to observe the landscape and work out a composition for my sketchbook at the lake at the toe of the Kennicott Glacier

Project 22

WORKING WITH A GRID: GLACIER LAKE

In this example, we will use a 3 x 4 grid on a photo so we don't need to line up our grid each time, like we would if we were out in the landscape. The grid will create a framework for breaking down the complex landscape.

MATERIALS: a pencil, a ruler, a pen, watercolor paper, and watercolors

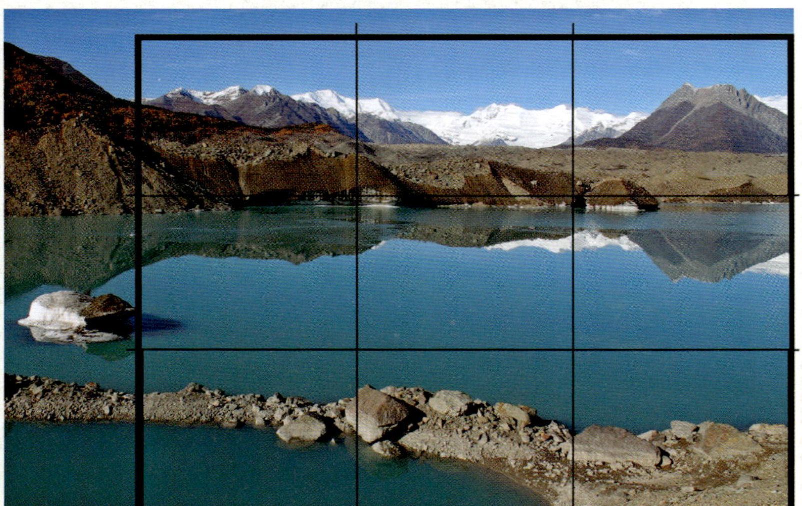

One of my favorite places to take sketching workshops is this lake at the toe of the Kennicott Glacier, surrounded by moraine (a mass of rocks and sediments deposited by a glacier). The landscape is unique and dynamic, and we often hear rocks falling into the water while the glacier melts around us.

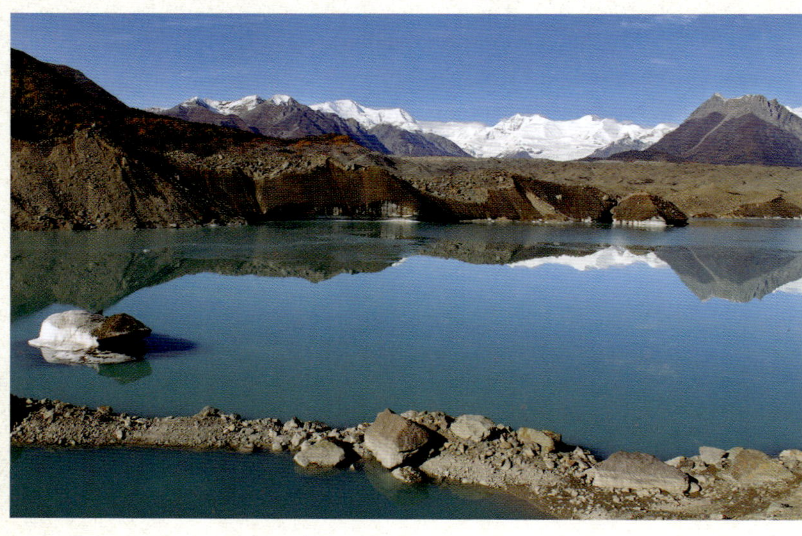

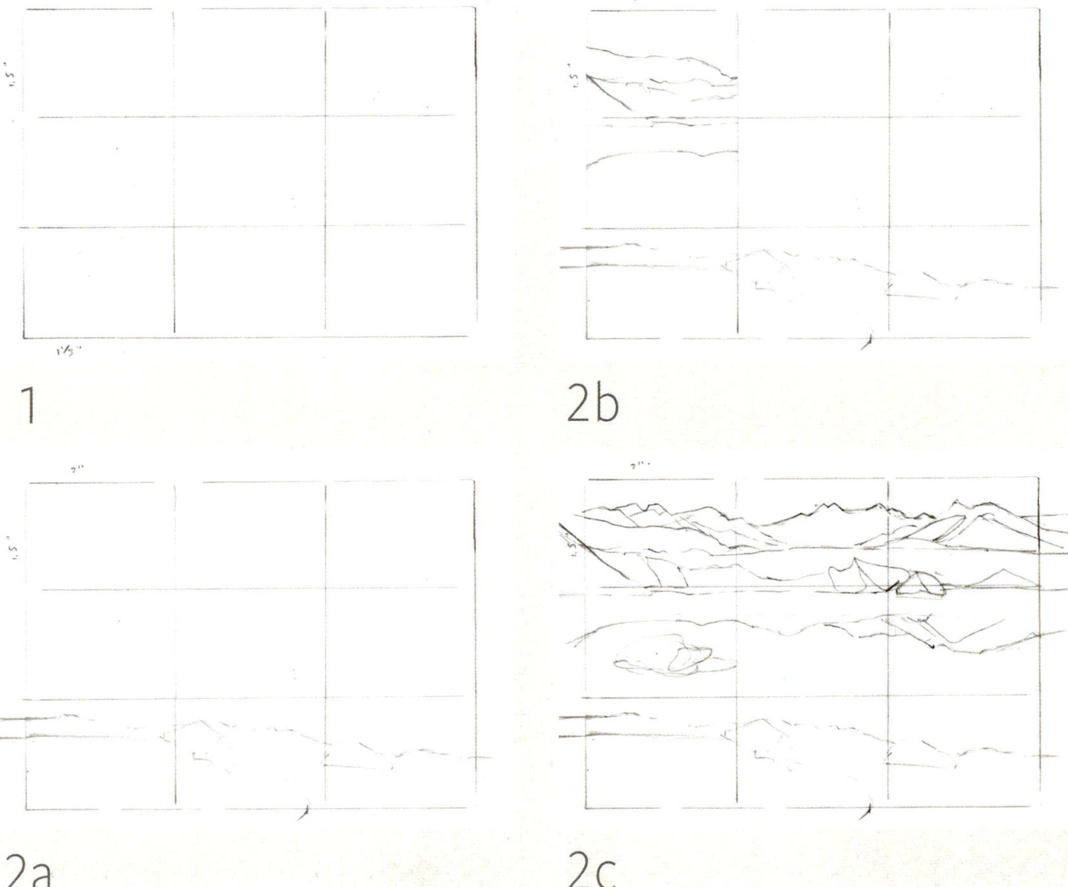

STEP 1: Draw a grid with the same proportions as the one in the photo reference. I drew a grid that is 4½ inches tall by 6 inches wide, with each rectangle or section being 1½ x 2 inches. You can make your own grid with a 3:4 ratio and divide each section into thirds.

STEP 2: Work from the grid in the photo, observing rectangle by rectangle, to draw in the main elements of the landscape. I started with the bottom left rectangle and the rocks in the foreground to draw in that shape that juts out into the lake.

Next I drew in the lakeshore, the moraine along the lakeshore, and the reflection. I decided to include the iceberg, even though that was outside my photo, so I added that to the middle-left rectangle. The mountains in the distance were the most complicated, but I worked on the main shapes first, erased them, and refined the ridges, again going square by square. At the end of this step, I had an accurate map of my landscape, which will be very helpful to paint from.

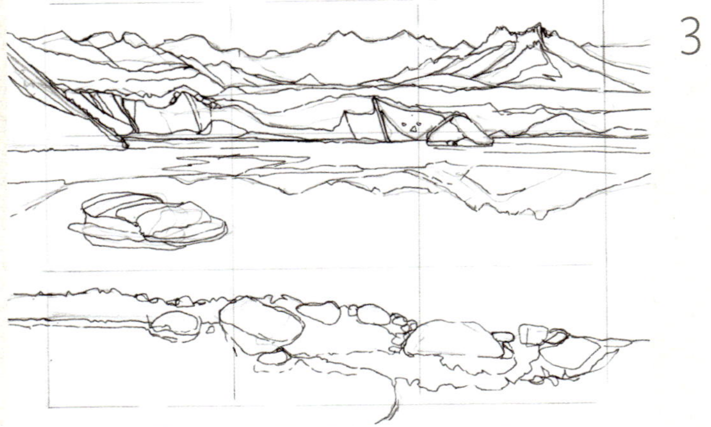

3

4

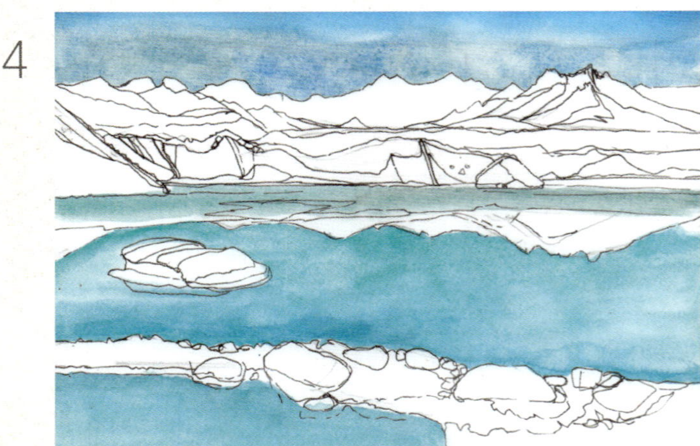

STEP 3: Go over the pencil lines with a pen. Refine and change things if you notice that some details are slightly off. Add some more texture and detail to some areas. Continue to use the grid if it is helpful to work square by square.

STEP 4: Once the pen dries, erase the pencil grid lines to clean up the image. Then, we are ready to paint, starting with the sky because it is the farthest away. Mix Cerulean Blue for the sky and add some Cobalt Teal Blue for the sky reflection in the lake. Leave the part of the lake with the reflection of the mountains and moraine blank for now. There is also a layer of ice along the shore of the lake that obscures the reflection. I painted this in with the same blue as the water but with a bit of brown to muddy it up.

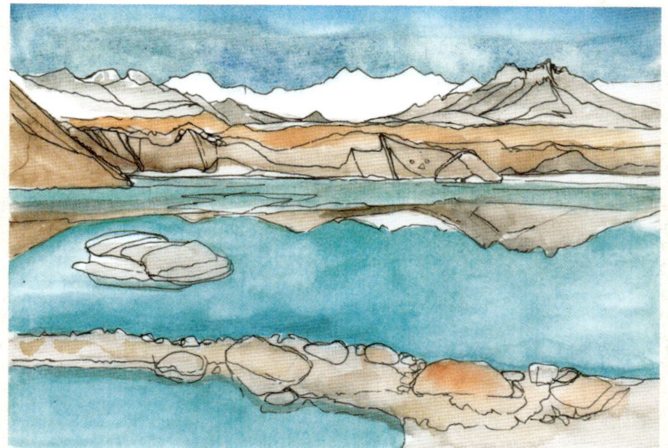

6

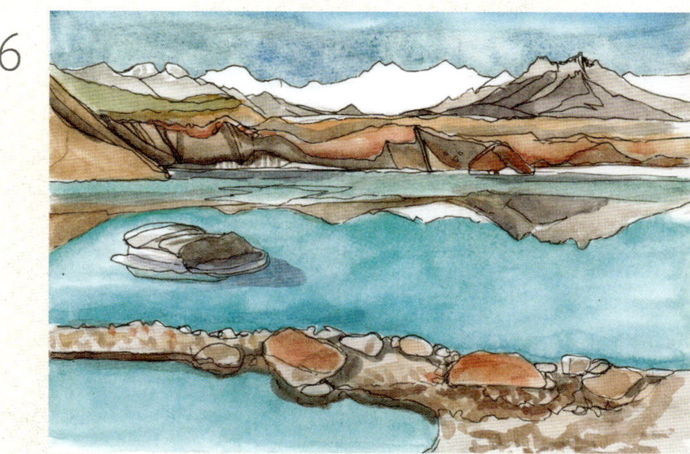

STEP 5: Begin painting in some browns and grays for the rocks and land. I used Burnt Sienna and Raw Umber for the different strips of rock that I observed in the landscape. The stones in the distance are more umber in color, and the closer ones are more Burnt Sienna in color. The moraine's different colors represent different rock layers carried down by glaciers from different areas up high.

STEP 6: Add more layers of watercolor. I painted some of the green parts of the landscape on the left. I also painted in some shadowy areas with a gray that I mixed from Burnt Sienna and Indanthrone Blue. I added some more Burnt Sienna to some of the rocks in the front of the moraine and the rocks in the foreground.

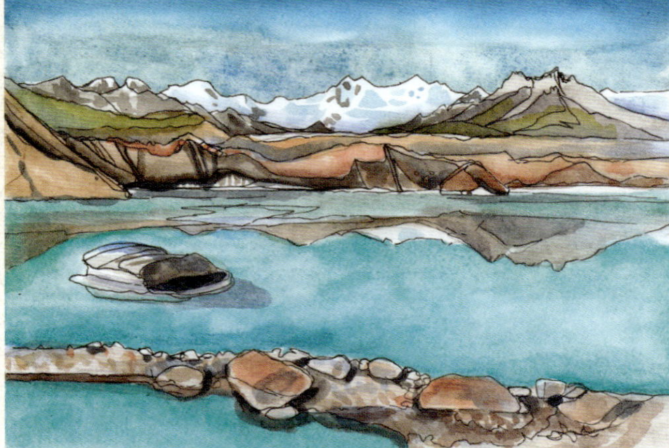

7

8

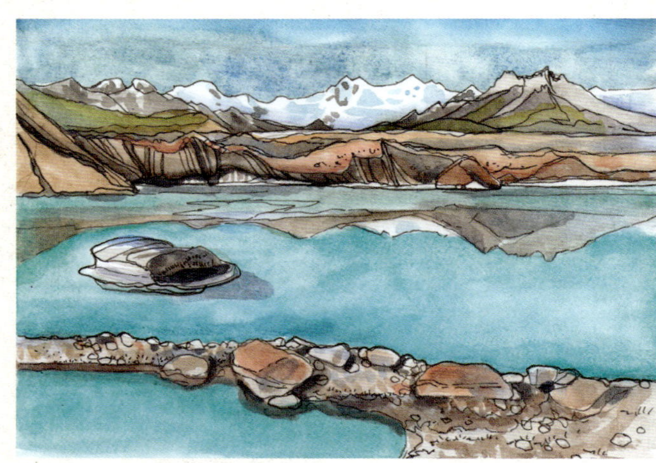

STEP 7: Add some shadows and cool colors to the landscape. I used Ultramarine Blue for the shadows in the distance and Ultramarine Blue mixed with Quinacridone Rose for the shadows in the foreground. The warmer violet helps those shadows feel closer. I added some shadows on the icefalls between layers of moraine in the distance to show where rocks and ice were casting shadows on the lake.

STEP 8: Once the watercolor is dry, come back with a pen to add some last details and textures. I wanted to add more texture and details to the foreground to make it feel closer. I drew in more rocks on the peninsula at the bottom and added texture to the iceberg. I also drew more lines on the melting face of the moraine on the lakeshore. These added details help the foreground feel closer in the sketch.

Project 23

SKETCHING NEAR AND FAR IN THE ALPINE TUNDRA

Capture the alpine tundra by zooming into the foreground and emphasizing some of the tiny alpine plants

MATERIALS: a pencil, a pen, watercolor paper, watercolors

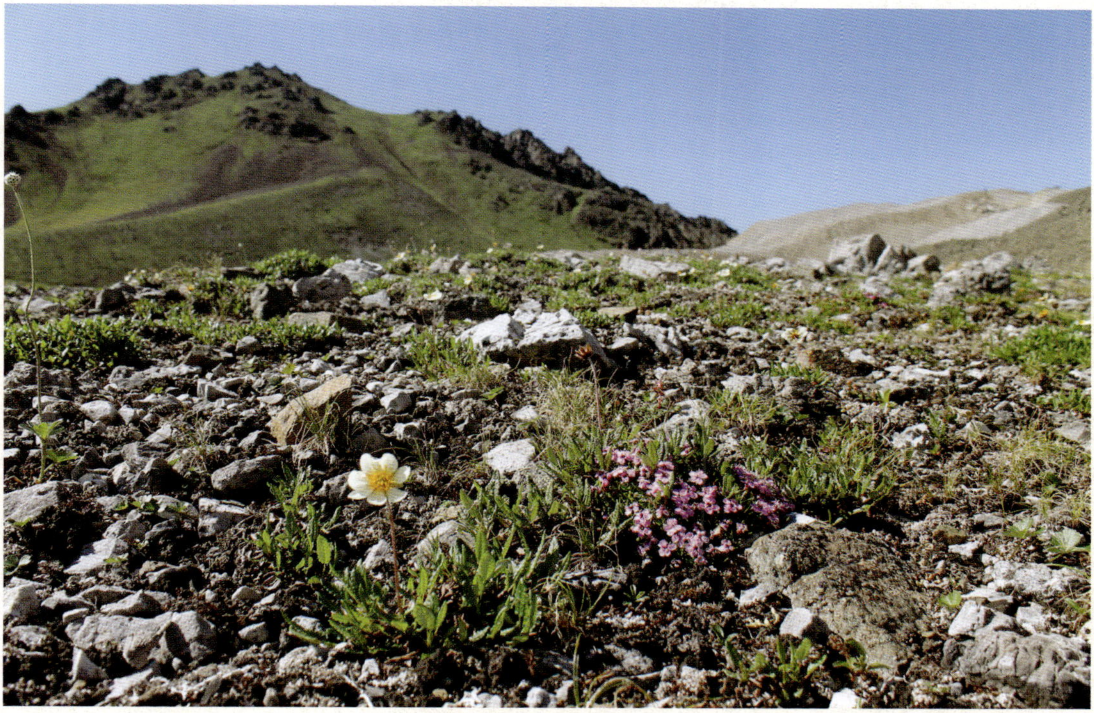

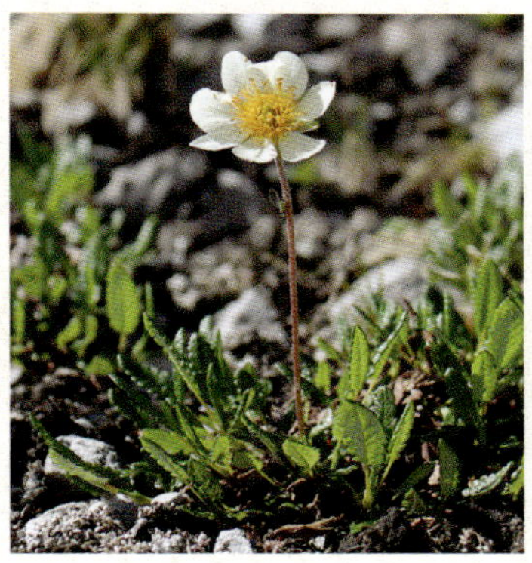

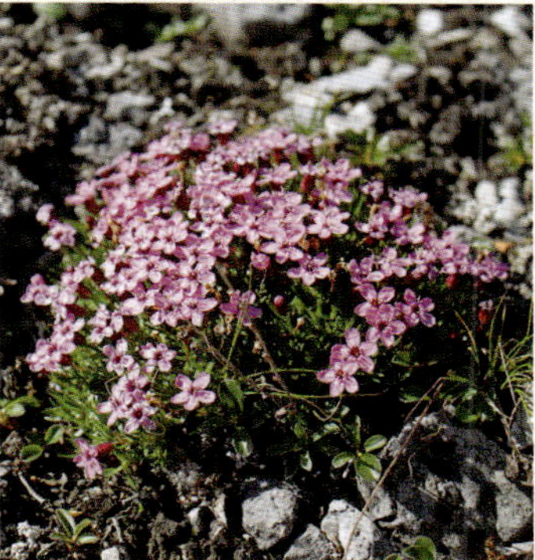

The alpine tundra is one of my favorite places to hike. Once you get above the tree line, you can admire spectacular mountain views and marvel at the worlds of tiny plants specially adapted to grow in this extreme environment. In this example, we see mountain avens (the white flower) and moss campion (the pink cushion plant) growing amongst the rocks.

Project 23

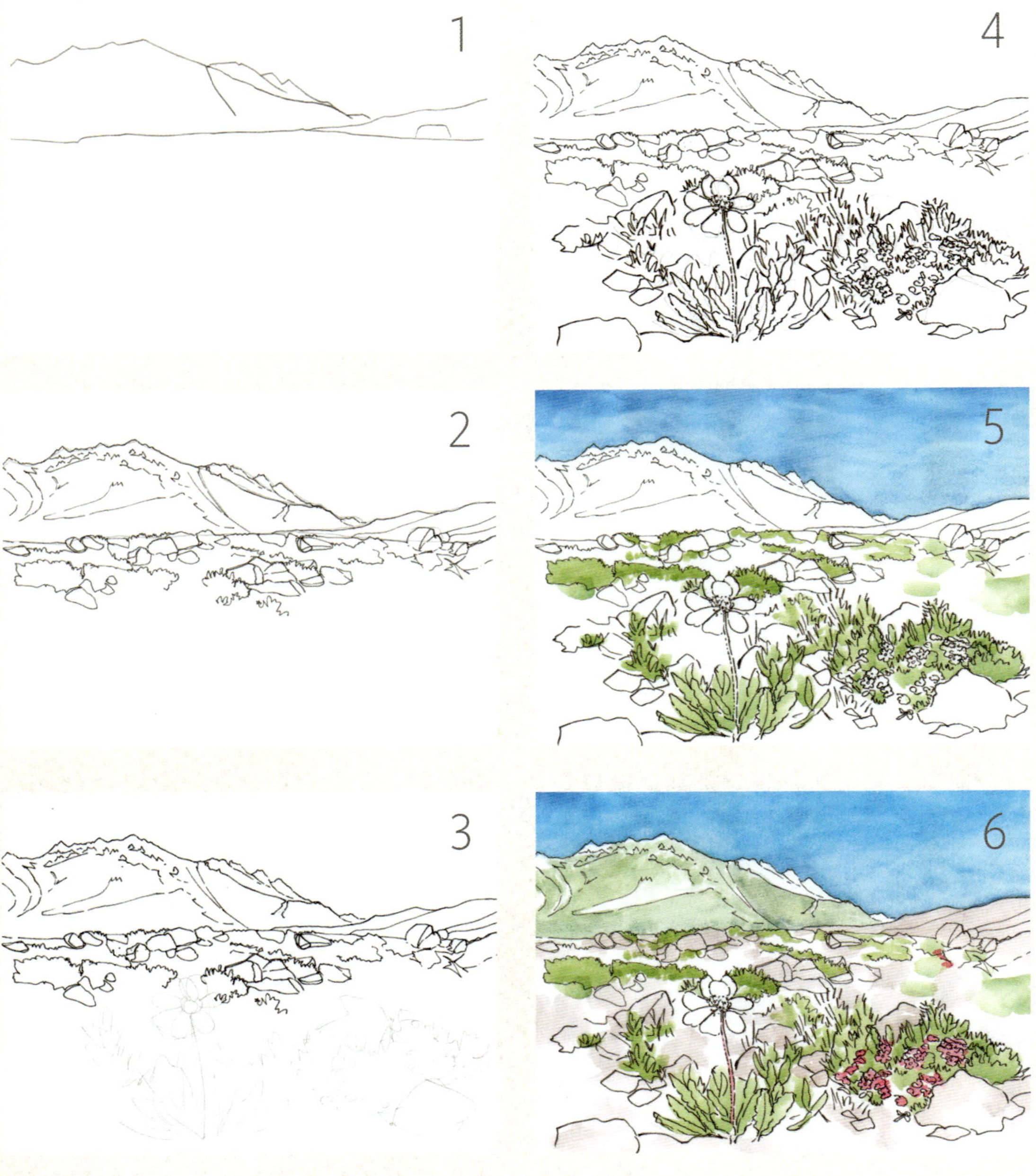

STEP 1: I wanted the focus of this sketch to be the tiny alpine plants in the foreground and planned to make them larger to increase the sense of scale. However, beginning the sketch with the background makes sense to help map the setting where those plants are growing. To do this, I drew a line across the paper where the tundra ridge meets the mountains in the background and then sketched some basic shapes for the peak in the background and the rock glacier on the right side.

STEP 2: Go over the pencil sketch with a pen and mark some of the main features you notice, drawing shapes where the terrain is rocky or vegetated. You don't need to draw each rock or leaf, but you can generalize clumps of things.

STEP 3: I wanted to magnify the alpine plants in the foreground to be a bit larger than they are in the photo so that they could be the focus of the sketch. Use a pencil to sketch the shapes of these plants roughly. The mountain avens flower has petals arranged in a circle around a central part, so I drew the stem, the center, and a circle. The moss campion clump is more complicated, so I sketched the main shape of the clump and the rocks around it.

STEP 4: Go over the foreground section of your sketch with a pen. I used a fine brush pen to sketch in the foreground so that it would have some thicker lines and more contrast. Start with the flowers that you want to be the main subject of the sketch. For the moss campion, I sketched in a few of the flower shapes where I noticed them and then added some spikey texture for the rest of the pin cushion. Once I had the focus elements sketched, I added some more marks for the other vegetation and the rocks. I kept the sketch loose but tried to pay attention to the different textures between the avens leaves and the sedges.

STEP 5: Erase any pencil marks you do not want and switch to watercolor. Paint in the sky with a wash of light blue. I used Phthalo Blue because the sky was so vibrant that day. I mixed Quinacridone Gold with Phthalo Blue to make a warm green and painted some areas of vegetation in the tundra. I was careful to paint around the flowers, which I wanted to be pink for the moss campion.

STEP 6: Start painting in some of the rocky areas. I mixed Cobalt Teal Blue with Burnt Sienna to make gray and painted where the landscape is rocky. This time, I was careful to paint around the white petals of the mountain avens flower. I used Quinacridone Rose to mark where the pink campion flowers are. I also painted some of the background with blue-green.

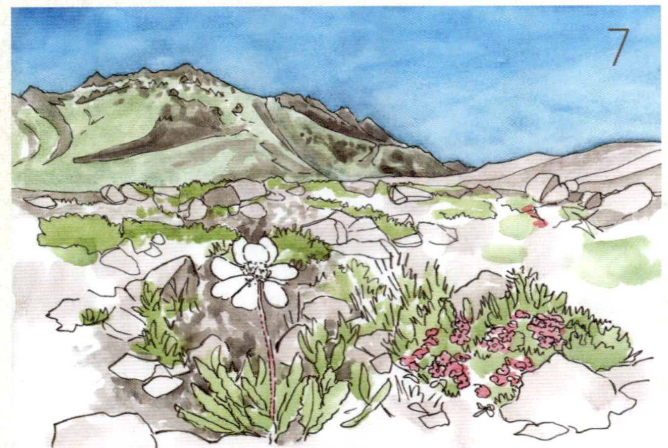

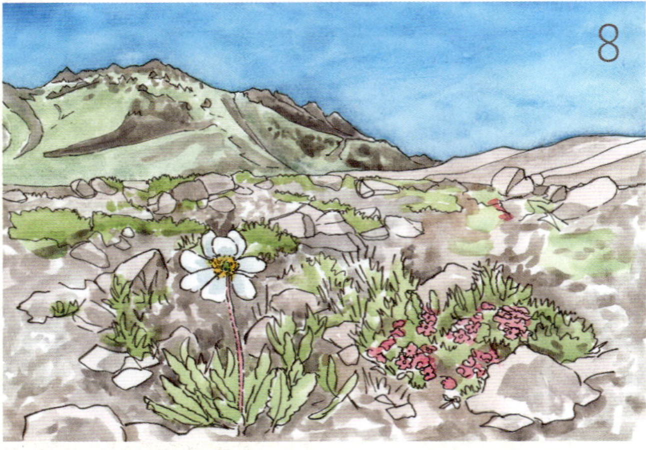

STEP 7: Mix brownish gray with Burnt Sienna and Indanthrone Blue to add some of the darker rocky areas. I painted in some of the darker rocks on the ridge in the background and painted around the mountain avens flower again. This contrast in negative space will help the flower stand out and pop forward. Because of the rocky ground, I dabbed my brush to create a mottled texture instead of making one smooth wash.

STEP 8: Continue spreading that grayish brown across the rest of the landscape. Keep using that mottled texture and leave some lighter spots to vary the ground texture. Paint in some very pale shadows on the mountain avens flower. I used light blue for the shadows on the petals, yellow for the center, and magenta for the stem.

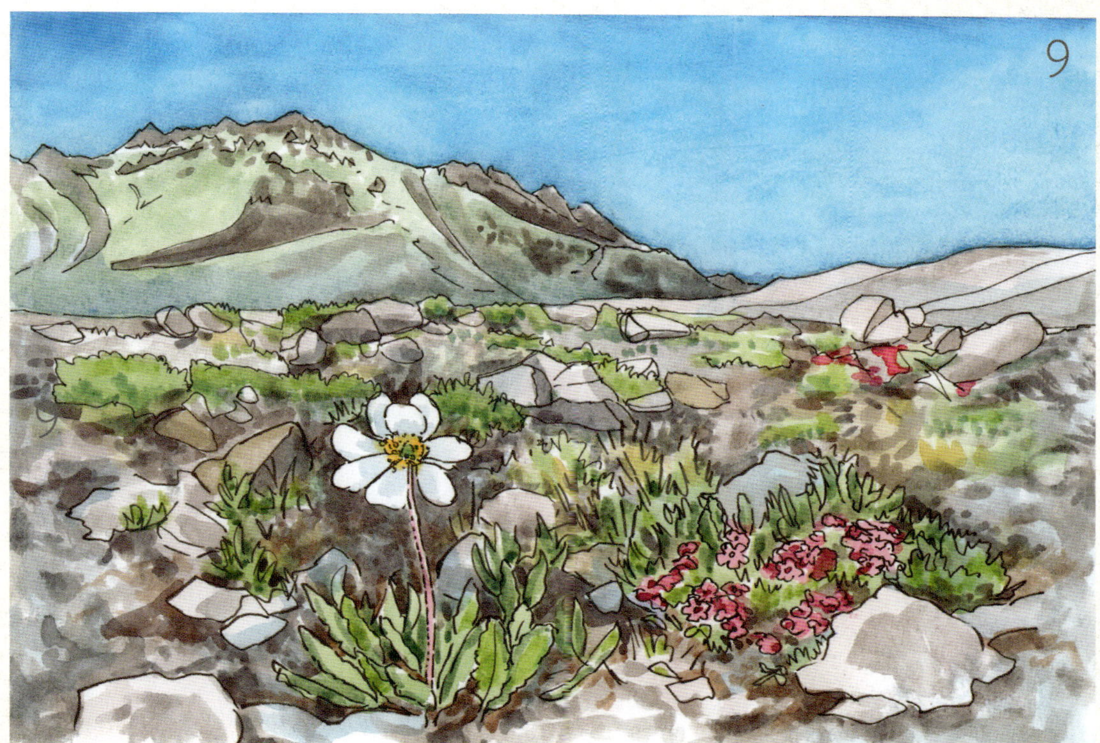

STEP 9: Add some more watercolor layers of shadow and detail. For shadows, I used Ultramarine Blue in a light wash to make the tundra area stand out from the background and add some cool places in the rocks. To create more variation in the ground, I dabbed some Burnt Sienna around the stones. I also added brighter greens, pinks, and gold to the vegetation, especially in the foreground, where we can notice more detail.

Project 24

WORKING ON TONED PAPER: GLACIAL MORAINES

Capture layers of ice and moraine by working with dark and light media on gray paper.

MATERIALS: toned paper (I used Steel Gray Canson Mi-Teintes pastel paper), a pencil, a pen, gouache or Bleedproof White, watercolors, and colored pencils

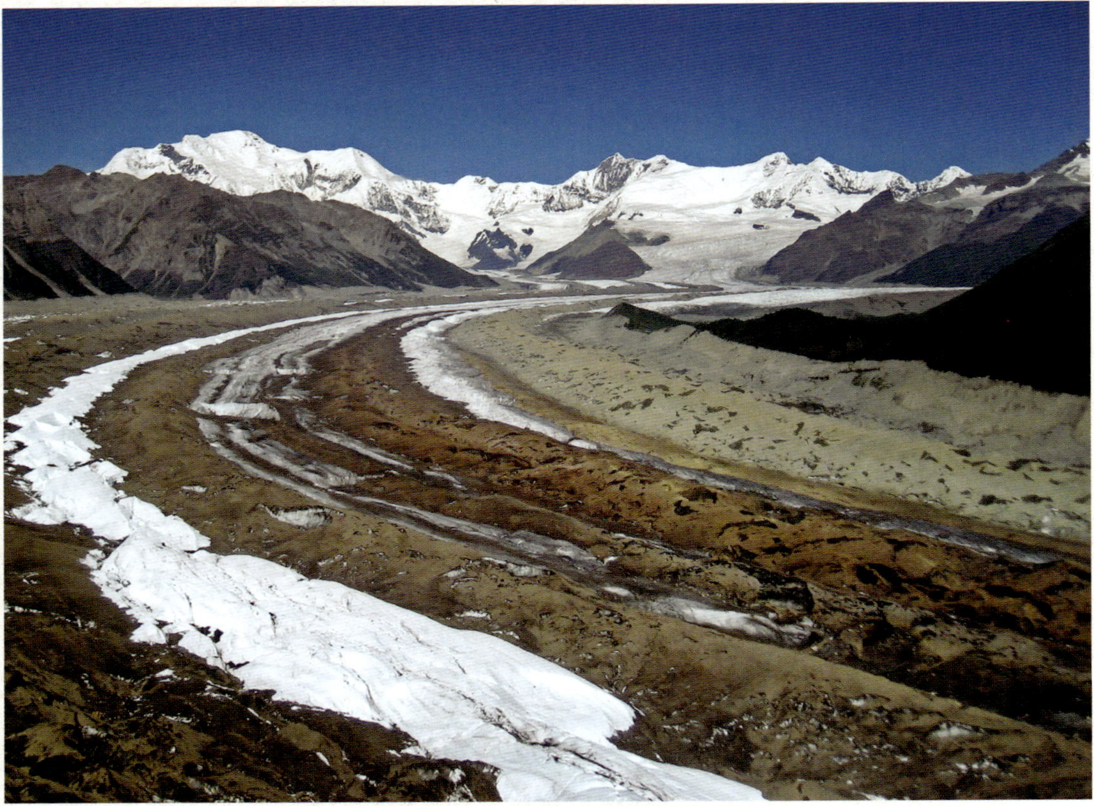

I took this photo from a small plane looking down at the Kennicott Glacier. Notice the stripes of ice and different colors of rock, called medial moraines, that flow off of Mount Blackburn, the white mountain on the left side of the ridge. This photo shows how glaciers work as conveyor belts for rocks and can be called "highways of ice."

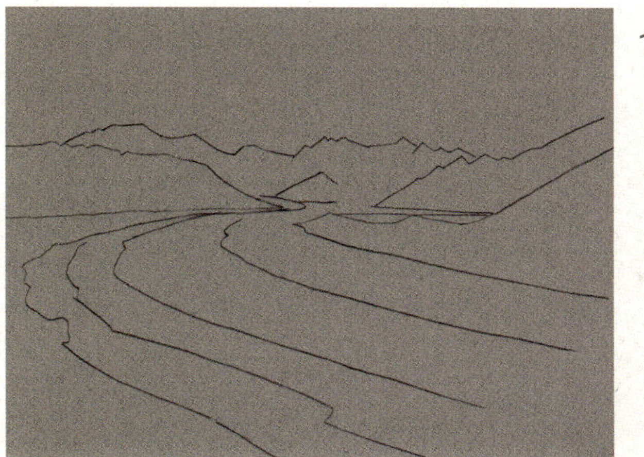

1

2

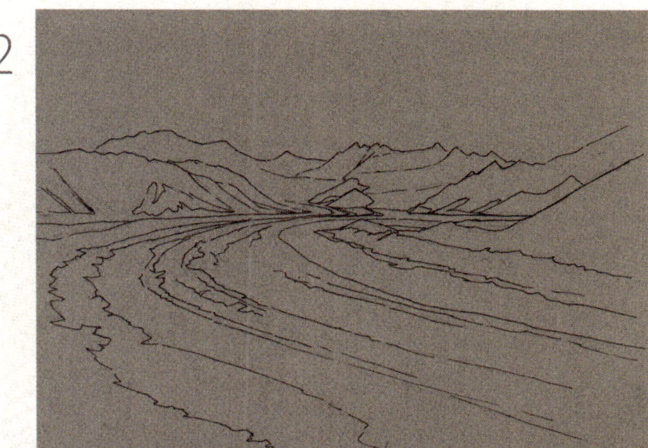

STEP 1: Lightly sketch some of the main shapes you see in the landscape with a pencil. The horizon line where everything converges is about two-thirds of the way up the paper. From there, a few curved lines of ice and rock define the glacier. Some rocky and vegetated ridges are on the left and right sides of the composition. There are also a series of white, glaciated mountains in the background. Work one section at a time, sketching the general shapes you can refine later.

STEP 2: Go over and refine your pencil sketch with a pen. Add more detail and information to the lines of moraine and ice in the foreground. The rock-covered moraine is often taller than the white ice, and there are many little ridges and micro-valleys. You can use your pen lines to show some of the direction and topography of this complicated terrain. Draw some of the shapes of the ridges and shadows on the icefalls in the distance. We are working with a pen, so if you make a mistake, that is fine; either draw over that line again or accept it as part of the sketching experience. I made one mountain in the middle the wrong shape, so I painted over the top of my pen line with gouache in the next step.

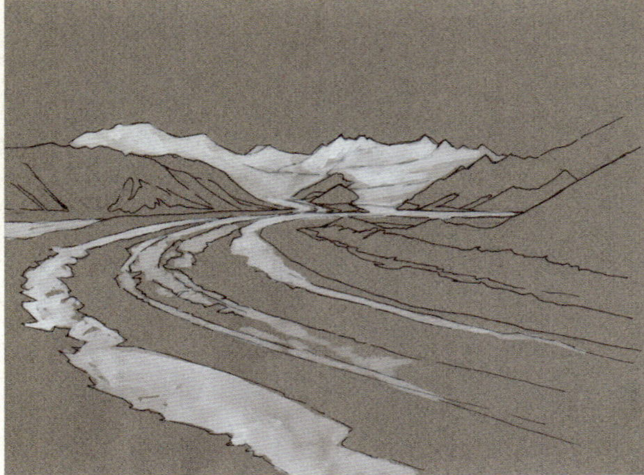

3

4

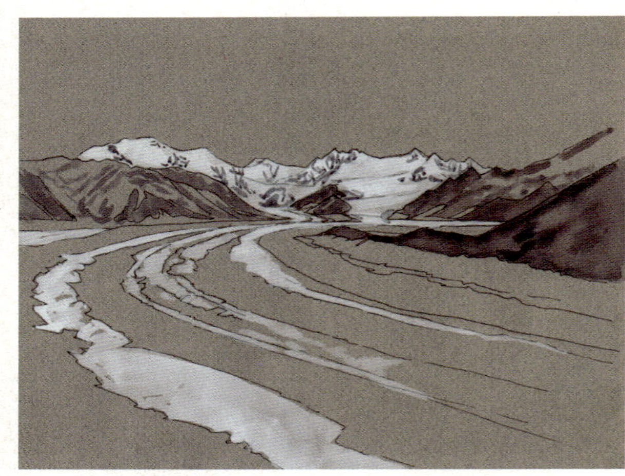

STEP 3: Paint in the white parts of the landscape using gouache or Bleedproof White. With less water, you will get an opaque wash, and the white can vary in brightness. If the first layer dries and isn't bright enough, you can lay down more than one wash.

STEP 4: Mix a darker gray than the tone of the paper with Indanthrone Blue and Raw Sienna. Paint in some of the darker areas, focusing on parts of the mountains in the distance and the middle ground. Remember that the gray of the paper is also a color we can use, so let that come through in some areas.

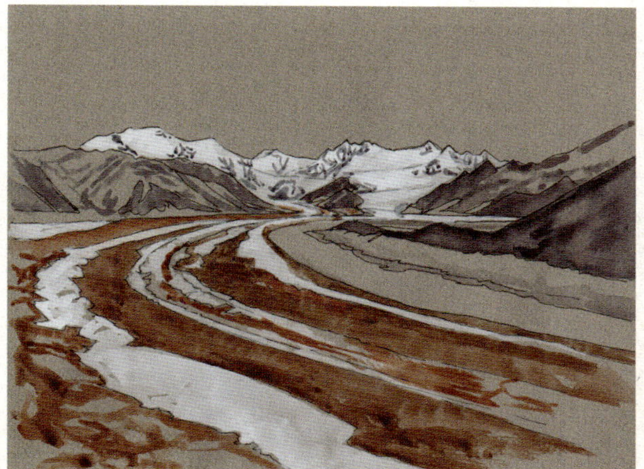

5

6

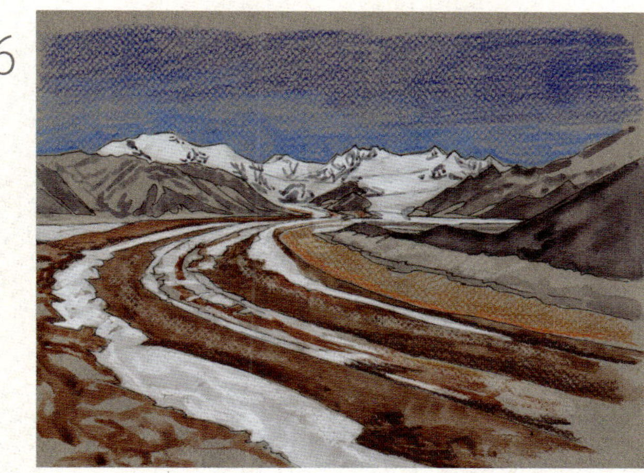

STEP 5: Paint in the brown strips of moraine. I mixed Burnt Sienna and Raw Umber to paint the moraine strips and rock between the ice. Again, leave some gray paper. I also mixed a very light gray for the shadows along the strip on the right side.

STEP 6: Let the paint dry and add colored pencil shading on top of the paper. The slight texture in the paper will help the colored pencil sit on top so that you can see the watercolor come through underneath. This texture works well for the variation in rocky terrain. I used blue to sketch the sky and some different browns and light grays on the moraine. In some areas, I went darker, and in some areas, I went lighter, again getting more variation in the final texture.

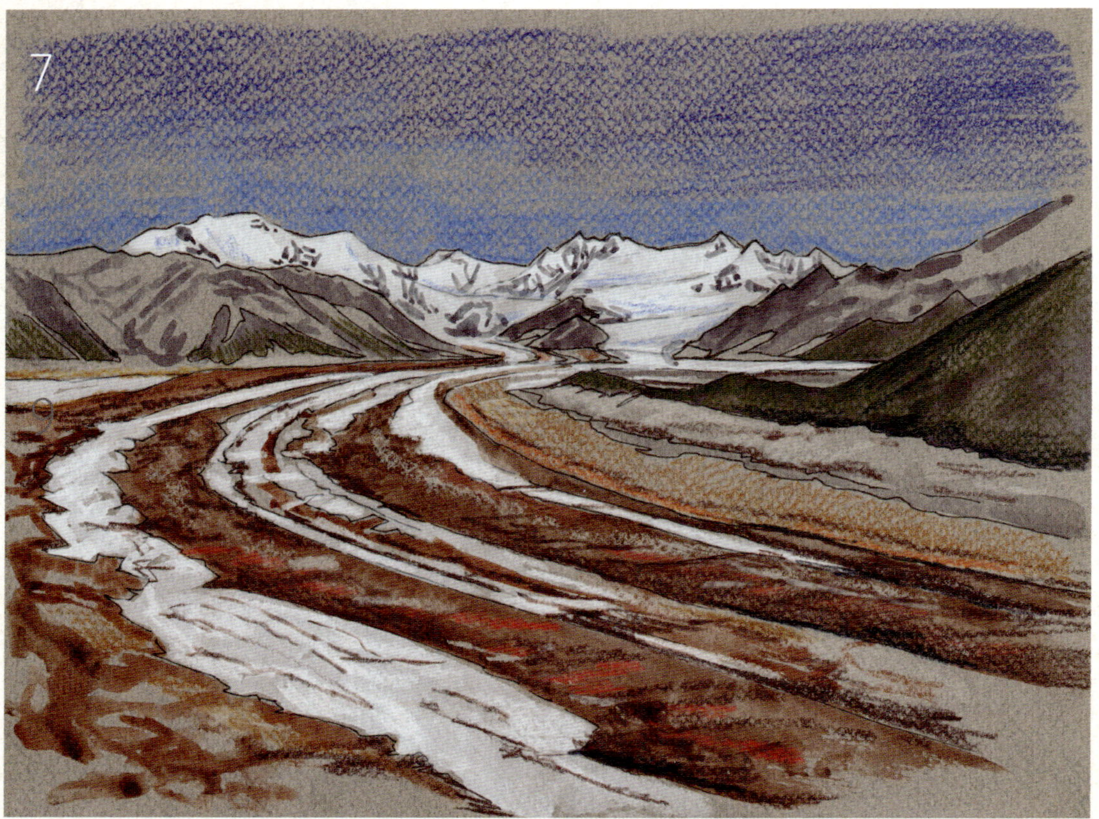

STEP 7: Add some last details. Use a green pencil to color the vegetation on the middle-ground mountains. I also added more red and dark gray to the moraines in the foreground to bring in some detail and get them to pop forward a bit. Finally, add a bit of light blue to some of the glaciers in the distance over the gouache.

Project 25

SKETCHING MOVING WATER: ARCTIC TUNDRA STREAM

Capture the shapes of the shadows and highlights that flowing water forms as it travels across the rocks and through the tundra landscape.

MATERIALS: a pencil, watercolor paper, and watercolors

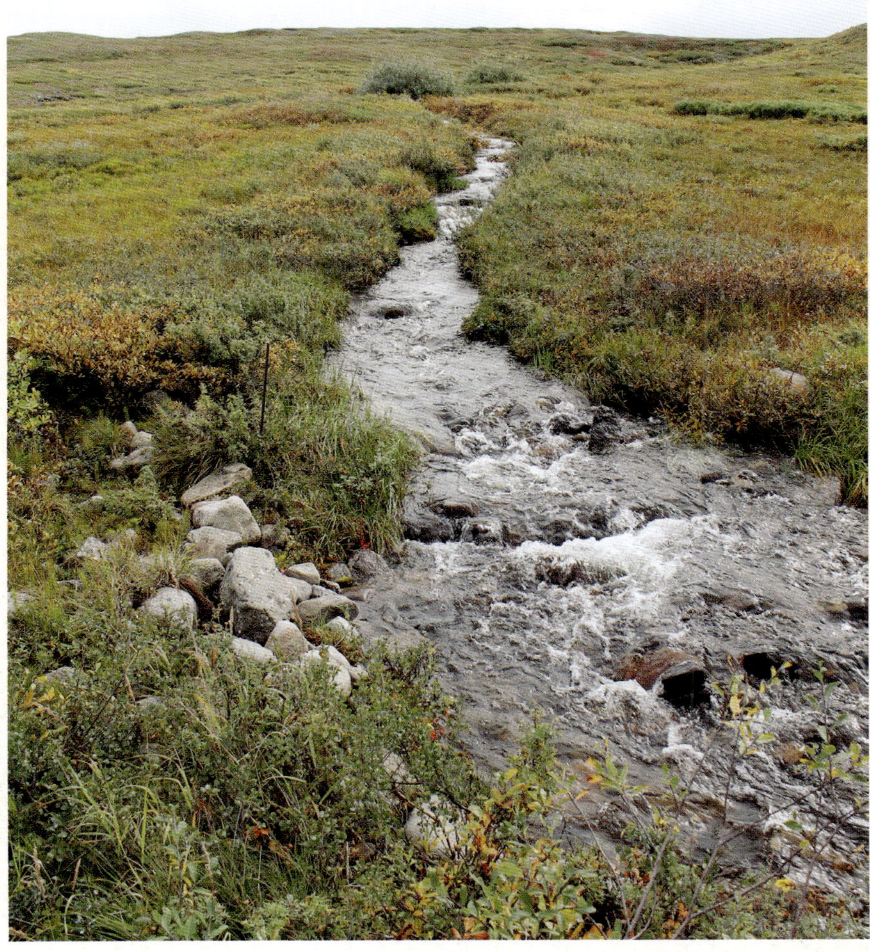

This beautiful, clear stream flows through the arctic tundra near Toolik Field Station on the North Slope of the Brooks Range mountains in northern Alaska.

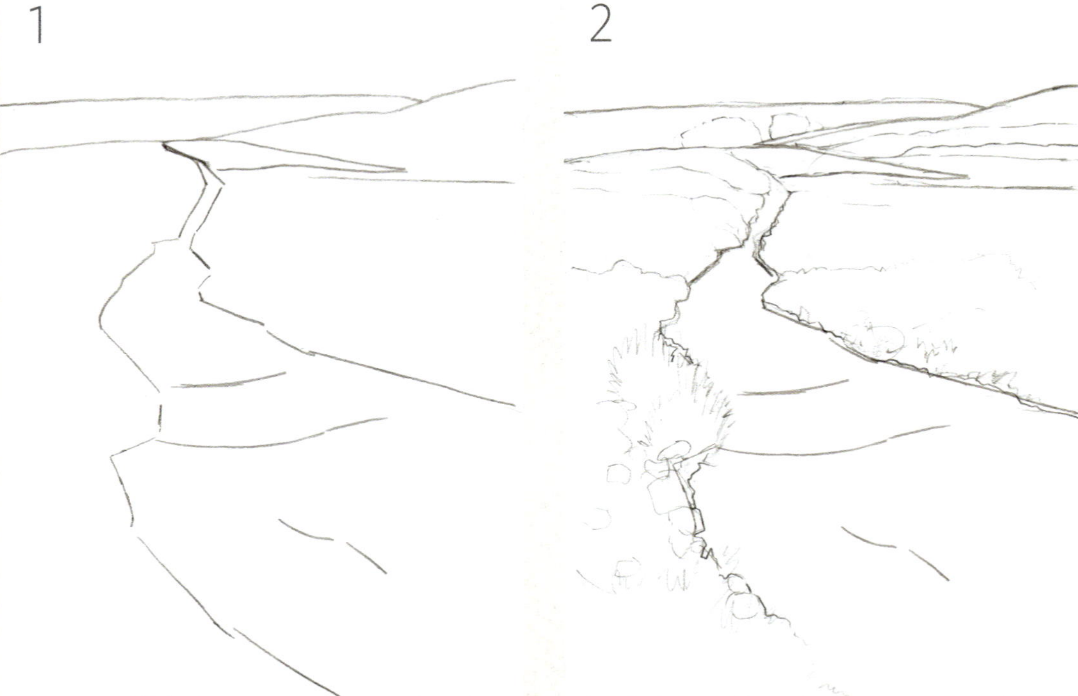

STEP 1: Begin sketching the landscape elements with some pencil lines. I noticed three overlapping tundra ridges in the distance, giving way to a gray sky. The horizon line is relatively high on the page, and you can't see much in the distance. Use a series of straight lines to sketch the area around the stream. I also added some lines where I noticed that the water dropped over a series of rocks. These will be important later.

STEP 2: Sketch the vegetation and rocks around the stream. Generalize clumps of grass, bushes, and rocky areas.

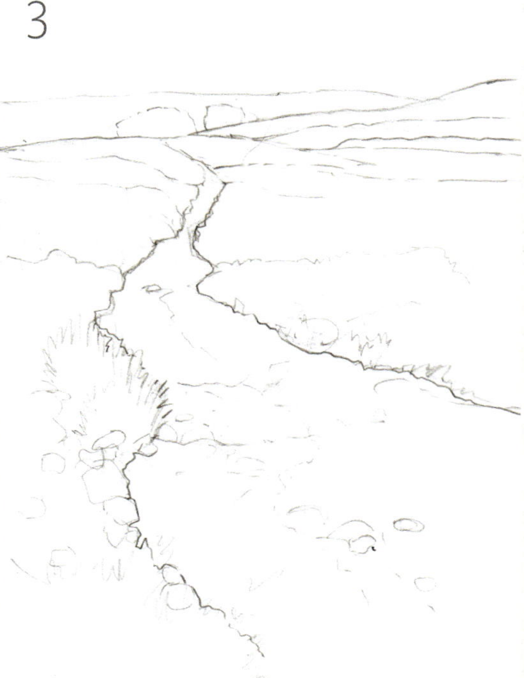

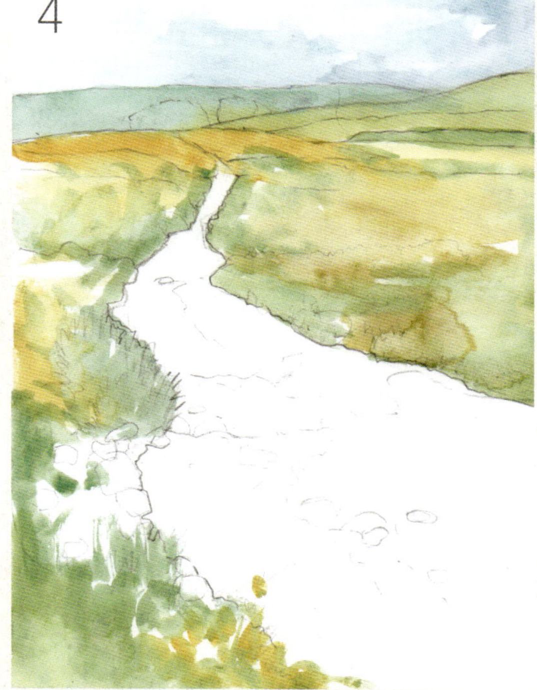

STEP 3: Look closely at the water and find the shapes that the highlights and shadows form. This is easier to see in a still photo than when looking at moving water, but in both cases, the water will form these shapes that show how it is moving. Draw some of the shapes you see in the water, focusing on light and dark areas. The light areas occur when the water is stirred up and aerated as it goes through a mini rapid. Mark in some places where you notice rocks through the water.

STEP 4: Begin painting the vegetation around the water. I started with a blue-gray sky, mixing Cerulean Blue with a tiny bit of brown and magenta and painting in a wash that left some white on the paper for the clouds. For the vegetation in the distance, I mixed Cerulean Blue with Quinacridone Gold and then mixed more Gold, some Cobalt Teal Blue, and Burnt Sienna as I moved toward the foreground. I worked wet-in-wet so that the colors would blend into each other independently.

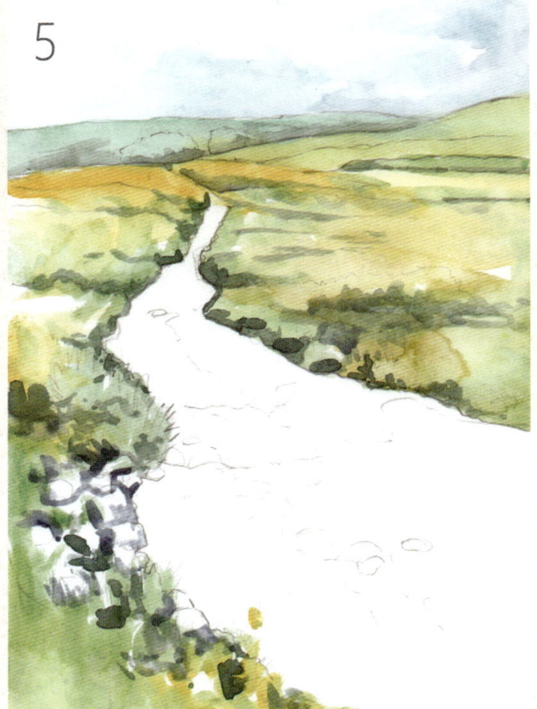

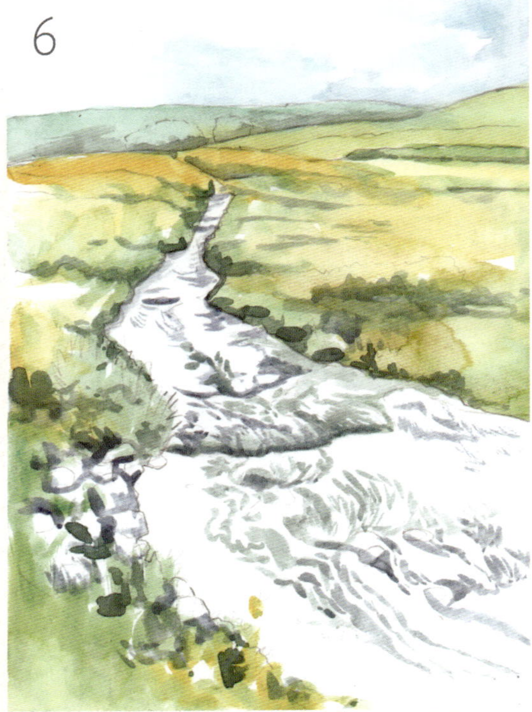

STEP 5: Paint the shadows on the sides of the stream. I mixed a shadowy gray color with Ultramarine Blue and Burnt Sienna. I painted this along the edges of the stream and in some parts of the rolling tundra to help define different patches of vegetation. I tried to ensure this wash got lighter as it receded into the background.

STEP 6: Begin painting in the water, starting with the shadows. I used the same purply shadow color from the previous step but also mixed that color with some of the green from earlier, mixing Ultramarine Blue, Burnt Sienna, and a tiny bit of Quinacridone Gold. I used these colors to paint in little marks to show the direction the water was flowing. I also painted bigger shadows where the water dropped over rocks, from the lines marked in the first step. Let this dry before moving on.

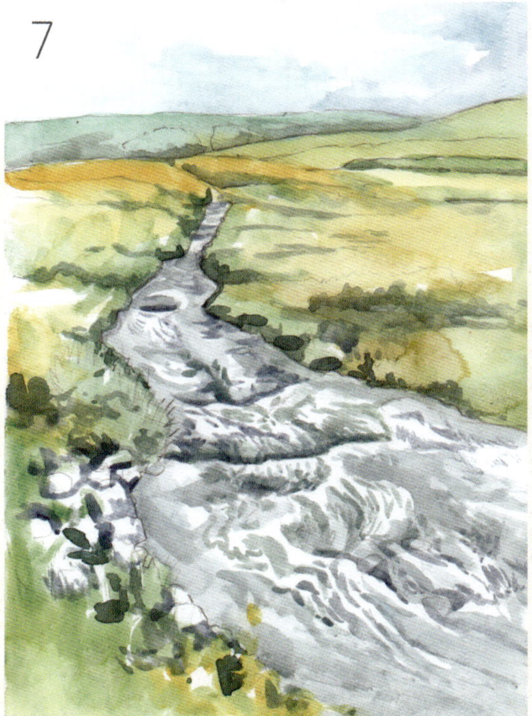

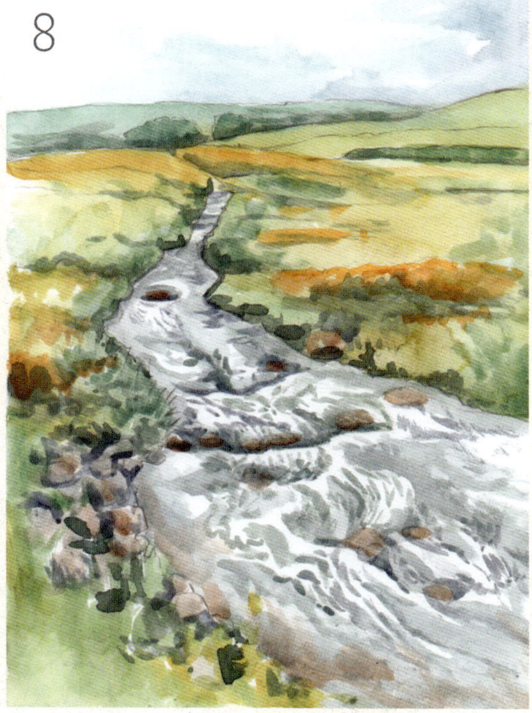

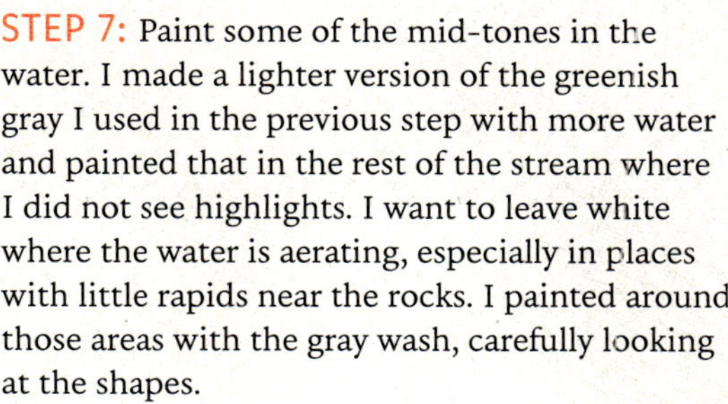

STEP 7: Paint some of the mid-tones in the water. I made a lighter version of the greenish gray I used in the previous step with more water and painted that in the rest of the stream where I did not see highlights. I want to leave white where the water is aerating, especially in places with little rapids near the rocks. I painted around those areas with the gray wash, carefully looking at the shapes.

STEP 8: Paint some rocks around the stream and under the water. I used Quinacridone Gold and Burnt Sienna to mix a warm brown. I painted this along the sides of the stream where I noticed rocks, under the water, and in the vegetation where it was brown.

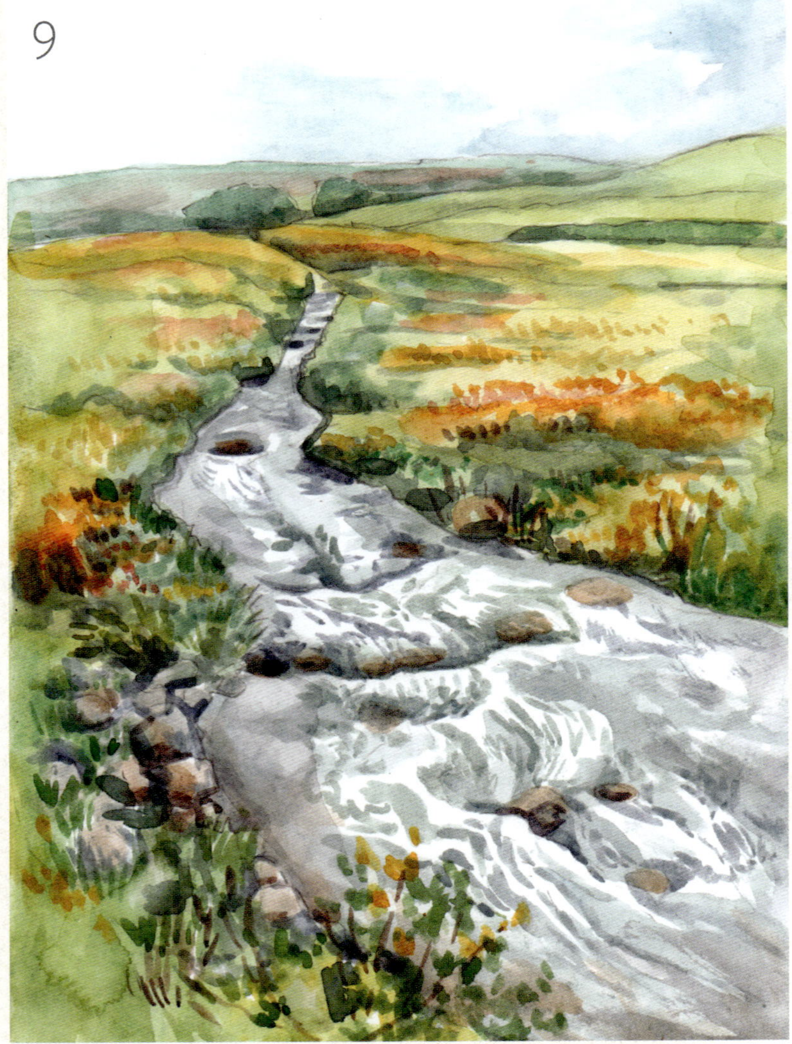

STEP 9: Add some detail and texture to the foreground. Bring in some of the reds and browns to emphasize the fall colors. Deepen the shadows in the foreground and the stream where you want it to pop forward, especially towards the bottom of the page.

SITTING STILL FOR A MOMENT WHILE THE WORLD CHANGED AROUND US

Nine high school girls, a few other instructors, and I headed out into the backcountry northeast of Fairbanks, knowing the forest fire danger was high. It was late summer, and it had been hot and dry, sometimes pushing 100 degrees Fahrenheit. We spent a few days out before the smoke came. We monitored the air quality, texted people in town on the satellite phone, and checked the visibility distance. Forest fires are a normal part of the summer in Alaska, though the frequency, severity, and overall fire regime change with climate change. We had just discussed and decided to stay out in the field, so I sat down to teach a lesson on landscape sketching. The smoke in the air changed the atmospheric perspective, shortening the distance that we could see, but we could still make out the rolling hills in the distance and see how the green got lighter and grayer farther away. The vegetation along the far lakeshore was bright and warm in color.

As we sketched, the air got worse. The fire wasn't close enough to be dangerous, but the air quality was deteriorating rapidly as the wind switched directions. The sky turned orange and then very dark. It was amazing to witness the light change as we sat and worked on our sketches, studying it. It got more challenging to see the colors in the orange light. Ash started to

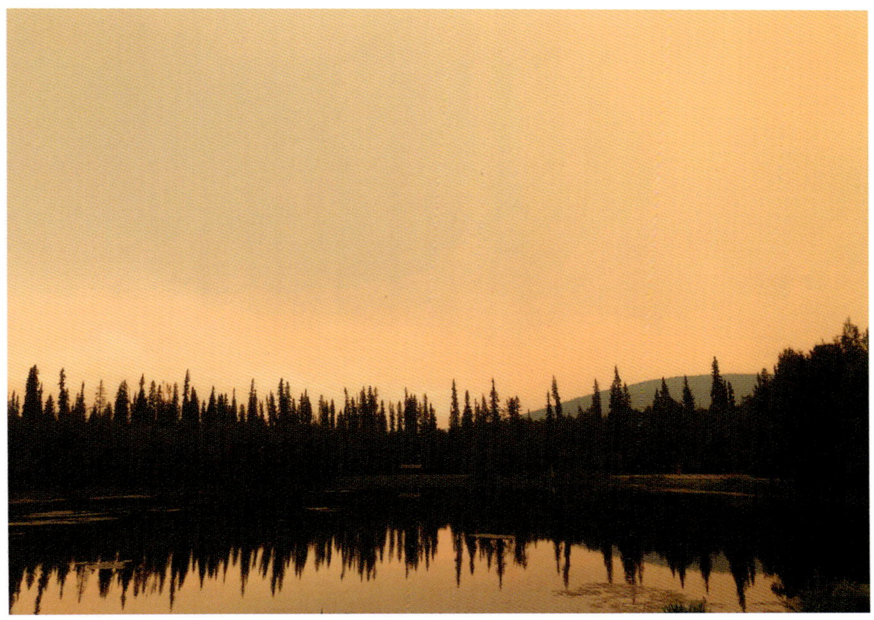

An orange sky during forest fires near Fairbanks

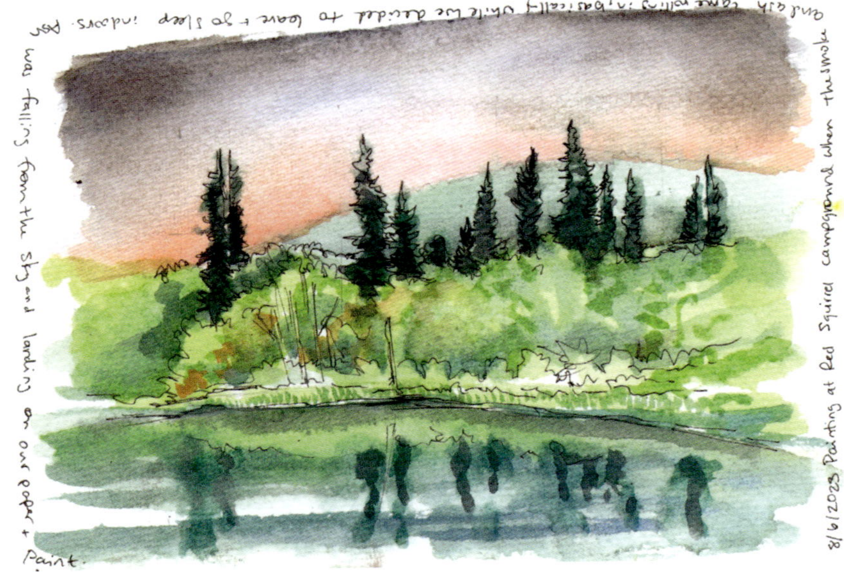

Sketch made while the smoke was blowing in from forest fires and the environment was changing very quickly

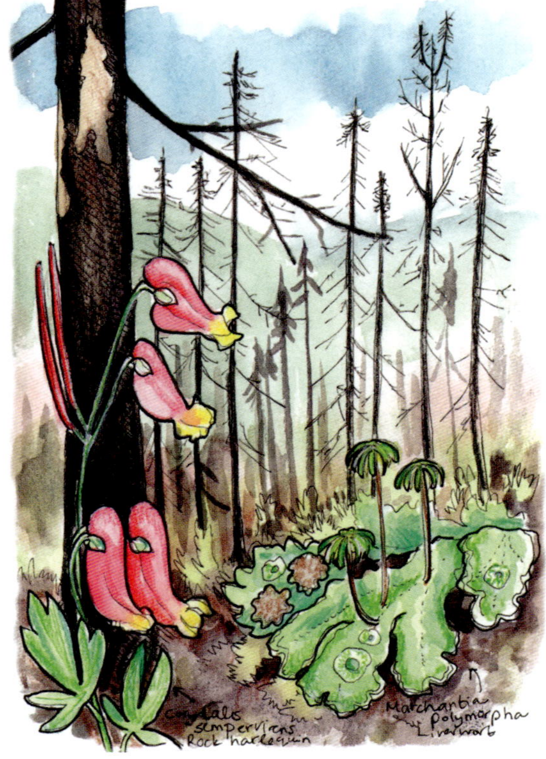

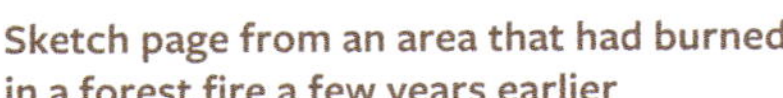
Sketch page from an area that had burned in a forest fire a few years earlier

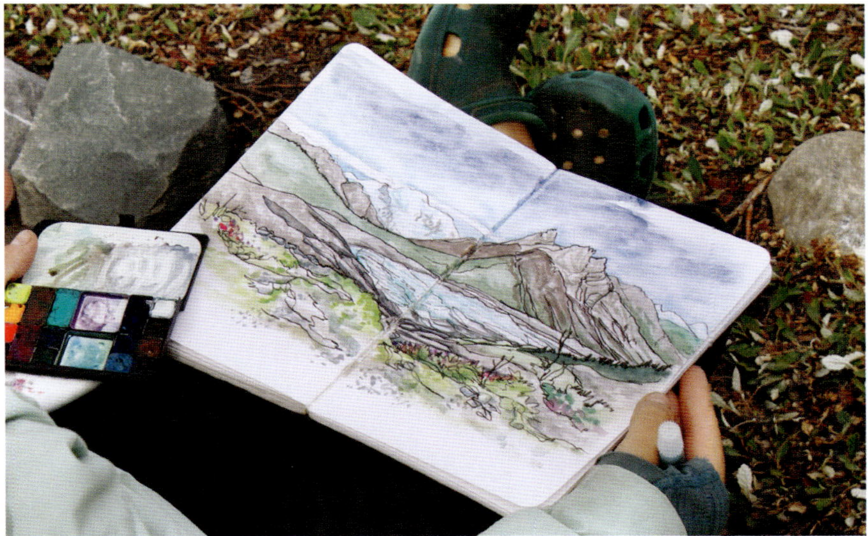

Finished sketchbook spread with watercolor and brush pen in the Wrangell Mountains of Root Glacier, Donoho Peak, and Mount Blackburn in the distance

fall on us and mixed in with our paint. People's sketches got more dramatic, and we talked with each other about the sudden change. It was clear that we would need to change our plans—to stop camping and head into the shelter where we could find better air. And we would do that soon, but in this moment, we sat, sketched, and witnessed the dramatic change in the landscape around us. I'll never forget that moment.

A few days later, the air cleared, and we returned and visited an area that had burned a few years earlier. We collected some charcoal to make paint from. The vegetation was scorched in the burn, and most of the forest was gone, but it was amazing to see the undergrowth and the plants that thrive after fire. I found some of the best blueberries of the summer in that burn. The forest would yield surprising pockets of bright green liverwort, the softest moss, the lovely tall, delicate flowers of rock harlequin, and swaths of magenta fireweed. The woodpeckers flitted about, enjoying the standing dead trees. That landscape felt overwhelmingly changed, but up close, I noticed so many tiny passages of life and beauty.

Reflection

How is sketching something farther away different from sketching something up close? Think of a place you know and love. What would be essential to capture in that sketch? What technique or style would you use to do that? Would your approach be more scientific, artistic, or a combination? Or something else?

Sketching Through the Seasons and Celebrating Winter

Over the years the content of the journals has broadened to include every aspect of my life. I try to see it all as natural history, and have become a naturalist of my own life.

—HANNAH HINCHMAN

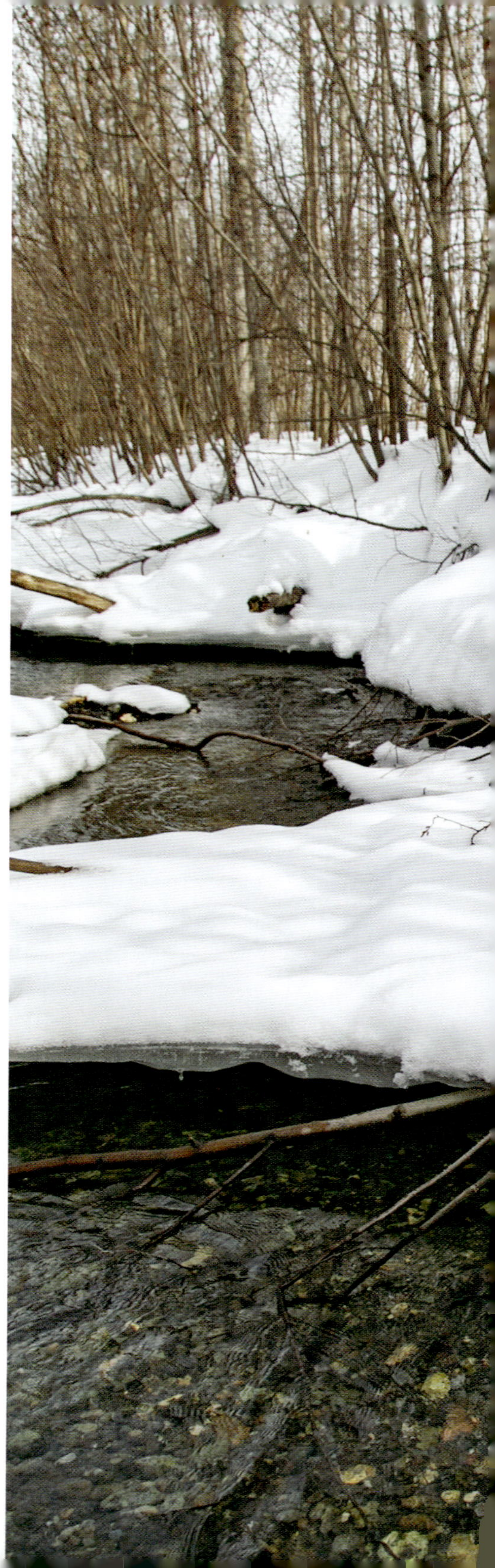

▶ **Sketching through the winter has deepened my understanding of the environment around me. This is a special spot where a spring comes out of the forest and stays open and unfrozen year-round.**

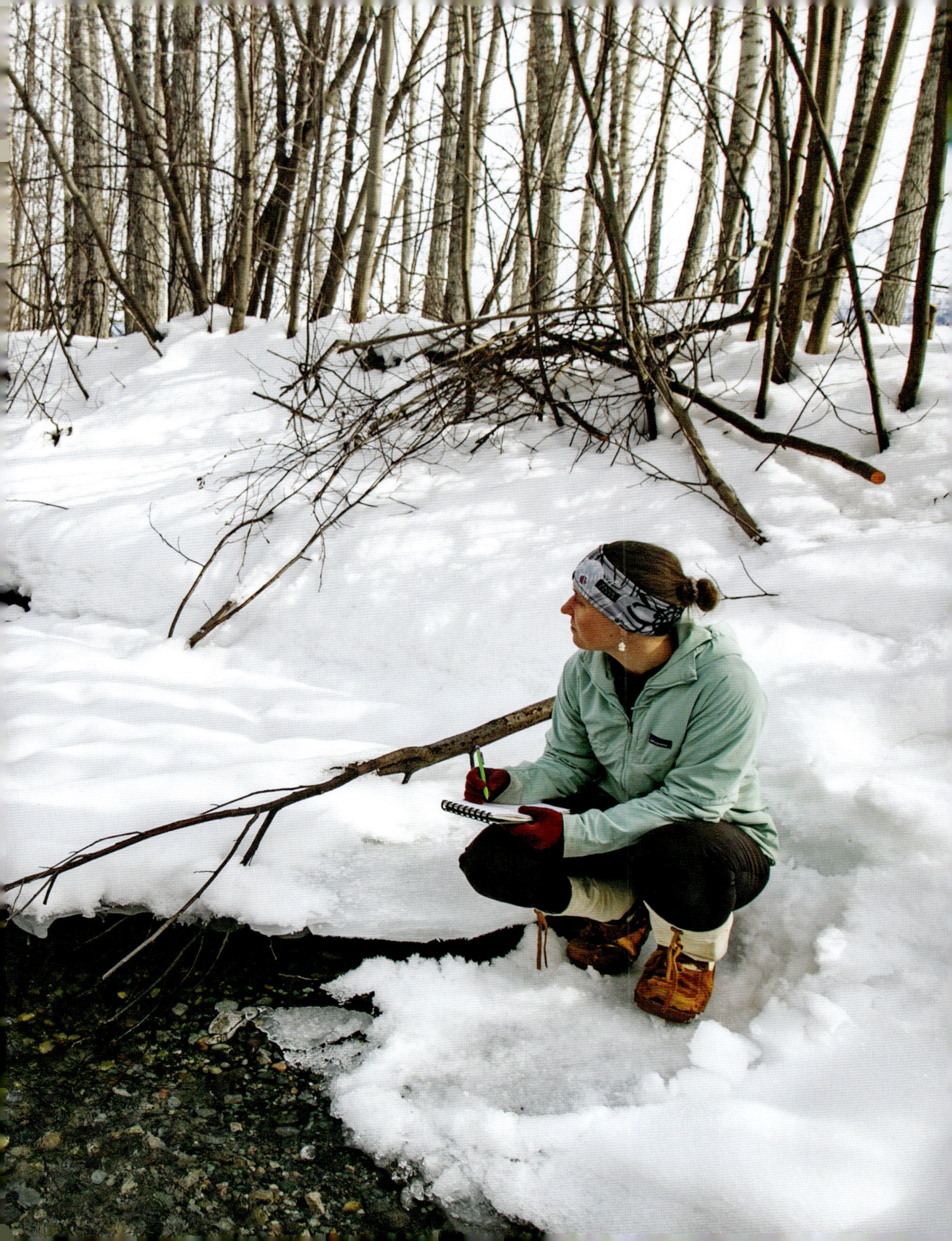

By going out and sketching during all seasons, I've become a better naturalist and better neighbor to the plants and animals around me. Sometimes, it is hard to find things to draw in the middle of the winter or when the weather is not great, but I think the challenge makes us better at noticing things and working in good weather.

At this point in the book, we have tried many techniques and sketched various subjects. I've shared approaches for sketching many different things outside on a nice day. Of course, a critical factor about sketching outside is that the weather and conditions are not always pleasant for taking a leisurely time. During the summer, it might rain or there might be too many mosquitos to stay still and sketch for long. In Alaska, we also have a lot of winter, and the ground is more or less covered with snow from October through April. Many animals hibernate and migrate away, and sometimes the landscape seems to be a monolithic, snow-covered place and it takes some extra effort to find new subjects to study.

After sketching my way through a few winters, it has become one of my favorite times to make observations we can't see at other times of the year. Animals leave their tracks in the snow. Winter light is remarkable, with spectacular sunrises and sunsets, long shadows, and extended twilights. We get some beautiful star- and aurora-filled nights. When the full moon shines on the snow, it feels almost as bright as day. I love getting to know the plants and animals during this quiet time of year.

I have made a simple kit that I can use to create a quick sketch in any weather. My all-weather kit consists of waterproof paper in a binder and some pencils, both colored and graphite, which I carry in a small zipper case. These pencils won't run if they get wet, and they work well even when frozen. I've used them at -20 degrees Fahrenheit. Some people use watercolor below freezing and replace the water with alcohol, but even with alcohol, it will still freeze and smudge, especially when it is well below freezing, so I have better luck working with simple pencils and paper in the cold. Having fewer supplies also ensures I keep my sketching process quick and straightforward. If it is raining or very cold, I cannot stand still and sketch for very long, so I will make a quick pencil drawing, maybe add some color, and revisit it later.

▶Walking outside when it is -20 degrees Fahrenheit or colder means bundling up with many layers and taking advantage of the short winter days. On days like these, I will make a very quick sketch or take some photos and memories to work from later.

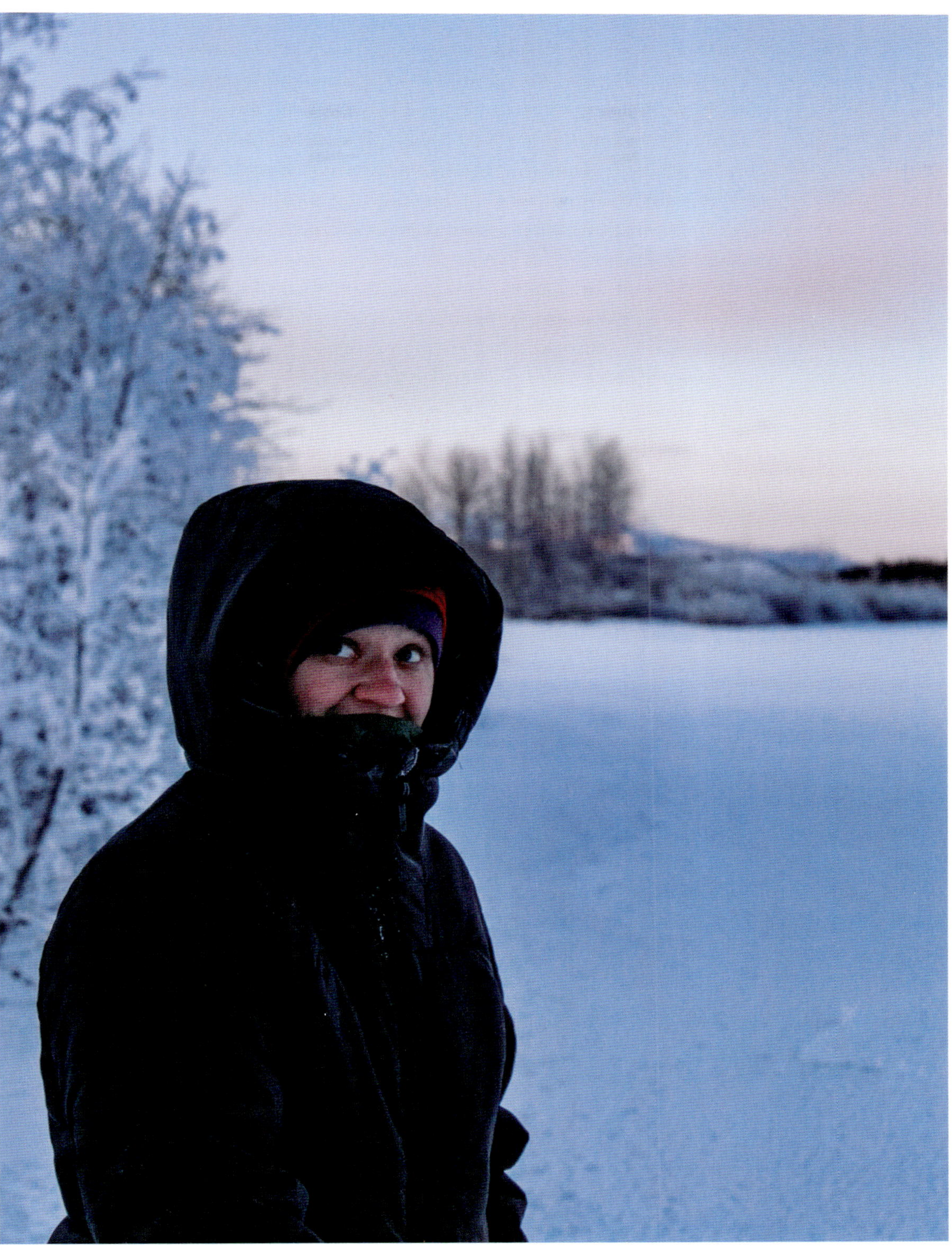

Another strategy is to work quickly outside and then revisit your sketches from a place of shelter. I might make a simple pencil sketch, snap a photo, and then redraw my notes from the day inside the comfort of my cabin. This strategy works well during winter days when we have limited daylight but long nights, when I find time to add notes and develop my sketches next to my desk lamp. Having even five minutes of observation time outside adds a lot of information to the finished sketch. Learning to draw from limited information later also makes me better at paying attention when I am outside.

In the rest of the chapter, I'll share some of my favorite subjects to sketch in the winter. The winter landscape, covered in snow, is beautiful, and I love the way the snow captures and reflects the light and shadow of what is around it. Ice is challenging but fun to paint, especially with watercolor,

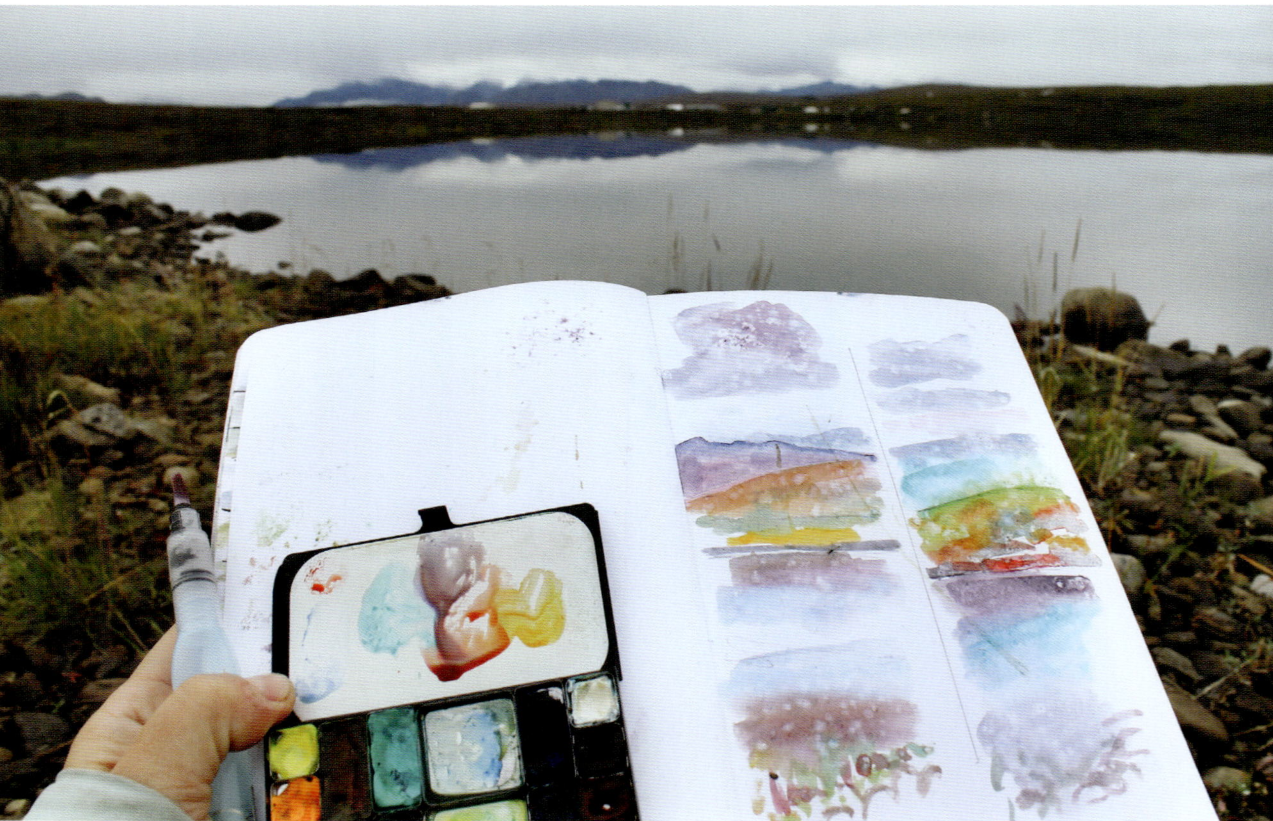

I was painting some swatches to study the color of the landscape when it started raining. Watercolor and rain don't mix very well—or they mix too well—and the raindrops started dissolving my work. At this point, it is time to put my book away and go for a walk or to switch my materials to something more waterproof.

where we can build up layers of transparency. Snow is also an excellent medium for finding animal tracks, so even when we don't see an animal in person, we can learn who walked through a particular patch of land before us. I've noticed voles disappear into tunnels that continue under the snow, crossed highways that hares stamp down for easy travel, followed a squirrel to its many caches, followed a lynx family who also seemed to be following those hare highways, and noticed the print of an owl who pressed its wings into the snow while hunting for small prey, all without seeing any of those animals. I've also learned to identify dormant plants so that I can recognize them without their leaves, flowers, and fruits. This helps me pay extra attention in the spring, when they start changing subtly, when the buds swell, and when the flowers start to show.

Using simple materials like paper and pencil works well in the winter because they will not freeze. You can still capture a great deal of information and have fun sketching even when it is cold outside.

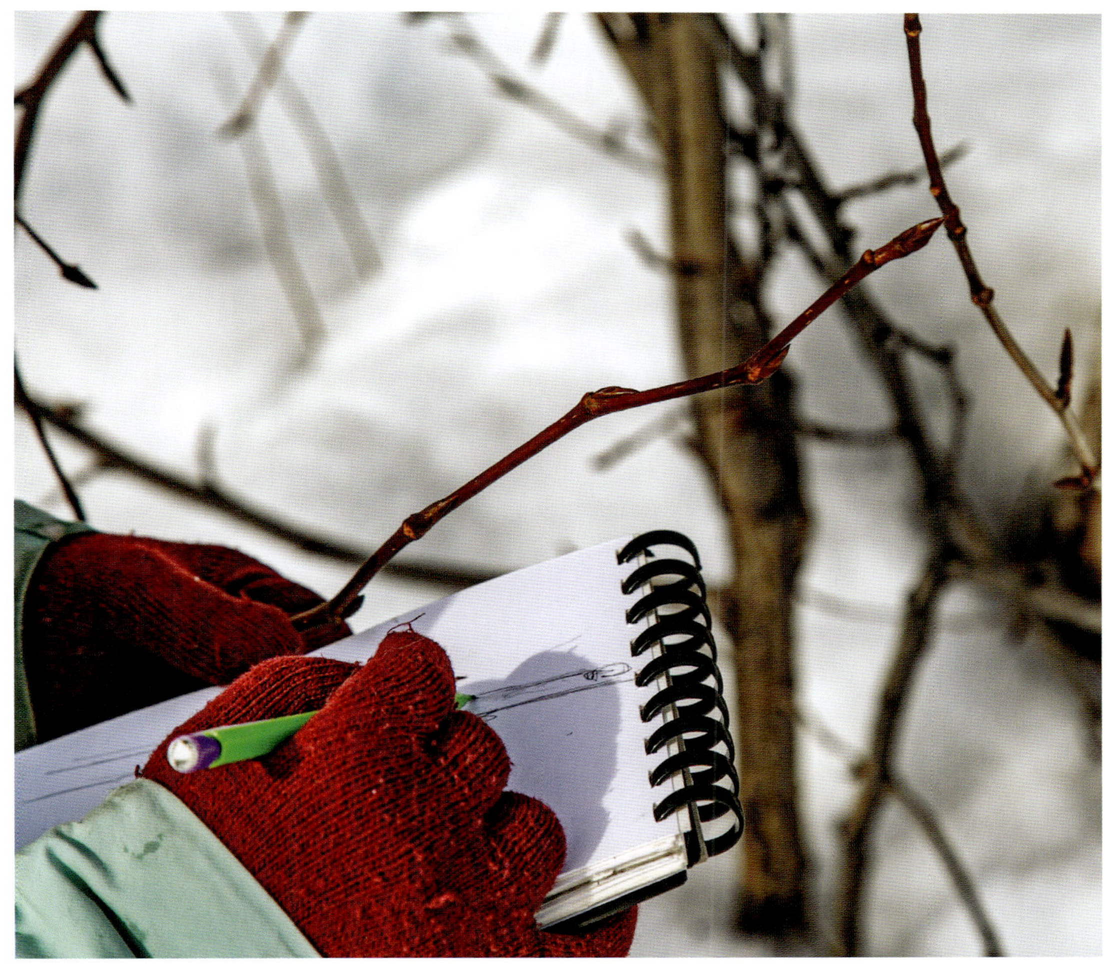

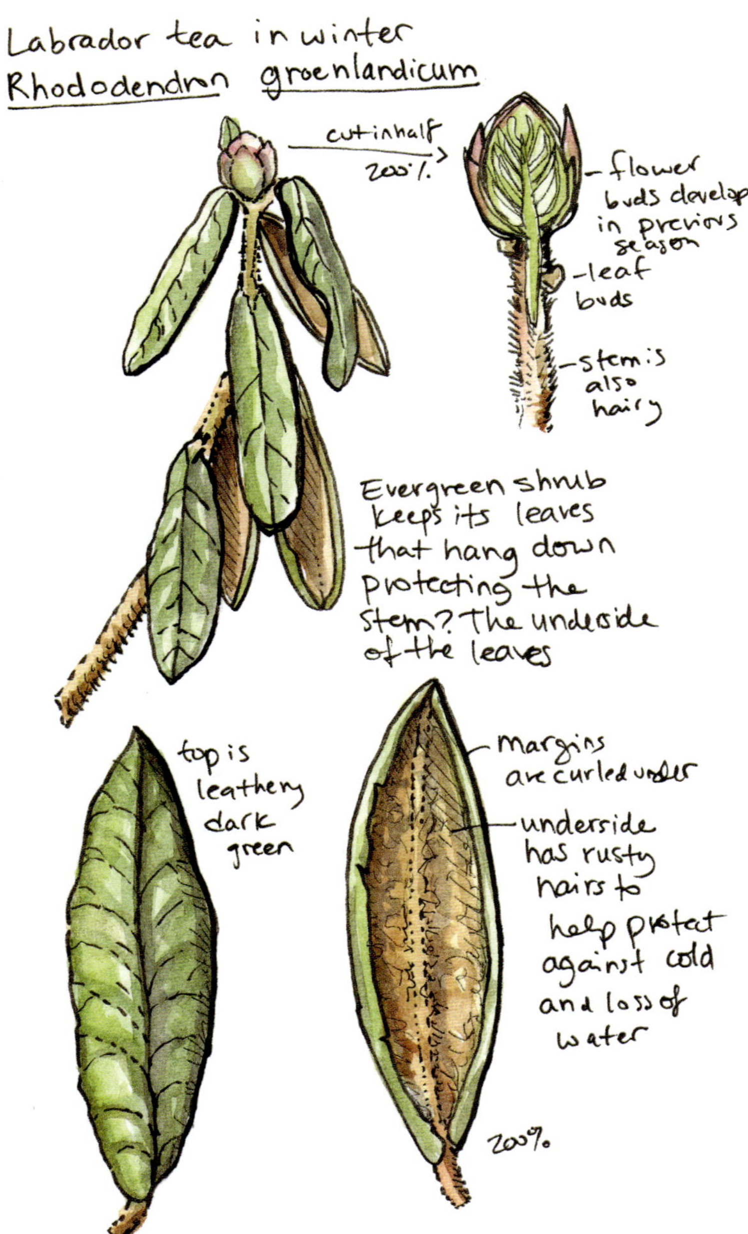

I learn so much by studying and sketching plants in their dormant stage. Labrador tea (*Rhododendron groenlandicum*) plants stay green through the winter. The fuzzy evergreen leaves help them stay warm and retain water.

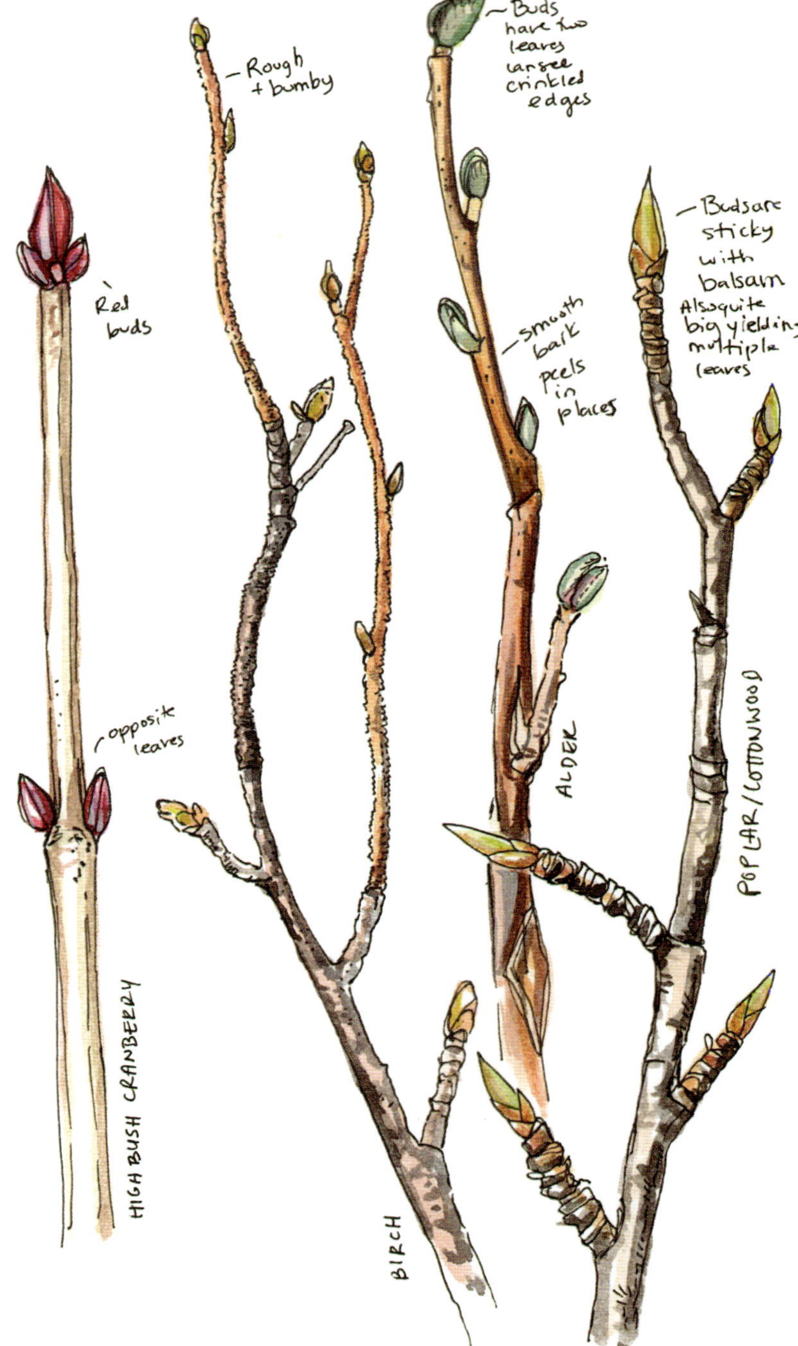

I taught myself to recognize most shrubs without leaves by sketching them. This sketch was made at the end of winter when there was still snow on the ground. It was freezing at night, but the days were getting warm and sunny. The buds are beginning to swell where last year's leaves and flowers have been stored and are waiting to pop.

Project 26

DORMANT PLANTS AND WINTER TREES: BIRCH TREE

Birch trees are a favorite subject because they are primarily white but have so many different colors when you look at them closely.

MATERIALS: a pencil, a pen, watercolor paper, and watercolors

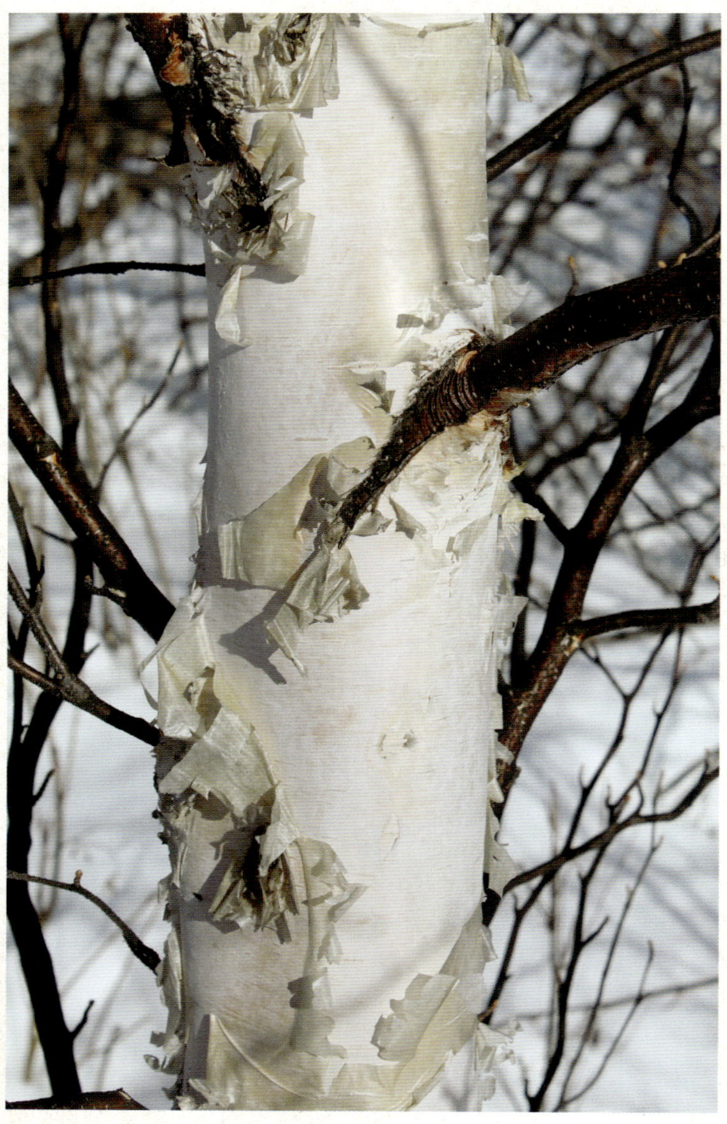

I once thought plants and trees were mostly dead in the winter, but I've learned that they are still doing quite a lot. I love sketching dormant plants. One thing I enjoy about winter is looking at all the tree bark, getting to know the different types of trees, and learning the stories each tells on its bark.

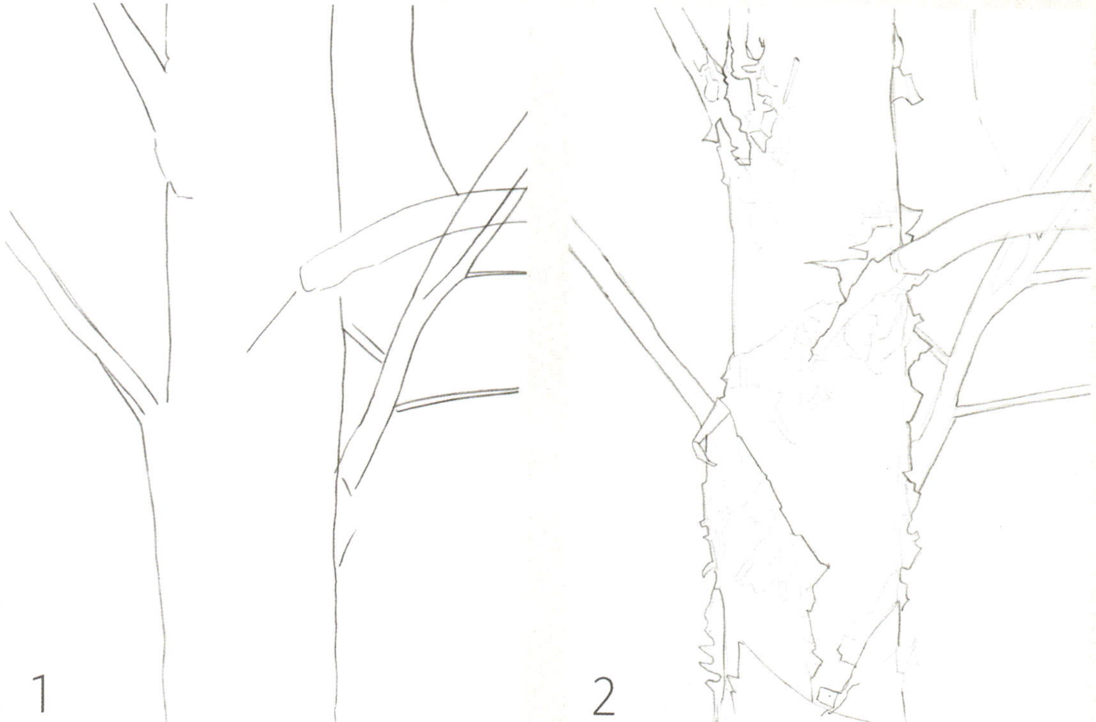

STEP 1: Sketch the main components of the tree. Make two vertical lines for each side of the trunk, then draw in the main branches. My focus for this sketch is the tree bark, so I won't sketch all the branches or most of the background.

STEP 2: Refine your sketch from the previous step and add more detail to the bark and branches. Mark out the main shapes where you notice the bark peeling.

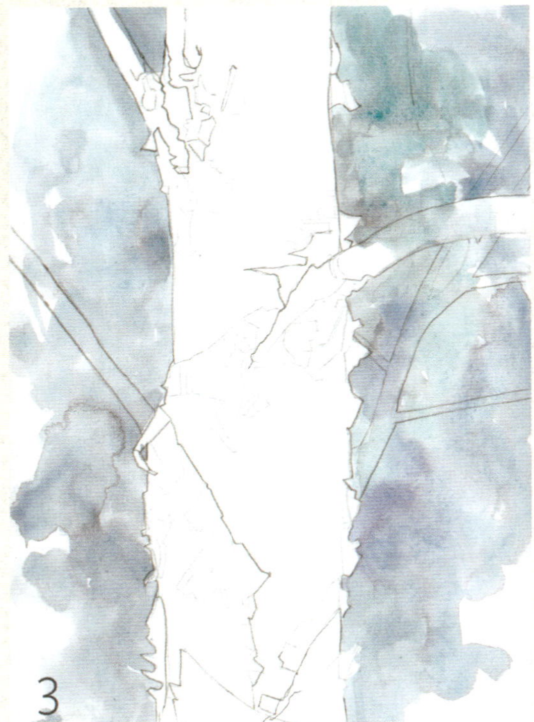

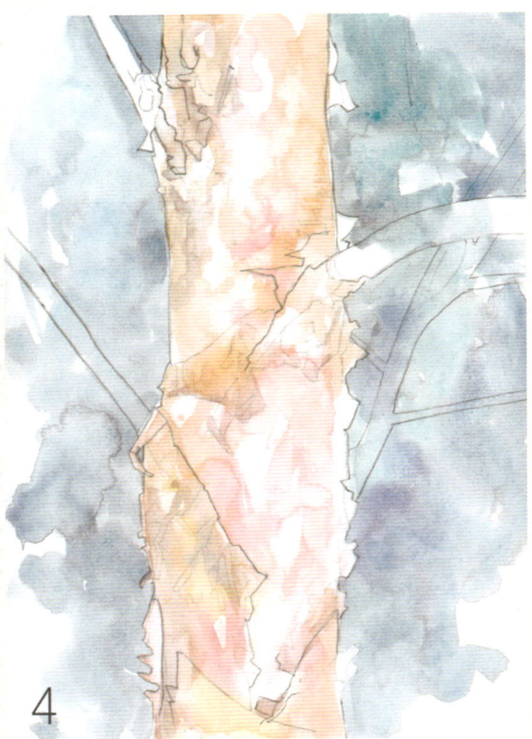

STEP 3: Add more detail to the bark drawing. Use contour drawing to notice all the little shapes and patterns. Don't worry about each piece being correct, but try to capture the overall shapes and patterns you notice. Mix a varied blue-gray wash for the background. I used Cobalt Teal Blue, Ultramarine Blue, and Burnt Sienna. The Cobalt and Ultramarine will separate due to the granular pigment so that the result will have some blotches and variety. Since the branches will be darker, you can paint over them. Be careful to paint around the lighter-colored birch bark.

STEP 4: Mix another varied wash for the light sections of the bark. I used Quinacridone Rose, Burnt Sienna, and Buff Titanium and painted the central part of the trunk wet-in-wet so that some of the paint would mix on the paper and have variation. Leave some white spaces for the paper to show through.

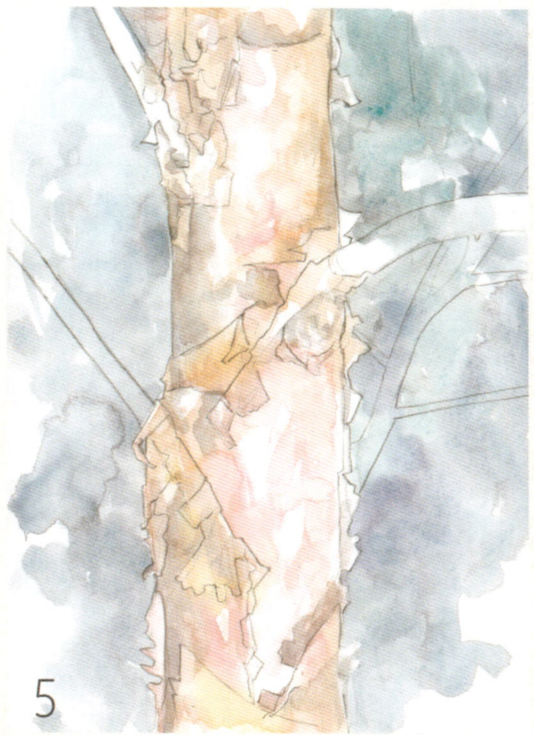

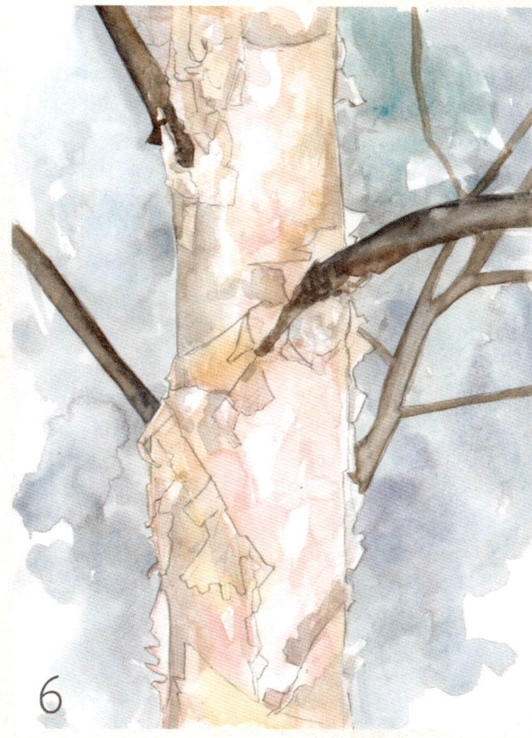

STEP 5: Mix a color for the shadows on the bark. I used Ultramarine Blue, Burnt Sienna, and some Quinacridone Rose to make a light violet-gray. Paint this to show the roundness of the trunk and some regions where the peeling bark is casting a shadow. At this step, I also realized that I painted the background color over a section of bark in the upper left, so I started adding some of the bark colors over the top of that wash. It is possible to fix mistakes with watercolor.

STEP 6: Paint the branches of the tree with a dark brown. I mixed Burnt Sienna and Ultramarine Blue. Use a graded wash so the branches are lighter in the center and appear round.

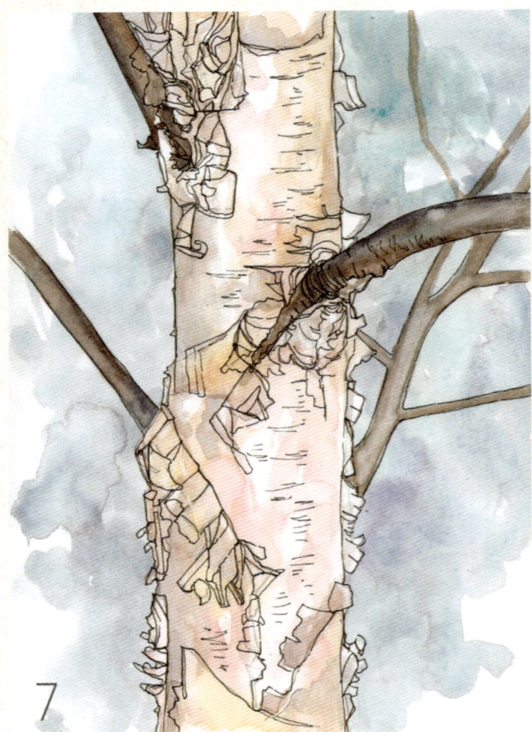

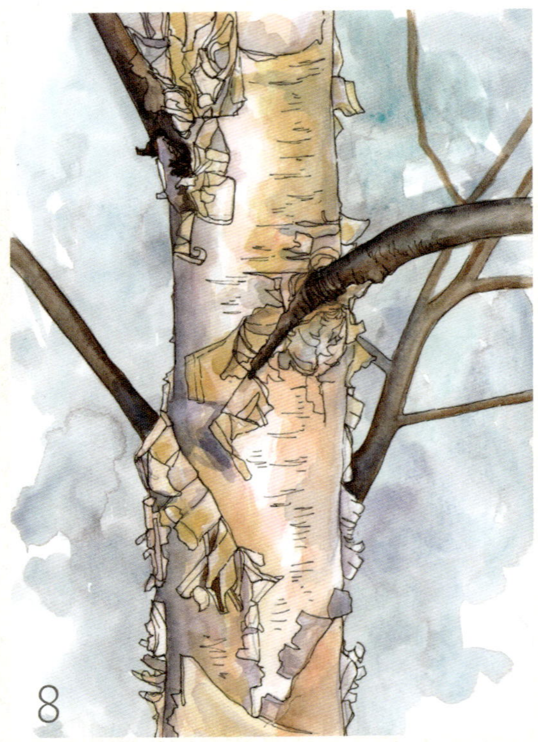

STEP 7: Once the watercolor is dry, use a fine pen to go over the lines. Think about abstracting the whole tree and focusing on one section of texture at a time. Play back and forth between the loose watercolor marks you've painted and the photo reference. Think about how the direction of the marks can show the roundness and the shape of the tree.

STEP 8: The tree sketch comes together with the linework added. Add another wash to the shadow layer to show which parts of the bark overlap. Also, deepen the shadows in some of the branches. Add more variation of color to the birch tree by building up some of the gold and pink tones and continuing to work on the shadows. I used Quinacridone Gold and Quinacridone Rose mixed with Buff Titanium to deepen the colors of the bark in some places.

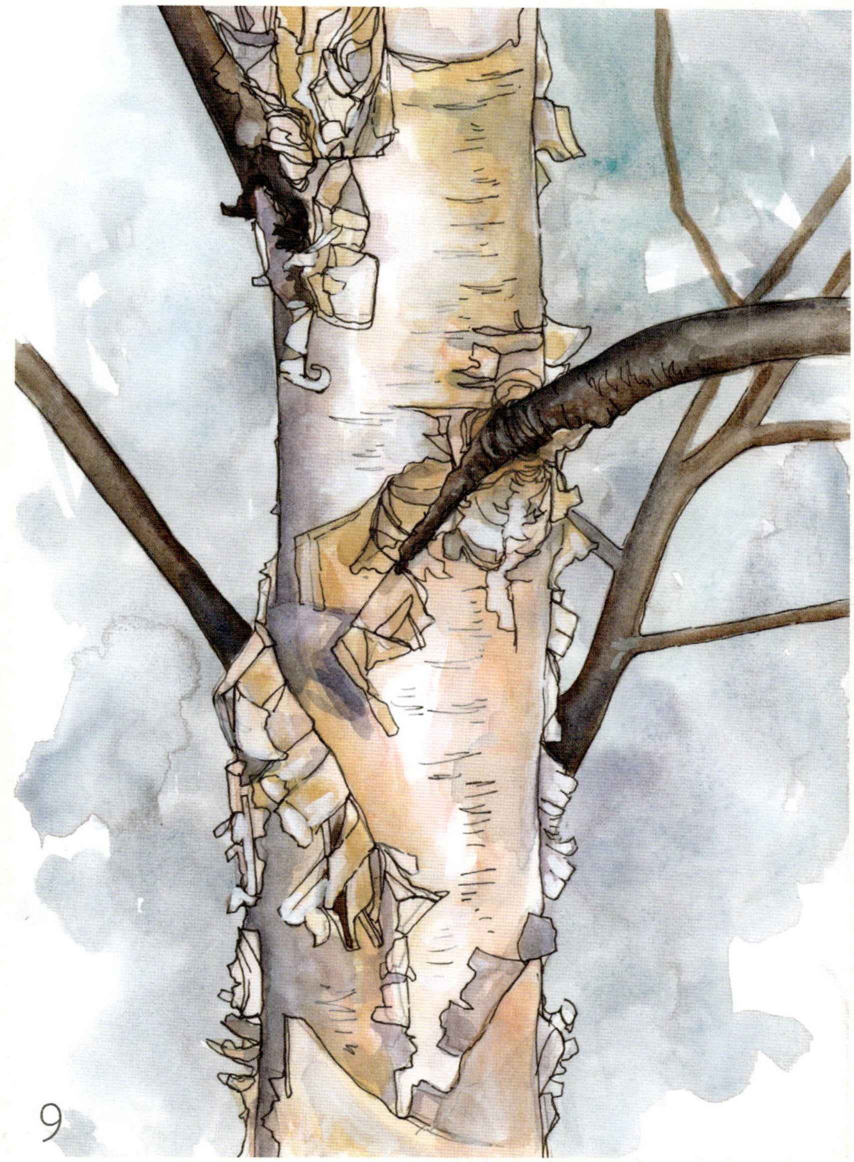

STEP 9: At the end of the sketch, you can bring back some white to show how the bark feels bright and shiny in some places. Use white gouache, Bleedproof White, or a white colored pencil to go over some areas where you notice the brightest highlights. Add a few details to the branches as well.

Project 27

ANIMAL TRACKS IN THE SNOW

Use layers of blue and gray watercolor to sketch the prints animals leave in the snow.

MATERIALS: a pencil, watercolor paper, and watercolors

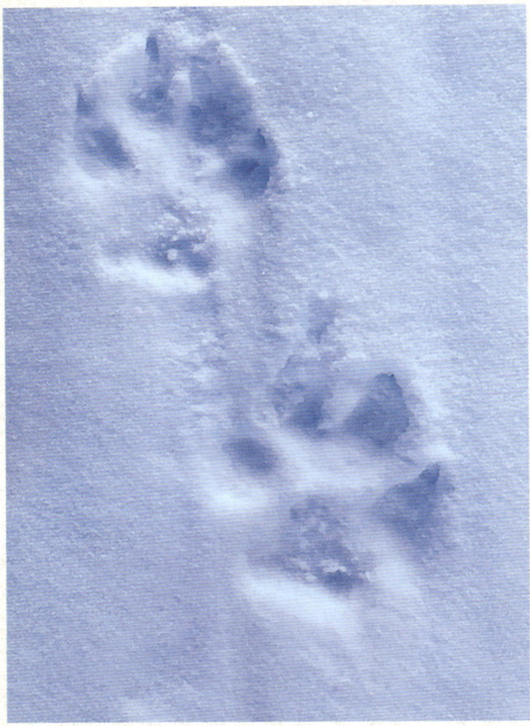

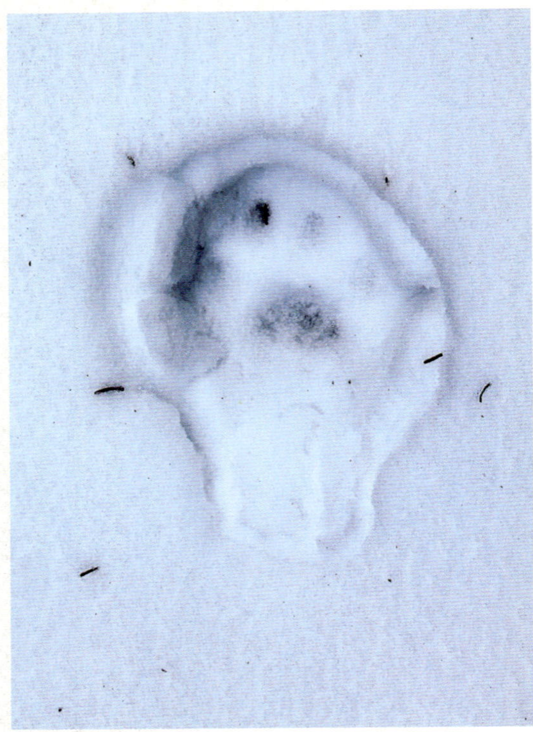

This project allows us to compare two similar animal tracks in the snow, a wolf (left) and a lynx (right). By sketching both next to each other, we can pay special attention to their similarities and differences.

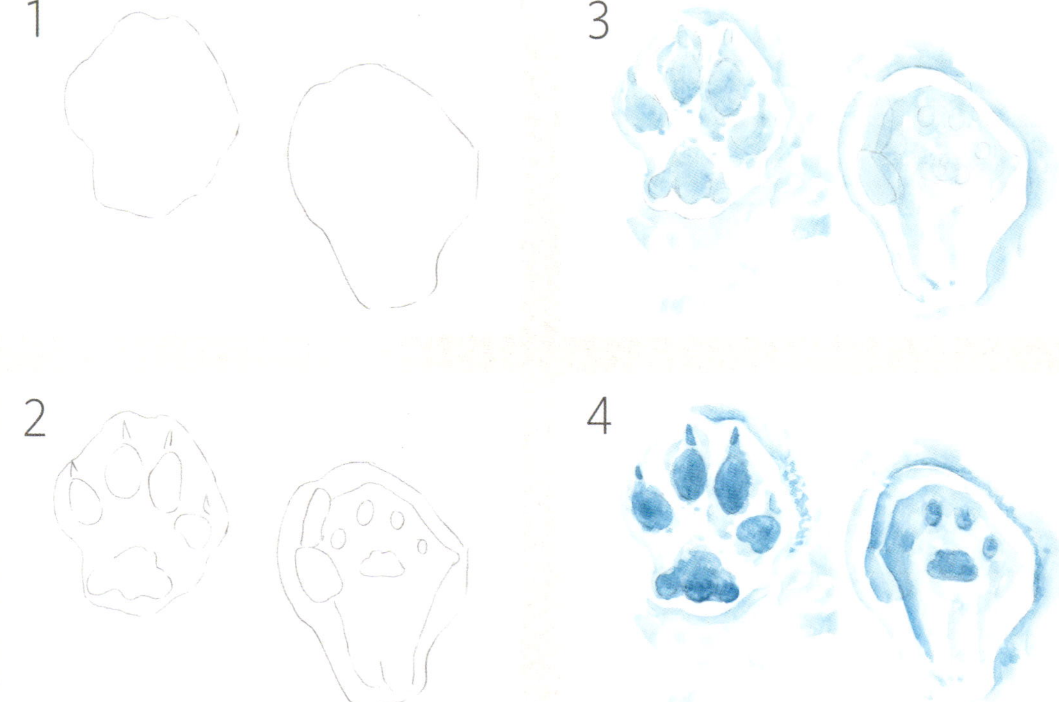

STEP 1: Sketch the outline of each track. I chose to sketch one wolf track and one lynx track to compare the two. Though the pads on the lynx are smaller and closer together, they have a large "snowshoe," so the tracks are relatively similar in size.

STEP 2: Sketch the interior of each track, marking the pads and claws, if present. It is typical to see the claws on a canine track but not on a feline because their claws are retractable. The lynx track is in crusty snow, so I sketched in some of the chunks of snow on the edge of the depression. Notice the difference in the pads' size, shape, and arrangement. The lynx foot has smaller, rounder pads arranged in a half circle. The wolf has larger, more oval pads arranged in a diamond or triangle shape.

STEP 3: Begin to paint in the shadows using a light wash of Cerulean Blue. We will build up value with multiple layers. Sketch in the mid- and dark tones inside each track and also in the snow surrounding them.

STEP 4: Paint another layer with Cerulean Blue to build up the mid-tones. This wash can have the same concentration of pigment and water as the previous step, but layering two washes on top of each other will make the color darker. I focused on building up the darkest parts of the track in the middle of the imprints of each pad or claw.

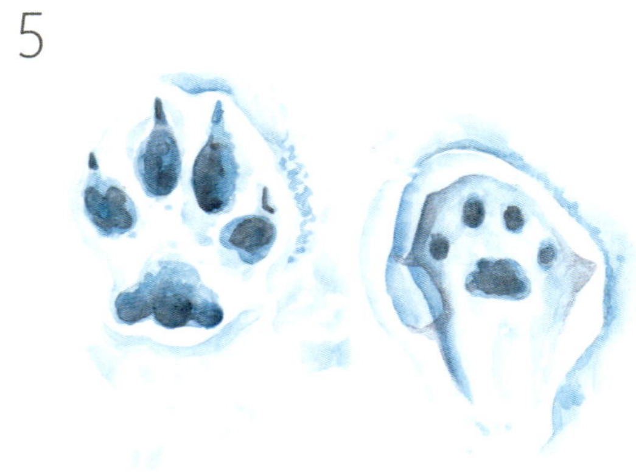

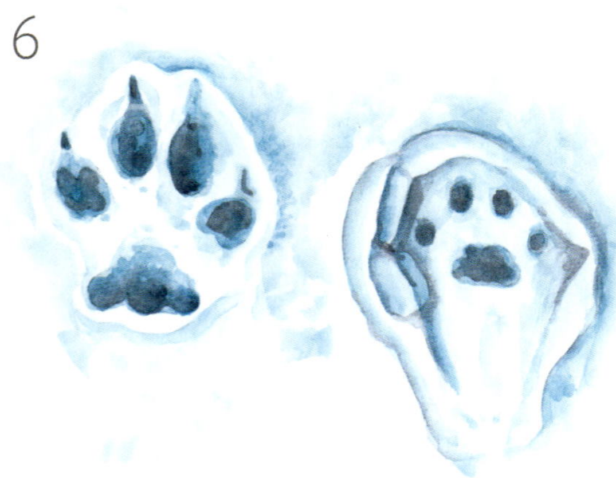

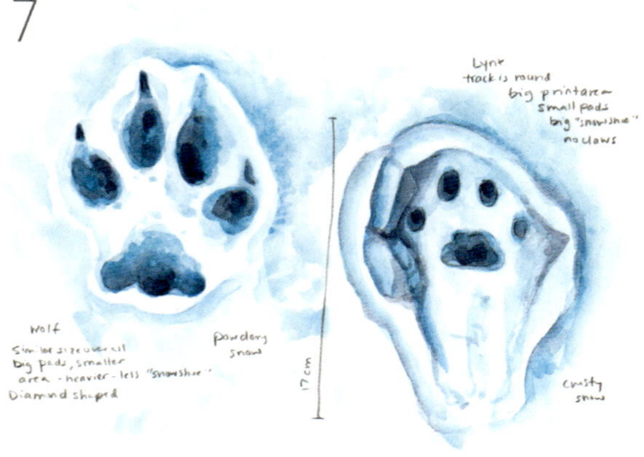

STEP 5: Mix a blue-gray for the darkest section of the tracks. I mixed Indanthrone Blue with some Burnt Sienna and Cerulean Blue. I painted this on top of the wash from the previous step to deepen some areas. At this point, I noticed which section of each pad imprint was darker and could better understand how the animal was walking.

STEP 6: Use the light blue (I used Cerulean Blue) to paint a light wash in the area surrounding each track. This gives the sense that the tracks are in the snow and that the ground around them also has texture and shadow.

STEP 7: Use the blue-gray to deepen some areas and details in the tracks. Add notes and measurements. You can pay attention to both similarities and differences.

DRAWING TO LEARN

One way to embrace the long nights we get during our Alaskan winters is to draw the night sky. It is hard to make a complicated sketch in the dark, but you can make some notes with a pencil and a headlamp, especially if you use the red mode that doesn't hurt your night vision. The night sky is a fun subject to explore with watercolor and white media, capturing the moon, constellations, the aurora borealis, and other effects. The more I sketched the night sky, the more I got to know the constellations and some features of the moon.

I usually sketch something I see and try to learn more about it or identify it from the sketch. However, sometimes, I work the other way around: drawing something from a reference and then trying to find it in the wild.

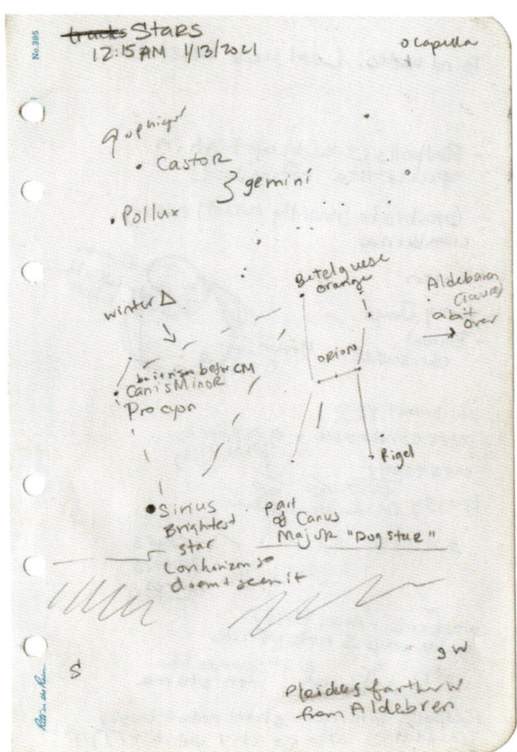

I made this sketch looking out the window at midnight in January, with simple marks for the stars that I recognized from studying star charts. I used a red light so that I could see my paper in the dark and keep my night vision to study the sky.

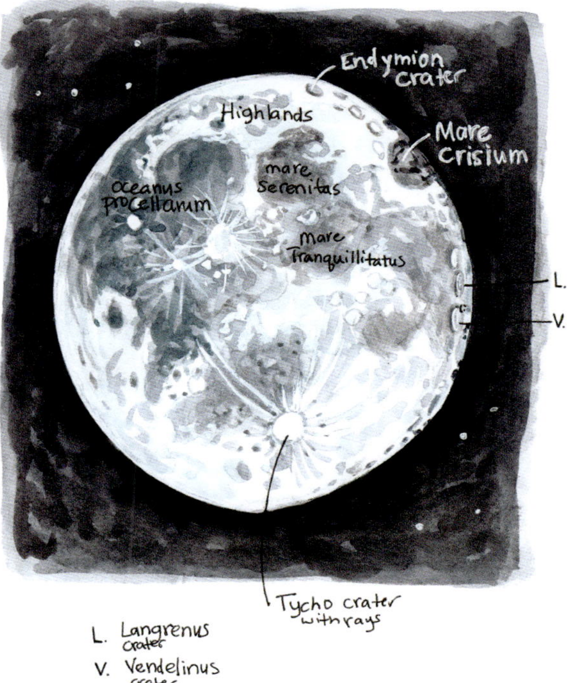

I drew this sketch of the nearly full moon for the winter solstice. NASA publishes a Daily Moon Guide that you can reference to help identify what features you see. A pair of binoculars can also help you see more detail.

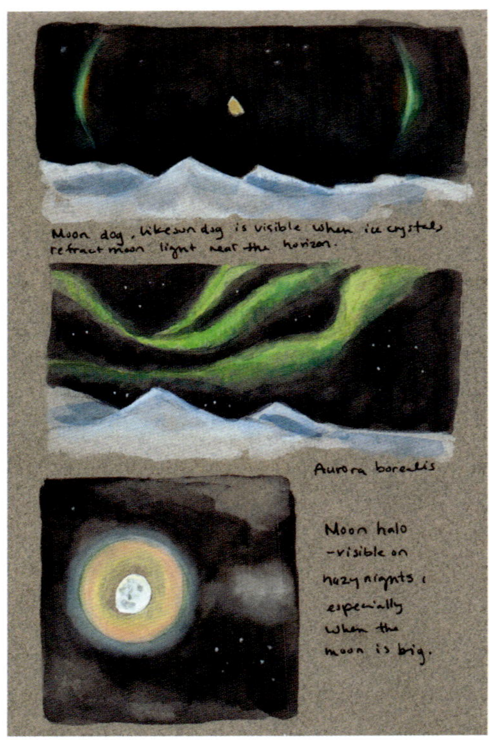

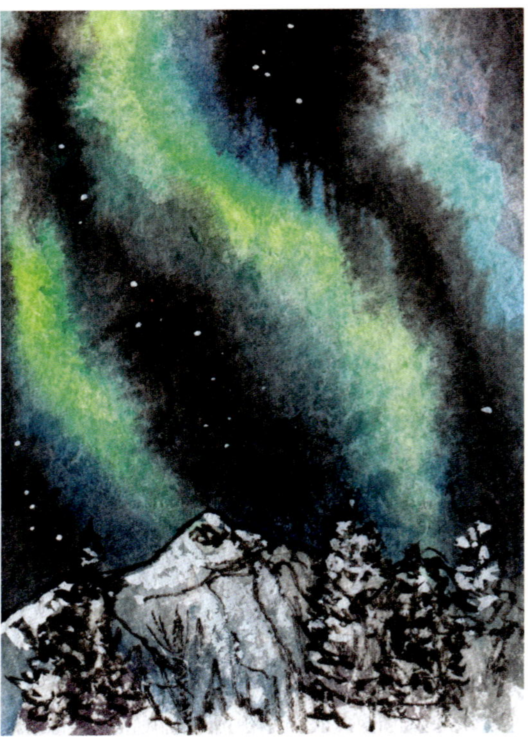

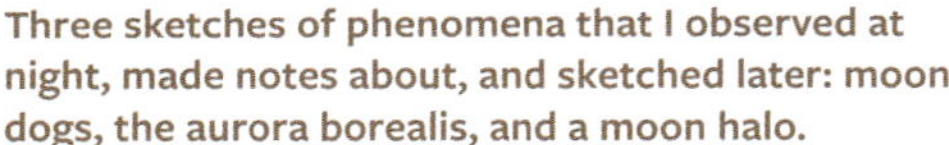

Three sketches of phenomena that I observed at night, made notes about, and sketched later: moon dogs, the aurora borealis, and a moon halo.

Wet-in-wet painting of the aurora from memory with watercolor and ink

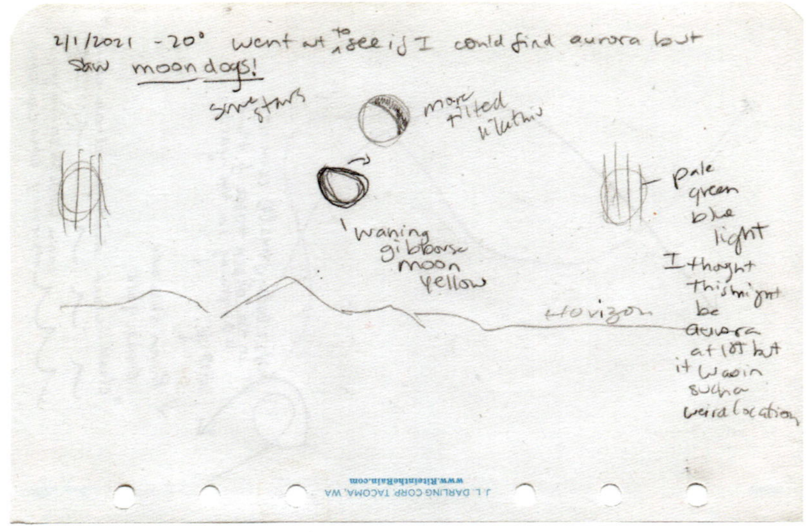

Simple pencil sketch of moon dog observations on a cold night

It is fun to discover how sketching helps you learn about things even if you haven't experienced them in real life. As a science illustrator, I cannot often draw my illustrations from life; I have to combine a series of reference photos, for example, to draw alpine flowers in the middle of the winter. Sometimes, I'll draw an unfamiliar plant and stumble upon it in real life a year or two later. That moment is always filled with joy, like meeting a person you talk to on Zoom all the time face to face: "I know you! So nice to actually meet you!"

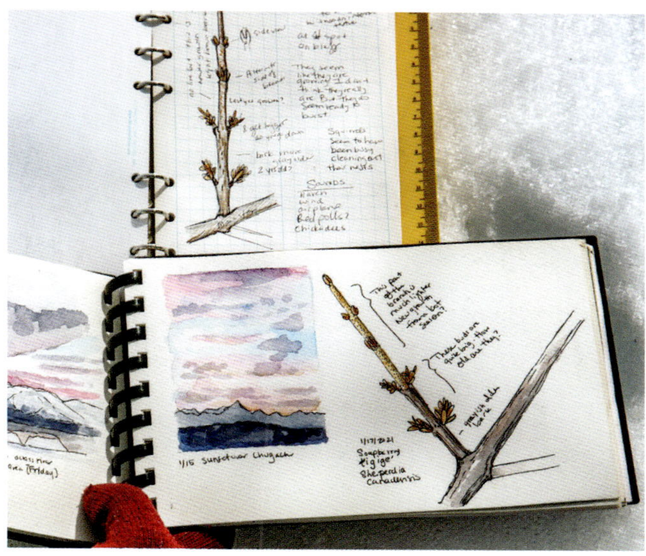

Sometimes, I make a simple sketch with colored pencils and pencil on waterproof paper (top) and then rework that sketch into a larger sketchbook with more detail using pen and watercolor (bottom). The bottom sketchbook is a collection of observations from the winter but made with watercolor inside where the paint won't freeze.

I've been learning this way by drawing the night sky, and it has brought me great delight to start sketching the night sky and to get to know the constellations. It is easy to look up star charts that outline what should be visible in the sky where you live monthly. I've sketched from these and then found those constellations outside. I've also sketched with the lights off in my cabin, headlamp in red mode, making simple diagrams looking out the window. Once I recognize a few critical stars, I can orient myself from them to find more. When I started, most of the stars looked the same and jumbled together, but over time, I noticed how they were different colors with different brightnesses. I've now learned to recognize some landmarks and see things in greater detail.

Reflection

In this book, we've practiced sketching different types of subjects found in nature. What is your favorite subject to sketch? Why?

I love sketching plants because they stand still. I am also obsessed with small worlds, drawing structure, and learning form and function. When you look closely, plants have many interesting structures that are fun to observe and wonder about why and how they work. But I also love learning about and sketching all different things.

Project 28

NIGHT SKIES: ORION CONSTELLATION

This project focuses on the Orion constellation that dominates the winter sky facing south and is one of the first spots that I can easily recognize in the night sky from my cabin.

MATERIALS: a white pencil, a white pen, gouache, watercolor paper, and watercolors

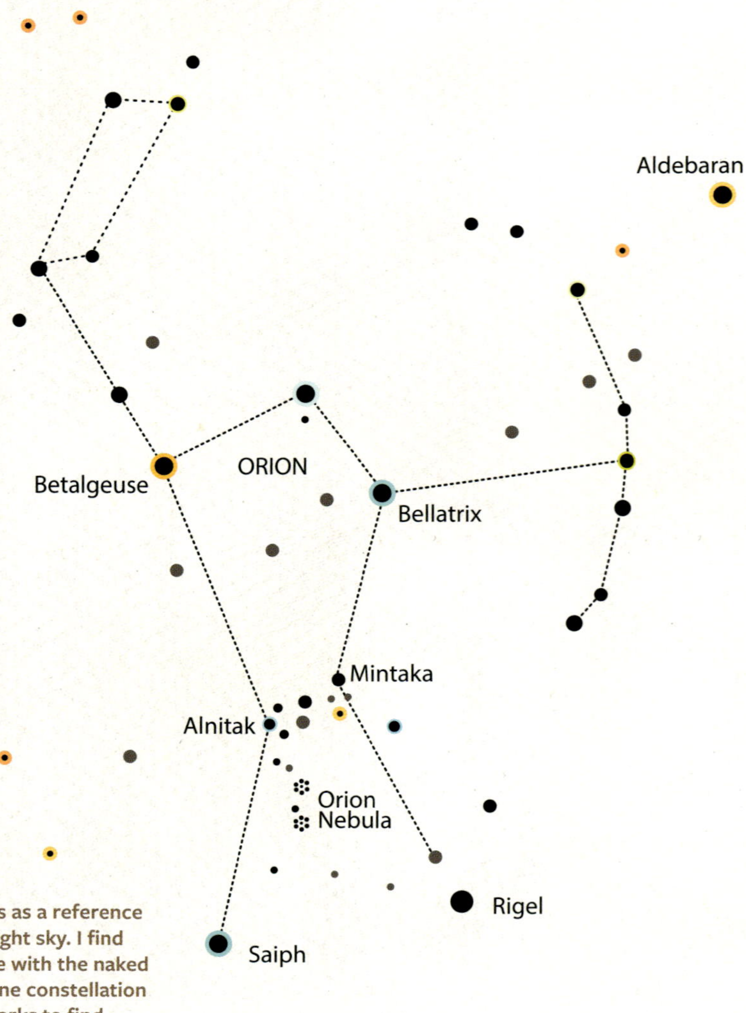

I often use star charts and diagrams as a reference when studying and sketching the night sky. I find references that show what I can see with the naked eye or through binoculars. I learn one constellation at a time and then use those landmarks to find other features and constellations.

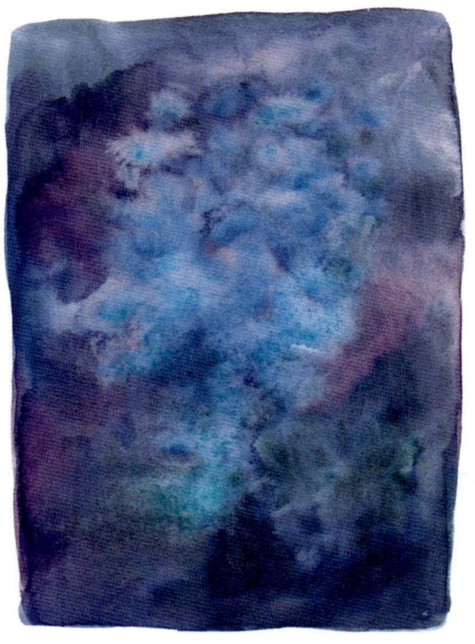

1

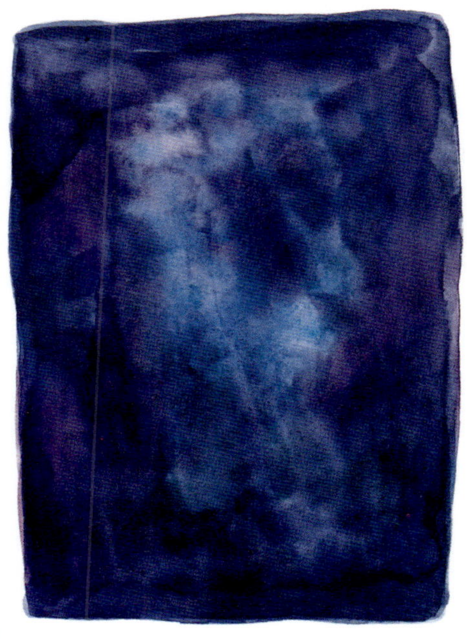

2

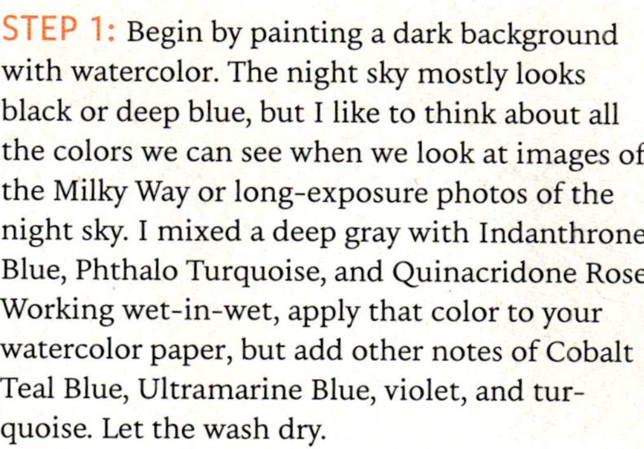

STEP 1: Begin by painting a dark background with watercolor. The night sky mostly looks black or deep blue, but I like to think about all the colors we can see when we look at images of the Milky Way or long-exposure photos of the night sky. I mixed a deep gray with Indanthrone Blue, Phthalo Turquoise, and Quinacridone Rose. Working wet-in-wet, apply that color to your watercolor paper, but add other notes of Cobalt Teal Blue, Ultramarine Blue, violet, and turquoise. Let the wash dry.

STEP 2: Make another wash. Working wet-in-wet with granulating colors yields a somewhat splotchy and uneven wash. I like this effect, but I often add a second layer to even the wash and make things darker. Let the second wash dry.

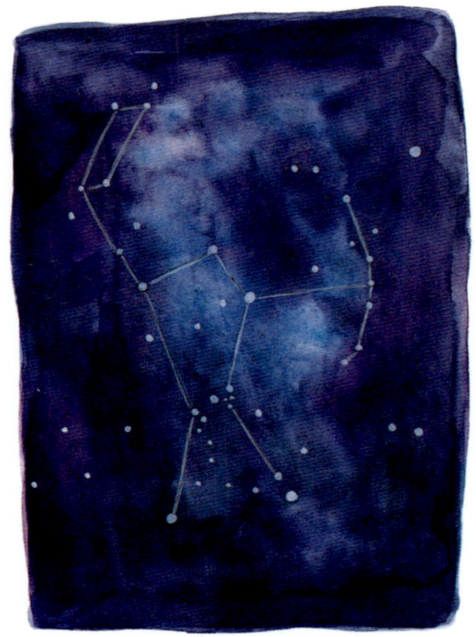

3

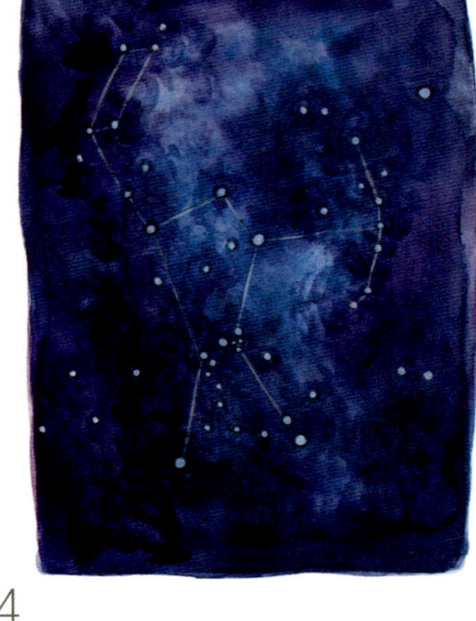

4

STEP 3: Use the star chart or a sketch as a reference to draw the main stars using a pencil. The graphite on a dark background can be challenging to see, so you can also use a white colored pencil if that is easier. I often use a graphite pencil and tilt the paper to see the shine. Measure the distance and angles from one point using pencil measurements or dividers. Once the stars are marked, you can draw lines to connect the main segments of the constellation with a white colored pencil and paint over the spots where the stars are with Bleedproof White or gouache.

STEP 4: To make the stars stand out more, I increased the contrast around them using another layer of dark watercolor paint. Paint around each star with the dark gray paint from the first two steps. Feel comfortable painting over top of the colored pencil lines because these will resist the watercolor. Continue a blotchy pattern into the sky, working with water to add variation to the background.

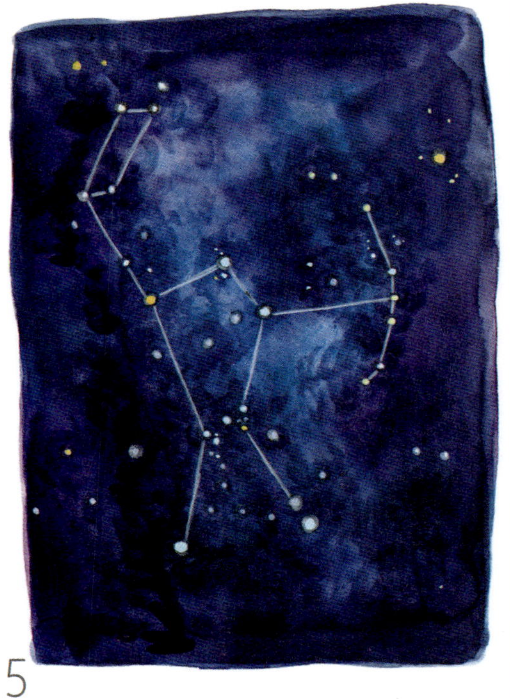

5

6

STEP 5: Once the watercolor is dry, brighten the white pencil lines and stars by going over them again with a white pencil. Stars are different colors, ranging from blue to white to yellow and orange. Use colored pencils or gouache mixed with watercolor paint to color in some stars. This should stand out more on the paper since there is already a layer of white underneath the colored layer of paint.

STEP 6: Add labels to name the stars or other essential features using a white gel pen.

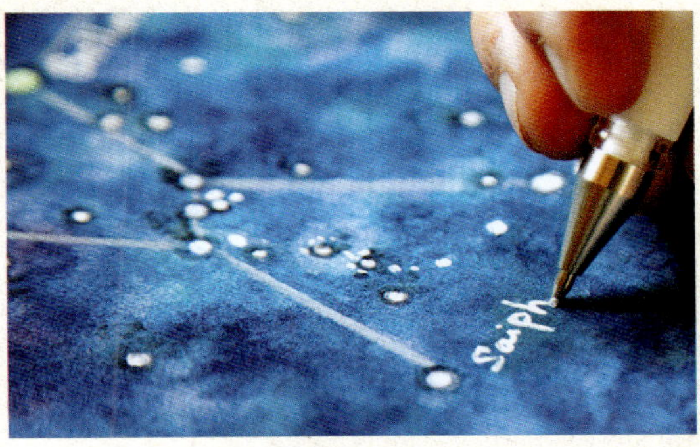

Adding labels and details with a white gel pen

Project 29

WINTER LANDSCAPES, WINTER LIGHT, AND ALPENGLOW

Capture the pink alpenglow light on the mountains with layers of watercolor.

MATERIALS: a pencil, watercolor paper, and watercolors

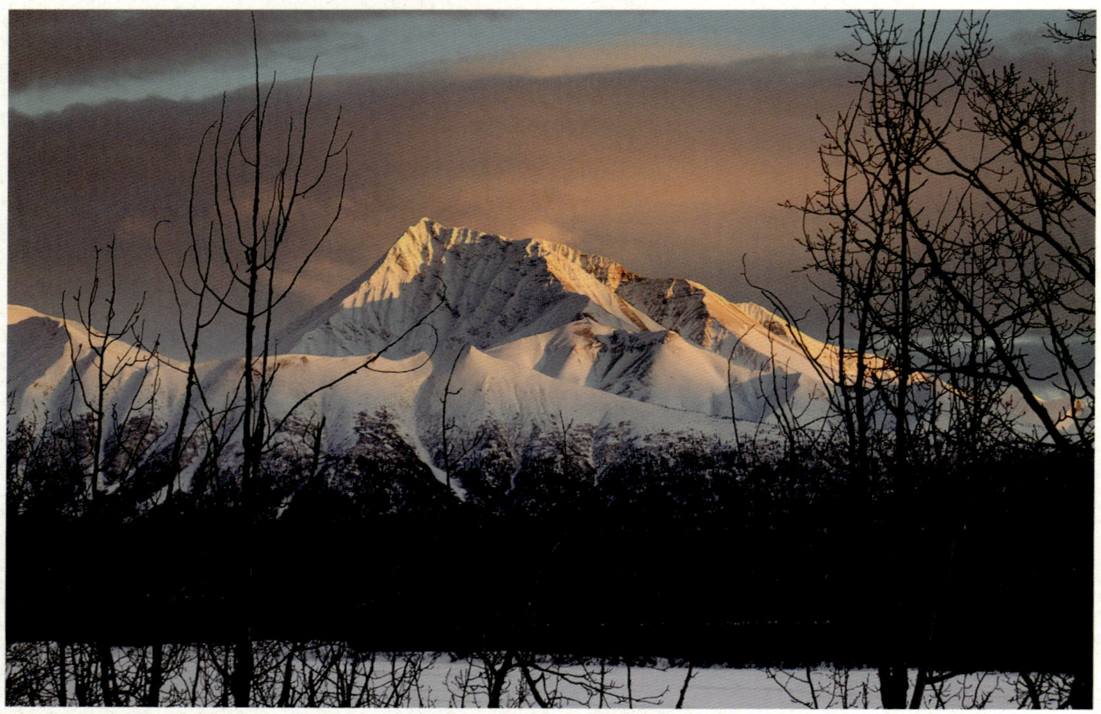

Winter has some of the most spectacular light shows of the year, and around the time of the spring equinox, we get lovely drawn-out sunsets where the setting sun reflects its light on the snow-covered mountains and turns them gold, magenta, and violet. This effect is called "alpenglow" because it looks like the mountains are glowing.

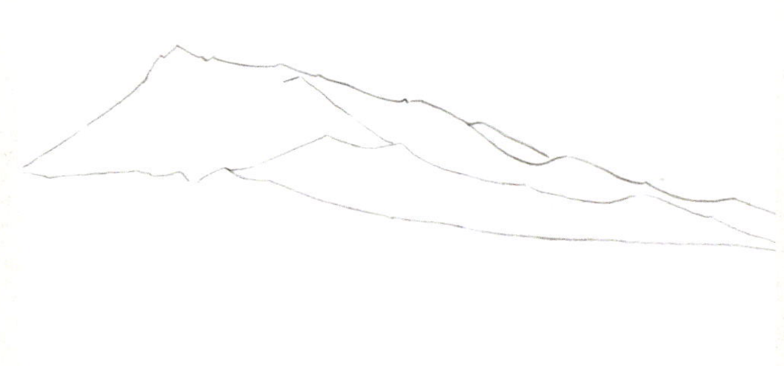

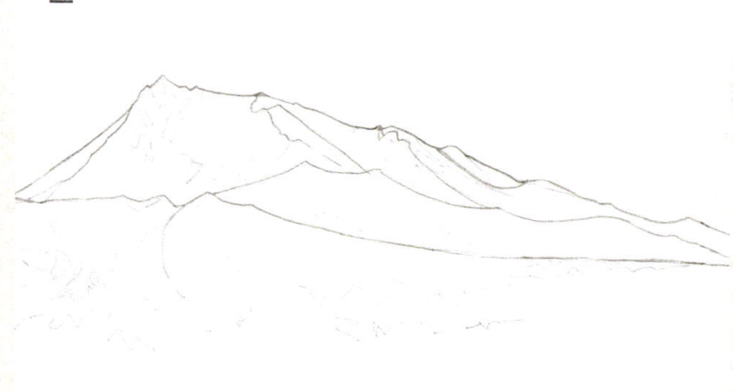

STEP 1: Draw the main shapes of the mountains, measuring the angles with a pencil. I started with the ridge in the foreground and then added the peak in the background and some of the ridges in between. I decided to focus my sketch on the mountains with the bright evening light and ignore the trees in the foreground.

STEP 2: Add more detail to the drawing. Squint your eyes to look closely at the shapes of the shadows and the ridges. Draw in the main shadows, the shapes of the rocky areas, and the shapes of the vegetated areas.

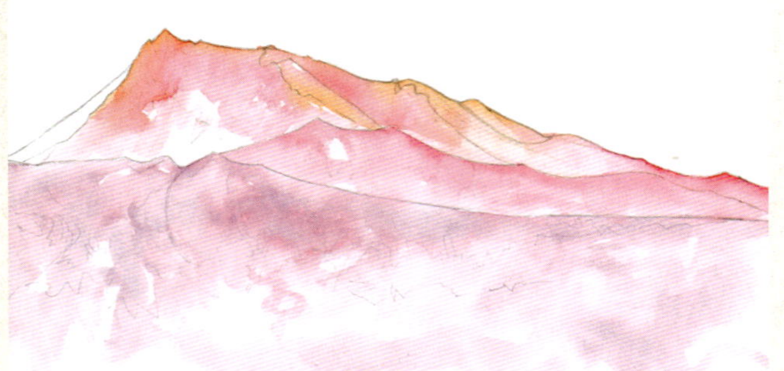

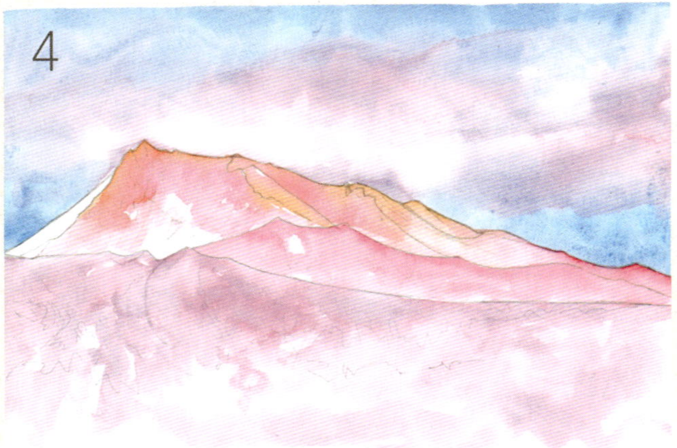

STEP 3: We want to capture the vibrant pink color that the evening light casts, so I started my painting there. Notice how the light is pink and gold at the top of the mountain, and then it gets more violet lower down. I mixed Quinacridone Rose with Quinacridone Gold for the top part and Quinacridone Rose with some Ultramarine Blue for the bottom part. Apply the watercolor in a light wash, working wet-on-wet, going from gold-magenta to pure magenta to violet-magenta. Let that wash dry.

STEP 4: Paint in the sky. I worked wet-in-wet with Cerulean Blue for the blue part of the sky and some of the Quinacridone Rose with Ultramarine Blue for the middle of the cloud. I dabbed up some of the paint right above the peak with a paper towel so the cloud would be lighter in the middle.

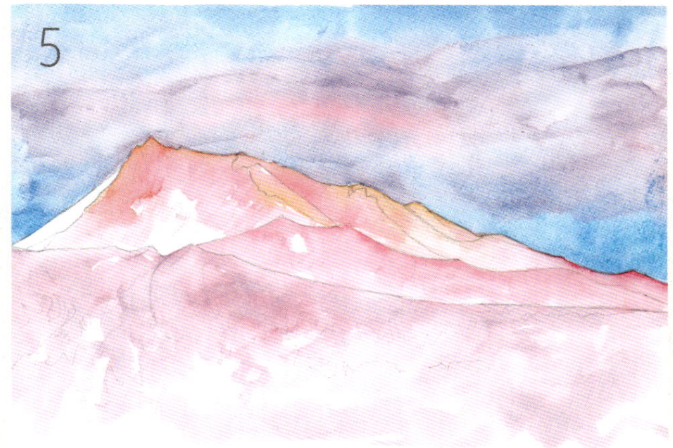

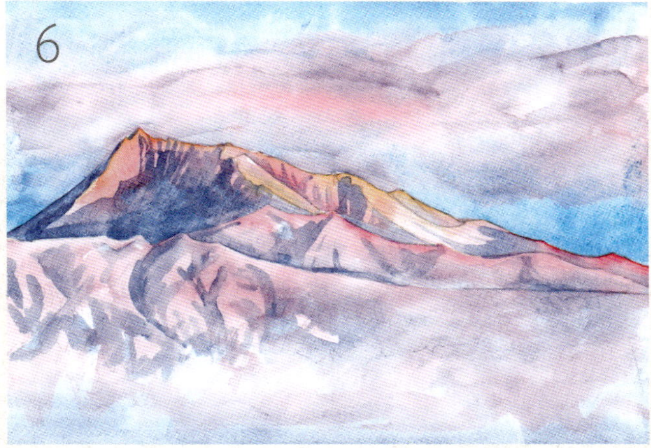

STEP 5: Add another layer of magenta and violet around the cloudy area in the sky. Work with a graded wash, going from pink in the middle to more violet and then blue along the edges.

STEP 6: With a light wash, paint in the areas and shapes where you notice shadows on the mountains. I used Ultramarine Blue, which turned blue-violet when layered on top of the magenta that I painted in an earlier layer. The shadows help define the form and shape of the mountains.

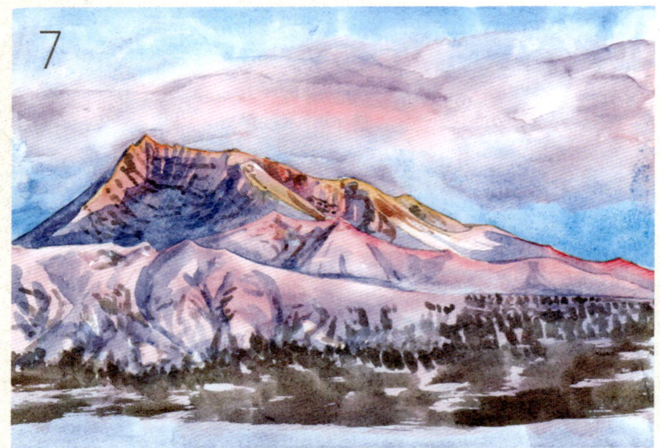

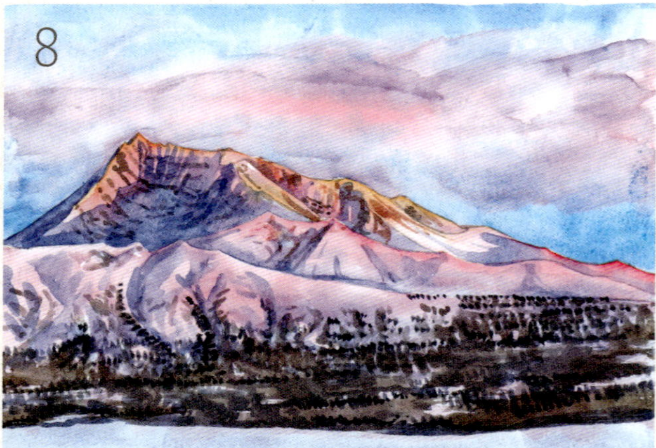

STEP 7: Next, paint some of the vegetation and rocky layers on top of the shadow layer. I mixed Raw Umber with some Ultramarine Blue to make a grayish brown. This wash will layer over what has already been painted so that it will be cooler in the areas with shadow. You can also vary the brown color to be warmer by using more Burnt Sienna in the places where sunlight hits. I painted some of the rocks and trees with tiny dots. Use a dry brush, making horizontal strokes to paint the bottom of the vegetation where the forest hits the flat frozen river.

STEP 8: Mix a darker brown with Raw Umber and Ultramarine Blue and paint another layer of vegetation on the closest ridge. I deepened the color in the valleys where the drainages are, on the bottom edge where the forest hits the river, and along sections of the far ridge.

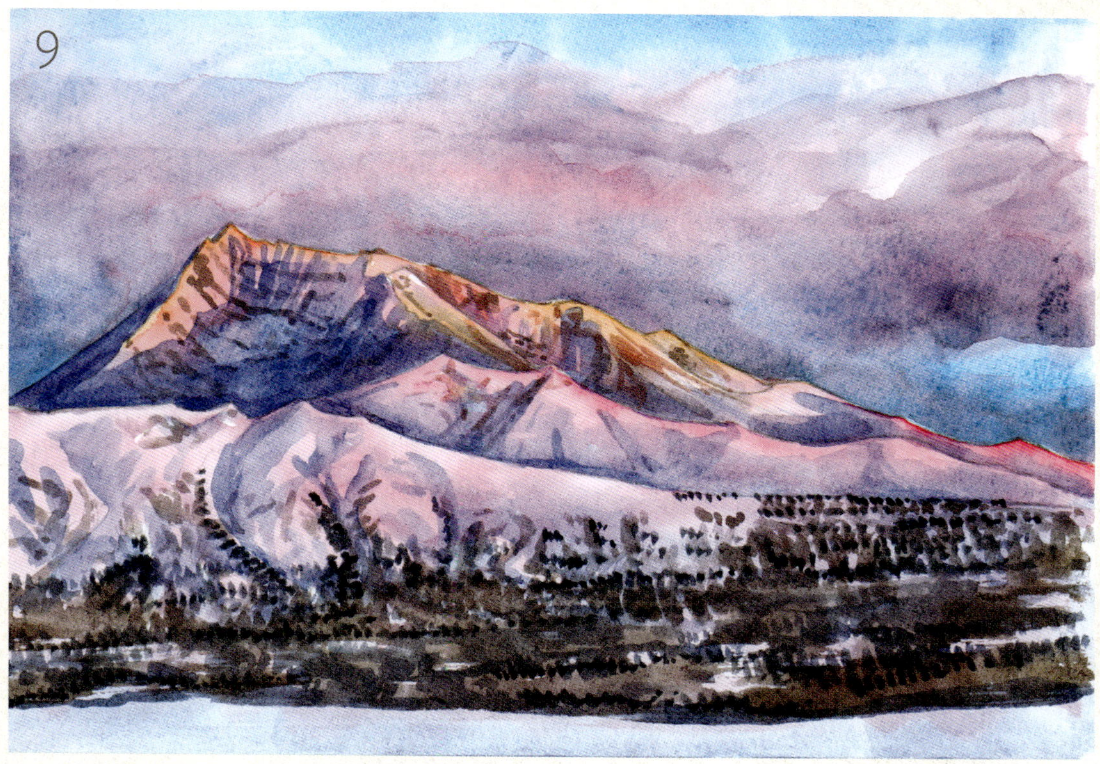

STEP 9: I noticed the sky in the photo was still slightly darker than my sketch. I wanted the glowing mountains to stand out, so I added another wash to darken the sky and create more contrast. I mixed Ultramarine Blue with magenta to create a light wash between the mountain ridges so they felt more separated. I also added some Burnt Sienna to that wash and painted purple-gray into the sky around the mountain.

Taking It with You and Making It Your Own

The journal is a place to decant the stuff of life; reassuringly, none of it is wasted. It remains fresh, still tasting of its source. Transferring experience from the vat of life into the vessel of the journal is distillation: it sieves, concentrates, and ferments. If after many seasons we develop some mastery of the process, the stuff can become as clear and fiery as brandy.

—HANNAH HINCHMAN

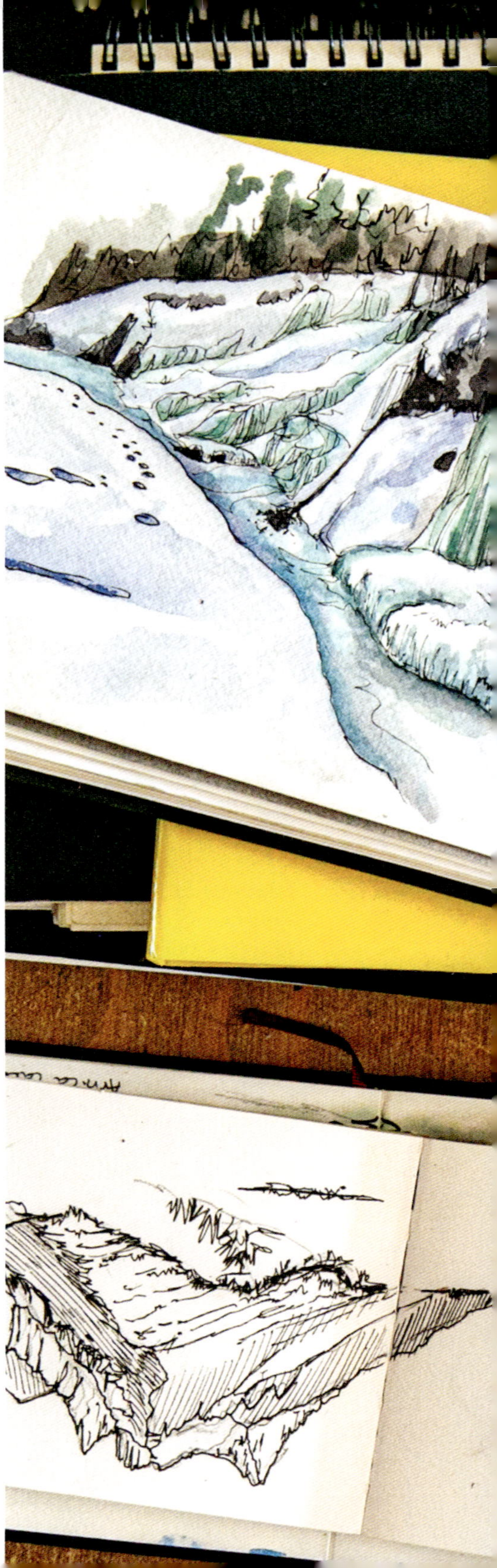

▶ **Some people like to sketch in the same format and keep a consistent record. I like to mix things up and try different sizes and types of paper. I often don't even sketch in a bound book. As long as I am sketching then I don't think it matters what the format is.**

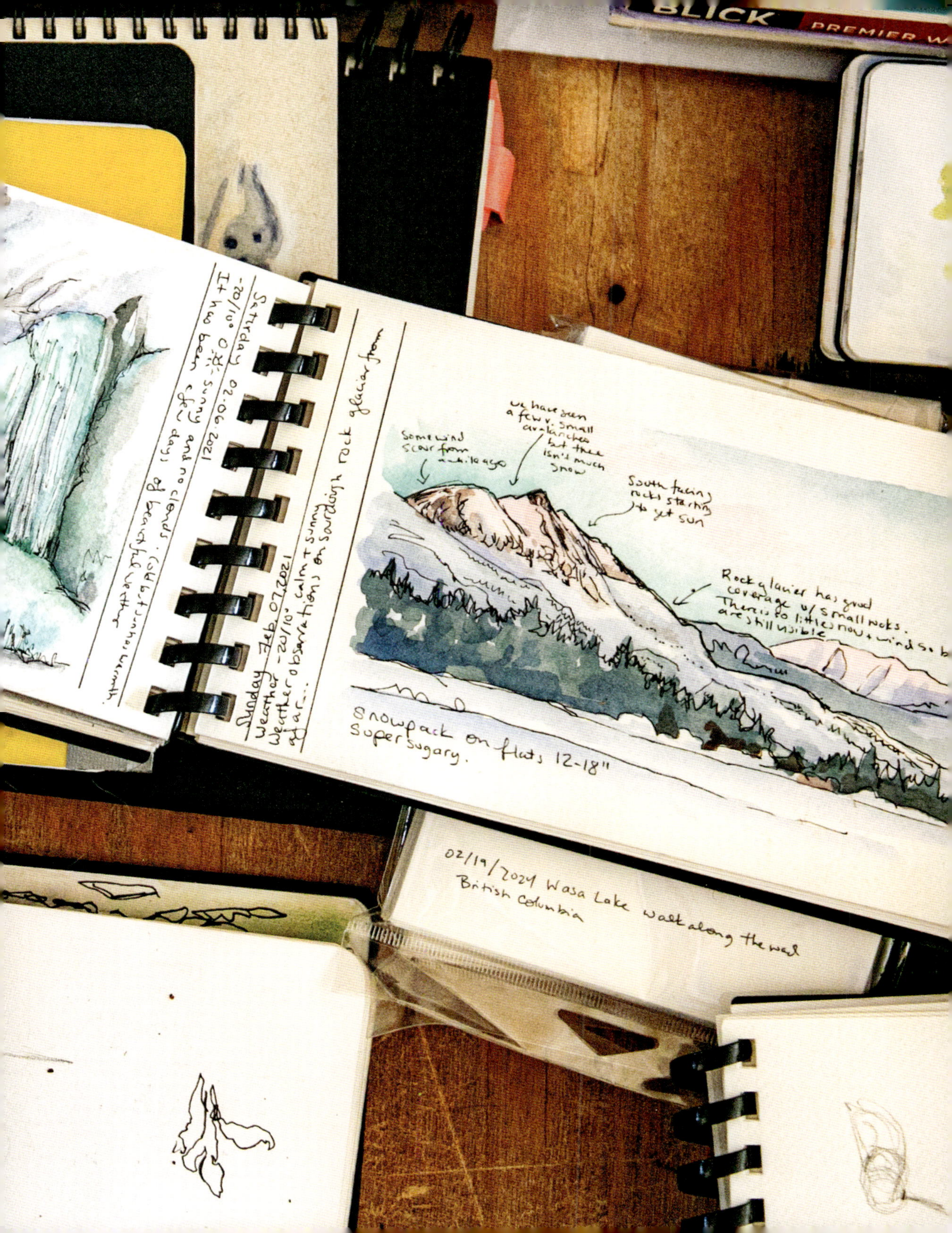

BLICK
Saturday 02.06.2021
It has been sunny and no clouds.
Sunday Feb 07, 2021
Weather -20/10° calm + sunny
Weather observations on sourdough rock glacier from
Some wind scour from a while ago
we have seen a few v. small avalanches but there isn't much snow
South facing rocks starting to get sun
Rock glacier has good coverage w/ small rocks.
Snowpack on flats 12-18"
Super sugary.
02/19/2024 Wasa Lake walk along the wall
British Columbia

Sketching is a process and a journey; there is always more to see and learn. I'm still developing new ways to capture information and learn more about the natural world around me. In all the hours of practice on these pages, you have probably learned how you like to work and what you like to sketch. I hope you feel ready to take this practice out into your surroundings, whatever that looks like for you. There is so much to experience there, and sketching is a beautiful tool.

Sometimes, there is so much to see and sketch that a blank page can feel overwhelming. Below are some of my favorite ways to start a sketch or to break into a blank page.

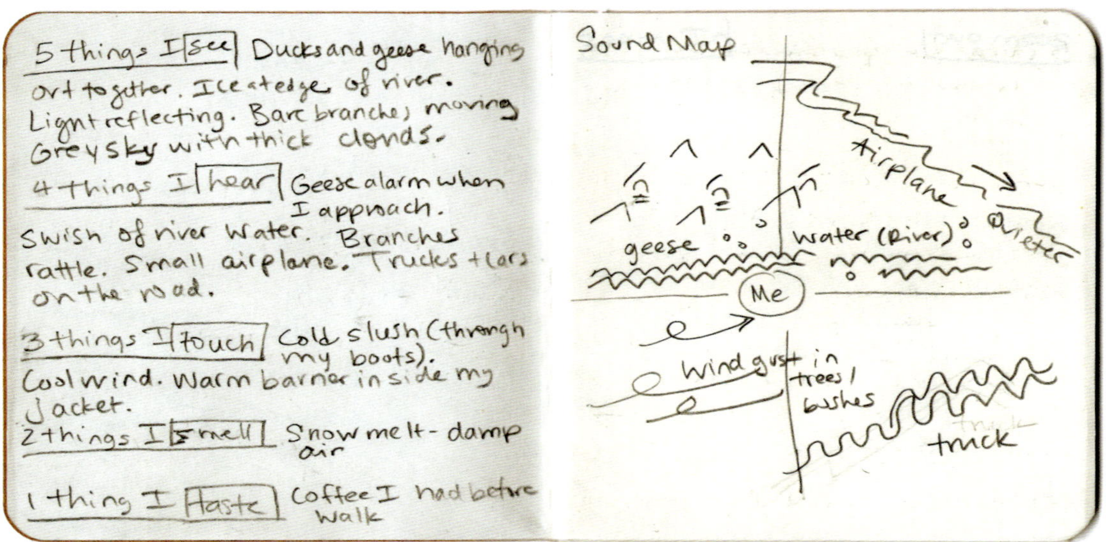

Some days, I would rather pay attention to all my senses than focus on careful observation of one thing. On this page, I spent some time writing down five things I saw, four things I heard, three things I felt, two things I smelled, and one thing I tasted. On the other page, I drew a sound map with marks and diagrams of what I could hear.

▶ This is one of my favorite ways to fill a sketchbook page and practice different techniques. I start by entering the metadata or weather and write a few sentences. Then I make a few contour sketches of plants or things that I find up close and a quick gesture sketch of the landscape.

Friday September 24, 2021 - Nizina

Clouds are moving around. Big temp change + high pressure coming in?

◐ ☁ 30°/44°

○ waning

☼ 7:22am → 7:26pm

12:04 hrs daylight

8:14pm → 12:08pm

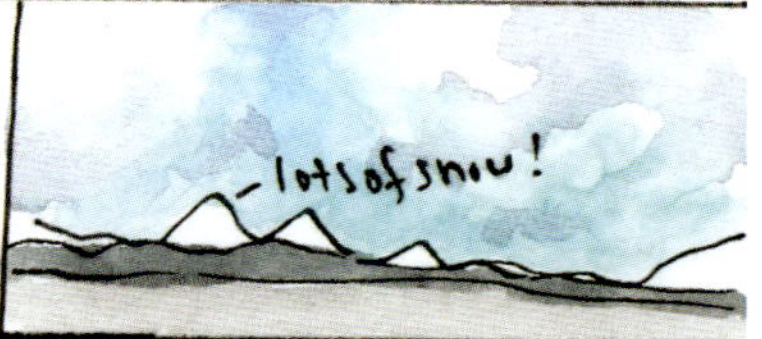

It poured rain here last night. Dumped snow on the Chugach. Woke up to frost and patches of blue sky moving in. Lots of leaves still falling but the snow and cold sapped a bunch of their color.

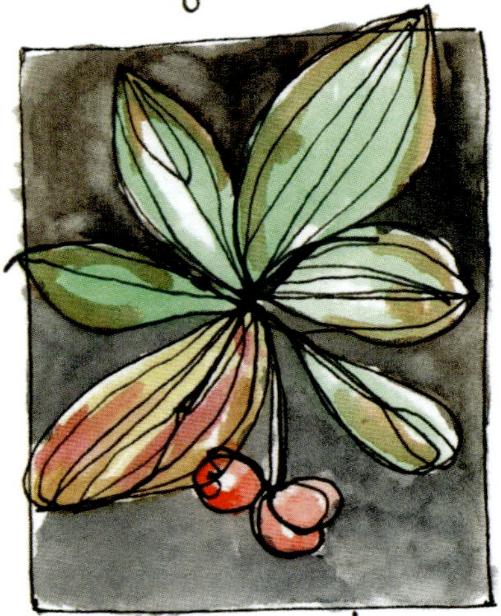

Dwarf Dogwood

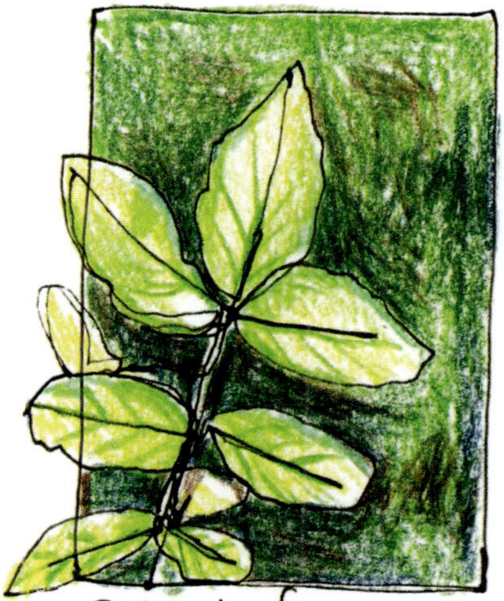

Rose leaf

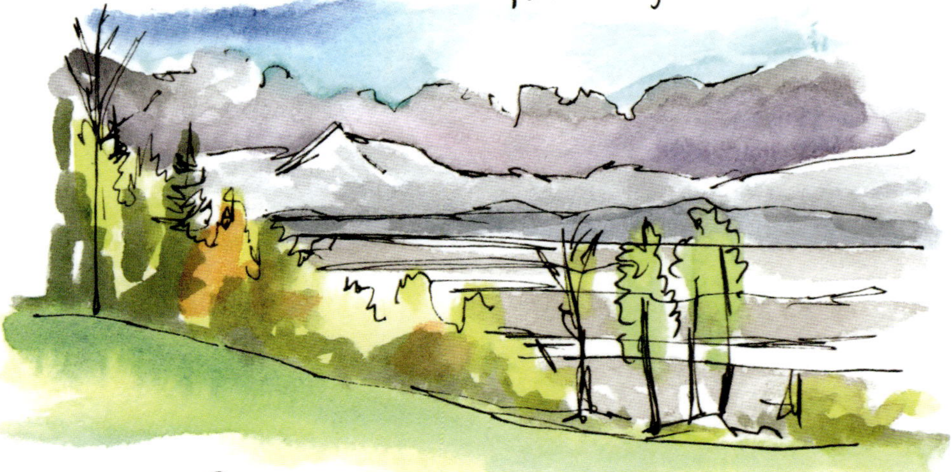

view east from the yard

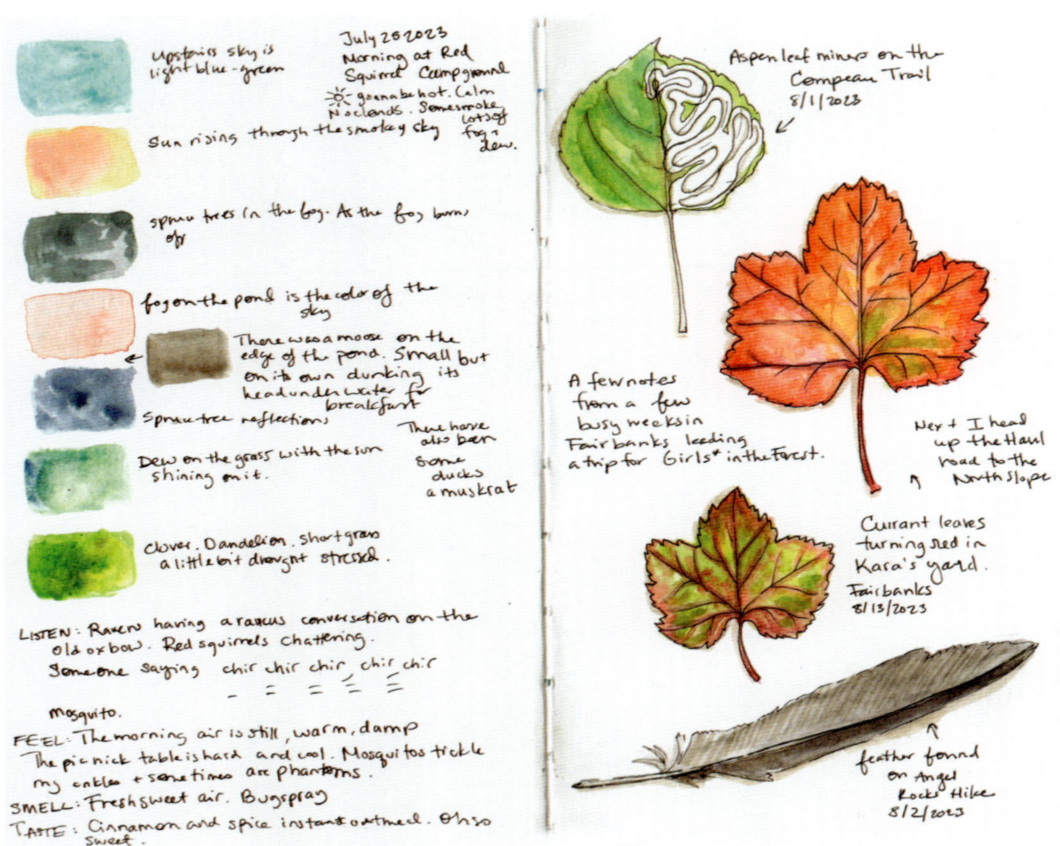

Including observations from all five senses on a sketchbook page can be a relaxing and grounding practice.

METADATA

Metadata means information about information, and in a sketchbook, metadata is usually a set of measurements you make in a standard format for each entry. It can be about the weather, the location, your mood, or anything, and it can be fun to come up with your metadata. My friend who lives near the ocean includes information about the tides. I keep track of the aurora index (KPI) in the winter. My metadata entries include words, pictures, and numbers, which are an excellent way to warm up my hand and set my intention for journaling. I will draw a small diagram of the sky, write out the date and location, and look up and record the temperature, cloud types, sky cover, precipitation, day length, and moon phase. I will also usually add a sentence about myself and how I feel.

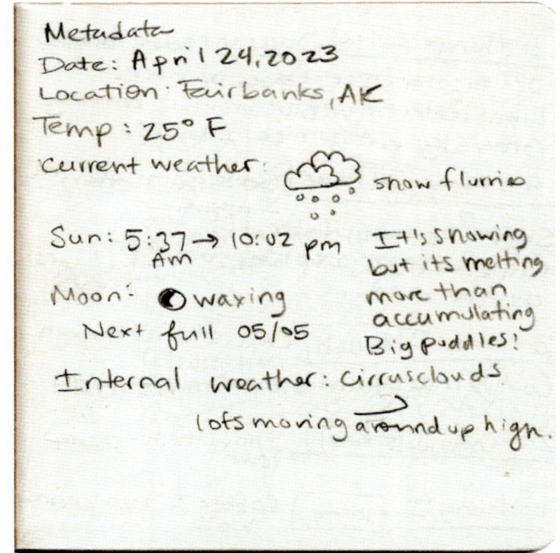

▲ Metadata entry in a small 2 x 2 inch sketchbook using words, pictures, and numbers

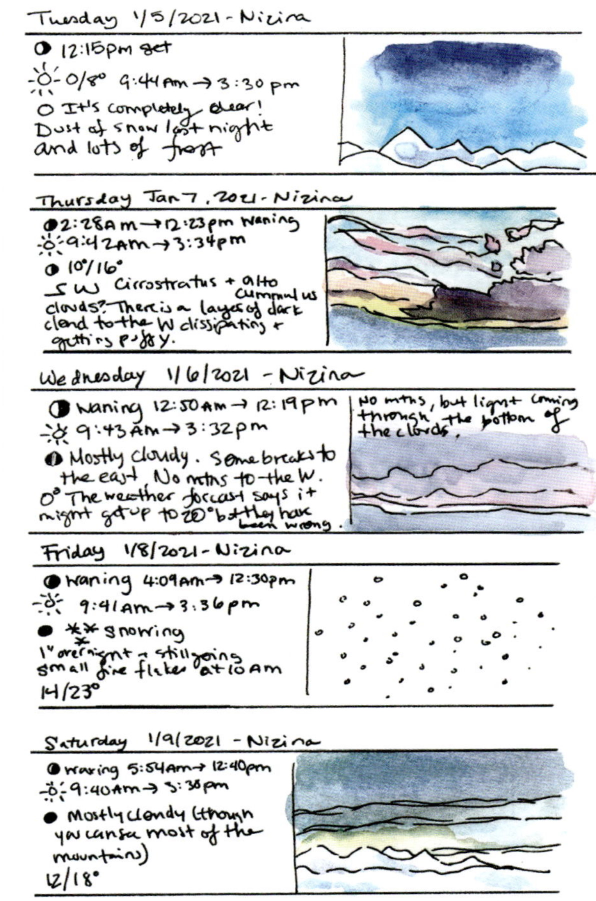

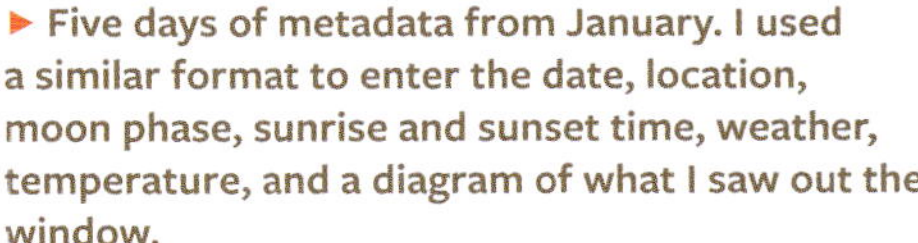

► Five days of metadata from January. I used a similar format to enter the date, location, moon phase, sunrise and sunset time, weather, temperature, and a diagram of what I saw out the window.

5.4.3.2.1. GROUNDING THROUGH THE SENSES

I learned this exercise in a wilderness mental health first aid class and started using it while sketching. It is a beautiful way to get to know your surroundings, pay attention to your senses, and relax your nervous system. I journal about five things I see, four things I hear, three things I feel, two things I smell, and one thing I taste. I love to find colors and textures to describe what I hear, smell, and taste and translate these into visual information, but I often write them out. For taste, I don't usually taste what is around me, but I will pay attention to my body and notice what flavors are already in my mouth—maybe a cup of tea—before I head out.

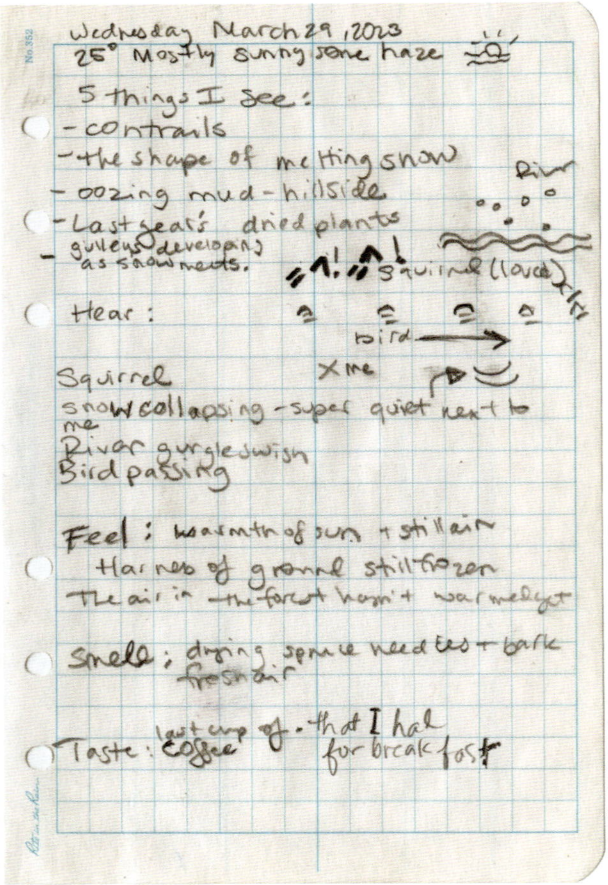

A sketchbook entry that focuses on my senses, made with words and diagrams

MAKE A MAP

Maps can take many forms, but they are a great way to begin a sketch page. You can create an event map for your walk by drawing a line to represent the path you traveled and different symbols and notes for the things you experienced along the way.

I will often draw a map as a part of my research before I go on a trip. I'll sketch a page by looking at satellite imagery or other maps I find online to get to know more about a place before I get there.

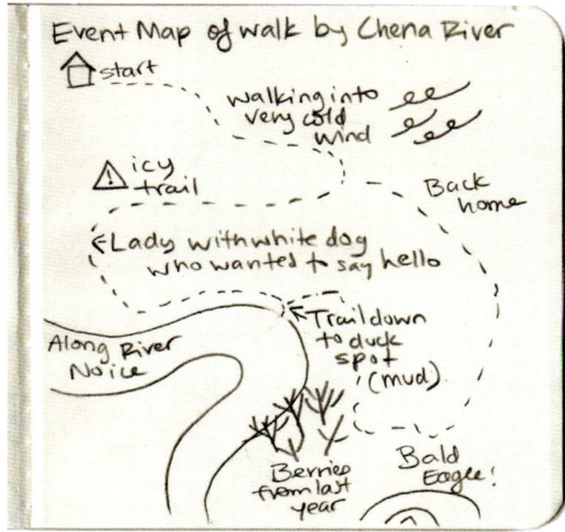

▲ A map of a walk I took, sketched with a simple diagram and labels

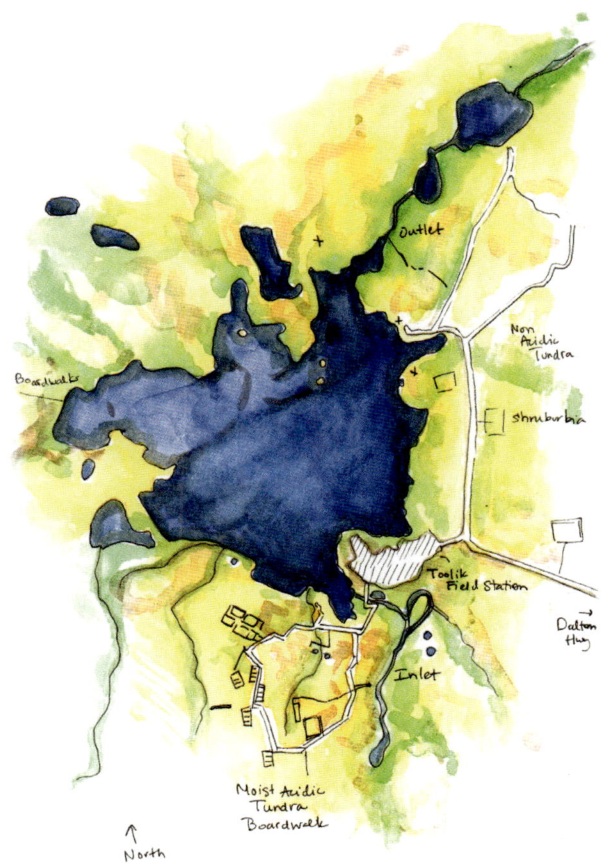

► A more artistically rendered map of Toolik Lake that I made during an artist residency there. This helped me learn the landscape and remember where I went on different walks.

I created this accordion book by sketching one plant or leaf a day during the fall. I also added notes and observations as I drew. The whole collection tells a story of what is happening during a particular time of year.

COLLECTION OR PERPETUAL JOURNAL

One way to cultivate a regular art practice is to make one small drawing a day. I often do this by drawing one leaf, flower, or part of a plant each day on the same page or in the same journal. It helps me slow down and notice how things are changing around me. I like to keep accordion books for certain times of the year and add drawings over multiple weeks. Some people make a perpetual journal where each spread represents a week of the year and is filled in with drawings made over several years, so each year, in the first week of April, you'd open to that spread and draw what you notice. It can be wonderful to have sketchbooks that you continue to build year after year. You can compare past seasons and see how much you have developed as an artist.

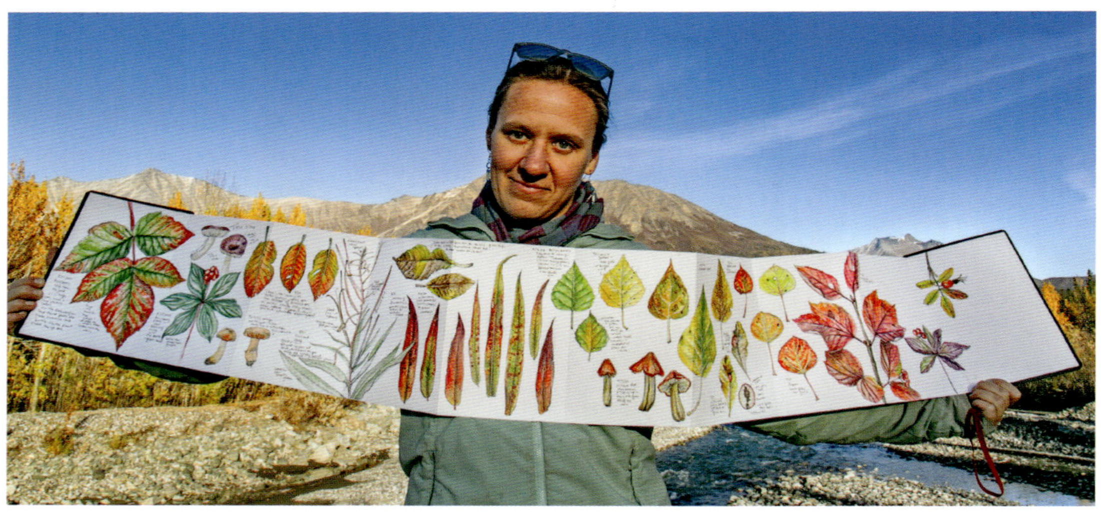

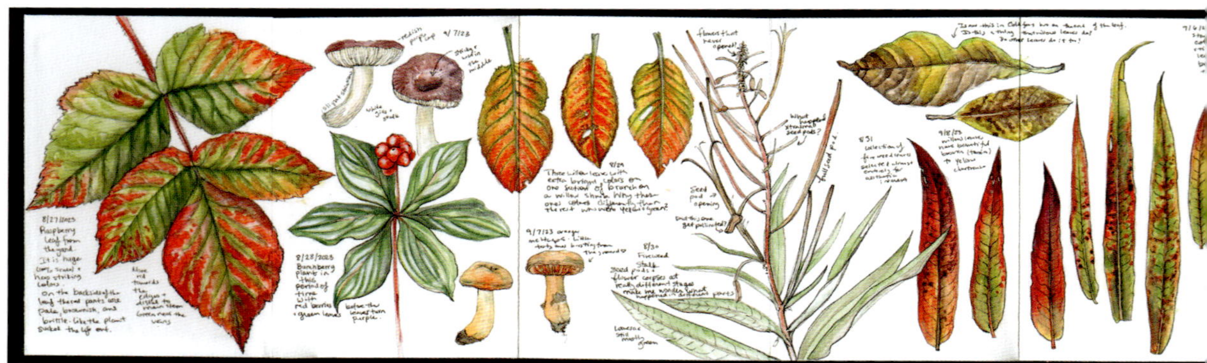

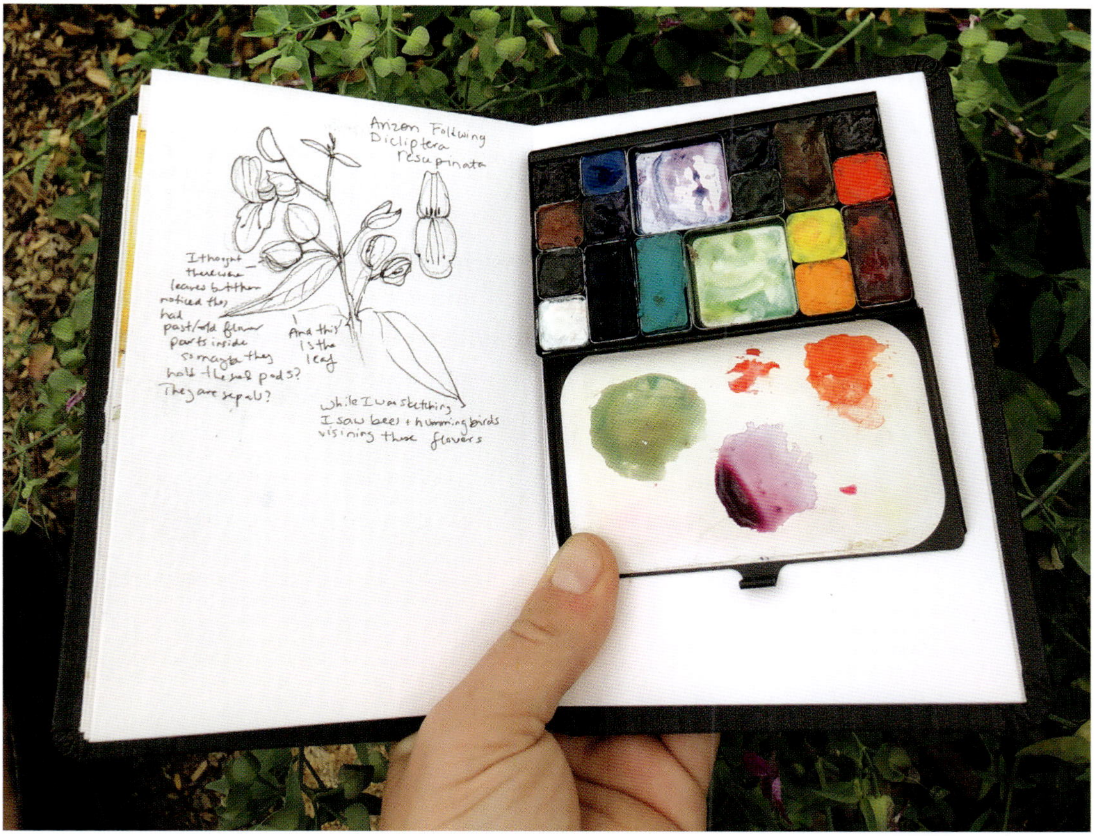

While traveling in the Southwest, I started a sketchbook of different plants that I encountered there. I made this sketch at the Tucson Botanical Gardens. It was a nice way to get to know some of the plants growing in a different environment from where I live in Alaska.

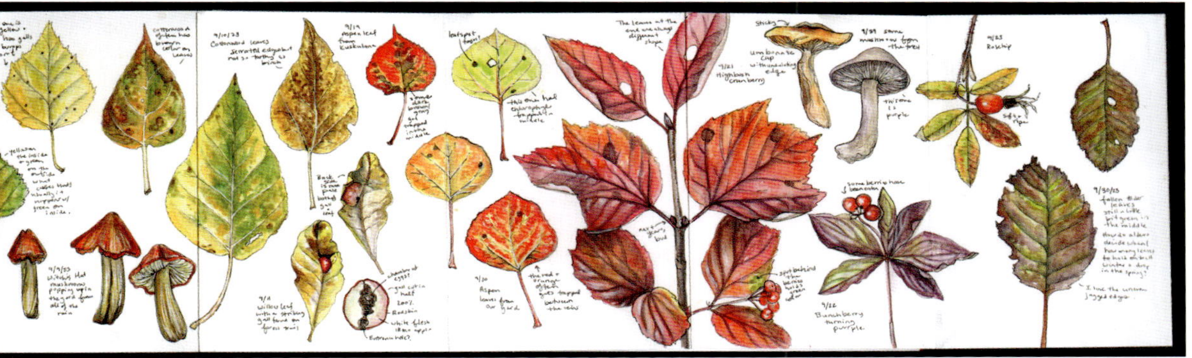

Project 30

ONE PLANT DRAWING A DAY IN LATE SPRING

We will make one drawing a day for five days from plant observations and photos that I took at the end of spring around my cabin.

MATERIALS: a pencil, a pen, watercolor paper, and watercolors

Day 1: scarlet elf cup

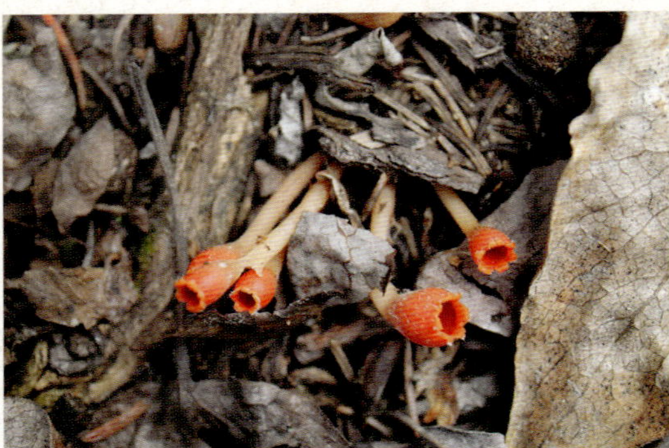

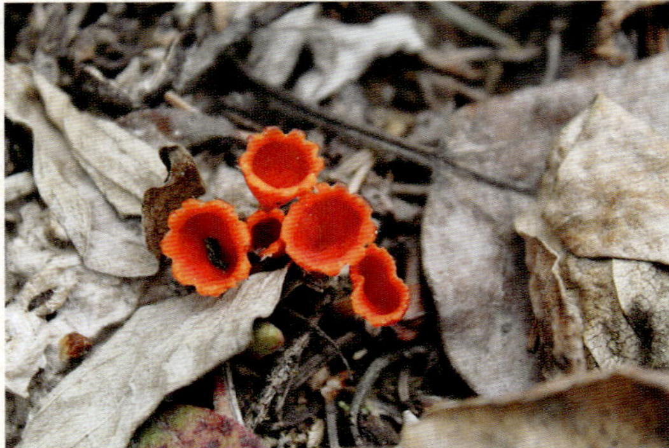

Day 2: bluebell leaf

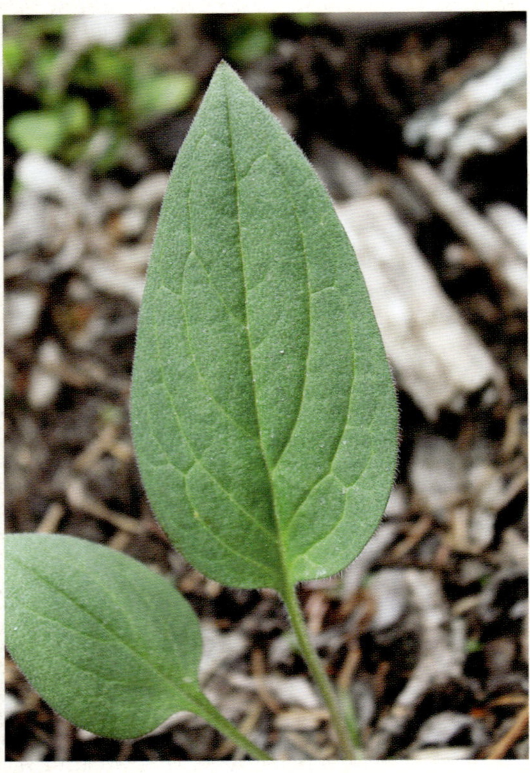

In the late spring, plants are coming out and changing rapidly. I easily get overwhelmed because so many things change simultaneously, and I can't keep track of and draw them all! Focusing on one drawing helps me slow down and still capture some of the incredible change.

Day 3: calypso orchid

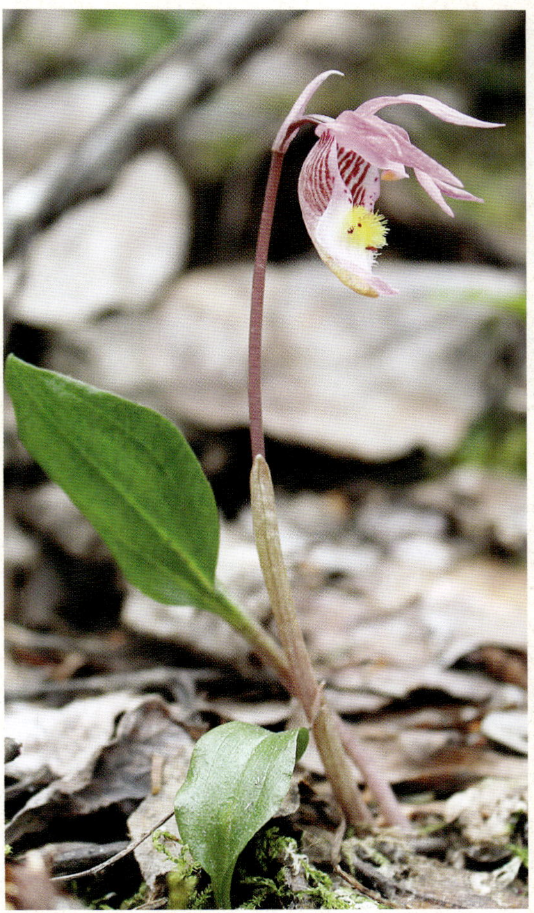

Day 4: raspberry leaf

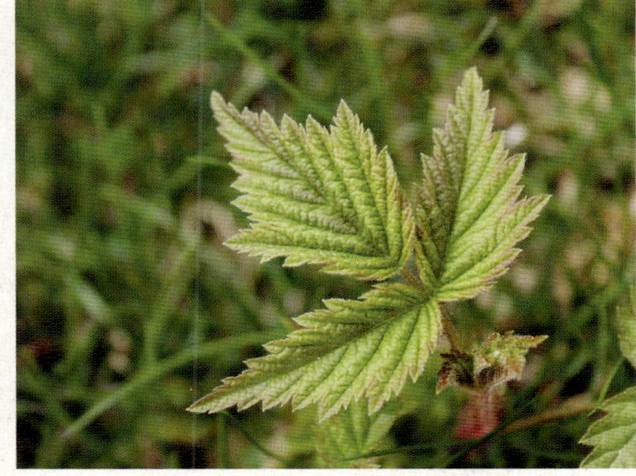

Day 5: white violet

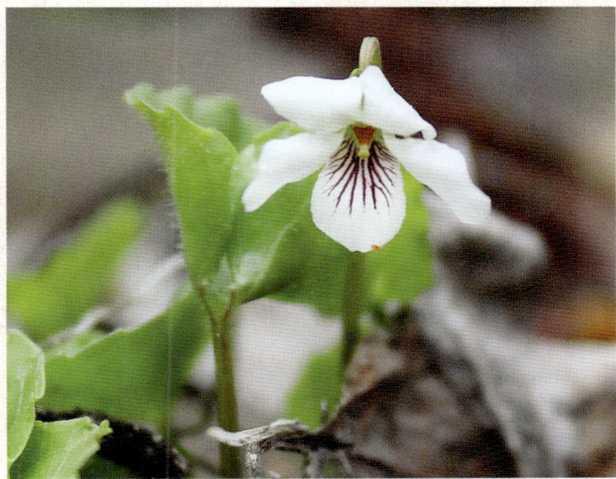

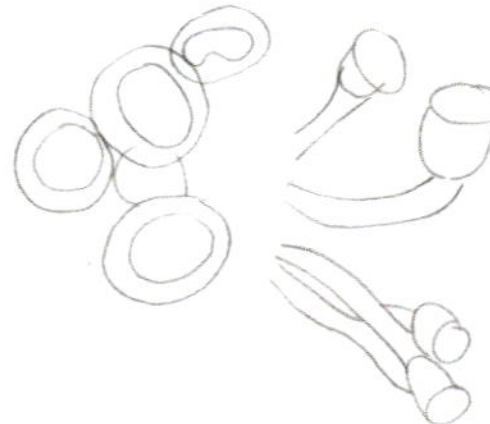

1

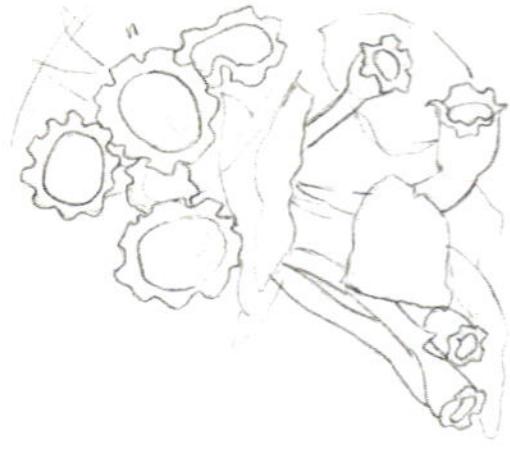

2

DAY 1

SCARLET ELF CUP: ***These bright red fungi come out in the spring. They are pretty small (under 1 cm), but we can enlarge them in our sketchbook.***

STEP 1: Using a pencil, draw circles and ovals where the orange cups will go. I started at the top-left corner of the page and will fill the paper day by day. Some of the fungi are viewed from the side and look like little cups on long stalks.

STEP 2: Go over the pencil drawing again with another layer to add detail to the edges, where the margins are fringed. Draw some of the leaves and vegetation.

STEP 3: Go over the pencil drawing with a waterproof pen.

STEP 4: Use the negative space to paint brown ground around the fungi. I mixed Burnt Sienna with Ultramarine Blue.

STEP 5: Working light to dark, fill in the fungi with a light shade of orange. For the fungi stalks, seen from the side view, I mixed Pyrrol Scarlet with Quinacridone Gold and some Buff Titanium.

STEP 6: Add another layer of watercolor to deepen the shadows in the middle of the lichen and the ground around it. Add in some notes and the date with a pen.

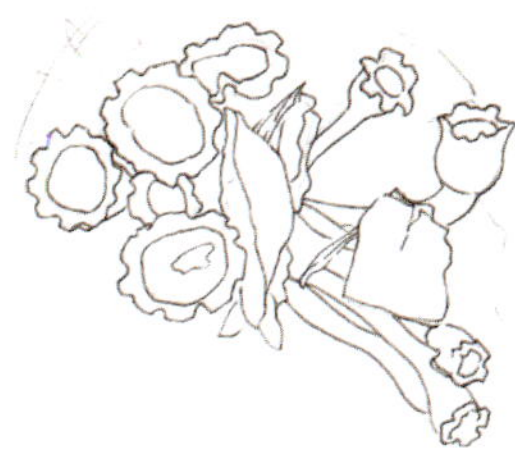

3

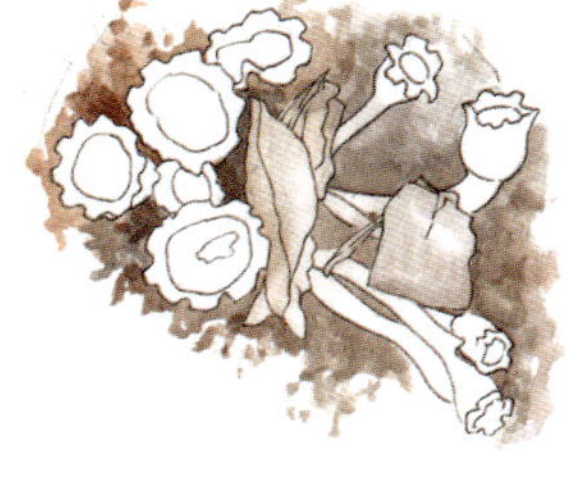

4

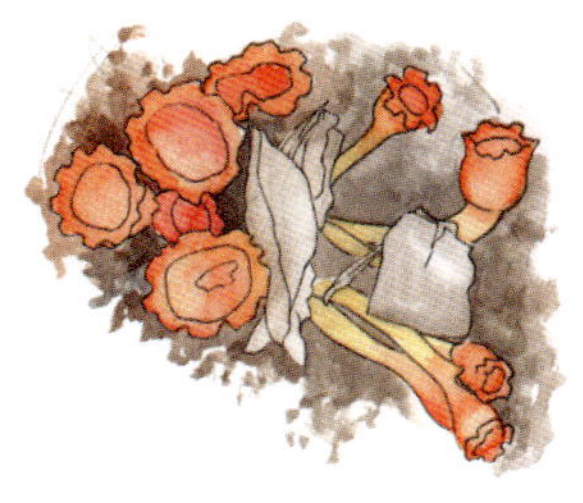

5

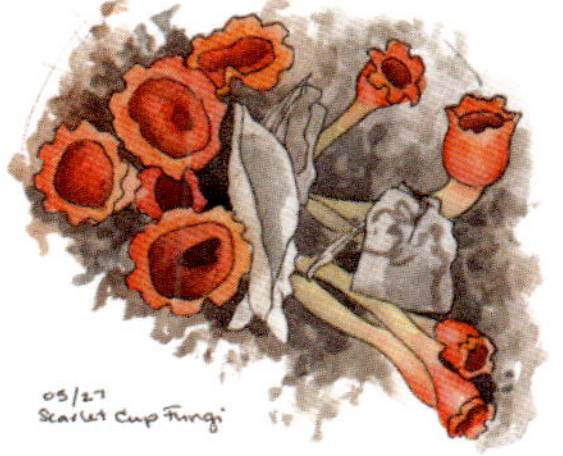

6

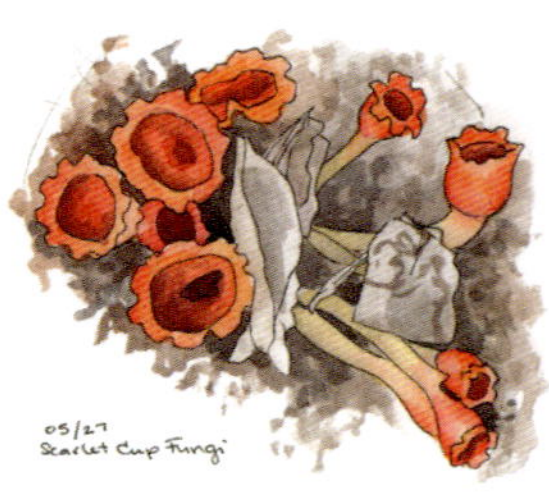

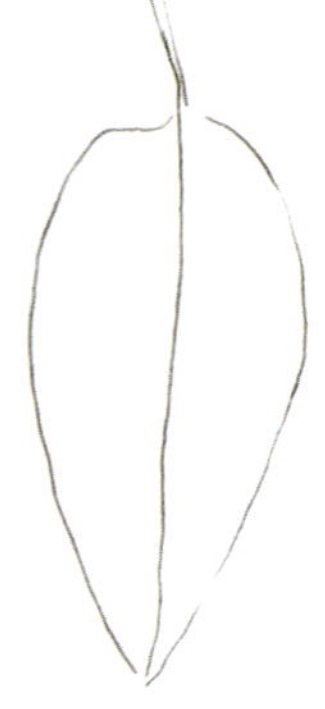

1

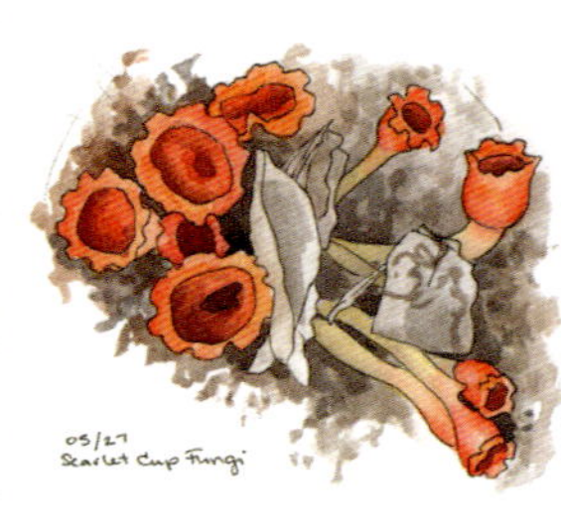

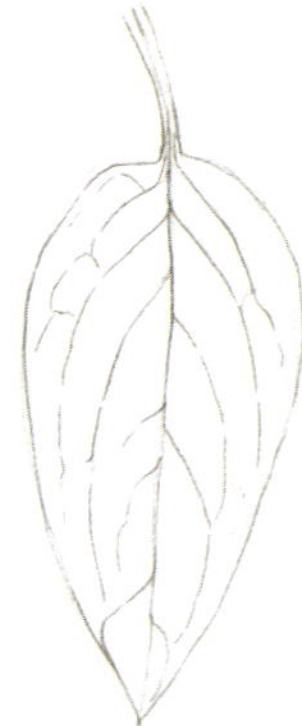

2

DAY 2

BLUEBELL LEAF: ***These are in the borage family and bloom early. The leaves are fuzzy and taste and smell like cucumber.***

STEP 1: Sketch the leaf with a pencil. I started with the middle vein and then the outer margin.

STEP 2: Refine the sketch from the previous step, adjusting the lines and adding more detail, such as the veins in the leaf.

STEP 3: Go over the pencil drawing with a waterproof pen. I added some texture along the margin to show that the leaf is furry and wrote some notes in a pen while I drew. I don't always finish each sketch each day, so I ended this one here and might add watercolor the next day.

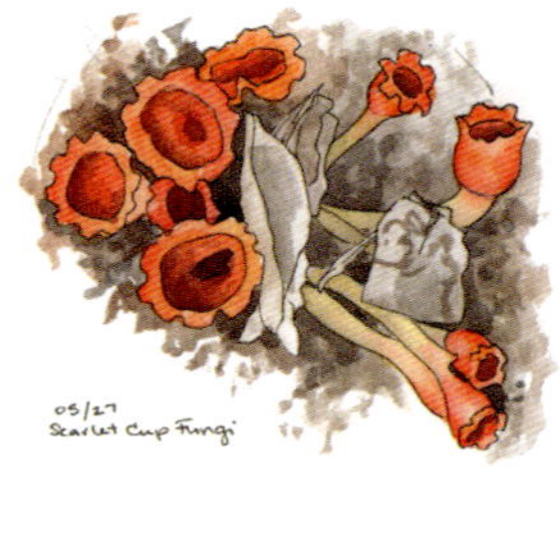

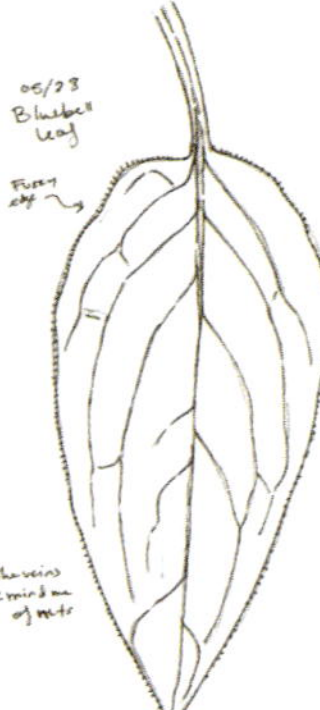

3

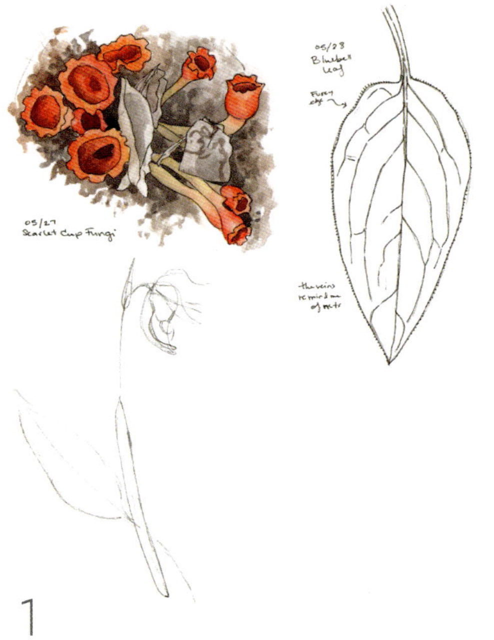

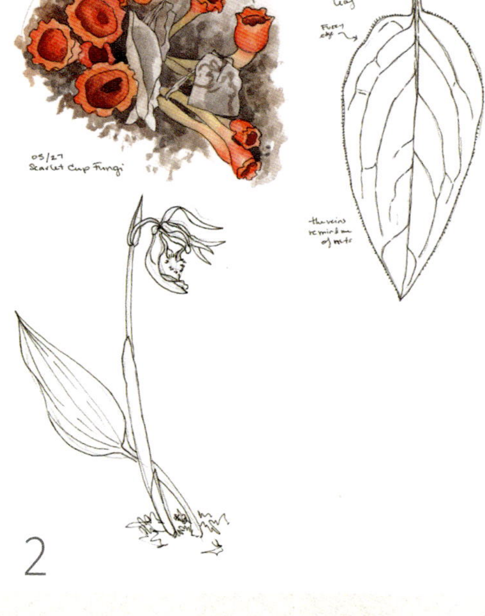

DAY 3

CALYPSO ORCHID: ***These little pink flowers are a welcome treat to find dancing in the forest.***

STEP 1: In light pencil, sketch the main shapes of the flower. I started with the stem and then drew the main part of the orchid flower head, adding lines to indicate where the top petals will go. Then, I drew the leaf.

STEP 2: Go over the initial sketch and add to the drawing with a pen. Using my pencil lines as a guide, I sketched the whole orchid. I added the sheath for the stem and all the little parts of the flower, the leaf with its parallel veins, and some scribble markings for the ground.

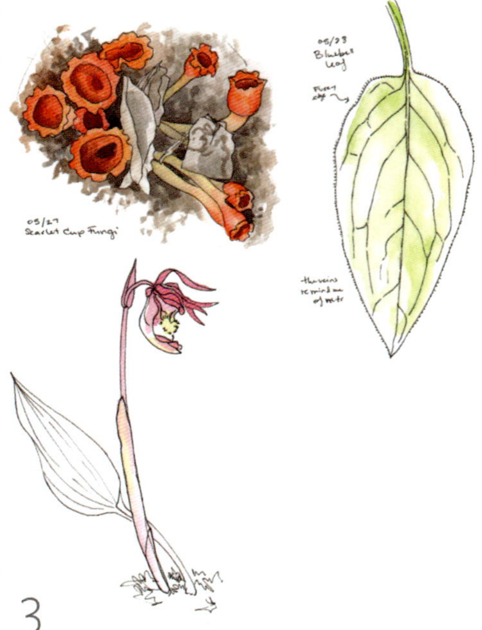

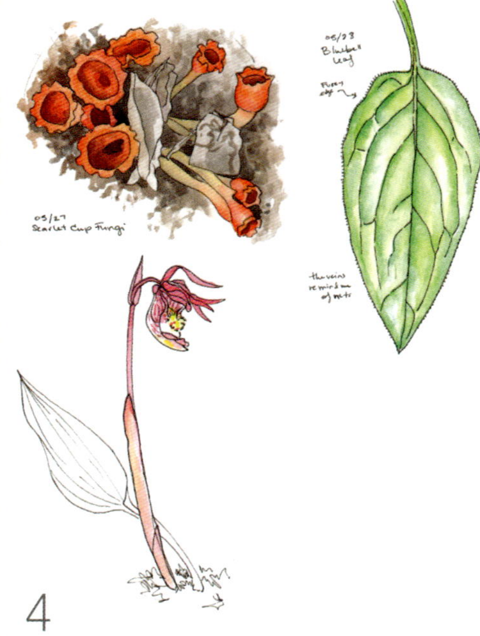

STEP 3: Begin painting the orchid. I used Quinacridone Rose for most of the orchid flower, with Hansa Yellow Light for the flower, and Buff Titanium. I also decided to paint the leaf from yesterday. I mixed Cerulean Blue with Quinacridone Gold and painted a wash over the middle of the leaf.

STEP 4: I added another layer of watercolor to both sketches. On the orchid, I added some stripes and textures to the flower. For the leaf, I mixed a blue-green and painted that wash along the veins and the margin of the leaf, leaving the middle area and the highlights the lighter color.

STEP 5: I mixed Quinacridone Gold with Ultramarine Blue to make an even darker green and used this to deepen some of the shadows in the bluebell leaf and to paint the leaf on the orchid. I also mixed Quinacridone Rose with Burnt Sienna and Ultramarine Blue to make a brownish purple to add details to the orchid stem. I added the date and a few more notes.

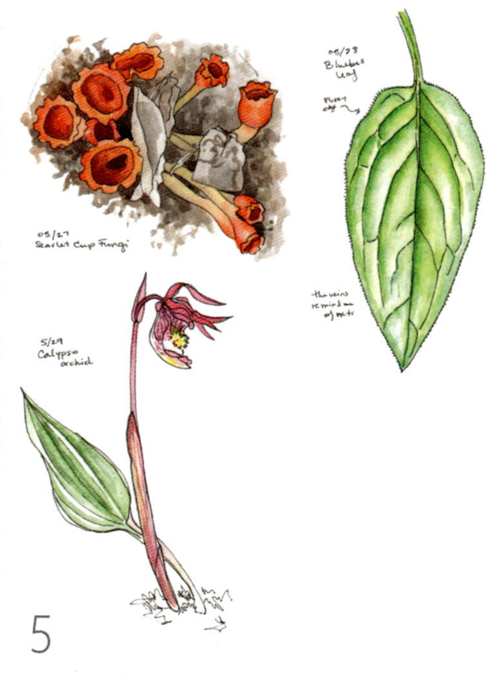

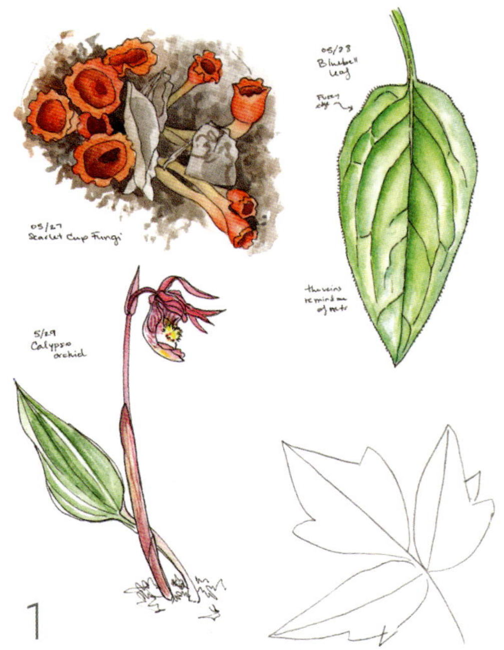

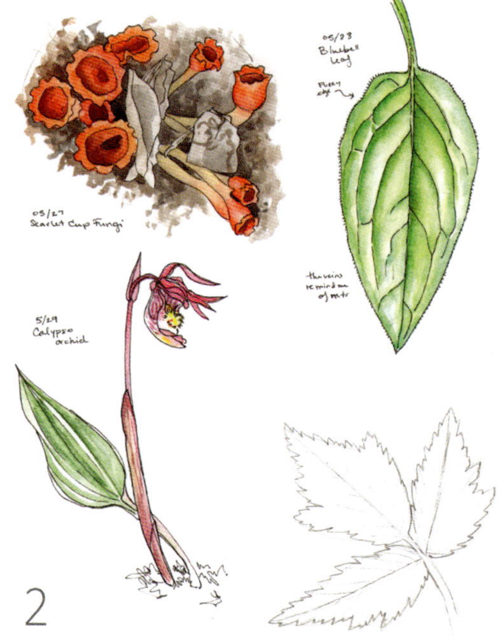

DAY 4

RASPBERRY LEAF: ***Raspberries love to grow wild in the sunny sections of my yard.***

STEP 1: In the bottom-right corner, I began sketching out the main shapes of the raspberry leaf. This is a compound leaf with three sections. I kept my first sketch rough, focusing on the bigger shapes.

STEP 2: Refine your pencil sketch from the previous step. Add details such as the jagged leaf margins and the veins where the leaf is still unfolding.

STEP 3: Go over the pencil sketch with the pen and erase the pencil if you want when the pen is dry.

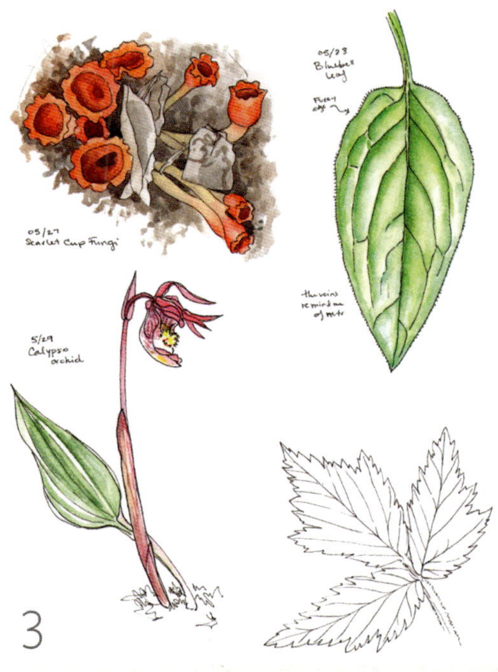

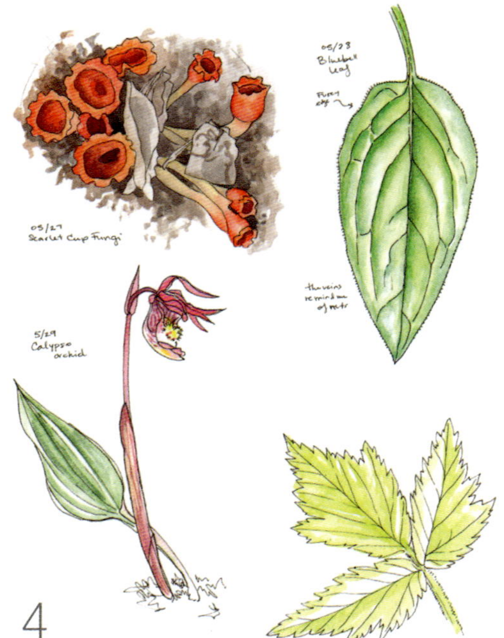

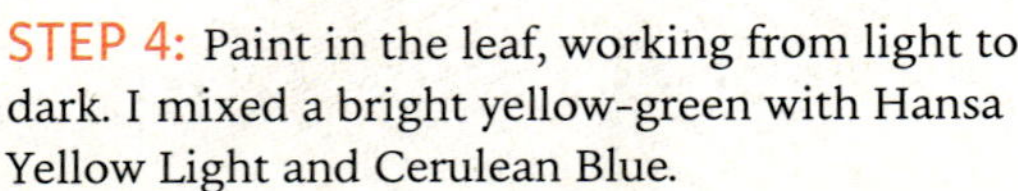

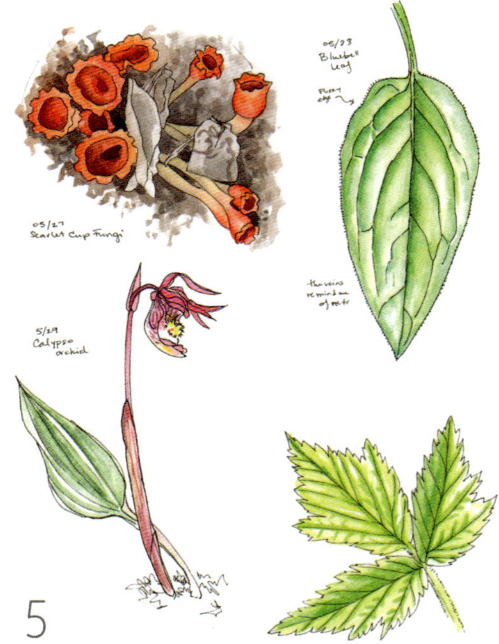

STEP 4: Paint in the leaf, working from light to dark. I mixed a bright yellow-green with Hansa Yellow Light and Cerulean Blue.

STEP 5: Mix a mid-tone green by adding more blue from the first wash. Paint this where you notice shadows, especially along the veins.

STEP 6: Add some of the reds along the edge of the leaf with Quinacridone Rose. Laying this over top of the green will tone the magenta down a bit. Add in the date and some notes with a pen.

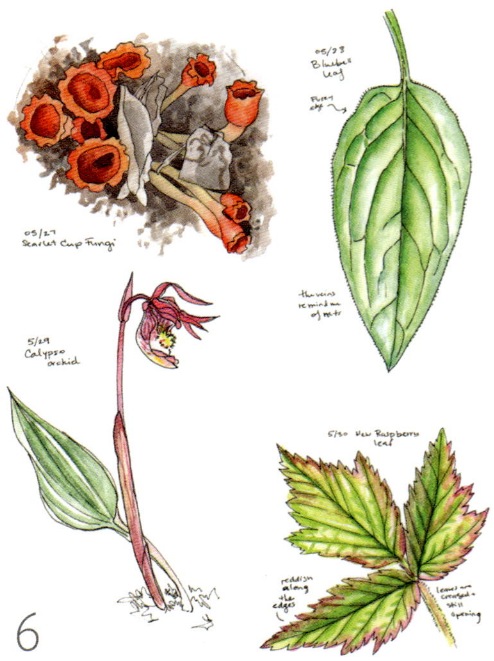

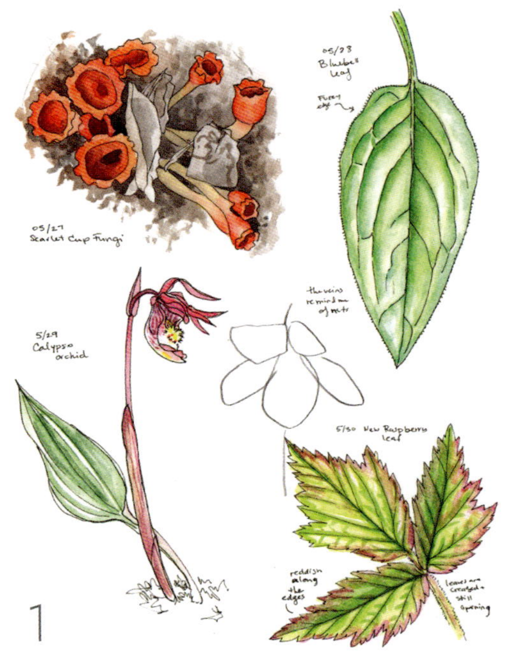

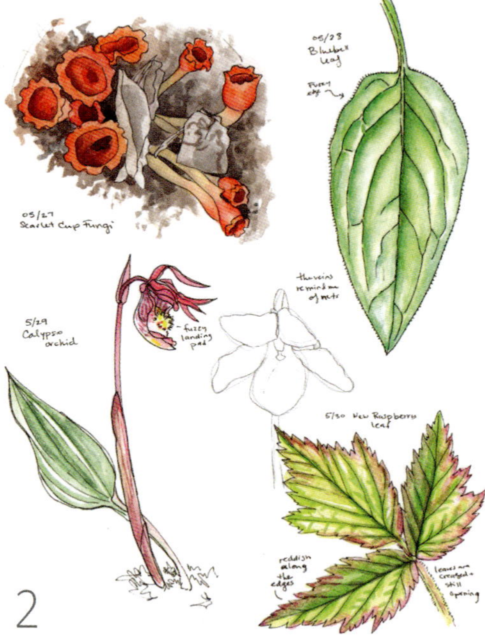

DAY 5

WHITE VIOLET: ***These are also early flowers that are a treat to find in the forest.***

STEP 1: Most of the page is taken up with sketches from the previous four days, but there is some space in the middle for a small sketch. I decided to sketch the violet flower in that area, overlapping it slightly with the raspberry leaf. Roughly draw in the stem and the five petals.

STEP 2: Refine the sketch from the previous step, adding more detail to the center part of the flower.

STEP 3: Go over the pencil drawing with a pen. Add notes as you go. Sometimes, I add notes to the sketches from the previous days. The more I look at them, the more questions come up.

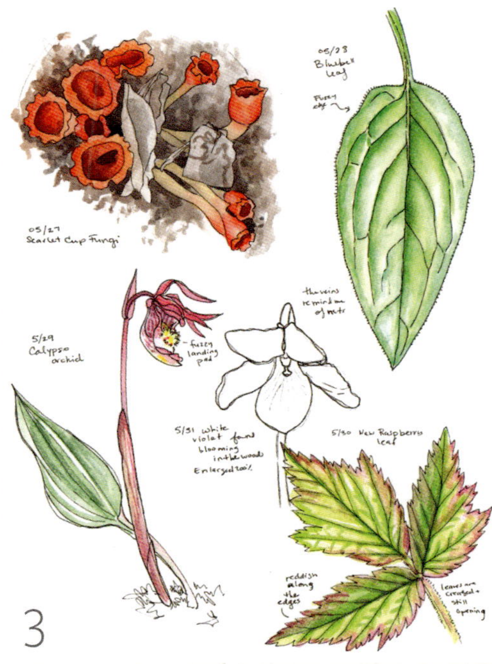

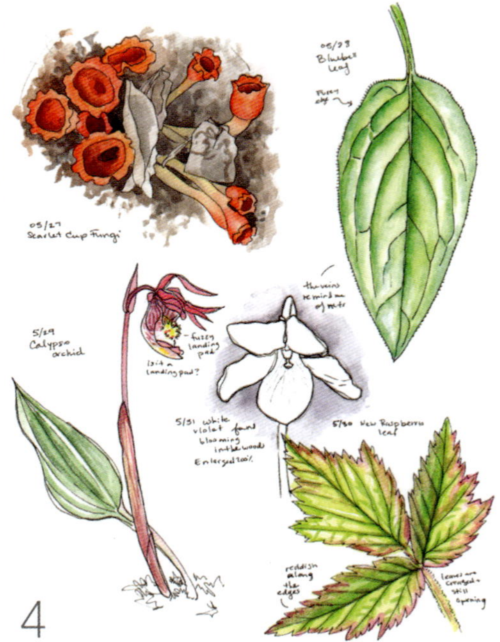

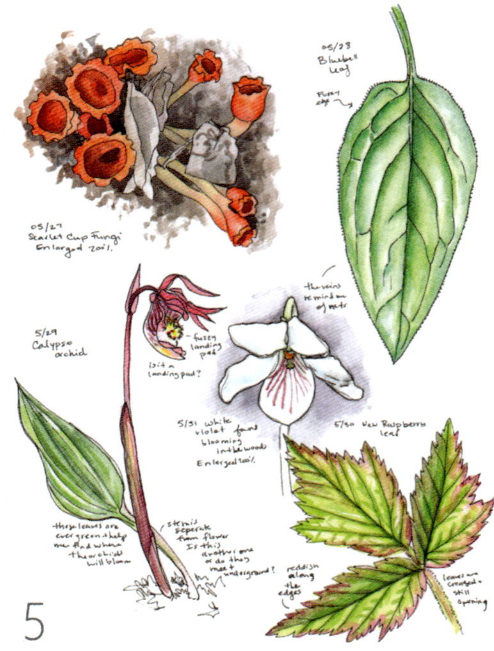

STEP 4: Since the violet petals are white, I decided to paint around them with a violet-gray and utilize the negative space. This adds more depth to the overall page and balances out the background in the top left.

STEP 5: Paint some details in the violet using a very light shadow for the petals and magenta for the lines and detail in the middle bottom petal. Go back and make any changes or adjustments to the page overall.

BUILDING COMMUNITY

One of the best ways to stay motivated and grow as a sketcher is to share the process with others. I've met with clubs online, joined and led local nature journal groups, gone hiking and sketching with a friend, and led and attended more formal workshops. It is lovely to share our different areas of expertise, whether in making art, organizing logistics, knowing a good place to go, or having knowledge of natural history. People who enjoy sketching are usually welcoming and friendly, and we enjoy nature and art in common. I encourage you to see what sketching and nature journaling groups exist in your area or meet online at a time that works for you. You could also consider starting your own group. You don't necessarily need to teach people; you just need to be a catalyst for bringing people together and getting sketching supplies out.

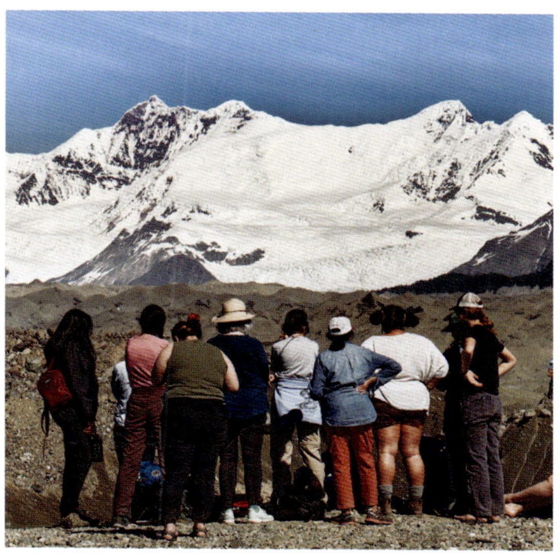

▲ A group of students gathers at the toe of the Kennicott Glacier for a field sketching workshop. Sketching is even better when shared with others.

(*next spread*) A watercolor and pen sketch of the mountains on the Nizina River

Final Reflection

Review some of the projects you've done working through this book. How have you changed as a sketcher? What is still challenging for you? What breakthrough did you have? How does it feel when you sit down to sketch? How do you feel after? What do you plan to work on next, and how will you cultivate a regular sketching habit?

I've been sketching for years, and I don't think there is one right way to make it a habit, but the more I practice, the better I get. I also feel more calm, relaxed, and connected to the world around me. I go for periods of time where I don't sketch at all, work in bound books, and then change to working on sheets of paper. I like to switch things up so I don't get bored. I take long breaks from keeping a regular practice, but when I want to get back into it, I like to try to start small, making a quick contour drawing a day, a gesture sketch, or sketching a leaf a day. Once I get my muscle memory back, it gets easier to keep going.

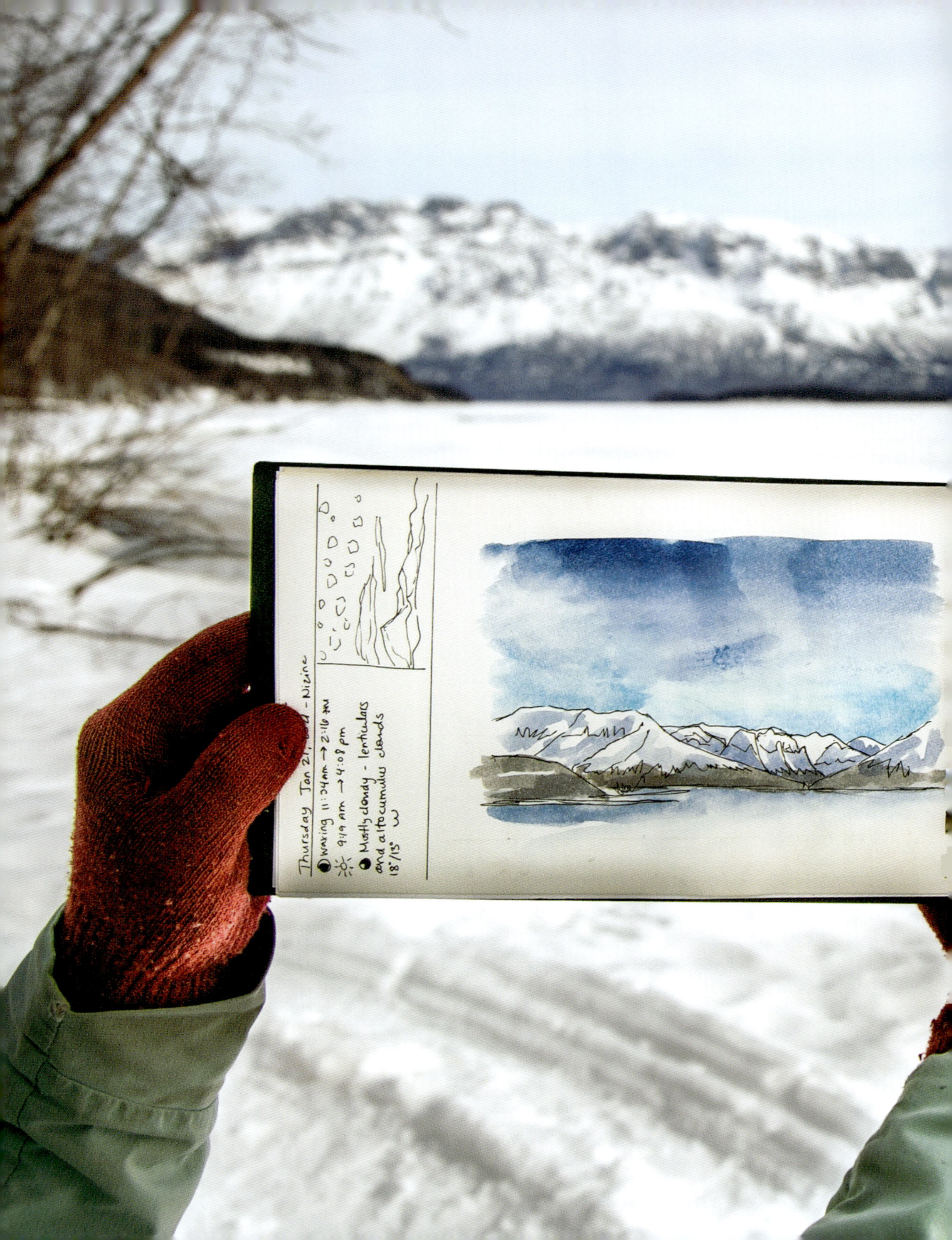
Thursday Jan 21,
- Nizine
waxing 11:24am → 2:16 am
9:19 am → 4:08 pm
Mostly cloudy - lenticulars and altocumulus clouds
18°/13° W

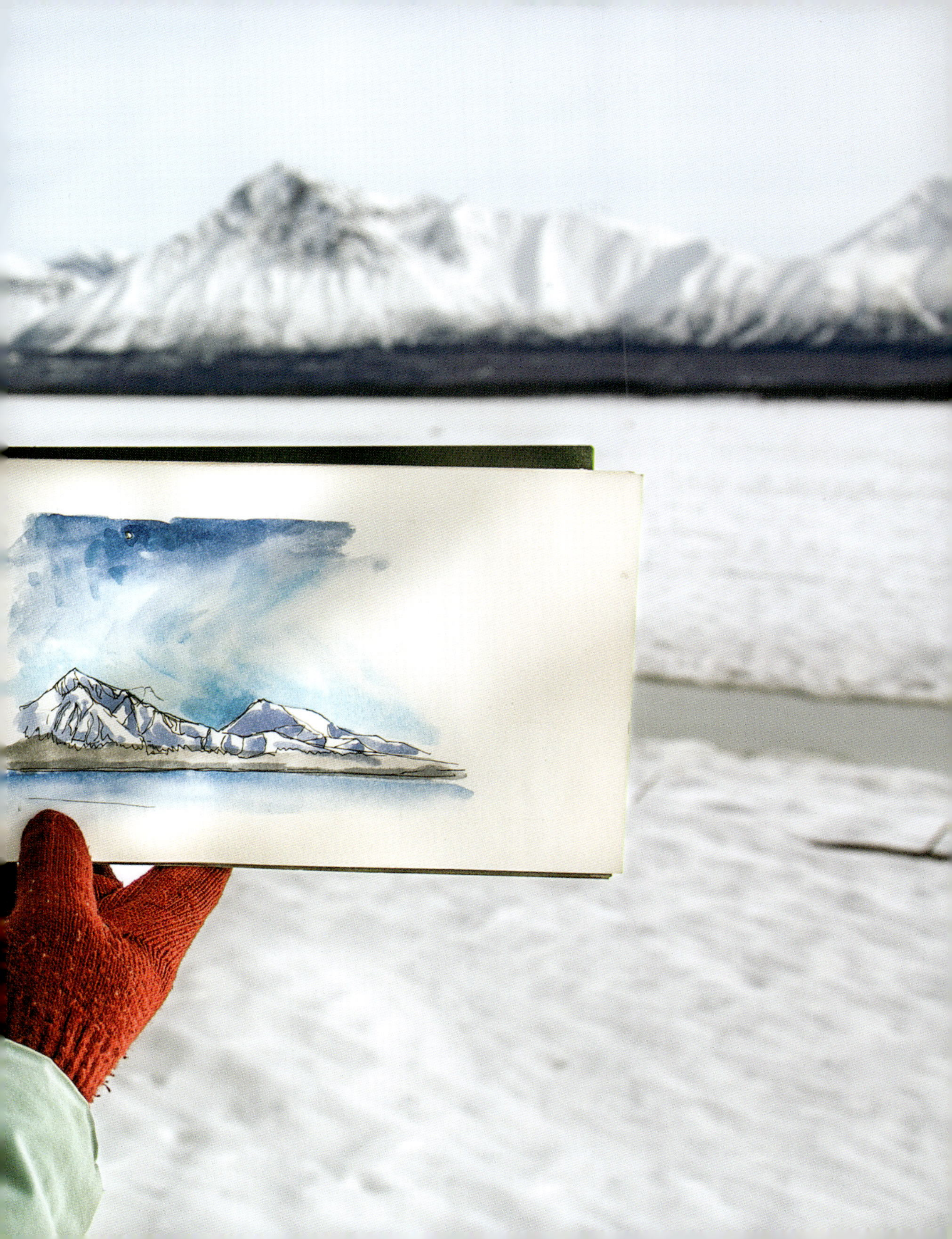

Glossary

ATMOSPHERIC PERSPECTIVE: Explains how the atmosphere influences the way distant objects appear in two-dimensional art. As an object recedes into the distance, it becomes less detailed, lower in contrast, and takes on the value and hue of the background.

COMPOSITION: Refers to the arrangement of visual elements in an artwork and guides the viewer's eye through the artwork

CONTOUR: An outline, especially one representing or bounding the shape or form of something

CONTRAST: The representation of two elements of design in opposite ways. For example, an area of bright light next to an area of dark, or two hues opposite of each other on the color wheel. The difference between the two elements is used to intensify the properties of the work.

CROSSHATCHING: To mark with two series of parallel lines that intersect, creating a tonal or shading effect

FLAT WASH: A visual arts technique resulting in an even, semitransparent layer of color

GESTURE: Quick and loose application of paint, pencil, etc., to describe movement and direction

GOUACHE: Water-based paint medium; similar to watercolor but more opaque

GRADED WASH: A visual arts technique resulting in a semitransparent layer of color that goes from light to dark

GRANULATION: A unique textural effect in watercolor paint when certain pigments settle into small, grain-like particles on the surface of the paper instead of settling evenly. Pigments with larger and more irregular granular sizes, like earth pigments, tend to granulate.

HATCHING: To mark with a series of parallel lines to create a tonal or shading effect

LINEAR PERSPECTIVE: A mathematical system for creating the illusion of space and distance on a flat surface in which parallel lines converge towards one or more vanishing points

NEGATIVE SPACE: The space around and between the subject of the image

PATTERN: The repetition of specific visual elements, such as a single unit or a multitude of forms

PERSPECTIVE: The representation of three-dimensional objects or spaces in two-dimensional artworks, creating the illusion of distance

PIGMENT: A substance that gives color to other materials. Pigment is combined with a binder and water to make watercolor paint. Different pigments have different properties, including transparency and opacity, lightfastness, granulation, staining, purity, intensity, and color shift.

SATURATION: An attribute of color that refers to the intensity and vividness of the color. Bright colors are highly saturated. Muted colors have low saturation.

SHADING: Darkening or coloring to suggest the degrees of light and dark in a picture or a drawing

STIPPLE: To mark with a series of dots to create a tonal or shading effect

TEXTURE: The visual or tactile surface characteristics and appearance of something

VALUE: An art element that describes how light or dark a color or hue can be

WASH (WATERCOLOR): A visual arts technique resulting in a semitransparent layer of color

WET-IN-WET: A painting technique in which wet paint is applied to a wet surface. The wet color will bleed, spread, and bloom in the wet area.

Acknowledgments

Thank you to everyone at Timber Press for making this book possible. I am especially grateful to Ryan Harrington for asking what kind of book I wanted to create and for his encouragement throughout the process. Matthew Burnett, Kevin McConnell, and Sarah Milhollin helped shape the final work and reminded me to track down missing pieces and images. Thanks to Brooke Littrell for careful editing and to the many others who brought this project to life. I am grateful to my friends and family who helped me test early lessons: Mollie, Victoria, Kara, and Linda. Thank you to Jenna Schnuer for pitching my sketching workshop to *The New York Times* Travel section and writing an article that drew wider attention.

This project was supported by an Individual Artist Award from the Rasmuson Foundation. The Dalton Highway Artist Residency, organized by Toolik Field Station and the Bureau of Land Management, provided time to sketch in an inspiring place. It was instrumental that other people and organizations also believed in this project.

I am deeply grateful to my partner, Greg, for support, adventures, editing, and the many art critiques he never expected to give. Thanks to my parents, Gary and Linda, for encouraging me to keep making art, and to my grandparents for sharing creativity from a young age, especially Mor Ellen, who taught me to watercolor and to watch nature. I am thankful for all my art teachers, especially Cindy Wasley, who encouraged me to take art seriously in high school, and Jennie Keller, whose field sketching class at the CSUMB Science Illustration program gave my career direction. Thanks to the Wrangell Mountains Center, and especially Jeremy Pataky, for supporting my first field sketching class in 2010, and for providing many teaching and learning opportunities over the years. Thanks also to Jeremy and Dave Sarbell for their photographs and for helping me share the beauty of this place.

I continue to learn from every teacher and student I meet, and I am especially grateful to all who have shared their sketchbooks with me over the years. Last but not least, thank you to my readers and students for making art.

Resources

These books were instrumental in my learning journey:

Cerruti, Courtney. *Make Art Where You Are: A Traveler's Guide & Sketchbook.* New York, NY: Abrams Noterie, 2020.

Franck, Frederick. *Zen Seeing, Zen Drawing: Meditation in Action.* New York, NY: Bantam Books, 1993.

Hanson, Roseann Beggy. *Nature Journaling for a Wild Life.* Tucson, AZ: Natural Selection Press, 2020.

Hinchman, Hannah. *A Trail Through Leaves: A Journal as a Path to Place.* New York, NY: W.W. Norton & Company, 1997.

Laws, John Muir and Emilie Lygren: *How to Teach Nature Journaling: Curiosity, Wonder, Attention.* Berkeley, CA: Heyday Books, 2020.

Leslie, Clare Walker and Charles E. Roth: *Keeping a Nature Journal: Discover a Whole New Way of Seeing the World Around You.* Adams, MA: Storey Publishing, 2021.

Martin, Rosie and Meriel Thurstan. *Botanical Illustration Course: With the Eden Project.* London, UK: Batsford Books, 2008.

I also recommend:

PERPETUAL JOURNAL
Lara Call Gastinger
laracallgastinger.com/perpetual-journal

THE GROWN-UPS TABLE
Wendy MacNaughton
wendymacnaughton.com/grown-ups-table

WILD WONDER FOUNDATION
wildwonder.org

Photography and Art Credits

All photos and illustrations are by the author except the following:

Jeremy Pataky, 14–19, 22–23, 30, 32, 41, 48–49, 70–71, 73, 123 (top), 132 (right), 142 (bottom), 146–147, 149 (bottom right), 171 (bottom), 172–173, 177 (top), 202–203, 205, 230–231, 233, 235, 249, 253 (bottom), 260–261, 268 (top), 282–283, 296

Dave Sarbell, 29, 128, 134 (right), 281

Index

A

accordion books, 268–269
Alaska, 11, 16, 20, 89, 104, 112, 116, 152, 160, 164, 172, 175, 204, 227, 232, 247
alder, 79
alpenglow, 254–259
alpine tundra near and far project, 211–215
alpine tundra stream project, 221–226
analogous colors, 97
anemone flower project, 100–103
angles, measuring, 41
animals
  anatomy, 148–149
  gesture sketching, 150–151
  moose gesture sketching project, 152–156
  moving, 39, 146–148, 150–151
  red squirrel project, 160–163
  skeletons, 148–149
  sketching, 148
  sketching dead, 170–171
  tracks, 235, 244–246
  See also birds
aquatic mammals, 149
arctic tundra stream project, 221–226
atmospheric perspective, 175–176, 285
meadow sketching project, 184–188
aurora borealis, 248

B

bark, 46, 47
Barred Owl, 150
beauty, finding, 46–47
Bee Paper Company Super Deluxe Mixed Media sketchbook, 31
BIC #2 mechanical pencils, 25
birch tree, 40, 238–243
birds
  Kayak Island hummingbird, 170–171
  owl feather with pencil project, 53–58
  owl skull anatomy study project, 157–159
  raven iridescence and feathers project, 164–169
  robin's nest colored texture project, 143–145
  skeletons, 149
Birn Zeta sketchbooks, 31
Black, 27
black morel mushroom project, 139–142
blank pages, breaking into, 262–263
Bleedproof White, 127
blooms, 75
bluebell leaf, 270, 274
Bodelin microscope lens attachment, 33
bones
  jawbone in pen project, 64–66
  owl skull anatomy study project, 157–159
  skeletons, 148–149
  skull drawing and shading project, 59–63
  studying, 149
Brooks Range, 20, 221
brushes, 27, 72, 134
Buff Titanium, 27
Burnt Sienna, 27, 84–88, 95, 98

C

calypso orchid, 271, 275–276
canines, 148
Canson Mi–Teintes paper, 28
Cape St. Elias, 170
Carbazole Violet, 27, 98
Carson, Rachel, 70
Cassiar Highway, 200
cast shadows, 52
Cerulean Blue, 26, 99
cholate lily, 78
Chromium, 26
circles, shading, 51
Cobalt Teal Blue, 26, 95, 98, 99
colored pencils, 26, 122, 127, 143–145
color(s)
  analogous, 97
  anemone flower project, 100–103
  complementary, 97
  cool, 97
  diary, 110
  fall leaves with complementary colors project, 112–115
  layering, 100–103
  lupine botanical study project, 104–110

mixing, 87, 95–96, 97–98, 99, 164–169
neutral, 27, 98
primary, 26, 94
relative nature of, 92, 94
secondary, 27, 94
swatches, 95, 111, 119
tertiary, 94
value, 92
warm, 97
wheel of place, 111
color wheel, 94–97
community, 281
complementary colors, 97, 112–115
composition, 178, 202, 285
constellations, 249, 250–253
contour, 285
contour drawing, 38, 40, 176, 262
K'esugi Ridge meditative sketching project, 194–199
contrast, 285
cool colors, 97
The Copper River Record, 46
Cordova, 146
Cotman watercolors, 22
cottonwood leaf, 42–45
creating, 18
crosshatching, 50, 285

D

Daniel Smith watercolors, 26
Dease Lake, 200–201
diaries
color, 110
daily, 110, 268–269
dimension, 48, 52
drawing and shading a skull project, 59–63
Donoho Basin, 11–13
Donoho Peak, 48, 229
drawing
contour, 38, 40, 176, 194–199, 262
gesture, 39, 40, 134, 176, 178, 179–183, 189–193, 262, 285
leaf line drawing project, 42–45
as meditation, 34, 40
owl feather with pencil project, 53–58
skull drawing and shading project, 59–63
warming up with, 36
drawing-a-day practice, 268
late spring plant project, 270–280
drawing paper, 36
drawing tools, 25–26
Dr. Ph. Martin's Bleedproof White, 33
Dryas drummondii, 19
dry brushes, creating texture with, 134

E

editing, 18
Edwards, Betty, 22
erasers, 25
Escoda brushes, 27

F

Faber-Castell Polychromos pencils, 26
feathers
owl feather with pencil project, 53–58
raven iridescence project, 164–169
felines, 148
ferry sketching, 89–91
fireweed complementary colors project, 112–115
Fireweed Mountain, 14
5.4.3.2.1. grounding through senses, 262, 264, 266
flat wash, 74, 78, 285
flowers
alpine tundra near and far project, 211–215
anemone flower project, 100–103
one drawing a day project, 270–280
forest fires, 227–229
fosses, 124
Frank, Frederick, 48, 92
French Ultramarine, 26
fur, red squirrel project, 160–163

G

Gentianella amarella, 67
gesture drawing, 39, 40, 134, 262, 285
animals, 150–151
landscapes, 176, 178
moose project, 152–156
sunset and lake gesture sketch, 189–193
tree sketching project, 179–183
glacial moraines toned paper project, 216–220
Glacier Lake grid project, 206–210
glaciers, 216
glazing, 75
gouache, 127, 285
graded wash, 74, 285
granulation, 286
green colors, mixing, 99

grids, 202–205
  Glacier Lake grid project, 206–210
grounding practice, 262, 264, 266
Gulf of Alaska, 59, 170

H

Hahnemüle sketchbooks, 31
hand-eye coordination, 36
hand lens, 33
Hansa Yellow Light, 26, 97, 99
hatching, 50, 286
highbush cranberry plant, 36
highlights, 52
Hinchman, Hannah, 230, 260
Hockney, David, 120
horizon line, 178
human eye, 37
hummingbird at Kayak Island, 170–171
hummingbird moth project with pen and watercolor, 129–132

I

ice, 234–235
illusion of space, 175–176
  meadow sketching project, 184–188
Indanthrone Blue, 26, 98
iridescence, raven project, 164–169

J

Jansson, Tove, 202
jawbone in pen project, 64–66
Juneau Icefield, 103

K

Kayak Island, 59, 170
Kennicott Glacier, 17, 204, 205, 281
K'esugi Ridge meditative sketching project, 194–199
kinnikinnick inflorescence, 37
Klee, Paul, 34

L

Labrador tea plant, 236
lake and sunset gesture sketch, 189–193
landscapes
  alpine tundra near and far project, 211–215
  arctic tundra stream project, 221–226
  changes in, 227–229
  composition, 178
  Dease Lake, 200–201
  Donoho Basin, 11–13
  glacial moraines toned paper project, 216–220
  Glacier Lake grid project, 206–210
  illusion of space, 175–176
  K'esugi Ridge meditative sketching project, 194–199
  meadow sketching project, 184–188
  perspective, 175–176
  starting a sketch, 176–178
  sunset and lake gesture sketch, 189–193
  tree sketching project, 179–183
  winter light and alpenglow project, 254–259
  working with grids, 204
Laws, John Muir, 146
layering
  color, 100–103
  red squirrel project, 160–163
  shapes, 77
  winter light and alpenglow project, 254–259
leaves
  fall leaves with complementary colors project, 112–115
  flat leaf watercolor project, 79–83
  line drawing of a leaf project, 42–45
  one drawing a day project, 270–280
lichen, 46, 47
light sources, 52
linear perspective, 176, 286
line drawing of a leaf project, 42–45
lines, 36, 76
locations, 16
loose gesture approach, 72
lupine botanical study project, 104–110

M

MacNaughton, Wendy, 13
maps, 267
Marion Creek, 20
mark-making, 75, 89–91
marks, 36, 68
meadow sketching project, 184–188
measuring dividers, 26, 41
measuring techniques, 41
mechanical pencils, 25
meditation, 17, 34, 40, 89
  K'esugi Ridge meditative sketching project, 194–199

metadata, 262, 265
microscope lens for phone, 33
mid-tone, 52
mixed media
combinations, 122–123
creating texture with, 133–134
fast sketching with, 124–125
hummingbird moth with pen and watercolor project, 129–132
robin's nest colored pencil and watercolor project, 143–145
rock sketching project, 136–138
mixing colors
color swatches, 95
greens, 99
neutrals, 98
raven iridescence and feathers project, 164–169
warm and cool, 97
mold, 46, 47
monochromatic shell project, 84–88
moon, 247
moon dogs, 248
moose gesture sketching project, 152–156
Mount Blackburn, 229
Muir, John, 13

N

nagoonberry, 37
nature journaling, 19–20
negative space, 78, 286
anemone flower project, 100–103
owl skull anatomy study project, 157–159
neutral colors, 27, 98
New Gamboge, 26, 97
night sky, 247–249
Orion constellation project, 250–253
Nizina River, 16, 281
Northern Hardwood Forest, 13
nunataks, 11

O

observational skills, 67, 146, 148, 232, 262, 264
Oliver, Mary, 14
Orion constellation project, 250–253
owl feather with pencil project, 53–58
owl skull anatomy study project, 157–159

P

paintbrush flower, 78
paper
drawing, 36
sizes, 28
toned, 28
watercolor, 22, 24, 28
waterproof, 232
patterns, 36, 286
owl feather with pencil project, 53–58
pencil drawings
initial, 21
lightening, 21
lupine botanical study project, 104–110
owl feather with pencil project, 53–58
pencils
ability to use in cold weather, 232
angle measuring with, 41
colored, 26, 122, 143–145
mechanical, 25
proportion measuring with, 41, 177
shading with, 50
starting with, 120
uses of, 68
watercolor and, 122–123
pencil sharpeners, 33
pens
ballpoint, 24
brush, 25
and colored pencil, 122–123
drawing over pencil with, 122
fine, 25
focusing on texture, 68–69
hummingbird moth project with watercolor and, 129–132
jawbone in pen project, 64–66
permanent ink, 24, 25
shading with, 52
uses of, 68
watercolor and, 122–123
watercolor ink, 25
water-soluble ink, 25
white, 25, 33, 126
white colored, 127
perpetual journals, 268
perspective, 175–176, 227, 286
photos
reference, 37, 68–69, 78, 249
sketching from, 20
Phthalo Blue, 26, 97, 99
Phthalo Teal, 98, 99
Phthalo Turquoise, 27
pigment, 286
Pileated Woodpecker, 13
plantigrade animals, 148

plants
alpine tundra near and far project, 211–215
describing unknown, 67
dormant, 238–243
lupine botanical study project, 104–110
one drawing a day project, 270–280
sketching whole, 103
structures of, 249
plastic card scrapers, 134
plastic wrap, creating texture with, 133
primary colors, 26, 94
Prince William Sound, 170–171
proportions, measuring, 41
Pyrrol Scarlet, 26, 97

Q

Quinacridone Gold, 26, 98, 99
Quinacridone Rose, 26, 97, 98

R

raspberry leaf, 271, 277–278
raven iridescence and feathers project, 164–169
Raw Umber, 27, 98
red squirrel project, 160–163
reflections, 52
rhodiola plant, 103
Rhododendron groenlandicum, 236
robins, 150
robin's nest texture project, 143–145
rock sketching project
rock sketching project, 136–138
Root Glacier, 31, 120, 229
rose hips, 127
Rufous Hummingbird, 170–171
rulers, 26, 41

S

Sakura pens, 25
salt, creating texture with, 133, 136–138
sandpipers, 146
Sap Green, 27, 98
saturation, 286
scarlet elf cap, 270, 272–273
scribbling, 50
secondary colors, 27, 94, 97
senses, grounding through, 262, 264, 266
shading
adding, 48
defined, 286
drawing and shading a skull project, 59–63
jawbone in pen project, 64–66
owl skull anatomy study project, 157–159
value scales, 50–52
shadows
arctic tundra stream project, 221–226
casting, 52
shapes, layering, 77
shells, monochromatic project, 84–88
shrubs, 237
skeletons, animal, 148–149
sketchbooks, 28, 31
sketching
community, 281
as meditation, 17, 89
as a practice, 14, 16, 116, 262, 281
skill-building, 17–18
skulls
drawing and shading project, 59–63
owl skull anatomy study project, 157–159
snow, 234–235
animal tracks project, 244–246
space, illusion of, 175–176
spheres, shading, 52, 76
splatter, 134
spruce tree, 179
star charts, 250
Stillman sketchbooks, 31
stippling, 50, 286
summer sketching, 232
sunset and lake gesture sketch, 189–193

T

tertiary colors, 94
textures, 36, 286
black morel mushroom project, 139–142
creating with watercolor, 133–134
focusing on, 68–69, 117
owl feather with pencil project, 53–58
robin's nest colored pencil and watercolor project, 143–145
rock sketching project, 136–138
thumbnail sketches, 125
toned paper glacial moraines project, 216–220
Toolik Field Station, 36, 221
Toolik Lake, 174
tracing, 41
tree sketching project, 179–183

Tucson Botanical Gardens, 269
two-color wash, 74–75

U

the "ugly," finding beauty in, 46–47
Ultramarine Blue, 84–88, 97, 98, 99
ungulates, 149

V

value
  color, 92
  defined, 286
  drawing and shading a skull project, 59–63
  lupine botanical study project, 104–110
  owl feather with pencil project, 53–58
  use of term, 48
value scales
  in pen, 52
  shading with, 50–51
  with watercolor, 76
Varda, Agnès, 172
viewfinders, 68, 78, 178

W

warm colors, 97
warm-ups, 36, 40
washes
  adding white back in, 126–128
  amount of water, 72
  defined, 286
  flat leaf project, 79–83
  layering shapes, 77
  making, 72–73
  marks, 76
  negative space, 78
  types of, 74–75
water, moving, 221–226
watercolor
  adding white back in, 126–128
  benefits of as a medium, 70
  brushes, 27, 72
  and colored pencil, 122–123
  creating texture with, 133–134
  flat leaf project, 79–83
  focusing on texture, 117
  hummingbird moth project with pen and, 129–132
  lupine botanical study project, 104–110
  materials, 24
  monochromatic shell project, 84–88
  neutral colors, 27
  owl skull anatomy study project, 157–159
  paints, 22, 24, 26–27
  paper, 22, 24
  and pen, 122–123
  and pencil, 122–123
  primary colors, 26
  robin's nest texture project, 143–145
  secondary colors, 27
  sketchbooks, 31
  using alcohol instead of water, 232
  See also washes
wax resist, 133
wet-in-wet wash, 75, 91, 119, 189–193, 248, 286
white, adding back in, 126–128, 139–142
white colored pencil, 127
white pens, 25, 33, 126
white violet, 271, 279–280
willow, 20
winter sketching, 232–237
  animal tracks in the snow project, 244–246
  birch tree project, 238–243
  night sky, 247–249
  Orion constellation project, 250–253
  winter light and alpenglow project, 254–259
Wrangell Mountains, 124, 229
Wrangell–St. Elias National Park, 16

Z

Zebra pens, 25
Zinc White Gouache, 27

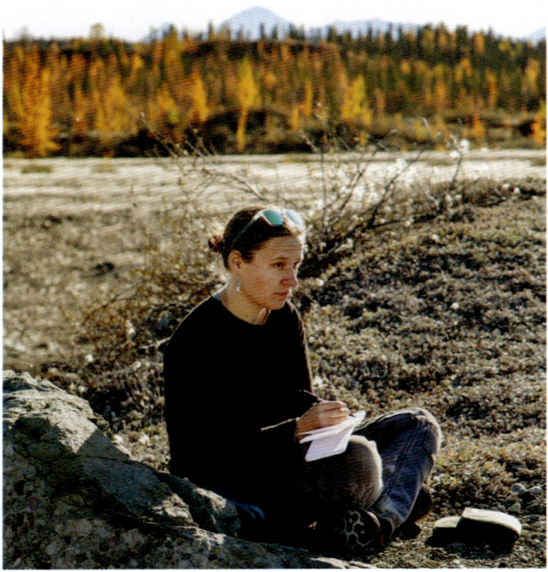

About the Author

KRISTIN LINK's art is rooted in curiosity and beauty, capturing the details of landscapes, wildlife, and seasonal changes. With a graduate certificate in science illustration from California State University, Monterey Bay, she combines storytelling with scientific precision. Her work has been featured in museum exhibits, fine art shows, periodical publications, interpretive education materials, and her own illustrated products.

For the past 15 years, Kristin has called Alaska home and lives in an off-the-grid cabin near McCarthy, surrounded by the Wrangell–St. Elias National Park. Kristin has extensive experience in the backcountry and glaciated mountains of Alaska. From climbing Denali to guiding teenage students on wilderness pack-raft trips to skiing at -20 degrees Fahrenheit with her partner and dog on the Nizina River, she is always finding inspiration in the natural world and striving to share it with others through her art.

She has been hired to create art displayed inside National Park buildings and along scenic Alaska highways, to teach and help rural students create murals reflecting their local environment and subsistence culture, and provide original artwork for museums, galleries, and individuals. Kristin teaches field-sketching workshops and joins undergraduate students on wilderness courses to teach science communication and field sketching.